Lecture Notes in Artificial Intelligence 2160

Subseries of Lecture Notes in Computer Science
Edited by J. G. Carbonell and J. Siekmann

Lecture Notes in Computer Science
Edited by G. Goos, J. Hartmanis, and J. van Leeuwen

Springer
Berlin
Heidelberg
New York
Barcelona
Hong Kong
London
Milan
Paris
Tokyo

Ruqian Lu   Songmao Zhang

Automatic Generation of Computer Animation

Using AI for Movie Animation

Springer

Series Editors

Jaime G. Carbonell, Carnegie Mellon University, Pittsburgh, PA, USA
Jörg Siekmann, University of Saarland, Saarbrücken, Germany

Authors

Ruqian Lu
Songmao Zhang
Academia Sinica, Institute of Mathematics
Beijing 100080, P.R. China
E-mail: {rqlu/smzhang}@math08.math.ac.cn

Cataloging-in-Publication Data applied for

Die Deutsche Bibliothek - CIP-Einheitsaufnahme

Lu, Ruqian:
Automatic generation of computer animation : using AI for movie animation / Ruqian Lu ; Songmao Zhang. - Berlin ; Heidelberg ; New York ; Barcelona ; Hong Kong ; London ; Milan ; Paris ; Tokyo : Springer, 2002
(Lecture notes in computer science ; 2160 : Lecture notes in artificial intelligence)
ISBN 3-540-43114-4

CR Subject Classification (1998): I.2, I.4, I.3, J.5

ISSN 0302-9743
ISBN 3-540-43114-4 Springer-Verlag Berlin Heidelberg New York

Springer-Verlag Berlin Heidelberg New York
a member of BertelsmannSpringer Science+Business Media GmbH

http://www.springer.de

Printed in Germany

Typesetting: Camera-ready by author, data conversion by Boller Mediendesign
Printed on acid-free paper SPIN: 10840290 06/3142 5 4 3 2 1 0

Preface

We are both fans of watching animated stories. Every evening, before or after dinner, we always sit in front of the television and watch the animation program, which is originally produced and shown for children. We find ourselves becoming younger while immerged in the interesting plot of the animation: how the princess is first killed and then rescued, how the little rat defeats the big cat, etc. But what we have found in those animation programs are not only interesting plots, but also a big chance for the application of computer science and artificial intelligence techniques. As is well known, the cost of producing animated movies is very high, even with the use of computer graphics techniques. Turning a story in text form into an animated movie is a long and complicated procedure. We came to the conclusion that many parts of this process could be automated by using artificial intelligence techniques. It is actually a challenge and test for machine intelligence. So we decided to explore the possibility of a full life cycle automation of computer animation generation. By full life cycle we mean the generation process of computer animation from a children's story in natural language text form to the final animated movie. It is of course a task of immense difficulty. However, we decided to try our best and to see how far we could go.

After nearly ten years of effort, we have been successful in developing a rough prototype of this technique which resulted in a software package called SWAN. A cartoon produced by SWAN, called "the three brothers", was shown on CCTV (Chinese Central Television Station) in October 1995. We are aware of the fact that this prototype is rough, because our technique is still far from being mature enough to produce delicate animated movies of commercial value. Nevertheless, we have been encouraged by the conclusion of an appraisal committee chaired by Academician, Prof. Yunmei Dong: the industrialization of the SWAN technique would hold great potential for economical and social benefits.

It is appropriate to make a note here about the contents of this book. Following the completion of our SWAN project, we carried out a review and assessment of the techniques developed in it. Based on the review, we have improved and redesigned many parts of its methodology, partly in the interest of scientific research, partly for the sake of preparing the implementation of the second version of SWAN. In this sense, the contents of this book conforms to the new design, not quite to the originally implemented one.

The SWAN project has received a grant from a special foundation of the President of the Chinese Academy of Sciences. We owe special thanks to the former President of the Chinese Academy of Sciences, Current President of the Chinese Association of Science and Technology, Academician, Prof. Guangzhao Zhou; the former Vice-President of the Chinese Academy of Sciences, Current Vice-President of the Chinese Association of Science and Technology, Academician, Prof. Qiheng Hu; and the former head of department of the Bureau for High-Tech, current Vice-Director of the Institute for Software, Mr. Wenzeng Yang. We are grateful to the Institute of Mathematics, Institute of Computing Technology, Lab for Intelligent Information Processing, Lab for Management, Decision, and Information Sciences, Center for Brain and Mind Science of the Chinese Academy of Sciences for their financial support. SWAN has also been supported by the Chinese Natural Science Foundation (especially project 69733020), by Key Projects of the Ministry of Science and Technology and by 863 High-Tech Projects.

More than 30 graduate students have participated in the SWAN project and made their contributions. Following is a list of some of their names: Qing Geng, Wenhong Zhu, Xiaobin Li, Lixin Yu, Zhenghao Jin, Dejie Yang, Yue Xu, Haihu Shi, Ronglin Wan, Zhaobin Chen, Ying Zhao, Yuan Li, Yi Luo, Bo Gao, Yuejiao Zhou, Yinghao Ma, Yizhen Li, Yujie Wang, Haixia Du, Lu Li, Ping Yang, Lu Fan, Guangfeng Ji, Xuesheng Zhang, Lengning Liu, Fan Yang, Xiaolong Jin, Chengmin Sun, Xiangliang Meng, Jingwei Cai.

We are also very thankful to Prof. Zichu Wei, who has made an important contribution to the SWAN project during discussions about the design and implementation of the SWAN software, and through his involvement in the management of the project.

We thank Prof. Christian Freksa of the University of Hamburg, Prof Bernd Krieg-Brueckner and Prof. Manfred Wischnewski of the University of Bremen for their invitation to give a series of seminar talks about SWAN at these universities. We also thank Prof. Manfred Broy of the Technical University of Munich and Prof. Jörg Siekmann of the University of the Saarland for their invitation to introduce SWAN at these universities. We owe special thanks to Prof. Jörg Siekmann. Without his encouragement and support the publishing of this manuscript would have been impossible. While preparing the talks, the first author of this book had the opportunity to further improve the manuscript.

Last, but not least, we would like to thank Ms. Wenyan Zhang and Dr. Cungen Cao for their valuable help in the final editing of the manuscript. We also thank the editors of the LNAI series and Springer-Verlag, and Ms. Karin Henzold for their kind support and help in the editing and publishing of this manuscript.

June, 2001

Ruqian Lu
Songmao Zhang

Contents

1 Overview of Research on Computer Animation and Related Topics

Although commercially available animation packages provide sophisticated facilities for generating computer animation interactively, although the products of these packages often seem quite attractive for users, the real use of these tools is nevertheless not so easy and requires a lot of tedious work.

Lots of papers have been published on the techniques developed in this field. In this chapter, we summarize shortly the research work on computer animation and related topics reported in the literature. Note that our focus of attention is the automatic generation of computer animation, not the animation itself. Furthermore, we have been focusing on the automatic generation of plots and motions of characters. Therefore, we have paid relatively little attention to the graphics aspects. For example, numerical models for generating physical phenomena, e.g. fire, water, fog, rain, etc. are not included in this survey. Because of the limited access to the current and past literature, this survey is by no means complete. Just as one Chinese idiom says: "for one thing cited, ten thousand may have been left out". The source of the material includes journal papers, proceedings, technical reports and also survey papers of other authors, for example, [Arnold, 1989], [Platt and Barr, 1988] and [Jin, Bao and Peng, 1997] contain quite comprehensive and rich material. Apart from that, we cite also material contained in the survey part of other published papers. We owe many thanks to all of these authors.

1.1 Key Frame Based Computer Animation

1.1.1 Basic Ideas and Numerical Techniques

The most successful technique may be that of key frame based animation generation which is probably the most mature technique of computer aided animation generation. With this technique, human painters design and draw a few animation frames as key frames, then the computer performs interpolation to supplement the missing intermediate frames.

Since interpolation is the key technique used in this approach, the numerical mathematics plays an important role. Steketee et al. proposed to use both position splines and motion splines as interpolation parameters. He called this method double interpolation [Steketee and Badler, 1985]. Brotman proposed to use differential equations of classical mechanics to describe the motion of objects and to con-

R. Lu and S. Zhang, Automatic Generation of Computer Animation, LNAI 2160, pp.1-27, 2002.

sider the key frames as constraint conditions [Brotman, 1988]. In order to calculate the position of an object in some frame, which moves along a trajectory, one needs methods for numerical integration. The traditional technique for that is the Simpson algorithm. Guenter et al. proposed to use instead a combination of a Gauss type numerical integration and a Newton-Raphson iteration to solve the problem [Guenter, 1990]. More important was the work of Shoemake who for the first time introduced the quaternion space as a mathematical tool for Bezier spline interpolations [Shoemake, 1985]. This quaternion method has been widely used by animators since then.

The key frame based method has its own disadvantage. As pointed out by [Bruderlin and Calvert, 1989], in this approach, the quality of a motion is directly proportional to the number of key frames specified. If the desired movements are complicated, then it is the animator, not the system, who controls the motion. On the other hand, though this approach is effective in some cases, it is not suitable for a system for automatic generation of animation, like SWAN [Lu, Zhang and Wei, 1999].

1.1.2 Example of a Desktop System for Animation Generation: The Life Forms

This is a product of the Simon Fraser University, developed by Tom Calvert, Armin Bruderlin, John Dill, Thecla Schiphorst and Chris Welman [Calvert, Bruderlin, Dill, Schiphorst and Welman, 1993]. The work started in 1986 as a project to develop computer-based tools to assist in choreographic for composing dance. Then, they found that this prototype, which was originally aimed at assisting working choreographers, could be further developed into a front-end of general-purpose systems for animation generation and a storyboard style tool for cartoon producers. Initially developed on Silicon Graphics workstations, Life Forms has been now transplanted to Apple Macintosh. Noticeable is the fact that this Macintosh version of Life Forms now interacts with Macromedia Director, Electric Image and Hypercard. This work combined key frame based method with articulate planning. Therefore we cite it in this section.

As a general-purpose desktop animation system Life Forms should have the following characteristics, as proposed by the authors, a relative complete platform for animation manufacturing, a flexible and easy to use tool for non-professional animators and a powerful and less expensive desktop workstation for personal use. In fact, the functions of Life Forms include full modeling, rendering and composition capabilities.

In the following, we summarize the functions of Life Forms in form of an algorithm:

Algorithm 1.1.1

Part One: Make a concept plan about the animation one wants to have

1. Call for the screen windows of animation generation.
2. Select bodies for characters (which can also be simple tokens at this moment) from menus and place them on the stage in appropriate positions and facing appropriate directions.
3. Consider the result of the last step as a key frame and store it in the computer.
4. Repeat this process to get a series of key frames
5. Add some background if needed.
6. Adjust the key frames with rotations, translations and zooms if needed.

Part Two: Implement single character movements

7. Design postures of characters in key frames by selecting and mounting limbs of characters and adjusting their directions, where constraints for limb positions and directions are posed to limit the various possibilities.
8. Using "forward kinematics" to build up body instances by successively adjusting the distal segments.
9. Using "constrained inverse kinematics" to calculate the interpolated positions and angles of articulates.
10. Develop new stances or modify old stances to get a series of body stances.
11. Edit this sequence to get the optimized one with controlled tempo of joint movements (by stretching or squeezing its sub-sequences, i.e. by changing the parameters).
12. For those parts where there is a locomotion (e.g. walk here and there), use procedural methods.

Part Three: Implement multiple character movements

13. Assemble the movements of characters together by using a stage window with a time axis, where the time intervals of character movements are registered and are subject to adjustments.

Part Four: Postproduction

14. Design body models for animation
15. Take human skeletons with 22 to 26 segments for building up characters.
16. Select one from the four possibilities listed in the menu: stick figures, outline figures, contour figures and solid models, for body representation.
17. Run the produced movement sequence of characters to get the animation.

End of Algorithm

1.2 Articulate Planning: Kinematics and Dynamics

Models of kinematics and dynamics are widely studied in the literature. There are two kinds of kinematical models. In the forward kinematical model, motion, rotation and scaling of objects and their articulates are described as functions of time. The success of this approach depends largely on the knowledge, skill and experience of the animator. Another kind of the kinematical approach is the inverse kinematics. In this approach, the animator may draw trajectories of movements as a set of constraints and let the computer calculate the motion of articulates. The number of constraints one can impose on the articulates depends on the number of degrees of freedom (DOF) of the objects. Generally speaking, each constraint "consumes" a degree of freedom. The complexity of the corresponding algorithms may be very high and may increase drastically with the increase of articulate numbers. Therefore, one tends to use numerical methods to obtain approximate solutions. An advantage of kinematical models is the possibility of defining constraints for the motions. For example, the system may let a character pick up an apple from the table while keeping a fixed distance off the table and fixing the feet on the ground. Both kinematical models have the disadvantage that the produced articulate movements are often not natural and smooth enough.

Pure (forward or inverse) kinematics ignore any influence from the existence of inertia. Mathematically, it was Denavit and Hartenberg [Denavit and Hartenberg, 1955] who was the first to propose a matrix method for describing the relative positions of articulates based on a relative Cartesian system. This method was then widely used by animators [Strurmann, 1986]. Korein proposed a method whose principle was to minimize the articulate translation. This principle brought the problem that the solutions thus obtained are not necessary natural. Girard and Maciejewski [Girard and Maciejewski, 1985] [Girard, 1987] used a pseudo inverse Jacobian matrix to find solutions in their inverse kinematics method and obtained better methods. Jack [Badler, 1991] is a multi-faceted system which was strongly based on pure kinematics. It was aimed at the description and generation of articulated body movements by interactively modeling, manipulating, and animating geometrically accurate human bodies. This human body model can be used in compliance with anthropometrical statistical data.

The goal-oriented technique is a special form of inverse kinematics method. Zeltzer [Zeltzer, 1982] developed a task-oriented system to animate human body motions such as walking and jumping. He used methods of kinematics and measured data interpolation to calculate joint rotation angles. These methods have difficulty in changing motion speed and step lengths. An improvement of his work was made by Bruderlin and Calvert [Bruderlin and Calvert, 1989], who implemented the KLAW (Keyframe-Less Animation of Walking) system. This is a hybrid approach which combines goal-directed and dynamic motion control. The overall architecture is a hierarchical control process. The user first specifies the wanted locomotion at the top level as tasks which are then decomposed in subtasks. These subtasks are solved by dynamic models of legs and calculated by numerical approximation.

On the other hand, a pure dynamics method does not make use of kinematics principles. The dynamics simulation is an much more difficult task, it includes complicated calculation of force and torques. This has the advantage that the animation designer does not have to care much about the trajectories of object motion in four-dimensional space (three space dimensions plus one time dimension). For example, to describe the trajectory of an object thrown forwards by some person, we only need to let the computer solve a differential equation. Another advantage of this approach is the naturalness and smoothness of the resulted animation. Generally speaking, in case of full passive systems (no autonomous internal force or joint torque) the dynamics approach is a good choice. But the computational complexity may be very high. And the resulted motion pattern may not be a very well controlled one.

Many authors tried to combine the kinematics approach other methods. One example was Van Overveld and Hyeongseok Ko who proposed feasible way of combination [Overveld and Ko, 1994]. They studied the simulation of bipedal locomotion. As input, they used a 14 DOF simplified human body model, together with walk directions and gait lengths. Using kinematics they calculated the trajectories of feet over time. Then trajectories of some other body parts (head, shoulder, etc.) may be derived from the known ones. All these trajectories form motion constraints for the dynamics algorithms. Thus the motion of all components is driven by their trajectories (if any) plus additional forces and torques (if any). All components without trajectory specifications will be driven by inertia effects. Recently, a software package called IKAN has been developed by the center for Human Modeling and Simulation. It is a complete set of inverse kinematics algorithms combined with analytical methods suitable for an anthropomorphic arm or leg. [IKAN, 2000]

We think that the idea of Zeltzer is closer to that of ours. He even proposed a motto: "Knowledge-based animation" [Zeltzer, 1983] which is similar in some aspects to our knowledge based method of SWAN. Another approach which we think is useful for us was adopted by Maiocchi [Maiocchi, 1990] who has developed an animation system called Pinocchio which records articulated body movements and builds a library of them for use during animation generation. His approach is similar to the one used by our system in the last stage of cartoon generation.

1.3 Path Planning

While planning the motion of a character in a movie, an obvious desire of the animator is to give only commands at task levels. For example, you may wish to let a cat run from under the window up to the top of a tree. Then it is comfortable to write down the command

Run (cat, under (window), top (tree))

Is this command still effective when there are obstacles between the window and the tree? Will it happen that the cat goes through the wall of a house or even goes through the body of its master until it arrives outdoors? We all want to avoid such circumstances. But to avoid obstacles of different sizes, forms and distances requires too many details in motion description such as "turn right with an angle of 90 degrees" and "go forwards 10 meters" etc. What we want to have is to keep the simplicity of descriptions like "run from under the window up to the top of a tree" and avoid the cumbersome task of writing detailed path descriptions. This is the task of path planning.

There has been a lot of research on this topic. Most of them simplified the problem in that they assumed the obstacles having simple forms, e.g. polygons or circles. Various results have been obtained. Most of them are related to two-dimensional cases, because the two-dimensional case is much simpler than the three-dimensional one. A straightforward way of dividing the two-dimensional space in several sub-spaces solves this problem with a time complexity of O (n^2 log n). A well known result was due to T. Lozano-Perez and M.A.Wesley [Lozano-Perez and Wesley, 1979] who developed a method called visible graphs, using which the authors proved a better result for finding a shortest path with the time complexity O (n^2).

This result was then improved. Two sub-problems are often addressed. One is to find a shortest path between two points within a polygon. Another one is to find a shortest path between two points outside of a polygon. In both cases the wanted path should not penetrate the border of the polygon. For the first sub-problem, [Lee and Preparata, 1984] proposed a method of constructing a tree of shortest paths based on a triangulation of the polygon. The time complexity for tree construction is O (n), and that for the triangulation is O (n log n). The total complexity is O (n log n). Thus the complexity of triangulation plays the decisive role. The complexity for solving the second sub-problem is similar. Shi improved the two results to a lower complexity of O (n) [Shi, 1996].

Other results about two-dimensional path planning have been published. [Lozano-Perez and Wesley, 1979] also proved an O (n^2log n) complexity for finding a shortest path in an area with a set of n obstacles all of which are convex polygons. This complexity is also valid for the problem of a moving circle with polygon obstacles [Sharir, 1985].

However, in three-dimensional space, the path planning problem becomes much more difficult. To our best knowledge, until present, only exponential results are obtained [John and James, 1994]. It was not until recently that researchers have proved that the problem of finding a shortest path between two points in a three-dimensional space with a finite set of polyhedral obstacles is a NP complete problem [Canny and Reif, 1987]. Nevertheless, some limited results have been obtained. For the case of an arbitrary number of polyhedral obstacles, the exponential complexity can not be further improved [John and James, 1994]. If the number of polyhedral obstacles, k, is equal to one, [Sharir and Schorr, 1986] has proved a complexity of O (n^3 log n), which was later improved to O (n^2) [Joseph, 1987]. For k = 2 one obtained O (n^3 log n) [Baltsan and Sharir, 1988], for k = 3 O (n^{4k}) [Sharir and Baltsan, 1986] [Sharir, 1987]. Shi reported an O (n^2) result for k = 2 [Shi, 1996].

The results mentioned above have been used to solve a variety of different motion planning problems, including the problem of moving a rectangle object (piano movement, [Schwartz and Sharir, 1983]), the problem of moving rigid obstacle objects in two-dimensional space [Lozano-Perez and Wesley, 1979], the problem of cooperative movement of several circle objects in a two-dimensional space with polygon obstacles [Sharir, 1985], and a generalization of the piano moving problem to the three-dimensional space [Sifrony and Sharir, 1987], etc. For the two-dimensional stick moving problem, Leven and Sharir [Leven and Sharir, 1987] have found a solution with time complexity O (n^2 log n) which improved the result of [Schwartz and Sharir, 1983] (time complexity O (n^5)) a lot. Later, the result of Leven and Sharir was proved to be almost optimal.

In case that the obstacles are movable, the complexity is significantly high. Some researchers assume that a robot may move away obstacles he meets in his way. An analysis of this problem proved that the complexity is NP if the goal place is not fixed, otherwise the complexity is PSAPCE [HuangYK and Ahuja, 1992]. In case that there is only one obstacle, the complexity reduces to O (n^3 $\log^2$ n) [HuangYK and Ahuja, 1992].

In our SWAN system, we did not use these algorithms with high complexity. We have adopted a series of heuristic methods to reduce the problem to a two-dimensional one. The only useful algorithm for us is that of T. Lozano-Perez and M.A.Wesley. We have implemented it which solves our problem most of the time. Besides, we have developed another principle of path finding. Namely, we have found that in many cases it is not the shortest path which is the most suitable, but the "most safe path", a concept we have developed ourselves.

1.4 Camera Planning

One of the most salient features of a movie as compared with a drama is the multiplicity of view angles and viewpoints of the same plot. The audience can observe the progress of the plot from all possible directions and all possible distances, of course guided by the director's camera. This fact reminds us of the necessity of an automatic camera planning as a component of automatic animation generation.

In SWAN, we have designed and implemented our camera planning module. As main sources of reference we have taken "Dictionary of Movie Arts", edited by Xu Nanming, etc. [XuN, 1986] (in Chinese), "Grammar of the Film Language" written by D. Arijon [Arijon, 1976], "Grammar of the Edit" written by Roy Thomson [Thompson, 1993], and several others. It was only after we have finished our work and started to write this monograph that we found and read the paper "The Virtual Cinematographer: A Paradigm of Automatic Real-Time Camera Control and Directing", written by He Liwei, Michael Cohen and David Salesin [He, Cohen and Salesin, 1996]. Much to our surprise that there are a lot of similarities between their work and that of ours. For example, we share the opinion that camera planning needs a formalized computer language to describe it, that one should summarize thumb rules used by cameramen in form of routines of this language, that a film should be considered as a structure consisting of scenes and shots (rather than just a linear sequence), that one should design a large set of film idioms to be called by camera planning modules, that these program modules have an additional task of reposition the characters in a scene to avoid people to be occluded, etc. Notwithstanding that such similarity exists, there are also a great lot of differences between their work and that of ours, which will be explained in more details below and in later chapters.

The Virtual Cinematographer (VC for short) forms one part of an overall architecture of a real time film producer. The other two parts are a real time application (e.g. real time communication in a 3D virtual environment) and a fast render. The working mechanism is as follows: the real time application sends to VC a description of events occurring at this moment, which are significant to the observer. The VC then produces a camera specification based on these events and on the previous state of animation, and sends it to the render which renders the scene in real time.

The VC itself consists of two parts: a set of film idioms (called camera planning primitives by us in SWAN) organized as a hierarchical state machine, where the cinematography rules are codified (knowledge base in our terminology), and a set of camera modules for low level geometrical placement (low level geometrical camera planning in our terminology).

Each idiom is implemented as a separate finite state machine (FSM), where each state (a typical scenario in our terminology) corresponds to a separate shot in the animation. Each state also includes a set of conditions. Each time when one of the conditions is fulfilled, a state change occurs which leads to another state (e.g. if the current state is 2Talk, i.e. two persons are talking to each other, and if a third person enters, then the state is changed from 2Talk to 3Talk). This state change may happen in form of going a level down in the hierarchy of FSM, or in form of going a level up. The up level and low level states are called parent and child states, respectively. Thus, the VC has in fact two hierarchies: one static hierarchy of idiom organization, and one dynamic hierarchy of idiom calls.

In VC, the idioms are written in C++ code. Let us consider an example:

Example 1.4.1 (The Idiom 2Talk)

```
DEFINE_IDIOM_IN_ACTION (2Talk)
    WHEN ( talking (A, B) )
      DO ( GO (1); )
    WHEN ( talking (B, A) )
      DO ( GO (2); )
END_IDIOM_IN_ACTION
```

Its camera modules are defined as follows:

```
DEFINE_SETUP_CAMERA_MODULES (2Talk)
   MAKE_MODULE (1, external, (A, B) )
   MAKE_MODULE (2, external, (B, A) )
   LINK_MODULE (1, 1, "A talks" )
   LINK_MODULE (2, 2, "B talks" )
   LINK_MODULE (3, 1, "A reacts" )
   LINK_MODULE (4, 2, "B reacts" )
END_ SETUP_CAMERA_MODULES
```

where MAKE_MODULE (<module id>, <type>, <parameter list>) creates a new camera module of the <type> with the specified <parameter list> and gives it the <module id> as the identification number. LINK_MODULE (<state>, <module

id>, <name>) associates the specified camera module with the corresponding state.

Now some words about the differences between VC and our camera planning technique. There are 16 idioms of VC already implemented, which are quite similar to the HLCP (High Level Camera Primitives) of our camera planning language Morning Glow. Many idioms of VC differ from the corresponding HLCP only in names. For example, their "apex" corresponds to our "rightangle", their internal and externals correspond to our in_contra and out_contra. This is understandable because the authors of the paper mentioned above have taken the same book of Arijon as the main reference book. Nevertheless, there is a significant difference that our Morning Glow is a wide spectrum language consisting of four layers. Their VC corresponds only to the second layer of Morning Glow. Our higher layer representations (DPRS and RCS) which are missing in VC have proved to be very useful in the automatic transformation from director's intention to the final implementation of the camera plan.

As to the state machines of VC, please note that although their ideas are roughly similar to that of ours, the levels of abstractness are different. Our basic scenarios are more abstract than their states. For example, we also have the scenario "talking" which has the same name as a state of VC. But the meaning of our "talking" is not limited to its original sense in natural language semantics. In our terminology, each scenario involving two main roles facing each other (e.g. two players playing tennis) belongs to this scope. Therefore, we think that our definition can cover a wider area of real situations.

Just as the authors of that paper, we have also noticed the problem that some characters in the final animation may be occluded by others due to inappropriate camera planning. But we have adopted different method to solve it. While VC chose the technique of repositioning the characters in the scene, we have gone another way of a fuzzy modification of camera placements to avoid any obstacles.

A good point of the design of VC is the inclusion of some basic principles of camera making. For example the "don't cross the line principle" and the "Avoid jump cuts" principle. We will consider these principles in the next version of SWAN.

1.5 Music Planning

Music is a very important factor in any movie, including (may be even more important for) animation. The automatic generation of computer animation should include the automatic generation of accompanying music.

To our knowledge, Hiller and Isaacson were the first authors who have attacked the problem of computer music composition [Hiller and Isaacson, 1959]. They completed a composition called Illiac Suite for string quartet. If we classify the computer music in stochastic and deterministic types, then their work will fall into the category of stochastic music. As basis for computer composition they took a set of constraints which were recognized as obligatory by most musicians. This set of rules include seven melody constraints and nine harmonic constraints. Based on these principles, the computer can produce music in a stochastic way. Let us take the choice of pitches as example. Each pitch was chosen at random from the major scale if it satisfies all constraints. The music was then composed by using a random number generator.

Since the composer was unable to take control over the thus produced music, another approach, called deterministic computer composition, was then proposed by Mathews [Mathews and Pierce, 1991]. They investigated pitch quantization as compositional strategy. They represented music as a set of functions over time, which can be generated by input or by algorithms. Although their rules are essentially deterministic, the result of the composition was still unplanned and could not be perceived in advance. That means, this approach was not completely deterministic.

Another work in computer composition, done by Koenig [Koenig, 1970a] [Koenig, 1970b], took three basic parameters: pitch, loudness and duration as basic material and used a combination of serial and stochastic composition procedures. They even used detailed rules to help these procedures.

All these methods and techniques seem to have one common disadvantage: they are not easy to use by common people, of course also difficult for those who want to implement automatic background music composition for computer animation. It was to this end that Jun-Ichi Nakamura et al. [Nakamura, Kaku, Hyun, Noma and Yoshida, 1994] developed a practical technique of music composition. Their music generation system includes four modules: a background music generator BGM, a MIDI data generator MDG which generates a MIDI file; a music performer MPF which generates MIDI data for the last component: the music Synthesizer (music producer). The following algorithm shows its working mechanism from the point of view of the user.

Definition 1.5.1 (Music Parameters)

The music parameters used in the following algorithm include:

1. A scene label (sequence number) for each scene.
2. A motif sequence for each scene, where for each measure there is a motif assigned.
3. A motif sequence for each main character.
4. A mode type (glad, happy, sleepy, sad, angry and tired) with its degree (1-5) for each role in each scene.
5. A time length for each scene.
6. A timbre for the sounds (piano-like, flute-like, etc.) which depends on the synthesizer.

Algorithm 1.5.1 (User Interface of the Music Generator)

1. Divide the animation into a sequence of scenes with clear transition boarders. Use a stop watch to measure the length (duration) of each scene.
2. Specify the "music" and "motion" parameters, where a motion parameter specifies the type of the action.

3. Transfer the MIDI file to the performer (a MAC SE/30) and run it together with the video player which displays the movie.

End of Algorithm

Algorithm 1.5.2 (Working Procedure of the Music Generator)

1. Determine the tempo of the scene based on the mood type and its degree. A table for this purpose is cited below. The basic tempo is represented by the number of quarter notes in one minute.
2. Determine the number of measures of each scene by using the tempo and the length of the scene.
3. Determine the scale and the volume of the music for each scene.
4. Generate a chord progression by using harmonic progression rules and the number of measures of the scene.
5. Generate a melody for the scene by repeating and transforming its motif based on the parameters generated so far. The repetition will be done so far until the whole scene is filled.
6. Generate harmony and rhythms accompaniments with the mood type as a key, supported by a database with 151 harmony accompaniments and 163 rhythms accompaniments.
7. Generate sound effects (e.g. hitting, blinking, falling, etc.) according to the actor's motions and emotions and adjust them to conform to the background music.

End of Algorithm

Table 1.5.1 Tempo Calculation

Mood Type	t_0	d
glad	100	10
Happy	110	8
Sleepy	100	- 8
Sad	110	- 10
Angry	100	10
Tired	90	6

The basic tempo will be calculated with the following formula:

$$t = k * d + t_0$$

where k is the degree of the mode type, d and t_0 are constants depending on the mood type as shown in the above table which is decided by experiments.

A similar effort has been made in the project COPPELIA by Detlev Zimmermann of DFKI, Germany [Zimmermann, 1995]. They call it automatic content-based composition. They claimed that there was a dilemma between deterministic and stochastic music composition. Whereas the former often produces products which are boring, the latter often produces uncontrollable and ugly music. They thought that intention-based composition (according to a presentation of e.g. an animation) was a way out of this dilemma. In composition, they used different musical styles as well as different kinds of orchestration styles. The production can be real time or optimized, in a full automatic or interactive mode. Their platform was implemented in the OZ language.

We have not yet implemented the music composition module in our SWAN system. In the first product of SWAN, called "the three brothers" (ten minutes long), which has been shown on the Chinese television, the music was composed by a professional composer. But we found that the idea of Nakamura (or the content-based idea of Zimmermann) is appropriate for us. SWAN has a director's module where many additional information, such as the mood of the scene (in our terminology: atmosphere), the sentiment and emotion of the roles, etc., is determined. All this information can be used to determine the tempo, the rhythms, the scale, the chord, the harmony, the melody, etc. of the accompanying music. In the next version of SWAN, we will incorporate such a module.

1.6 Natural Language Understanding and Story Analysis

The necessary condition for an effective generation of computer animation from natural language narratives is a good natural language understanding interface. In the literature, one tends to consider story understanding as a subtask of natural language understanding. However, there are significant differences. Generally speaking, we can divide the research topics which relate to natural language understanding in three levels. The first level is the conventional approach of natural language understanding. It is traditionally limited to the understanding of structure and meaning of individual sentences. In this approach, even if the researcher is interested in exploring the relation between two sentences, it is just for solving problems within the individual sentences themselves, for example, for solving the anaphoric or cataphoric problems. At the second level is the discourse understanding. Its job is to analyze and summarize the main content of a discourse and to produce an abstract out of it. This discourse may be a text from a newspaper or a journal. It can also be the protocol of a communication or the minutes of a meeting. Clearly, more delicate techniques are needed to accomplish this task. The story understanding is at the third level. It is more complicated than the discourse understanding, because it pays more attention to the pragmatic aspect which is the most difficult area in natural language understanding (for details see section 5.1). Therefore, we bear the opinion that we should differentiate between two meanings of the term "natural language understanding": natural language understanding in general and that in special. The story understanding is a subtask of the former, but not a subtask of the latter. In fact, it is another area of research.

1.6.1 Early Approach of Story Grammar

In the seventies, there were already works studying techniques of story understanding. In 1975, Rumelhart [Rumelhart, 1975] introduced a method of formal grammar based story analysis. He proposed 11 syntactic rules and corresponding semantic interpretations for his story grammar. For example,

Rule 1: Story → Setting + Episode
Rule 1': ALLOW (Setting, Episode)
Rule 2: Setting → (State)*
Rule 2': AND(State, State,......)

where rule 1 and rule 2 are syntactic rules, rule 1' and rule 2' are semantic constraints. Rule 1 says that each story can be divided into two parts: the setting and the episode. Rule 1' says that there is a semantic relation ALLOW existing between setting and episode. Rumelhart tried to use such kinds of rules to catch the syntax and also semantics of a story. Based on this idea, he also proposed thirteen so-called summarization rules which are responsible for mapping the semantic structures of a story onto a broad outline of it. These summarization rules correspond to the semantic relations (e.g. AND, ALLOW, INITIATE, MOTIVATE, CAUSE, THEN) mentioned above. For example, there is the following summarization rule:

S1: Summary(CAUSE [x, y]) → Agent (x) caused (y)

meaning that the agent x caused the event y to happen. This process of summarization can be done step by step until the final abstract (or theme) of the story is produced.

Rumelhart has published a series of further papers on this approach, [Rumelhart, 1977a] [Rumelhart, 1977b] [Rumelhart, 1980], which was also followed by some authors [Mandler and Johnson, 1977] [Thorndyke, 1977]. But there were also people who have criticized his story grammar [Black and Wilensky, 1979], because its expressive power was quite limited and it failed in understanding stories with complicated style or plots. The main reason of the failure was that the Rumelhart's story grammar was a context free string grammar which caused a serious problem that a text produced by such a grammar is not necessary a story, and, on the other hand, many meaningful stories can not be described by his story grammar. Another disadvantage of his grammar is that it is syntax oriented. This defect has limited its use in understanding a story, because to this end the semantic information, which is usually called deep level information, is necessary.

The criticisms of Black and Wilensky have raised heated discussions and arguments. Mandler and Johnson for example published a paper called "On throwing out the baby with the bath water: a reply to Black and Wilensky's evaluation of story grammars" [Mandler and Johnson, 1980]. One year later, Frisch and Perlis lunched even more heated counter criticisms in their paper [Frisch and Perlis, 1981]. In the following, we will summarize their divergence in points of view related to story grammars, where we insert our comments at appropriate places:

B & W: Finite state story grammars are too weak, because many stories can not be captured by finite state grammars. There are stories which are self-embedding. A grammar is a FSG if and only if it is not essentially self-embedding.

F & P : Please do not confuse grammars with languages. If a language is not of a particular type, then it cannot be generated by a grammar of that type. However, a grammar which is not of a particular type might generate a language of that type. In this case there is a grammar of a more restricted form which generates the identical language.

L & Z : To be more precise, we interpret this argument as follows: if a language is of type n in the Chomsky terminology, then it can not be generated by a grammar of type n + 1. However, a grammar which is of type n might generate a language of type n + 1. In this case there is a grammar of type n + 1 which generates the identical language.

B & W : For example, there are stories which are of the form $a^n b^n$ which can not be produced by FSGs.

F & P : You are wrong! Any story can be produced by FSGs. In fact, any string can be generated by a FSG.

L & Z : Finite strings are referred to here, because every story is finite. It seems that one should differentiate between "produce a text" and "produce a language".

B & W : But what happens if the story is infinite?

F & P : No problem. Even the set of all strings can be generated by a FSG.

B & W : But an infinite language may contain an infinite sub-sequence which can not be generated by a FSG! For example, the set $\{a^n b^m \mid n, m \geq 0\}$ is a FSL, but its subset $\{a^n b^n \mid n \geq 0\}$ is not a FSL.

F & P : But this says nothing about the set of stories themselves! I would agree with you if you took the set $\{a^n b^n \mid n \geq 0\}$ as the set of all stories. But you didn't say that.

B & W : It has been proved that the English grammar is not a FSG, even not a CFG. Stories are more complicated than the English language. Therefore the stories can even less be represented by FSGs.

F & P : We can not see why story texts should be more complicated than English. Although there are some similarities, these analogies are unsubstantiated and doubtful. In fact we even believe that the opposite may be the case.

B & W : Story grammars are syntactic in nature. Story understanding involves semantics. Thus they can not be represented by story grammars.

F & P : What is this distinction between syntax and semantics? For any language which can be recognized by any known computational device, there is a URS (universal recursive system) which also recognizes it. There is no formal deficiency in the "syntactic" URS. The semantic-syntactic distinction can only be practical and not a formal one.

L & Z : We agree with this comment of F & P. But at the same time we wish to point out that practical aspects are not unimportant. The key issue is not to prove whether or not the grammatical approach is theoretically enough for representing any story. This belongs to the area of the theory of computability. Our concern is much more on the following: how the representation tool can be effectively used for arbitrary stories.

F & P : A major flow of B & W's evaluation is that they have overlooked the purpose of the story grammars as intended by Rumelhart and others. Just as it was pointed out in [Mandler and Johnson, 1980], story grammars are not intended to define the set of stories, nor are they intended to be the sole component of a story comprehender. Rather, their purpose is to serve as one of the many sources of knowledge necessary in story comprehension. For example, the Rumelhart's "interactive model of reading" [Rumelhart, 1977b], which is based on the architecture of the Hearsay II speech understanding system, consists of a set of independent cooperating knowledge sources (KSs) each working on a different representation of the text. A story grammar, coupled with an appropriate parser, could be incorporated in such a system as an additional KS. A grammar could serve the above purposes whether or not the texts it could generate correspond precisely to our intuitive notion of stories.

L & Z : Yes, we agree. But this point was not made clear in Rumelhart's original paper.

F & P : There has been no intent to limit the grammars to a certain type. Though a specific story grammar may be a CFG, it should be noted that it is also a URS. The set of stories chosen for study were usually simple enough that restricted grammars were sufficient. As the stories investigated became more sophisticated, the form of the grammars used has become less restricted.

L & Z : Bravo! This is just the reason why we have developed two-dimensional and context-sensitive grammars to parse stories. The basic mechanisms of these grammars are presented in chapter four and are further referred to in chapter five.

1.6.2 Scripts and Frames

About at the same time as Rumelhart proposed his story grammar approach, Schank [Schank, 1977] proposed a theory of conceptual dependency (CD) and a script based technique to understand a story. This theory considers each story consisting of a series of script templates and each script template consisting in turn of a series of atom actions which are components of CD. According to Schank, there are not only temporal relations between the atom actions of a template, but also causal relations. One can imagine the existence of a causal chain. At the one end of this chain are the initial conditions of the script, whereas at the other end we have the results of the script. Each time when a story is given, the initial conditions of the template are used to match the key parameters of the story. If successful, this script will be activated. The information contained in the story will be then used to fill the slots of the template. On the other hand, the information contained in the script will be used to answer questions relating to the story.

Based on this idea, Cullingford developed a story understanding system SAM [Cullingford, 1978] which can understand simple stories and answer simple questions relating to these stories. SAM can also produce abstracts in multiple languages from stories. It contains three modules: the PARSER, MEMTOK (a memory module) and APPLY (application module). Based on the CD theory, PARSER produces a CD representation for each sentence of the story.

One year later, DeJong published his FRUMP (Fast Reading Understanding and Memory Programming) system [De Jong, 1979], based on a similar principle. The approach of Schank has further developed into the so-called MOPs (Memory Organization Packets) [Schank, 1980] [Schank, 1982]. MOPs understand a story by predicting the next coming scripts based on current information. This understanding depends largely on the way of organizing memory units.

SAM and FRUMP share the problems that knowledge structures cannot be shared and that they cannot understand the abnormal story plots beyond the script. Actually in real world very few stories meet the standards of scripts completely.

Charniak added time concepts into story skeletons and got the so-called temporal frames. Using the frame based method, Charniak implemented a story understanding system Ms. Malaprop in 1977 [Charniak, 1977] [Charniak, 1978], which can understand simple stories (including only a few sentences) about painting. The frame representation is similar to but more general than the script representation due to the fact that it is a modularized and shared schema. This program understands a story in three phases. In the first phase, it accepts a story represented in predicate form, transforms it into some internal representation which will be matched against some event frames in the second phase. If in this process there appears information which mismatches the frames about painting, then the program finds the missing link which is necessary for the understanding and tries to complete the story with the added link. For example, if the intention is to paint the wall green, but the story says that one has bought yellow and blue paint, then the program searches the knowledge base for the relation between different colors of paint and finds the missing link which is to merge the yellow and blue paint on some palette to get the green one.

1.6.3 The Plan Understanding Approach

In 1978, Wilensky implemented PAM using plans as knowledge structures [Wilensky, 1978]. A plan represents some human goal and the means used for realizing this goal. This plan schema is more flexible than script and frame ones. One disadvantage of PAM is that the relation among various goals of different roles has not been well dealt with.

In 1983 Lebowitz implemented IPP which could understand stories about international terrorism published in the newspaper [Lebowitz, 1983]. IPP adopts MOP as knowledge structure, which is a knowledge unit proposed by Schank in 1979 based on human memory model. As compared with script, MOP has more flexibility, higher modularity and closer connections with other MOPs. Moreover, MOP is a shared knowledge structure.

Lehnert proposed the plot unit method to obtain the summaries of stories [Lehnert, 1981] [Lehnert, 1983]. The main idea of this method is to understand stories according to the roles' emotions. This theory assumes that each role should be in some emotion state at each moment of story development. The state is "+" if the role is happy, otherwise the state is "-" if the role is unhappy. The third possibility is "M" which means don't care.

The relations between different states mean their transformations. There are four kinds of arcs: m (Motivation), a (Actualization), t (Termination) and e (Equivalence). Two states plus a semantic chain connecting them form a plot unit. From the graph of plot units one can inference various conclusions about the story, including its synopsis. For example, m: M → M and a: M → + are all plot units.

Complex plot units can be formed with simple ones.

Example 1.6.1

A Chinese idiom says: "Extreme joy begets sorrow. Out of the depth of misfortune comes bliss" which can be illustrated with Lehnert's notation as follows:

$$t(-, a(+ \rightarrow +)); \quad t(+, a(- \rightarrow -))$$

Example 1.6.2

A Famous love story in China:

"A beautiful girl Zhu Yingtai disguised herself as a boy, in order to enter a school which was only for male students, where she got a good friend Liang Shanbo. They became sworn brothers. At the end of three years study the students returned home. When they said good bye to each other, Zhu Yingtai told Liang Shanbo that she wanted to introduce her younger sister to Liang Shanbo as his wife. Liang was very happy and agreed. When Liang visited Zhu's home one month later, he was told by Zhu that Zhu was not a boy, but a girl and the "younger sister" whom Zhu wanted to introduce was in fact Zhu herself. Unfortunately, Zhu's father ordered Zhu to marry another person of a rich family. Liang was very sad. He became serious ill and died. After his death he became a butterfly. Zhu jumped into the grave of Liang and became another butterfly. They lived together forever in this way. "

A plot unit graph for this story in the sense of Lehnert is given below to show his idea.

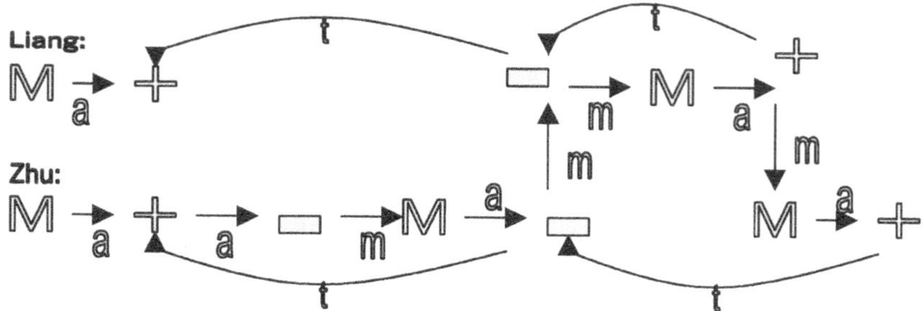

Figure 1.6.1 Plot Unit Graph for Liang and Zhu

Yet no story understanding systems have been implemented based on the plot unit approach.

In 1982, Dyer used a highly integrated method in BORIS [Dyer, 1983a] [Dyer, 1983b] to combine various kinds of knowledge structures together so that BORIS could understand extremely complicated stories, e.g. divorce, kidnapping, etc. Integrating various kinds of knowledge structures, BORIS avoids the limitations caused by single knowledge structure representation. But BORIS cannot synthesize various kinds of knowledge structures simultaneously. And it is very difficult to modify these complicated and specific knowledge structures.

Since almost all algorithms in the story understanding systems introduced above depend upon some specific knowledge structure, the knowledge inference mechanisms in one algorithm cannot be transplanted to fit knowledge structures of another algorithm. In this regard, research on the so-called weak methods has appeared in recent years. The weak method is a universal method independent of knowledge representation for solving some kinds of problems. Generally speaking, algorithms in these methods have high complexity.

The Lehnert's approach is closer and relevant to our technique used in SWAN. We did not use the concept of plot units. But we have used a simple method of counting the number of relations between roles in the story to determine the main content of the story, its main characters and main development threads. The results have shown that it was quite successful.

In the research about plan based speech understanding, many authors have invented various approaches for analyzing beliefs, desires and intentions of the speakers. A well known approach in this direction was that of Cohen and Perrault [Cohen and Perrault, 1979]. They have proposed four factors for constructing a plan in the speech-act theory. These factors are:

1. Operation: An action in the real world, e.g. walk, eat, sleep, etc.
2. Premise: The necessary conditions for performing an action.
3. Operation Body: The content of an action.
4. Effect: The influence and result of an action.

Among these four factors, we are mainly interested in the second and fourth one, namely the premise and the effect. Cohen and Perrault used three modal operators to represent the premise and the effect. They are: BELIEVE, WANT and CANDO, each with a set of axioms. Let us consider a few examples, where a denotes a speaker (partner of a conversation), P, Q denote predicates:

Examples of BELIEVE Axioms:

B1: a BELIEVE (all true statements of the predicate calculus)
B2: a BELIEVE (P) or a BELIEVE (Q) => a BELIEVE (P or Q)
B3: a BELIEVE (P) and a BELIEVE (Q) => a BELIEVE (P and Q)

Examples of WANT Axioms:

W1: a WANT (P) => not (a WANT (not (P))
W2: a WANT (P) => a BELIEVE (a WANT (P))
W3: a WANT (b BELIEVE (P)) => a BELIEVE (P) (Principle of honesty)

Examples of CANDO Axioms:

C1: there is C, a CANDO (C)
C2: a CANDO (C) or a CANDO (D) <=> a CANDO (C or D)

Cohen and Perrault used these modal operators for representing premises and results of actions occurring in a story, where they have summarized the actions in a few of classes just as Schank has done in his conceptual dependency theory. In the following, we list only the class of MOVE actions:

MOVE (role, start position, end position)
Premise (CANDO): LOC (role, start position)
Premise (WANT): role BELIEVE (role WANT MOVE (role, start position, end position))
Effect: LOC (role, end position)

1.6.4 The Story Structure

It is important to clarify the structure of a story. It was Lebov who has pointed out six key points which have to be made clear by any story understanding program. In some sense, it displays also a standard structure of stories, which is explained in the following.

1. The Abstract of the story, which is a short resume of the whole story.
2. The Orientation of the story, which describes the background of the story, including the time, the place, the roles and the objects, the environment where the roles and objects act, etc.
3. The complicated actions of the story, which include a series of events which have happened in the story, which imply in turn the changes of states during the development of the story plots. Apart from the statements, this part contains also the dialog of roles in the story.

4. The evaluation of the story. This part represents the points of view of the authors and readers on the story, including comments on the theme, the roles, the actions, the events and the style of writing, etc.
5. The result or resolution of the story. It describes the outcome of the story, including the fate of the roles, the success or failure of their goals and efforts, etc.
6. The coda of the story, which is an epilog of the whole thing. Usually it consists only of very few sentences.

As it is easy to see, the first point (abstract of the story) usually does not belong to the text of the story itself. It has to be written extra by the author, or has to be made by the reader him/herself after reading. But all other five points do appear in the story text and form the main structure of it. There is a rough order relation between these parts:

Orientation → Complicating Actions → Resolution → Coda

---------------------------------Evaluation ------------------------------

which means that the evaluation can appear at any place of the story text.

Another approach of studying story structures was proposed by Grosz [Grosz, 1985]. According to her opinion, a story should be analyzed along three lines: the utterance structure, the intention structure and the focus structure. One should not imagine that each sentence in a story has its own intention. Rather, a story has to be first divided into a sequence of segments. The intentions of the story writer are assigned separately to the different segments which can be nested. That means, while the whole story has a global intention, different segments should have their local intentions. In the case of nesting, the intentions of internal segments are components of the intention of the containing segment. On the other hand, the preceding segments prepare necessary conditions for following segments. For example, the preceding segments may play the role of introduction for the following ones.

Example 1.6.3

Discourse analysis according to Grosz:

DS0:
DS1: 1. Everybody likes watching film.
2. Especially the young people.
3. Now it's time to care about social effects of movie.
DS2: 4. Should the parents be careless about their children's behavior in this regard?
DS3: 5. No one can ignore the social effects of good films.
6. because they are really moving.
DS4: 7. But the problem is: should we take a laissez-faire attitude?
8. Isn't it a harmful attitude?
DS5: 9. First of all, there are too many bad films.
10. One may convince oneself by looking at the advertisements.
DS6: 11. Even the good films have problems.
DS7: 12. Some good films lack spiritual ballast.

13. Some films are too far from the reality.
14. No enough patriotism is reflected in films.
15. Is this not a bad thing for the young people?
16. The parents and teachers should ponder about this problem.

The study on discourse and story structure is not only of theoretical nature. In the SWAN system, it helps us in analyzing the themes and development threads of a story, and dividing the story into acts.

1.7 Plot Planning and Generation

One of the tasks in automatic generation of computer animation is to do detailed planning for abstract plots in a story, such as "wedding", because the forms of the wedding ceremony are so many and so different that the computer does not know where to start with the word "wedding" only. An early system for plot generation, called PEGASUS, was developed at the beginning of eighties [Meehan, 1981]. Using this system, stories are produced in real time by a cooperative play between pre-specified roles of the cast of the story.

One approach of interactive plot generation is to use story graphs which (are not the same concept as our story graphs explained in chapter five and) are quite similar to finite state machines. Each node of a story graph represents an episode of a possible story. The arcs leading from one node to others show the possible development trends of the story. By following the arcs the user may "create" event chains of a new story. The creativity provided by this approach is limited because the story graph is predefined.

The story grammar of Rumelhart was also used to generate stories, but in a controversial way.

Another approach for story generation is to simulate a real world by letting the user talk to computer simulated characters. Just as it was pointed out by N.M.Sgouros [Sgouros, 1999], this kind of work "has concentrated mainly on portraying the emotional state of these characters, on supporting full-body interactive video environments, or on developing directed improvisation paradigms in which computer characters improvise a joint course of behavior following users' directions".

Recently, Nikitas M. Sgouros has developed a technique for generating interactive plots based on the Aristotelian theory of drama [Sgouros, 1999]. According to this theory, the main development thread of a story is based on the appearing, development and resolution of conflicts between its roles. Most conventionally, "a conflict between antagonistic forces develops out of an initial situation. The plot moves from this initial situation towards its antagonistic climax, through a sequence of conflicts, and then towards an unambiguous solution at the end." This theory is the philosophy of the system DEFACTO developed by the author. DEFACTO invites the user to participate in the story development. In fact, he/she plays the role of a protagonist of the story. The plot planning is done dynamically during the process of interaction between the user protagonist and other members of the cast, all simulated by the computer.

DEFACTOR has a plot manager which is its main module. Each time when playing, the plot manager accepts as input a set of initial plot conditions written in predicate form to describe the roles, motivations and interrelations of cast members. It outputs a sequence of character actions together with their motivations and causal relations.

The plot manager consists of three parts: a Generation module which generates a set of possible interactions between the story characters, an Evaluation module which evaluates the interactions produced by Generation and chooses the most interesting ones among them for inclusion in the dynamic story, The control will return to Generation if the selection is successful, otherwise it goes one step down to the third module called Resolution which calculates the outcome of character interactions based on an importance hierarchy for character motives. All these three modules are supported by sets of criteria and heuristic rules, which we call knowledge bases in SWAN.

In interactive story systems, it is the user intervention which determines the progress and outcome of the story. In DEFACTO, there are two kinds of character intervention: the goal intervention and the normative intervention. The former tries to influence (badly or favorably) the efforts of other cast members in reaching their goals, while the latter seeks to influence the attitudes or behaviors of other cast members (called norms of these members). In the following, we cite from this paper some primitives used in the Generation module to show its mechanism of intervention:

Goal (x, g) # x seeks to achieve g #
Intervene (+, x, y, +, g) # y seeks to satisfy goal/norm g by helping x #
Intervene (-, x, y, -, g) # y seeks to impede goal/norm g by obstructing x #
Intervene (+, x, y, -, g) # y seeks to impede goal/norm g by helping x #
Intervene (-, x, y, +, g) # y seeks to satisfy goal/norm g by obstructing x #
Try (+, x, a, g) # x attempts to execute action a for achieving goal/norm g #
Try (-, x, a, g) # x attempts to execute action a for impeding goal/norm g #
Motivates (a, b) # action a motivates action b #
Rel (+, x, y) # characters x and y have positive relation #
Rel (-, x, y) # characters x and y have negative relation #

The meaning of these primitives will be more obvious if we cite some rules of plot generation from this paper:

Goal (x, g) → Try (+, x, a, Goal (x, g))
Intervene (+, x, y, +, g) → Try (+, y, a, g) ∧ Motivates (Intervene (+, x, y, +, g), Try (+, y, a, g))
Rel (+, x, y) ∧ Goal (x, g) → Intervene (+, x, y, +, g)

Example 1.7.1 (A Story Produced by this Approach)

"The user asks E for an interest free credit. Because E likes the protagonist, s/he proposes to him/her to marry A in exchange. The user accepts this proposal. Because D wants to marry A, she/he confronts the protagonist who decides to confront D as well. A likes D. Therefore s/he decides to defend D against the user."

It is not difficult to see that this approach has a similarity to our approach of abstract representation language Silver Beach presented in chapter five. In fact, by designing and using the Silver Beach language, we have also made benefit from the Aristotelian theory of drama in our SWAN system, but not for plot generation, rather, for story analysis.

Note that the approach taken in this paper is in principle not applicable for our purpose, because the plot generated in this way has a random character which may be not in compliance with the pre-specified story plot. But it is useful when we are going to add a user intervention module to help the development of abstract events into concrete ones (for their definition see chapter six). Another disadvantage which this approach seems to have is the lack of a commonsense knowledge base which could support it largely. We see this disadvantage by the simplicity of the story thus produced.

1.8 Generate Computer Animation from Natural Language Instructions

Ideas about using natural language instructions to generate computer animation have emerged since the seventies [Simmons and Bennett-Novak, 1975], [Badler, O'Rourke, Smoliar and Weber, 1978], where people have made attempts to use a set of task oriented motion control schemas to generate a computer animation. Badler et al. [Badler, O'Rourke, Smoliar and Weber, 1978] have tried to design a suitable architecture for animating natural language, which has met a large set of particular difficulties in implementation [Badler, O'Rourke and Kaufman, 1980].

The research in this field has made considerable progress in the eighties. Zeltzer, Girard et al. and Bruderlin et al. have studied the problem of locomotion control of mobile agents [Zeltzer, Pieper and Sturman, 1989] [Bruderlin and Calvert, 1989] [Girard and Maciejewski, 1985] and developed manageable models.

Badler et all. [Badler, 1991] have established a rather comprehensive framework for interpreting and executing natural language instructions. A simpler version of animating natural language instructions has been already done in 1989 by Esakow and Badler [Esakov and Badler, 1989] whose overall goal can be described with the following motto:

Instruction → Behavior

Example 1.8.1 (Instruction Sequences Elaborated in [Esakov and Badler, 1989])

Animated are two agents John and Jane in front of a switchboard.

John, look at switch twf-1.
John, turn twf-1 to state 4.
Jane, look at twf-3.

Jane, look at twlJ-1.
Jane, turn tglJ-1 on.

It is easy to see that this work has rather little to do with natural language understanding. In the 1991 publication, they have followed a much more ambitious goal. They wanted to build a system which can animate complicated natural language instructions. The new motto can be illustrated as follows:

$$\text{Instructions} \rightarrow \text{Beliefs} \longleftrightarrow \text{Plan} \longleftrightarrow \text{Behavior}$$

That means, instructions will be first turned into beliefs and then into plans and then into behaviors. There is feedback from behaviors to plans and plans to beliefs. This complication arises from the necessity to solve difficult tasks, such as:

1. There is a set of instructions which form a sequence. Their translation in animation is only possible if the whole sequence and the relations between the individual instructions have been understood.
2. The instructions may be conditional, which require the agents to perform actions under appropriate circumstances.
3. The instructions may be given at several levels of detailedness or in different ways.
4. The instructions may imply the changes of significant features of objects, even their creation or destruction.
5. The instructions may only provide circumstantial constraints on behavior but not specify when those circumstances will arise.

Example 1.8.2

For each of the above five situations:

1. Left out the door, down to the end of the street quickly, cross straight over Essex immediately, then left up the hill, take the first right, and it'll be on your left.
2. Diverter spout is provided with insert for 1/2″pipe threads. If supply pipe is larger than (3/4″), unscrew insert and use spout without it.
3. Clear away loose plaster. Make a new lath backing with metal lath, hardware cloth, or, for small holes, screen. Cut the mesh in a rectangle or square larger than the hole. Thread a 4-to 5-inch length of heavy twine through the center of the mesh. Knot the ends together. Slip the new lath patch into the hole.
4. Mix plaster compound according to package directions. With a flexible putty knife or scraper, force the thick creamy into the opening.
5. When you have to cut a sheet of paneling, try to produce as smooth an edge as possible. If you are using a handsaw, saw from the face side.

It is easy to see that the tasks to be solved in this system is much more complicated than those in [Esakov and Badler, 1989]. There is thus no wonder that the system includes a rather complete set of components, which we will explain one by one in the following:

1. A natural language processor which consists of a parser, a semantic interpreter and a discourse processor. Its output is a set of descriptions of actions involved in performing the task, relationships among the actions and constraints on their performances.
2. An incremental planner to develop a plan gradually in compliance with the possible change of the environmental world and the actors' capabilities. Its output is a partial global plan. The word "partial" means the content of this plan depends still on circumstances which are going to come up.
3. A semantic mapper elaborates the output of the incremental planner (a set of actions) and outputs a set of parameterized event templates, which combine the temporal constraints, kinematics and dynamic features with geometric constraints related to these events.
4. A simulator, which solves a temporal constraint satisfaction problem (TCSP) among the parameterized templates, maintains the event queue, schedules the active events, and outputs basic animation commands with parameters such as motion paths and forces.
5. Six motion generators, including a forward kinematics-guided motion generator; an inverse kinematics motion generator; a strength-guided motion generator; a forward dynamics motion generator; a walk generator and a facial expression generator.
6. A display processor which is based on Jack [Phillips and Badler, 1988], a powerful interactive graphics system for manipulating articulated actors. Using Jack, a visualization plan consisting of scenes, cuts and camera views is defined and executed. This module was not yet completed as it was reported in the 1991 paper.
7. A narrative planner and generator to explain the actions in the animation.

The entire process is viewed as a pipeline with feedback, including a variety of knowledge bases to support these functions.

It is interesting to have a look at the capabilities these motion generators can perform. We list them in groups (according to their nature and the motion generators used) as the authors originally presented.

1. Reach, touch, place, position;
2. Orient, align;
3. Attach, detach, grasp, ungrasp;
4. Put, take;
5. Look at;
6. Lift, push, pull;
7. Stand up, sit down;
8. Follow path;
9. Exert force or torque;
10. Walk along a path, walk to a goal point;
11. Produce facial expressions from speech intonation and emotion;
12. Walk.

Although the overall design and architecture are quite ambitious, there are still some key techniques of the SWAN system which are missing in their system. The goal of SWAN is to transform a children story into a cartoon. This is very different from that of transforming a set of instructions into an animation. First, a children story requires a cooperative play of multiple roles in the same space. Thus the planning task is much more complicated than if there were only one single role for performing the instructions. Second, the work of SWAN is based on a thorough analysis of the whole story, which can not be performed by an incremental planner alone. This is also the main difference between the framework of [Badler, 1991] and that of us. On the other hand, some interesting things of Badler's system are missing in SWAN. We do not have modules like narrative planner and generator, which are not needed for producing cartoons from children stories. Also the two modules "strength guided motion" and "forward dynamics" of Badler's six motion generators are missing in SWAN.

1.9 Generate Animation from Natural Language Stories

The point of focus of the MULTRAN project [Noma, Kai, Nakamura and Okada, 1992] is different from that introduced in last section. In that project, studies are made to address the problem of translating a story written in natural language to an animation. The MULTRAN project (MULtimedia TRANslation) was started in 1990. It was aimed at developing a system for understanding, generating and translating multimedia information, including reciprocal translation between natural language texts and images. For the language-to-animation direction, they focused on studying temporal relations among events narrated in the story, each with a temporal constraint. The following four tasks are included: derivation of events from texts; determination of time constraints for events; finding a solution of the constraint satisfaction problem; constructing the motion sequence and completing the animation. The goal is to obtain an optimal solution with these constraints. Let us compare the following two stories:

Example 1.9.1 (A Story Processed by MULTRAN)

"John started to walk from the market. Mary started to walk from the station. He arrived at the bridge. She also arrived there."

Example 1.9.2 (Another Version of the Story)

"John started to walk from the market. Mary started to walk from the station. He arrived at the bridge. She also arrived there simultaneously. "

There is only one difference between the two versions of the same story. The second version has the temporal constraint word "simultaneously" while the first one does not. This difference will influence the final result produced by the movie planner, because the product of the second version should respect the time constraint but that of the first one does not need to do so.

There are two kinds of time constraints in MULTRAN:

Definition 1.9.1

The ordering of sentences prescribes the temporal order of the events animated. This is called the weak time constraint. The temporal words (adverbs, etc.) in the sentences determine the final order of events. This is called the strong time constraint.

In example 1.9.2, the temporal word "simultaneously" is a strong time constraint. Of course there are also spatial constraints, such as "at the same place", etc.

Definition 1.9.2

Each actor has an evaluation function for each of its actions. We denote it with f (a, b), where a is the actor name, and b is the action name. Consider f (a, b) as a distribution over the time axis, called Action Time Estimation Function (ATEF), we may define:

$$f(a, b): [0, \infty) \rightarrow [0, \infty)$$

The smaller the value f (a, b) (t) is, the more plausible is t the time length of the action f (a, b). A possible choice of the function form is

$$f(a, b)(t) = k(t - t_0)^2$$

Algorithm 1.9.1 (Temporal Optimization)

1. Use a lexical functional grammar to parse the story and to obtain an intermediate representation.
2. Determine the anaphoric referents.
3. Use spatial constraints to determine the places of actions.
4. Each event is treated as a point of time.
5. List all the strong temporal constraints.
6. Let the actors calculate the time lengths s/he needs for performing the actions.
7. Arrange the time points on the time axis in the way that the total sum of all f (a, b) (t) reaches its minimum under the condition that all temporal constraints are fulfilled.

End of Algorithm

Note that the concept "event" is a micro one. For example, it is not the action "the rabbit runs" which is taken as an event, because such events would not be able to be represented as a time point. Rather, "the rabbit starts to run" or "the rabbit stops to run" will be considered as events.

Obviously, the type of stories considered in MULTRAN is much simpler than that considered in SWAN. In fact, these stories are designed to show the main function of the optimization module of MULTRAN. Many other problems relating to the transformation of natural language texts into animation form are not discussed here. As to the problem of time constraints, we have adopted another approach. We followed the principle of divide and conquer and introduced the two step (qualitative and quantitative) planning method which has been proved to be efficient, see chapter six.

2 SWAN: Full Life Cycle Automation of Computer Animation

2.1 An Overview of SWAN

2.1.1 How SWAN Was Born

After nearly ten years effort, supported by a special foundation of President of Academia Sinica and several other foundations, a research group in Institute of Mathematics, Academia Sinica, has developed a technique of full life cycle computer aided animation generation, called FLICA, and implemented a prototype software, called SWAN. By FLICA we mean the computer should provide whole life cycle aid during animation generation. Given a story written in natural Chinese language, the computer should be able to convert the story into a cartoon ready to be shown on the screen. Starting from the understanding of stories written in some natural language (here Chinese), until the generation of the cartoons, the whole process should be done automatically by the computer (Of course, user intervention is available, see below). A cartoon produced by SWAN, called "the three brothers", has been shown on CCTV (Chinese Central Television Station).

Many works reported in the literature are masterpieces of really good contribution to this field. But most of them seem to only form part of an ambitious unfinished project. To our best knowledge, the full cycle of automatic computer animation generation from children stories in natural language has not been reported in the literature before SWAN. We have implemented a prototype of SWAN, and thus the FLICA methodology in 1995 on two SGI workstations. SWAN has more than 50000 lines of C codes, and a large volume of the animation library. SWAN is supported by Explore™, a graphics package of TDI (later Wavefront).

2.1.2 The FLICA Methodology

The transformation from a natural language story to an animated movie is very complicated. In order to complete this process successfully, we follow the principle of stepwise refinement , which has been used as a guideline in the practice of software engineering for many decades. More precisely, we divide the process of animation generation from a natural language story in eight stages.

Stage 1. Comprehension of text written in a limited Chinese natural language, and its conversion into a form of semantic representation.

R. Lu and S. Zhang: Automatic Generation of Computer Animation, LNAI 2160, pp. 29-63, 2002.

Stage 2. Understanding the content of the story and doing corresponding story analysis with necessary commonsense knowledge checks.
Stage 3. Qualitative planning of cartoon shots and plots.
Stage 4. Director planning.
Stage 5. Qualitative camera planning.
Stage 6. Qualitative light and color planning.
Stage 7. Quantitative cartoon script planning, camera planning, and light and color planning.
Stage 8. Cartoon generation based on the quantitative description mentioned above and a comprehensive animation knowledge base.

2.1.3 Five Levels of Representation

When researching the possibility of generating cartoons automatically, we do not overlook the need of providing system support to the users so that they can intervene in the generation process and modify the decision made by the computer, thus develop their creativity in arts and animation techniques. In fact, for each stage mentioned above, we provide a corresponding representation language. The user (movie director, animation creator) can revise the "program" of animation represented in any of these languages at his will.

Roughly speaking, there are five different levels of representation. The first level is the limited natural Chinese language which is used to write the story. After a parsing process, the natural language text will be transformed into its deep semantic representation which is based on a modification of the case frame theory of Fillmore [Fillmore, 1968]. That means, the basic content of the story has been understood by the SWAN system. Then a series of qualitative planning can be started to produce the script. The result of this series of planning is represented in a qualitative script description language, where many parameters, including the location parameters and the temporal parameters of roles and actions, are either open or given in a fuzzy way. Then, a quantitative calculus is introduced at this stage to determine the exact values of the fuzzy parameters contained in the qualitative description language. In this way, we get a quantitative description of the story where all fuzziness has been resolved. The last step is to transform this quantitative representation into an assembler level language called SCRIPT. A SCRIPT program will be performed by a TDI interpreter to produce the final animation.

Among these five levels of languages, only the language of the last level, the SCRIPT™ language, was a part of the Explore graphics package. New versions of SCRIPT are now products of the Wavefront company. Names are given by the authors of this book to the representation languages to honor their contributors (students).

Level 1. A Limited Chinese Natural Language, called Moon Light.
Level 2. A Semantics Description Language, called Golden Forest.
Level 3. A Qualitative Script Description Language, called Rainbow.

Level 4. A Quantitative Script Description Language, called Evergreen.
Level 5. A Low Level Computer Animation Language, called SCRIPT.

2.2 Moon Light: The Natural Language Level Representation

2.2.1 The Limited Chinese Natural Language

Taking into consideration the current state of art of natural language understanding techniques, we think it is reasonable in the SWAN project to deal with limited natural language texts only. We have designed a small language of limited natural Chinese for writing children stories. This language, called Moon Light, should be powerful enough so that a large class of children stories can be written in it. By this large class we mean children stories, which can be told to, say, three to five years old children such that they can understand the rough content of these stories quite well. The limitation is not very strict, since many others can be first simplified and then written in it. This language should also be natural enough so that it is really a subset of the Chinese language used in daily life. At the same time it should also be concise enough so that a parsimonious parser could be built up to analyze its syntax and semantics clearly.

Following is a tiny example written in Moon Light. The structure of these sentences should not be compared with the syntax listed in next chapter, because they are English sentences translated from Chinese, and the syntax in next chapter is only valid for Chinese texts.

"The mother of Princess Snow White died. Snow White was very sad. The king married a new queen. The new queen believed that she was the most beautiful woman in the world. But a magic mirror told the new queen that Snow White was more beautiful than her. She was very jealous. She let a hunter kill Snow White. The hunter set Snow White free. Seven dwarfs accepted Snow White. The magic mirror told this to the new queen. The new queen became a peasant woman. She visited Snow White and gave a poisonous apple to her. Snow White ate the poisonous apple and died. A prince came and saw the dead Snow White. He rescued Snow White. He killed the new queen. The prince married princess Snow White."

2.2.2 Check the Validity of the Story Based on Commonsense Knowledge

When designing our story grammar for the Moon Light language, we have paid attention to two important aspects. The first one is the characteristics of the Chinese language. There is a remarkable difference of grammatical structure between Chinese and languages of other families, such as English or French. On the other hand, this grammar should be context sensitive, since otherwise it could hardly be used to describe a meaningful real story. For example, a context free story grammar would consider the following sentence as legal:

Princess Snow White eats princess Snow White. (1)

Furthermore, the following micro-story would be also considered as legal:

Princess Snow White died.
Princess Snow White eats an apple. (2)

A human-being can not eat him/herself. A dead person can not do anything. All these belong to commonsense knowledge. We call the sentence (1) as a sentence with local commonsense knowledge error, and the sentence (2) as one with global commonsense knowledge error. The first type of errors can be detected on the basis of analyzing one sentence only, independent of the situation described by other sentences. The second kind of errors can only be detected with respect to at least two sentences.

In order to check the huge amount of commonsense knowledge, we have introduced a new kind of attributed grammar, the commonsense oriented unification grammar, CSU grammar for short. This grammar is divided into two levels. The first level is a context free grammar which serves as a basis of story description. The second level is a decoration of this context free grammar with commonsense constraints which are collected in frames called commonsense constraint frames whose form is similar to the attribute frames used in a unification grammar.

The commonsense constraint frames may be attached to each production rule of the Moon Light grammar. Therefore the task of parsing a story is twofold. First, parse the sentences of the story just like parsing a text of a conventional programming language. Second, the reduction performed by each rule is accomplished with a check of all commonsense constraint frames attached to this rule.

Note that any violation of commonsense knowledge detected by the parser will not be considered as a fatal error, but only as a warning message to the user, since in a children story there may very well be commonsense violation. For example, people may go through a wall or just fly in the sky. The user may ignore this warning if the effect of the violation of commonsense knowledge is just what he wanted.

2.3 Semantic Analysis and Its Representation

2.3.1 A Representation Based on Case Frames

We use a context sensitive parser to parse a Moon Light text and to transform it into its deep semantic form: GF (means Golden Forest), which is a series of case frames. Each sentence corresponds to a case frame. We call this series of case frames a forest of case frames. In Chapter Four the reader will see that we have designed a grammar, called forest grammar, to analyze the content of a story. For the moment, we are interested only in natural language parsing. The parser assumes in general that the order of the sentences in the case frame series denotes the direction towards which the time of the story elapses. That means a flashback is in general not allowed. In the example above, the prince rescued Snow White and then married her, not the contrary. This limitation, which has eased the story parsing a lot, is reasonable for writing small children stories. But sometimes this limitation brings also inconveniences. In order to solve this problem, SWAN allows a story writer to use some special keywords to produce flashbacks in a story text.

The form of a case frame used in SWAN system is a little bit different from those proposed by Fillmore originally. In order to meet the need of story description, we have generalized it to allow nouns and pronouns to be the key of a case frame. They include those physical entities which appear often in a story, such as persons, objects and backgrounds. We call those case frames whose keys are actions as main case frames. They form a chain of the action series. Other case frames are called auxiliary case frames. We call this representation a GF.

It would occupy too much space if we were to list the complete syntax of GF in this section. But we can at least give a short summary of the main part of this syntax to let the reader get some flavor of it. The GF language has two formats. The first format, GF1, is used to represent the story after natural language understanding. It consists of a continuous flow of case frames in its original sense. The second format, GF2, is a higher level form of GF1, where all statements are written in form of procedure calls. The form of a GF2 statement is very similar to that of a RAINBOW statement (to be explained below). The only difference is that a Gf2 statement may represent an abstract action, while a RAINBOW statement doesn't. All GF2 statements representing abstract actions will be replaced by those with concrete actions in the process of plot planning. In the following section 2.3.2 we give a short introduction to GF1.

2.3.2 A Short Introduction to the GF1 Syntax

The deep semantics representation of a story in SWAN is called a GF1 script which consists mainly of four parts: the roles, the objects, the environments and the actions. Note that not every syntactical item is necessary.

<GF1 script> ::= GF1 Script : <Script Name>;
Role List: <Sequence of Role Declarations>;
Object List: <Sequence of Object Declarations>;
Environment List: <Sequence of Environment Declarations>;
Action List: <Sequence of Action Declarations>;
End of GF1 Script

2.3.3 The Roles

The main difference between a role and an object is a pure technical one. It prescribes that the former may have articulates but the latter does not. The difference between articulated and not articulated things is a requirement of the SCRIPT language which is the last level in the representation hierarchy of SWAN, whose interpreter is provided by the TDI company.

<Role Declaration> ::= # Role Key : <Role Key>,
  # Role Name : <Role Name>,
  # Role Number : <Thing Number>,
  # Role Identity : <Role Identity>,
  # Role Difference : <Role Difference>,
  # Role Sex : <Role Sex>,
  # Role Age : <Role Age>,
  # Role Decoration : <Role Decoration>,
  # Role Feature : <Role Feature>,
  # Role Affiliation : <Role Affiliation>,
  # Role Characteristics : <Role Characteristics>,
  # Role Relations : <Role Relation>
End of Role

A role declaration consists of those items which are useful for analyzing the role in chapter four, five and six, and/or for portraying the role in chapter five, six, seven, eight and nine. The role number item denotes the number of a group of similar roles. The role identity denotes a role directly taken from the role base. The role difference specifies the reconfiguration of a role figure after it is taken from the role base. For example, the declaration "replace (head, head (lion))" replaces the role's head by one of a lion. The declaration "add (tail, coccyx)" adds a tail to the coccyx articulate of the role. Note that in a GF1 script one can not produce, nor change an articulate. All articulates are predetermined in the basic graphics package. The role decoration denotes attachments to a role. They may be objects, for example, a hat, a stick, a sword, a school bag, etc. They may also be other roles, for example, a bird or a fly (may be in the hand or on the shoulder of a role). The role feature denotes some outlook of the role. The role affiliation denotes the social position of a role. The role characteristics denote abstract and mental properties of a role. The role relations denote role's relationship with other roles.

<Thing Number> ::= <Positive Integer ≧ 2> | several | many
<Role Identity> ::= <Name of a Role Figure Stored in Knowledge Base>
<Role Difference> ::= <Sequence of Role Part Modifications>
<Role Part Modification> ::= <Role Part Replacement> | <Role Part Addition>
<Role Part Replacement> ::= replace (<Role Part>, <Replacement>)
<Replacement> ::= <Object Key> | <Role Part> (<Role Identity>)
  | <Role Part> (<Role Key>) | empty
<Role Part Addition> ::= add (<Sequence of Replacements>, <Articulate Name>)
<Role Sex> ::= male | female
<Role Age> ::= <Positive Integer> | baby | child | young | middle-aged | old |very old
<Role Decoration> ::= <Sequence of Attachments>

```
<Attachment> ::= attach (<Sequence of Thing Denotations>, <Articulate Name>)
<Thing Denotation> ::= <Role Key> | <Object Key>
<Role Feature> ::= <Sequence of R_Features>
<Role Affiliation> ::= <Sequence of Affiliations>
<Role Characteristics> ::= <Sequence of R_Characteristics>
<Role Relation> ::= <Sequence of R_Relations>
<R_Feature> ::= <R_Feature Class> ( <Sequence of R_Feature Values> )
<R_Feature Class> ::= appearance | figure | <Role_Part>.<R_Feature Class> | ...
<Affiliation> ::= king | queen | peasant | hunter | ...
<Role_Part> ::= leg | hand | arm | foot | eye | ear | mouth | head
            | <Role_Part>s | left <Role_Part> | right <Role_Part> | ...
<R_Feature Value> ::= <Appearance Value> | <Figure Value>
<Appearance Value> ::= beautiful | ugly | dirty | luxurious | good | gorgeous
        | stinking | exquisite | rich | worn-out | bad | ...
<Figure Value> ::= fat | thin | tall | short | very <Figure Value> | ...
<R_Characteristic> ::= kind | cruel | mad | honest | sly | ...
<R_Relation> ::= <Relation Class> (<Sequence of Role Keys>)
<Relation Class> ::= father_of | mother_of | sister_of | brother_of | son_of
        | daughter_of | friend_of | enemy_of | ...
```

2.3.4 The Objects

The declaration of an object is much simpler than a role.

```
<Object Declaration> ::= # Object Key : <Object Key>,
   # Object Name : <Object Name>,
   # Object Number : <Thing Number>,
   # Object Identity : <Object Identity>,
   # Object Feature : <Object Feature>
# End of Object
<Object Identity> ::= <Name of an Object Stored in Knowledge Base>
<Object Feature> ::= <Sequence of O_Features>
<O_Feature> ::= <O_Feature Class>(<Sequence of O_Feature Values>)
<O_Feature Class> ::= size | material | color | lightness | safety | ...
<O_Feature Value> ::= <Size Value> | <Material Value>
            | <Color Value> | <Lightness Value> | <Safety Value> | ...
<Size Value> ::= huge | large | middle | small | tiny | ...
<Material Value> ::= gold | silver | glass | wood | paper | ......
<Color Value> ::= red | green | blue | black | white | yellow
            | light <Color Value> | dark <Color Value> | ...
<Lightness Value> ::= dark | bright | very <Lightness Value> | ...
<Safety Value> ::= safe | crisp | poisonous | explosive | not <Safety Value> | ...
```

2.3.5 The Environments

An environment here means a physical environment, which may be a physical background or a natural phenomenon, or both. In the current version of SWAN, we have not yet integrated graphics packages which support the presentation of natural phenomena. Therefore, for the present, we use the trick of including the natural phenomena into the backgrounds. They are not live. But they do give the audience some impression about the environment, for example, a cloudy weather.

A background may also include objects, even roles. But they are an integrated part of this background. They are not live, either. This is the basic difference to the roles and objects declared in the last two sections 2.3.3 and 2.3.4.

<Environment Declaration> ::= # Environment Key : <Environment Key>,
Background Name : <Background Name>,
Bakground Identity : <Background Identity>,
Weather : <Weather>,
Season : <Season>,
Daytime : <Daytime>,
Role : <Sequence of Role Props>,
Object : <Sequence of Object Props>
End of Environment
<Background Identity> ::= <Name of a Background Stored in Knowledge Base>
<Weather> ::= sunny | cloudy | overcast | foggy | snowing | …
<Season> ::= spring | summer | autumn | winter | ...
<Daytime> ::= morning | noon | afternoon | evening | night | ...
<Role Props> ::= <Role Props Key> : <Role Key> (<Number> , <Position>)
<Object Props> ::= <Object props Key> : <Object Key> (<Number>, <Position>)
<Position> ::= <Relative Position> (<Background Name>)
| <Position> and <Position>
| <Relative Position> (<Role Props Key>)
| <Relative Position> (<Object Props Key>
<Relative position> ::= over | under | in front of | on | inside | outside | …

The background identity denotes a background directly taken from the background base. A background may be a mountain, a river, a forest, a street, a building or something else alike. There is a difference between the use of a role and that of a background. A role figure can be modified and decorated after it is taken from the role base. On the contrary, a background taken from the background base is not subject to any change. One can only produce a "virtual background" by adding some role props and/or object props to it. This is the meaning of role and object props declarations within a background declaration. As we said before, these declarations are not live. Note that a recursive definition of role props or object props is not allowed.

The weather, season and daytime conditions are, on the one hand, already taken into consideration during the selection of the background, but remain, on the other hand, still in the environment declaration, because they will also play a role in the story analysis, director planning, camera planning and light planning phases.

2.3.6 The Actions

The word "action" here has a generalized meaning. An action in GF1 may be a physical one (eating), a mental one (thinking), or just a predicate (being). But different kinds of actions have different numbers and types of cases. It is known from the commonsense, that even if some actions have the same numbers and types of cases, the values of their corresponding cases may be subject to different constraints.

<Action Declaration> ::= # Action Key : <Action Key>,
  # Action Name : <Action Name>,
  # Action Aspect : <Action Aspect>,
  # Action Tense : <Action Tense>,
  # Action Mood : <Action Mood>,
  # Action Case : <Sequence of Cases>
End of Action
<Action Aspect> ::= active | passive
<Action Tense> ::= past | future | present | ...
<Action Mood> ::= will | can | wish | <Action Mood> not
<Case> ::= <Case Type> (<Case Value>)
<Case Type> ::= subject | direct object | indirect object | tool | way | reason
  | location | time | start place | end place | ...
<Case Value> ::= <Role Key> | <Object Key> | ...

2.3.7 An Example

Let us now try to analyze a tiny story which will go through the whole chapter:

> "The new queen killed the beautiful princess Snow White with a poisonous apple.
> A prince made Snow White alive again.
> The prince married princess Snow White in a church."

It will be parsed by our natural language parser and transformed in the following GF1 format, where the title "the story about Snow White" is given by the user:

Script : The Story about Snow White;
Role List: # Role Key : r_1,
  # Role Name : Snow White,
  # Role Sex : female,
  # Role Feature : appearance (beautiful),
  # Role Affiliation : princess
  # End of Role,

  # Role Key : r_2,
  # Role Name : new_queen,
  # Role Sex : female,

```
            # Role Feature : appearance ( cruel ),
            # Role Affiliation : queen
            # End of Role,

            # Role Key : r_3,
            # Role Name : prince,
            # Role Sex : male,
            # Role Affiliation : prince
            # End of Role;

 Object List : # Object Key : o_1,
            # Object Name : apple,
            # Object Feature : safety (poisonous),
            # End of Object;

Environment List: # Environment Key : e_1,
        # Background Name : church,
        # End of Environment;

Action List: # Action Key : a_1,
        # Action Name : kill,
        # Action Aspect : active,
        # Action Tense : past,
        # Action Case :  subject (r_2),
                direct object (r_1),
                tool (o_1)
        End of Action,

        # Action Key : a_2,
        # Action Name : make alive,
        # Action Aspect : active,
        # Action Tense : past,
        # Action Case :  subject (r_3),
                direct object (r_1),
        End of Action,

        # Action Key : a_3,
        # Action Name : marry,
        # Action Aspect : active,
        # Action Tense : past,
        # Action Case :  subject (r_3),
                direct object (r_1),
                location (e_1)
        End of Action
End of Script;
```

2.4 Pragmatic Analysis and Qualitative Script Planning

2.4.1 Pragmatic Analysis

The GF1 representation obtained after the semantic analysis phase is just a "translation" of the original story. In most cases it is impossible to produce an animation just based on this form. Usually, a lot of information lacks. We list some of it in the following:

1. Information about the environment and background: where did the new queen kill princess Snow White, in the palace or outside the palace? Where did the prince rescue Snow White, at the same place or somewhere else? (The new queen may hide the dead body of Snow White somewhere else)
2. Information about the time of the events: when did these events happen, at daytime or at night? How was the weather of that day, sunny or rainy?
3. Information about the procedure of events: How did the new queen kill Snow White, by giving the apple to her as a food, or by hitting Snow White with the apple? If the first situation applies, then in which way did the new queen do it, by presenting her the poisonous apple as a gift, or by selling it to her? How did the prince rescue Snow White, by an injection or by some pills? How was their wedding ceremony, luxurious or simple?
4. Information about time and place of events: Actions a_1, a_2 and a_3 happened on the same day or different days? How is the distribution of roles and objects in the scene space? If there are obstacles in the space, how do the roles avoid them when performing some actions?
5. Information about the character, idea and moral of the roles. There are three people: new queen, Snow White and prince. Among these persons, who are the kind and good ones? Who are the cruel and sinister ones?
6. Information about the belief, desire and intention of the roles: Why did the new queen kill Snow White? Why did the prince rescue Snow White and then marry her?
7. Information about sentiment of the roles and the way of expressing it: Which was the feeling of the new queen before and after the murder? Which was the feeling of the prince before and after the rescue? And people's sentiment at wedding?
8. Information about the outlook of roles and objects: How do the different roles look like? How do the places where the events happen look like?

The above mentioned missing information can not be obtained in the syntactic analysis phase, nor in the semantic analysis phase of usual natural language understanding, as it was discussed in section 2.3. The solution of these problems, if available at all, can only be done partly by a pragmatic analysis, partly by an intelligent planning. In our terminology, we call them also story analysis and plot planning, which are performed based on the commonsense knowledge base Pangu. This knowledge base is supported by knowledge units of three different representation forms: the agents, the ontology bodies and rule sets of a formal grammar called Young Pine. See chapter ten for the detailed description of Pangu.

2.4.2 The Qualitative Planning

The aim of story analysis is to get enough information for qualitative script planning which is an important and decisive step on the way from the GF1 representation form of the script to the final animation. The jobs of qualitative planning include at least the following:

1. Transform all GF1 statements in their higher level form GF2.
2. For each GF2 statement containing an abstract action, choose a plot plan (consisting of drama agents or plot agents) for it from the knowledge base, and replace it with this plot plan. Do this recursively until no abstract action is remaining. This is the plot planning mentioned above.
3. Divide the continuous flow of GF2 statements (now containing only concrete actions) into a sequence of scenes, such that each scene is an independent component of the script. This is called scene planning.
4. Make decision about how to implement the theme (main idea) of the story, how to portray the main roles, how to determine the layout of each scene (distribution of roles and objects in the scene space), how to design new plots to display the atmosphere and sentiment of role and role groups, etc. This is called director planning,
5. Decide about how to design and implement the best point of view for the future audience by using a special-purpose language to simulate the techniques of movie photographing. This is called the camera planning,
6. Decide about how to design the best light and color use for implementing the director's intention and cameraman's intention, This is called the light and color planning.
7. Collect the results of all of this in a program written in an appropriate specification language which is called the qualitative planning language. We call this language Rainbow.

Note that it is difficult to find a unique order of performance of the jobs mentioned above. In fact these jobs depend on each other. For example the director planning's work is partially oriented to the individual scenes. Thus it seems the work of dividing the GF2 statements into scenes should be done before the director planning. But on the other hand, the principles of scene division are again partially based on the director's intention. Taking this into consideration, we may think that the director's planning should be done before scene division. So there is no simple and unique solution. In the practice of SWAN, we do these steps in an interleaving way.

In this section, we will only show the result of points 1 and 2 mentioned above. The results of point 3 and point 7 will be shown in section 2.4.6. The results of points 4, 5, 6 will be shown only in the following chapters.

As a preparation for the plot planning phase, SWAN first translates the GF1 statements into GF2 ones. After the translation, our ting story has the following form:

Role (Snow White, sex (female), appearance (beautiful), affiliation (princess)),
Role (New_queen, sex (female), appearance (cruel), affiliation (queen)),
Role (Prince, sex (male), affiliation (prince)),
Object (Apple, safety (poisonous), class (apple)),
Environment (Church, class (church)),
Kill (New_queen, Snow White, tool (Apple), t1, t10),
Make_alive (Prince, Snow White, t11, t20),
Marry (Prince, Snow White, location (church), t21, t30)
Where the ti's are time marks. It is assumed that for each i, ti < ti+1.

During the plot planning phase (point 2 above), SWAN detects that all three actions of the story: kill, rescue and marry, are abstract actions. They should be developed with plot plans. Fortunately, there exist such plot plans in the knowledge base. After development, all abstract action declarations are replaced by concrete actions. The knowledge base suggests at the same time a new background: garden.

Environment (garden, class (garden)),

The first action statement "Kill" of GF2 format is transformed in a sequence of new GF2 statements with concrete actions only. The main part of the GF2 statements is given as follows:

Give (New_queen, Snow White, Apple, garden, t1, t2),
Eat (Snow White, Apple, garden, t3, t4),
Fall_down (Snow White, garden, t5, t6),
Close_eye (Snow White, garden, t7, t10)

We see here something new in GF2 syntax, which does not exist in GF1. This is the action time [ti, tj], where ti and tj are time marks whose values will be determined in quantitative planning phase.

Among the various ways of rescuing, the knowledge base recommends the most simple way: praying. So the second case frame "rescue" of GF1 is transformed in a sequence of GF2 statements which contain the following five as its core part.

Come (Prince, outside (garden), garden, facing (Snow White), t11, t12),
Knee_down (Prince, facing (Snow White), t15, t16),
Pray (Prince, facing (Snow White), t15, t16),
Open_eye (Snow White, garden, t17, t18),
Stand_up (Snow White, garden, facing (Prince), t19, t20),

At last, the most simple plot plan for displaying the action "marry" is to show the bride and bridegroom leaving a church after wedding.

Walk_together ({Prince, Snow White}, in_front_of (gate (church)), forwards, slowly, t21, t30)

Note that there are constraints on the relations between time marks, which are partly inherited from the knowledge base, and partly calculated dynamically during animation generation.

2.4.3 The Rainbow Language

2.4.3.1 A Simplified Syntax of Rainbow

Rainbow is the language for representing qualitative planning in SWAN. It is also the most important intermediate language in the animation generation process of SWAN. A simplified and rough syntax of Rainbow is given in the following, where the difference between environment (role, object) specification and environment (role, object) selection is that the latter is a call (may be with refinement) to the former. It guarantees also the reuse of specifications. In order to save space, we omit the exact definition of these three items. The reader may get an impression about them in the example which will be given below. Since camera planning, light planning and color planning will only be discussed later, in chapters eight and nine respectively, their syntax and examples are not given in this section.

```
<Program> ::= # RAINBOW (<Program Name>):
            # Environment : <Environment Specification>;
            # Role : <Role Specification>;
            # Object : <Object Specification>;
            # <Sequence of Scene Specifications>
        # End of RAINBOW
<Scene Specification> ::= # Scene (<Scene Name>) :
            <Environment Selection>,
            <Role Selection>,
            <Object Selection>,
            <Camera Plan>,
            <Light Plan>,
            <Color Plan>,
            <Plot Specification>
        # End of Scene
<Camera Plan> ::= # Camera:
             <Sequence of Basic Camera Primitives>
            # End of Camera
<Light Plan> ::= # Light :
             <Sequence of Basic Light Primitives>
          # End of Light
<Color Plan> ::=# Color :
             <Color Signature>
```

End of Color
<Plot Specification> ::= #Plot:
<Sequence of RAINBOW Statements>
#End of Plot
<Basic Camera Primitive> ::= <Type of BCP> (<Sequence of Parameters of BCP>)
<Basic Light Primitive> ::= <Type of BLP> (<Sequence of Parameters of BLP>)
<RAINBOW Statement> ::=<MM Action>(<Subject>,<Object>,<Sequence of Case Parameters>,
<Sequence of Time Parameters>)
<MM Action> ::= <Macro Action Name>

Note that we have used a short notation <Sequence of Parameters of BCP> or <Sequence of Parameters of BLP> to represent the concrete content of BCP or BLP parameters. It is because that a concrete presentation of BCP and BLP syntax and semantics would involve too many details. We defer this job to the corresponding sections of the eighth and ninth chapter.

2.4.3.2 The Three Kinds of Actions

In SWAN, we differentiate among three kinds of actions: the generalized action, which is an abstract event with no details, like "wedding"; the macro action, which is a basic action of a person, usually in order to achieve some goal, and which can not be decomposed in a series of meaningful actions. For example "walking" is a macro action; the micro action, which is a basic action of articulate movement of a person or an object. In the "walking" example, the moving and rotation of legs and arms are micro actions, which together form the macro action "walking". These three kinds of actions are processed at three different stages. The generalized actions are transformed in a partially ordered set of macro actions during the scene and plot planning stage, and then macro actions are transformed in micro actions during the quantitative script planning stage

We call a description of a script with macro actions only (without generalized actions) a qualitative action hierarchy. Rainbow is a language for representing such qualitative action hierarchies, together with their role, background, object and camera descriptions. We will describe the macro actions in the next section. Micro actions will be explained in more details in chapter ten.

2.4.3.3 The Macro Actions of Rainbow

The classification of Rainbow macro actions was inspired by the idea of Schank about his conceptual dependency theory (CDT). In CDT, Schank proposed a set of eleven atomic actions to summarize all possible actions in a story. Our classification depends largely on the different mechanisms of implementing these actions in SWAN. In most of the cases, actions of the same class have the same number and type of parameters. Actually, the concept "action" is understood in a rather broad sense. "Being in some state" is also considered as an action. Following is a rough classification of macro actions in Rainbow.

1. The class of appearing actions (APP)

   It refers to those actions which denote roles who appear or disappear during some time interval limited by two time marks in the current scene. Examples of this class are appear, disappear, standing, siting, kneeling, lying, sleeping, etc. Parameters of APP include agents of APP, position of APP, directions of agents of APP, two time marks of APP, etc. They specify the way in which APP happen.

   Example: appear (princess, in-front-of (tomb), t1, t2)

2. The class of holding actions (HOL)

   It refers to those states in which some object (role) is kept fixed by another object (role). Thus, "A is being hold by B" is considered as an action. Examples of this class are holding, bearing, grasping, etc. Parameters of HOL include agent who holds, agent being hold, place of holding, etc.

   Example: holding (prince, flower, in (right_hand), t1, t2)

3. The class of change_state actions (CHS)

   It refers to state changes (color, form, size, etc.) of agents. These changes are also considered as actions. Examples of this class are change_color, change_scale, change_form, etc. Parameters of CHS include agents (or parts of agents) of CHS, initial values of changing states, final values of changing states, etc.

   Example: change_color (apple, green, red, t1, t2)

4. The class of sentiment expressing actions (SEE)

   It refers to the generation of facial expressions to show the agent's sentiment. Examples of this class are laugh, cry, speak, ponder, angry, disappointed, surprised, etc. The action "speak" does not contain any special sentiment. But since it involves also movements of facial muscle, this action belongs also to SEE. Parameters of SEE include agents of SEE, degree of SEE, etc.

   Example: laugh (princess, loudly, long, t1, t2)

5. The class of part actions (PAC)

   It refers to those actions by which the agents perform some articulate movements and at the same time keep their body position unchanged. Examples of this class are bend, kneel down, nod head, look around, raise hand, etc. Parameters of PAC usually have different number and type of parameters because the PAC are very different. Generally, they include agents of PAC, moved articulates, speed of PAC, times of repeating the actions, etc.

   Example: nod (king, repeatedly, t1, t2)

6. The class of moving actions (MOV)

   It refers to those actions which will change the body position of the agents who perform them. That this agent may at the same time perform part actions is not to exclude. Examples of this class are walk, run, fly, climb, jump, etc. Parameters of MOV include agents of MOV, start place, end place, moving direction, moving speed, etc. It is not necessary that all parameters appear in the same MOV statement. Thus the parameter "moving direction" is not necessary if both the start place and the end place are specified.

   Example: jump_to (frog, on (ground), bottom (well), quickly, t1, t2)

7. The class of group_moving actions (GRM)

   It refers to actions performed by a group of agents, where each agent performs the same action. The synchrony of group actions should be kept untouched. Examples of this class are move_together, walk_together, jump_together, etc. Parameters of GRM include sequence of agents, start place, end place, direction, speed, etc.

   Example: walk_together (king, queen, entry (church), tribune (church), slowly)

Based on the classification given above, we can see that our principles of classifying actions are different from those in CDT of Schank. All abstract actions and mental actions in CDT, like ATRANS (change of ownership) and MBUILD (information generation) are not present in our classification system, because they can not be shown on the screen.

2.4.4 Camera Planning and Light Planning

One basic difference of a movie from a theatre is that in a theatre, the audience is always in front of the tribune and can only watch the play from this fixed direction and fixed distance. In a movie, however, the audience is guided by the camera director. It is possible to watch the progressing of the story from any angle and any distance in the physical space where the event happens. Therefore, an important task of SWAN is to generate a camera plan (chapter eight) together with the script planning (chapter six). The generation of a camera plan in SWAN goes through a multi level process which consists of several representation levels. The basic camera primitives (BCP) form a qualitative description level which corresponds to the level of macro action statements in the scene planning part. In this section, we only give an overview of the structure and functions of BCP. A detailed description can be found in chapter eight.

Each BCP denotes a basic type of camera working. The camera may have a fixed position, may move around in the space, may crab left and right, may pan left and right, may mount up and down, may tilt up and down, may track in and out, etc. The parameters of a BCP include the targets (roles or objects the camera is pointing to), type of shot, direction, angle (of tilt and pan), speed (of move, tilt, pan, track, crab and mount), etc.

Let us consider some typical BCP statements.

fixed (LS (front (king)), long, t1, t1)

where LS denotes the shot type "long shot". It says that the camera is fixed and pointing to the front side of the target (king), and the distance between king and camera is quite large (for a more exact explanation see chapter eight). The meaning of the time interval [t1, t2] is similar to that in scene planning part.

move (LS (front (king)), MS (left (queen)), quickly, t1, t2)

where MS denotes the shot type "medium shot". It says that the camera is initially quite far from the target (king) and moves quickly from that position to a new position which is not very far, nor very close to the new target (queen). It is now pointing to the left side of queen.

track (MS (left (queen)), CU (queen), slowly, t1, t1)

where CU denotes the shot type "close up". It says that the camera is always pointing to the left side of queen and tracks in slowly from the shot type MS to the new type CU where the new position is very close to the target.

pan (CU (left (queen)), princess, very slowly, t1, t2)

which says that the camera pans very slowly from pointing to the left side of queen to the direction pointing to the princess. Note that one can not specify which side of the princess the camera should point to, because in a pan action the place of a camera does not change. The view angle from camera to princess determines already the direction of photographing.

A final note: in the camera planning part, the time intervals of different BCP must not overlap, because at any time moment there is only one point of view the audience could have. This is very different from the scene planning part, where the different macro actions may have overlapping time intervals to denote concurrent actions.

2.4.5 Light and Color Planning

The camera planning must be accompanied by a corresponding light and color planning. In fact, many people consider them as an integrated part of the camera planning. In SWAN, however, the camera planning, light planning and color planning are three separated program modules. The reason is a technical one. From the point of view of the programming technology, it is more natural and more straightforward to go ahead in this way.

The light and color effect play a great role in a movie. In particular, they can help to produce a wanted atmosphere of the environment and to set off the sentiment of the roles. In RAINBOW, one can consider a light definition as an object definition plus some particular light effect. It is implemented by the so-called Basic Light Primitives, BLP for short. However, it is more difficult to implement the color effect. On their technical details please see chapter nine.

2.4.6 An Example

Take a summary: what is new from GF2 to RAINBOW? Following is a list of progress we have reached during this step:

1. The GF2 statements are grouped in plot specifications.
2. After story analysis, the director module has decided to add more actions to the plot specifications to display the characters of the roles. For example, it excludes the possibility that the new queen lets Snow White commit suicide by ordering her to eat the poisonous apple, because there is no dispute between them shown in the story. There is no reason for the new queen to do that. A much better assumption is new queen's cheating. Therefore, the plot planning module adds some conversation between them to show the cheating procedure.
3. For each role and each object, a figure was selected from the knowledge base.
4. The time order between the actions is made complete.
5. Camera planning, light planning and color planning (explained later).

Instead of giving the details of the syntax of Rainbow, we will have a look at the representation of our tiny example in RAINBOW, where a more refined plot planning than that given above is done.

```
# RAINBOW (Story about Snow White):
    # Environment : # Background : garden,
                # Type : in (garden_1),
                # Object : apple_tree (several)
                # End of Background,
                # Background : church,
                # Type : in_front_of (church-1),
                # End of Background
    # End of Environment;
    # Props : # Object : poisonous_apple,
            # Type : apple_1,
            # Color : red
            # End of Object
    # End of Props;
    # Role : # Character : Snow White,
            # Type : girl_1,
            # Property : figure (small),
                    color (white, skirt_art),
                    color (white, chest_art),
                    face (beautiful)
            # Decoration : crown (on_top__of (head))
```

```
        # End of Character,
        # Character : new_queen,
        # Type : girl_2,
        # Property : figure (small),
                color (black, skirt_art),
                color (black, shirt_art)
        # End of Character,
        # Character : prince
        # Type : boy_1,
        # Property : figure (tall),
                color (red, costum),
                face (handsome),
        # End of Character
# End of Role,

# Scene (Kill Snow White) :
  # Background (garden),
  # Plot :
   Standing (Snow White, in_middle_of (garden), , t0,t11),
   Standing (new_queen, in_front_of (Snow White), facing (Snow White), t0,
      t11),
   Holding (new_queen, apple, in(right_hand), t0,t5),
   Speak (new_queen, Snow White, "would you like a delicious apple?", t1,
      t2),
   Speak (Snow White, new_queen, "oh, yes, it's very nice of you", t3, t4),
   Speak (new_queen, Snow White, "here you are", t5, t6),
   Give (new_queen, Snow White, apple, t5, t6),
   Speak (Snow White, new_queen, "thank you very much", t7, t8),
   Eat_2 (Snow White, apple, t9, t10),
   Speak (Snow White, , "oh! I get dizzy!", t11, t12),
   Fall (Snow White, on (ground), t11, t12),
   Close_eye (Snow White, t12, t13)
  # End of Plot
# End of Scene,
# Scene (Rescue Snow White) :
  # Background (garden),
  # Plot :
   Lying (Snow White, on (ground), t0,t11),
   Come (Prince, outside (garden), near (Snow White), facing (Snow White), t1,
      t2),
   Speak (Prince, Snow White, "oh! Poor princess! I will help you", t3, t4),
   Kneel_down (Prince, t5, t6),
   Pray (Prince, t7, t8),
   Open_eye (Snow White, t9, t10),
   Stand_up (Snow White, facing (prince), t11, t12),
   Speak (Snow White, Prince, "who are you? why are you here?", t13, t14),
```

```
  Speak (Prince, Snow White, "I am happy you are awake again!", t15, t16)
  # End of Plot
# End of Scene,
# Scene (Marry Snow White) :
  # Background : church,
  # Plot :
  walk_together (Prince, Princess, in_front_of (gate (church)),
            backing(church), forwards, t1, t2)
  # End of Plot
# End of Scene
      # End of RAINBOW
```

2.5 Quantitative Planning and Representation

What we now have at our hand is a program in the Rainbow language which provides a qualitative description of the cartoon script. There are yet two transformations to be performed: the transformation from Rainbow to Evergreen, a language for describing the script quantitatively; and the transformation from Evergreen to SCRIPT, a machine level animation language provided by the Explore animation software package.

2.5.1 The Evergreen Language — Global Definition

2.5.1.1 A Short Survey of Evergreen

Let us first give a short introduction to the Evergreen language. The intention of designing and implementing the Evergreen language was to establish an intermediate level of representation between our RAINBOW and the SCRIPT™ language of TDI company. Therefore, the design of Evergreen has adopted many ideas from that of SCRIPT. Nevertheless, it also possesses many new and high level features which do not exist in SCRIPT. An Evergreen program is divided in several segments. Each segment specifies a scene and may have six parts:

1. The image declaration. It specifies the serial number of the current scene and the beginning number, end number and step size (interval between two frames) selected to be shown from its frame series.
2. The object declaration. It describes all objects appearing in the cartoon script, their properties and relations to each other, including object's initial position, its rough size, direction, color, light reflexivity, and connection (Incidence) relation with each other. Note that the concept "Role" does not exist in Evergreen anymore. All Physical entities are here objects.
3. The scene declaration. This is the most important part of a segment. It is again divided in two parts:

3.1. The movement declaration which specifies the trace and speed of moving objects.
3.2. The environment declaration which specifies the background and its possible change.
4. The camera declaration. It specifies the camera's state (fixed or moving), position (if fixed), trace and speed (if moving), direction (pointing to), and focus.
5. The light declaration which specifies the light sources, their positions, directions, colors and movements.
6. The body action declaration. It specifies the articulate movements of object's body.

Following is a simplified syntax and the corresponding semantics of Evergreen.

2.5.1.2 General Syntax

```
<Evergreen Program> ::= <Program Head> {<Program body>}1-n <Program Tail>
    <Program Head> ::= Evergreen (<Program Name>);
    <Program Tail> ::= End of Evergreen
    <Program Body> ::= <Image Declaration> ; <Object Declaration>
            ; <Scene Declaration> ; <Camera Declaration>
            ; <Light Declaration> ; <Action Declaration>
```

The reader may wonder why there is no color declaration in the program body of an Evergreen program. We do not need a color declaration in an Evergreen program because the effect of color declaration in Rainbow is implemented in Evergreen partly via object declaration, and partly via light declaration.

2.5.1.3 Image Declaration

```
< Image Declaration > ::= Image { <Series of Image Statements> }
< Image Statement > ::= Name of Scene : <Parameter 1>;
            Number of Images : <Parameter 2>;
            Begin : <Parameter 3>;
            End : <Parameter 4>;
            Step: <Parameter 5>;
<Parameter x> ::= <Positive Integer>
```

The image declaration specifies the distribution of all frames to the individual scenes. The word "image" here means frame, which is a common concept in movie or TV, where every second 24 or 25 frames of pictures are shown on the screen. We have used the notation "image" because the word "frame" is used in chapter six in another sense.

The five parameters represent separately: name of this scene; total number of images in this scene; sequential number of the first image; sequential number of the last image; and the number of frames of each frame group from which only one is taken for display in the script.

2.5.2 The Evergreen Language — Detailed Definition

2.5.2.1 Object Declaration

The object declaration specifies static properties of objects. These properties may be changed later. The changes are specified in a scene declaration. In this case, they are called initial properties of objects.

The components of a complex object may be drawn separately. Bu they still form an integrated object. If one of them moves, the others move with it together. These components are declared as connected objects.

<Object Declaration> ::= Objects {<Simple Object Declaration> ;
<Connected Object Declaration>}
<Simple Object Declaration> ::= Objs { { <Object Name>[of size <Object Size>]}$_{1\text{-}n}$ }
<Object Size> ::= (<x-size>, <y-size>, <z-size>)
<x-size> ::= <y-size> ::= <z-size> :: = <Positive Real Number>
<Connected Object Declaration>::= Con-Objs {{<Object Name> of size <Object Size>}$_{1\text{-}n}$}

2.5.2.2 Scene Declaration

The macro actions are further elaborated and made perfect in the script planning stage. They are decomposed in a partially ordered set of micro actions during the quantitative script planning stage. Finally, the micro actions will be numerically calculated during the stage seven.

<Scene Declaration> ::= Scene (<Name of Scene>){<Series of Object Specifications> [<Background Declaration>] }
<Object Specification> ::= Object (<Object Name >)
{[< Object State> ,] < Object Behavior> }
< Object State > ::= <Rotation> | <Scaling> | <Color> | <Appearance>
| <Flotation> | < Object State> , < Object State>
<Rotation> ::= Rotation (<Axis>, <Speed>, [<T-interval>])
<Axis> ::= <First Pole> : <Second Pole>
<First Pole> ::= <Second Pole> ::= [<Point Name>] <Position>
<Speed> ::= <Rotation Number> | <Rotation Number> →
<Rotation Number>
<Rotation Number> ::= <Real Number>
<Scaling> ::= Scaling (<Rate>) [<T-Interval>]
<Rate> ::= <x-Rate> , <y-Rate> , <z-Rate>
<x-Rate> ::= <y-Rate> ::= <z-Rate> ::= <Positive Real Number>
<Color> ::= Color (<Color Degree>) [<T-Interval>]
<Color Degree> ::= <Color Name> | <Pallet> | <Color Degree> →
<Color Degree>
<Pallet> ::= <r> , <b> , <g>
<r> ::= <b> ::= <g> ::= <eight bit number>

<Appearance> ::= Appearance (<T-interval> , <A-Place> , <A-Frequency> ,
<A-Instance>) | Disappearance (<T-interval> , <D-Frequency>)
<A-interval> ::= < Initial Image Number> →
<D-interval> ::= → <Final Image Number>
<T-interval> ::= <Initial Image Number>→ <Final Image Number>
| <A-interval> | <D-interval>
<A-Place>::=<Position>| Inside <Object Name> | Outside (<Object Name>)
| Around : <Position> [Range : <Object Distribution>]
| <A-Place> → <A-Place>
<A-Frequency ::= <D-Frequency> ::= Every <Positive Integer> Images
| Randomly High | Randomly Low
<A-Instance> ::= <Positive Integer> | Randomly Many | Randomly Few
<Object Distribution> ::= (<Length> , <Breadth> , <High>)
<Length> ::= <Breadth> ::= <High> ::= <Positive Real Number>
< Object Behavior> ::= fixed (<Position>)
| lmoving (<Initial Position > → <Final Position>, <T-Interval>)
| cmoving (→ <Final Position>, <T-Interval>)
| tmoving (<Moving Trace>,<T-Interval>)
| <Object Behavior> , <Object Behavior>
<Moving Trace> ::=(<Sequence of Positions>) | (<x_function>,
<y_function>, <z_function>)
<x_function> ::= <y_function> ::= <z_function> ::= <Function Name>
<Initial Position> ::= <Final Position> ::= <Position> ::= (<x-coordinate>,
< y-coordinate >, < z-coordinate >)
<x-coordinate> ::= < y-coordinate > ::= < z-coordinate > ::= <coordinate>
::= <Real Number>
<Initial Image Number> ::= <Final Image Number> ::= < Image Number >
::= <Positive Integer>

2.5.2.3 Camera Declaration

We divide the camera effects in two classes, one caused by camera position and direction changes, another one caused by change of camera focuses. The former is similar to the description of object behavior. The latter is the main content of this section. Note that the target position may change together with the change of the focus.

<Camera Declaration> ::= Camera { <Sequence of Camera Statements> }
<Camera Statement> ::= { <Camera Position Specification> ;
<Focus Changing Specification>;
<T-Interval> }
<Camera Position Specification> ::= Position (<Object Behavior>)
<Focus Changing Specification> ::= Target (<Target>, <Focus>)
<Target> ::= <Object Name> | <Object Name> → <Object Name>
<Focus> ::= <Positive Real Number> | <Positive Real Number> →
<Positive Real Number>

2.5.2.4 Light Declaration

The light declaration of Evergreen is quite complicated. It includes a lot of functions to implement the various effects of lightning. In this section, we are not interested in its technical details and are limited only to that part which is in some sense a combination of object declaration and camera declaration. On the one hand, we can consider a light source as an object which can be fixed or can move. On the other hand, we can consider a light source as a camera which points always to a specified direction.

<Light Declaration> ::= Light { <Sequence of Light Statements>}
<Light Statement> ::= { Type (<Light Type>) ; [Position (<Light Position>) ;]
[Color (<Light Color>) ;][Target (<Light Target>) ;]
Intensity (<Light Intensity>) ; <T-Interval> }
<Light Position> ::= <Position>
<Light Type> ::= homogeneous | point | object (<Object Name>)
<Light Color> ::= <Color>
<Light Intensity> ::= <Real Number between 0 and 1> | <Intensity> →
<Intensity> | <Function Name>

The syntax of light position and light target is not given here, because this part of syntax is similar to that of an object. Light position includes fixed position, moving and rotating of the light source, where the fixed position may be outside of the screen, or infinitely far away. Light target involves the names and positions of targets delighted by the light source. For a homogeneous light there is no light position nor light target.

2.5.2.5 Action Declaration

This part of declaration corresponds to the PAC class of macro actions in section 2.4.3. Each PAC action of RAINBOW is decomposed in a set of articulate movements in Evergreen.

<Action Declaration> ::= Action { <State Declaration> , <Series of Action Statements> }
<Action Statement> ::= <Action Name> {<State Change>}
<State Declaration> ::= State { <Sequence of Articulate States> }
<Articulate State> ::= <State Name> (<Articulate Name>
(<Articulate Behavior>))
<Articulate Behavior> ::= <Object Behavior>
<State Change> ::= <Type of Change> {(<Sequence of Articulate Changes>,
<T-Interval>)}
<Type of Change> ::= loop | single
<Articulate Change> ::= <State Name> → <State Name> ,
<Repeat Number>
<Repeat Number> ::= <Positive Integer>

An articulate state includes several aspects like the position, direction, scaling, rotation, etc. We omit its detailed description here.

Let us have a look at the Evergreen version of our tiny example (further simplified). We take only its last statement:

The prince married Snow White in a church.

```
Evergreen (wedding)
Image { Name of Scene : 1;
    Number of scene : 1;
     Begin : 1;
     End : 200;
     Step : 1  }
Objects { objs {boy_1, girl_1, church_1} }
Scene (pmarrys)
    { Object (boy_1) { lmoving ( x1, y1, z1→ x2, y2, z2 ), 1→200 };
     Object (girl_1) { lmoving ( x3, y3, z3→ x4, y4, z4 ), 1→200 };
     Object (church_1) { fixed (x5, y5, z5 ) };
     Background { cloudy (gray) };          }
Camera { Position (lmoving (x6, (y1 + y3)/2, z6 → x8, (y1 + y3)/2, z6) ;
      Target (boy_1 → girl_1, girl_1);  1→ 200    };
Light { source (x6, y6, z6); intensity (bright) };
Action { ......omitted   }
```

In this example, all xi's and yi's are numerical values.

2.6 Geometric Planning

All spatial and temporal parameters of the plots, which remain qualitative in the previous stage, will be given exact values in this stage and turned into quantitative ones. Therefore this stage involves a lot of calculation. In order to get the Evergreen presentation of the example above, a lot of geometrical quantities have to be calculated.

2.6.1 Layout Planning

For all roles and all objects appearing in a scene, their initial positions have to be calculated. These positions are calculated based on the qualitative positions we have obtained during qualitative planning procedure. It is a process of defuzzying, turning fuzzy concepts into crisp values.

2.6.2 Path Planning: The Tiger Planner

On the way from a Rainbow program to an Evergreen program, moving traces of roles and objects have to be calculated. When a story involves the movement of roles or objects in an environment with other physical entities, there is a problem of avoiding the obstacles. In the Rainbow language, the user does not have to specify how to avoid the obstacles. It is enough to specify the starting point x and endpoint y of the movement. A planning module called Tiger will then automatically calculate a collision free path from x to y, if such a path exists at all. For the moment, Tiger is only capable to do two-dimensional path planning, which is enough in most of the cases.

In the case of two-dimensional space, where the obstacles are a finite set of polygons, the path planning problem was solved several years ago [Lozano-Perez and Wesley, 1979]. Our algorithm follows basically the same idea. We reproduce this algorithm in the following to make the things complete.

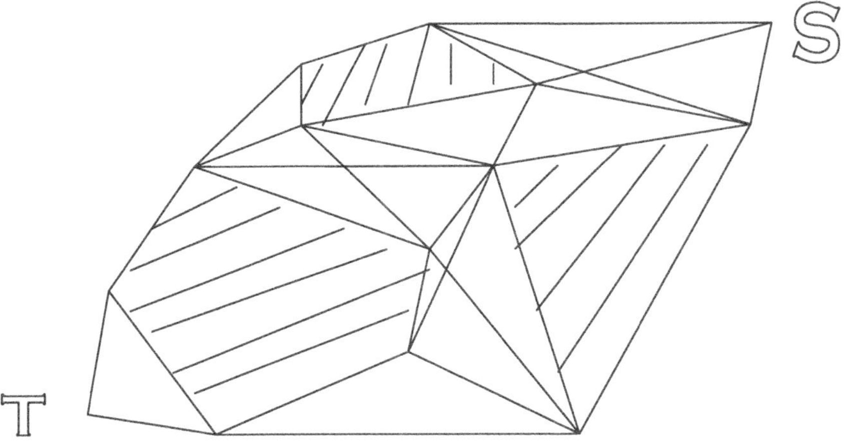

Figure 2.6.1 A Visible Graph with Three Obstacles

Definition 2.6.1 (Visible Graph)

A visible graph is a undirected graph VG (N, L), where N is the set of nodes : N = V ∪ {S, T}, where V is the set of all vertices of all obstacle polygons, S is the starting point and T is the terminal point of the wanted path. L is the set of all edges (a, b) of VG, where a, b are members of N and the segment (a, b) does not intersect any polygon (means: does not go into the intern of any polygon).

This graph is called a visible graph because the two endpoints of any segment are visible to each other. For example see figure 2.6.1.

Algorithm 2.6.1 (Polygon Obstacles for Point Movement)

1. Given a finite polygon FP, within which there is a finite set of polygon obstacles, which do not intersect, and a start point S, a terminal point T. S and T are inside of FP, but outside of any polygon. Construct a visible graph VG.
2. Assign a weight w to each edge e of VG, which is equal to its length.
3. Use a graph search program to find a shortest path from S to T.

End of Algorithm

It is easy to prove the correctness of this algorithm. It will find an optimal solution.

Definition 2.6.2 (Pseudo-Polygon)

A connected area whose border consists of linear segments only, is called a pseudo-polygon.

Note that a pseudo-polygon does not have to be simply connected. It is easy to generalize the definition of a visible graph to the case of pseudo-polygons.

Algorithm 2.6.2 (Pseudo-Polygon Obstacles for Point Movement)

1. Given a finite pseudo-polygon FP, within which there is a finite set FS of pseudo-polygon obstacles. Given also a start point S and a terminal point T . S and T are inside of FP, but outside of any pseudo-polygon of FS. Construct a visible graph VG.
2. Assign a weight w to each edge e of VG, which is equal to its length.
3. If S and T are connected in VG, then use a graph search program to find a shortest path from S to T. Otherwise, the algorithm fails.

End of Algorithm

Algorithm 2.6.3 (Pseudo-Polygon Obstacles for Circle Movement)

1. Given a finite pseudo-polygon FP, within which there is a finite set FS of pseudo-polygon obstacles, a start point S, a terminal point T and a circle C with S as its center and r as its radius. Assume that the circle C does not intersect any polygon.
2. Extend each edge of each pseudo-polygon P from FS towards the extern of FP with a distance of r.
3. Extend also each edge of FP towards the intern of FP with a distance of r.
4. If any two pseudo-polygons of FS intersect, then delete all parts of their edges, which intersect, to combine to larger pseudo-polygons.
5. If a pseudo-polygon P of FS intersects FP, then delete all parts of their edges, which intersect, and consider P as a part of FP.
6. Construct a visible graph VG.
7. Assign a weight w to each edge e, which is equal to its length.
8. If S and T are connected in VG, then use a graph search program to find a shortest path from S to T. This is also the wanted path of circle movement.

9. Otherwise, the algorithm fails.

End of Algorithm

For example see figure 2.6.2, where the two extended obstacles intersect and are thus combined to a single obstacle.

The solution of the above algorithm is a shortest path from S to T. But it is not necessary a most natural path in daily life. In general, a human being does not walk around some obstacle with a zero distance (his cloth just touches the border of the obstacle). So we think that in many cases the shortness of the path is not obligatory. Instead, we have the following definition.

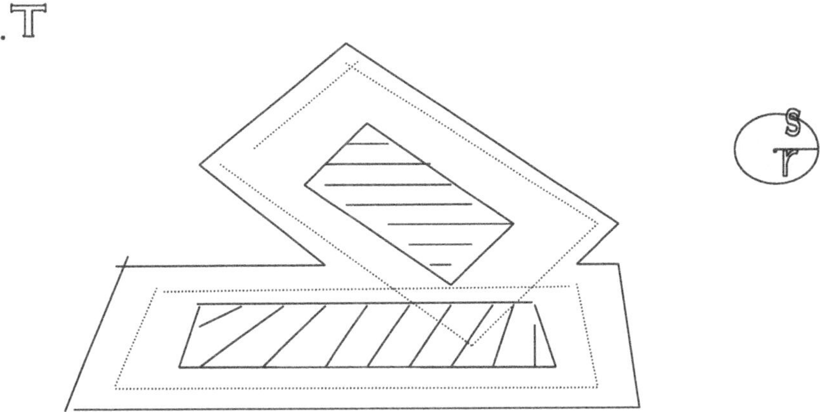

Figure 2.6.2 Extended Obstacles for a Circle Move

Definition 2.6.3 (Most Safe Path)

Assume FP is a polygon with some obstacles in it. The points S and T are also within FP, but outside of any obstacle. A path from S to T is called most safe, if it avoids touching any edge of FP and of the obstacles as much as possible.

For a more simplified case, the algorithm is given below.

Algorithm 2.6.4 (Find the Two-dimensional Most Safe Path)

1. Assume there are finitely many obstacles r_1, ..., r_n, all in form of rectangles, whose sides are parallel to the x or y axes. All obstacles are included in a square Q which is boarded by four lines $x = 0$, $x = a$, $y = 0$, $y = a$, where $a>0$. No obstacle is touching or intersecting another one.
2. Assume there is a circle C whose center S is going to move to the goal point T. C is initially situated in Q, not touching, nor situated in any rectangle in Q. So does the circle with T as center and having the same radius as C.

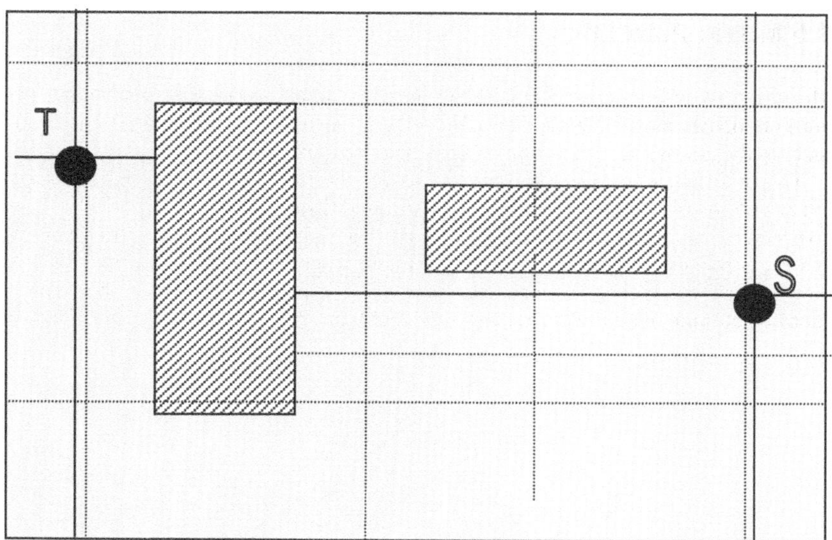

Figure 2.6.3 A Safe Graph with two Obstacles

3. For each pair of neighboring parallel edges of two different obstacles, draw a line parallel to these sides and halving the distance between them, provided that this distance is not less than the diameter of C. Do the same thing for each pair: (a boarder line of Q, the neighboring edge of a neighboring obstacle). We call all these new lines central lines.
4. Consider the set of all intersection points of the (vertical) central lines (with the horizontal ones), and of the central lines with Q boarder lines or with rectangle edges. We call each segment of a central line, boarded by two intersection points, a central segment. Delete all central segments which are included in some rectangles. Delete all central segments which do not halve the distance of the two neighboring rectangle edges on their both sides (or the distance between a neighboring rectangle edge and a neighboring Q boarder line). Delete all isolate intersection points. Call the set of the remaining intersection points RP and that of the remaining central segments RS. G = (RP, RS) forms a undirected graph.
5. Let the coordinates of S be (x1, y1), those of T be (x2, y2). Draw four lines x = x1, x = x2, y = y1, y = y2. Let FI be the set of the first intersection points of the four lines with each other and with the central segments. (An intersection point p is called a first one, if the segment (p, S) or (p, T) does not include any other intersection points) Add S and T to FI. Let SG be the set of segments which are boarded by two points of FI. Delete from SG all segments which traverse a space between two edges (or an edge and a boarder line) whose distance is less than the diameter of C. Add FI to RP and SG to RS.

6. If there is a connected component of the graph G, which is called a safe graph, which includes S and T as two vertices, then find the shortest path between S and T. To this end, well known algorithms are available. (For example, that one of Dijkstra) Otherwise, it is impossible to move C from S to T.

End of Algorithm

SWAN produces three-dimensional animation. Therefore, the path planning should also be in fact a three-dimensional one. But in the literature, this problem is still far from being solved. A general and feasible algorithm for finding a shortest path in three-dimensional space remains unknown. In our research, we have not yet found an efficient and powerful enough three-dimensional path planning algorithm, either. Fortunately, there are small tricks which help us to program practical algorithms which can meet our need in most of the cases.

Trick 1. Use a polygonal cylinder to envelop any physical object such that if we take any profile of the space, we get a set of polygons on the plane. Then we can use the algorithm above to produce a two-dimensional path which is also valid in three-dimensional space.

In case that there are not a lot of obstacles in the space, this trick is quite useful. It is, however, not appropriate for use if the form of physical objects biases a lot from a cylinder, especially, if the upper part of an obstacle is big, and its lower part is small so that the obstacle as a whole does not prevent human being from going through. A typical example is a tree. It is enough to consider only the trunk of the tree as an obstacle. Therefore, we have the following improved trick:

Trick 2. For things whose form is not uniform in horizontal dimension, we divide it in some segments, each segment enveloped with a different polygon. Then, when there is a need to do path planning, we consider only the relevant level of segments and construct a profile of these segments for polygon planning.

For example, the relevant level of segments of a tree for human walking is its trunk. The relevant levels of segments of a city for airplane flying are the very high buildings. The relevant levels of segments of a high building for human movements are the different floors in that building.

Trick 3. If the distribution of obstacles in the space is not uniform, we can divide the area where the story happens in several regions, each of which has a uniform distribution of obstacles.

For example, inside and outside of a room, inside and outside of a yard, upstairs and down stairs of a house, inside and outside of a forest can all be considered as different regions.

2.6.3 Path and Move Planning of Cameras

The qualitative camera statements (BCP) of Rainbow must be transformed in the corresponding quantitative ones (QCP) in Evergreen. During this process, positions, directions and moving traces of the cameras have to be calculated.

Note that this process is not just a calculation. It involves a procedure of heuristic search. The numerical quantities we got from the camera primitives are based on an estimate of the current script, because the camera primitives coming from the knowledge base match the current situation only approximately. It is possible that the calculated positions or movements of the camera are not appropriate, for example letting somebody be hidden by other people and thus become invisible to the observer. In this case the camera planner should adjust the parameters and calculate a new position.

2.6.4 Modification of Objects

No matter how comprehensive the animation library is, it can never provide any figure the cartoon wants. Therefore some modification of the objects taken from the animation library is almost inevitably. There are three kinds of modification.

1. Deformation. It makes the original figure larger, smaller, thicker, thinner, taller, shorter, etc.
2. Decoration. It includes coloring, clothing and other ornaments, such as hats, shoes, and things attached to the character or hold by the character.
3. Reconfiguration. The montage module is able to change parts of a figure, which are connected to the figure by articulates. For example, this module can replace a human head by a tiger head, or plant a tail to the back of a figure.

All these modifications are done automatically by the system based on the knowledge base.

2.7 Summary, Acknowledgements, and Prospects

In summary, with the support of animation knowledge bases, SWAN undertakes the step-by-step transformations from stories written in natural language to the cartoons. The outline of the working flow of SWAN is illustrated in figure 2.7.1.

The SWAN project has been granted by a special foundation of President of Chinese Academy of Sciences. We owe special thanks to the former President of Chinese Academy of Sciences, Academician, Prof. Guangzhao Zhou; the former Vice-President of Chinese Academy of Sciences, Academician, Prof. Qiheng Hu; and the former department leader, Mr. Wenzeng Yang. SWAN has been also supported by the Chinese Natural Science Foundation, by Key Projects of the Ministry of Science and Technology, and by 863 High-Tech Projects.

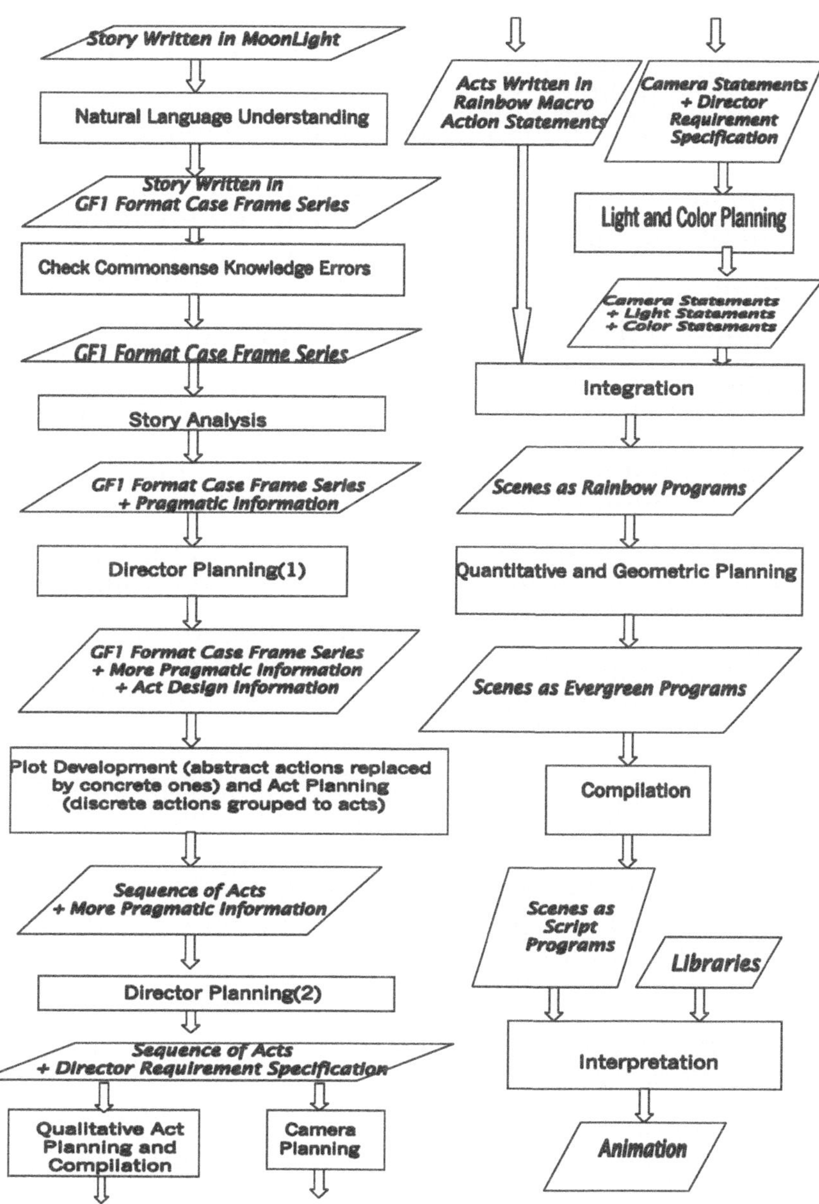

Figure 2.7.1 Working Flow Chart of SWAN

More than 30 graduate students have participated in SWAN project and made their contributions. Following is a list of their names: Qing Geng, Wenhong Zhu, Xiaobin Li, Lixin Yu, Zhenghao Jin, Dejie Yang, Yue Xu, Haihu Shi, Ronglin Wan, Zhaobin Chen, Ying Zhao, Yuan Li, Yi Luo, Bo Gao, Yuejiao Zhou, Ying-hao Ma, Yizhen Li, Yujie Wang, Haixia Du, Lu Li, Ping Yang, Lu Fan, Guang-feng Ji, Xuesheng Zhang, Lengning Liu, Fan Yang, Xiaolong Jin, Chengmin Sun, Xiangliang Meng, Jingwei Cai, etc.

We are also very thankful to Prof. Zichu Wei, who has made important contributions to the SWAN project during participating at discussions about the design and implementation of the SWAN software, and during participating at the management of the project.

We thank also Prof. Freksa of the University of Hamburg, Prof Krieg-Brueckner and Prof. Wischnewski of the University of Bremen for their invitation of given a series of seminar talks about SWAN at these universities. While preparing the talks, the first author of this book has got opportunity to improve further the manuscript.

Last, but not least, we would like to thank Ms. Wenyan Zhang and Dr. Cungen Cao for their valuable help in the final editing of the manuscript.

At last, we wish to make a note to the content of this book. After we have finished our SWAN project, we have made a review and assessment of the techniques developed in it. Based on the review, we have improved and redesigned many parts of the FLICA methodology. In this sense, the content of this book conforms to the new design, not quite to the originally implemented one.

2.8 Notation Used in This Book

In SWAN, we have designed and implemented a multi-level representation of knowledge. Each level has the form of a programming language. We basically use the traditional BNF notation for describing the syntax of our languages with a slight modification. Namely, we use the following meta-syntax notation to simplify the representation.

```
<X Name> ::= <Identifier>
<Name of X> ::= <Identifier>
<X Key> ::= <Identifier>_<Number>
<Identifier> ::= <Letter> | <Identifier><Letter> | <Identifier><Digit>
<Number> ::= <Sequence of Digits>
<Digital> ::= 0 |1 |2 |3 |4 |5 |6 |7 |8 |9
<Letter> ::= A |B |C |... |a |b |c |...
<Sequence of Xs> ::= <X> | <X>, <Sequence of Xs>
<Series of Xs> ::=  <X> | <X>; <Series of Xs>
<Line of Xs> ::= <X> | <X>. <Line of Xs>
<Group of Xs> ::=  <X> | (<X>, <Sequence of Xs>)
```

<Queue of Xs> ::= <X> | <X> <Separator> <Queue of Xs>
<Separator> ::= , | . | : | ; | ? | !

where X can be any non-terminal symbol.

<X> ::= Y | …

where X can be any non-terminal symbol, Y can be any form of right hand side of a grammar rule. The three dots "…" mean that the right hand side is not complete. The content of this right hand side depends on the content of the Pangu commonsense knowledge base. More content will be added to it, if the Pangu knowledge base will get more knowledge relating to it.

3 Understanding the Limited Chinese Natural Language

3.1 The Chinese Language

According to certain statistics, there are in total 5651 different languages and their dialects in the world. Not included are the many ancient languages which have already died out. Some thousands of current languages are declining. The number of people using these languages are getting less and less. Based on a study of the linguistics experts, about 2790 languages are independent ones. Seventy percents of them do not yet possess a written form. The number of languages which have been studied systematically by linguists is estimated to 500. Among them, only 13 languages are spoken by more than sixty million people. The Chinese language occupies the first place. About 36 percents of people in the world use Chinese Characters in their languages.

China is a country with 56 nationalities. Many nationalities have their own language. For example, the Man nationality (ruling nationality of the Qing dynasty, 1644 - 1911), the Monggol nationality (ruling nationality of the Yuan dynasty, 1271 - 1368), the Tibetan nationality, the Uygur nationality, the Korean nationality, the Russian nationality, the Dai nationality, etc. Most people of the Hui nationality are Moslems. Many of them know Arabic language. Now the language which can be used in whole China is the Han language. When we talk about Chinese, we mean the Han language.

One important characteristic of the Chinese language is its composition from individual characters. How many characters are there in Chinese? There is no unique estimation. The Kang Xi (Second Emperor of the Qing Dynasty) dictionary collected more than fifty thousands of different Chinese characters. But most of them are no more used nowadays. A committee led by the Chinese government has worked out a standard, called national standard of Chinese characters. It includes 3755 most frequently used characters as the first level, and further 3008 characters as the second level. Thus there are 6763 characters in the standard. That means, if you know these 6763 characters, then you will very rarely meet "unknown" characters if you read a book or a newspaper published in our time. A statistic has shown that about three thousands of characters cover 99.7 % of character use in Chinese literature.

Each Chinese character is a structure consisting of a set of character components. It is often that these components remind us of their pictographic origins. For example, the Chinese character means "bright". It has two components: 日 and 月,

R. Lu and S. Zhang: Automatic Generation of Computer Animation, LNAI 2160, pp. 65-92, 2002.

where 日 means the sun and 月 means the moon. It is not difficult to see that the form of 日 is similar to the sun and that of 月 is similar to a new moon (crescent moon). Note that by chance 日 and 月 are characters themselves. But not all components are characters. According to a statistics of the Song dynasty (960 – 1271), there were in total 540 different character components. But this number has largely decreased, just as the case of the number of characters. Nowadays, a conventional Chinese dictionary provides only more than 200 different components for the user to look up a word. The 6763 standard Chinese characters have in total 16725 components. That means, in average each character has 2.5 components.

Each character component consists of a set of strokes. For example, the component 日 has four strokes and 月 has four strokes, too. The least number of strokes in a character is one. But the largest number is 64! Strokes have different types. The estimations about the numbers of stroke types are different. The least number estimated by experts is five, while the largest number estimated is greater than forty.

The Chinese characters are also units of pronunciation. Each character is a single syllable. In modern Chinese, there are about more than 400 different syllables. If the dialects and variations are added, this number will be increased to more than one thousand. For a statistics see the following table:

Table 3.1.1 Syllables in Chinese

	Ancient	Nowadays
Number of vowels	36	21
Number of consonants	92	39
Number of syllables	3823	1332

Most Chinese characters have their independent meanings. Character combinations form words which are the most important syntactic units in Chinese. The set of Chinese words is very rich. A modest Chinese dictionary for pupils' use may contain more than 20 thousands of words. Since there is no marking between words in a sentence, the first problem met in lexical analysis is the segmentation of a sentence in words.

There is a big difference between the Chinese syntax and the English one. In Chinese, there is no concept of cases (the sentences "you see I" and "you go with I" are all correct) and no concept of plural or singular noun forms (the sentence "he have five apple" is correct). The tense of a verb is represented with extra auxiliary words, not with a postfix at the end of the verb. For example, I eat "le" five apple means "I have eaten five apples", where the word "le" is an auxiliary word which means some event has already happened. Therefore, the morphology of Chinese characters is simple. In any context, there is no variation of character forms at all. The ambiguity of meanings is resolved with auxiliary words and with the order of characters in a sentence. This order of characters has a key significance for understanding Chinese. For example, in Russian, the sentences "the officer killed the soldier" and "the soldier killed the officer" may have the same meaning, if appropriate endings are added to "officer" and "soldier" to display their cases. But in Chinese this is impossible.

Another characteristic of Chinese is a rich set of quantity words. In English, one uses a quantity word if the noun represents a concept which is not countable. For example, one talks about "a piece of paper", "a drop of water" and "a bottle of wine". But in Chinese, one uses quantity words almost for everything. They are very different. To list a few examples, a "pi" horse, a "tou" ox, a "tiao" dog, a "zhi" cat, a "kou" pig, etc. The number of different quantity words is estimated to more than one hundred.

3.2 The Moon Light Language

When designing our story grammar for the Moon Light language, we have paid attention to two important aspects. The first one is the characteristics of the Chinese language. There is a remarkable difference of grammatical structure between Chinese and languages of other families, such as English or French. On the other hand, this grammar should be context sensitive, since otherwise it could hardly be used to describe a meaningful real story. The grammar designed by us to complete this task is the commonsense oriented unification grammar (CSU grammar).

In our terminology, context sensitivity mainly means the constraints enforced by commonsense. Let us first have a look at the context free part of the CSU grammar in this section and postpone the discussion of that part of the CSU grammar which describes the context sensitivity to the next section. In this section, we will introduce the syntax, semantics and pragmatics of the Moon Light language. Note that it is difficult and in fact impossible to give a Chinese syntax in pure English. On the other hand, the Chinese sentences, once they have been translated into English, do not keep the ordering of the words any more. As a result, both the syntax and the examples of sentences of Moon Light given below are only "pseudo-English". Therefore, we ask the readers not to be surprised when they find something in the remaining part of this paragraph, which looks like English, but which is actually not English.

We will go ahead in a bottom up way. We first define the most basic constructs, then the more higher level ones, then the even more higher level ones, etc., until the global syntax is built up.

3.2.1 Characters and Words

As we said in section 3.1, a Chinese text consists of a sequence of sentences. Each sentence consists of a sequence of characters. A character can be considered as a "picture" of strokes. But the strokes have no meanings. So it is reasonable to start from the characters. A character may have a meaning, may also not. The basic units in Chinese, which have a meaning, are words. In fact, each sentence consists of a sequence of words which can only be recognized by an appropriate segmentation of the sentence. A word consists of one or more characters. Among the words, we differentiate between notional words and function words. The notional words play an independent role in language formation. They include nouns, verbs, adjectives, adverbs, pronouns, numerals, classifiers. The function words play an auxiliary role in language formation. It includes prepositions, conjunctions, auxiliary words and interjections. All kinds of words (but not all words) are accepted by Moon Light as its word constructs.

Some notes should be added here.

1. Verbs

   1.1. Tense of verbs

   In Moon Light, just as in conventional Chinese, we use temporal words to express the tense of verbs. Note that the verbs themselves do not change their form with respect to different tenses.

   1.1.1. "le" means the completion of an action. For example

   The leaves are red "le".
   (The leaves have become red)

   1.1.2. "zhuo" means the continuation of an action. For example

   They read "zhuo" a book.
   (They are reading a book)

   1.1.3. "guo" means that an action was completed in the past.

   They write "guo" a book.
   (They wrote a book)

   1.2. Double occurrence of verbs

   In many cases, two instances of the same verb can be concatenated together to mean (roughly speaking) repeated occurrences of the action denoted by this verb. More exactly, we can understand its meaning as follows: each of such kind of actions usually contains a set of sub-actions. The completion of this action requires a repeating execution of these sub- actions. In a sentence, the concatenation of two instances of a verb serves to emphasize the repeating execution of the sub-actions of the action denoted by this verb. For example, "discuss" is such an action. Its sub-actions are opinion exchanges. Then "discuss-discuss" means a repeating exchange of opinions.

   1.3. Omission of the "be" verb

   In many cases, the "be" verb can be omitted in a Chinese sentence of noun + be + adjective structure, For details see the SP construction described in 3.2.2.

2. Adjectives

   Unlike the adjectives in many western languages, the adjectives in Chinese, if used to modify a noun, are often followed by an auxiliary word "de1". Thus, instead of saying:

   The apple is red.

   we should say:

   The apple is red "de1".

On the other hand, both of the following two sentences are valid:

This is a red apple.

This is a red "de1" apple.

But if one uses n adjectives to modify a noun, n>1, then all adjectives but the last one should be followed by a "de", for example:

This is a big "de1" red apple.

3. Quantity words

This may be a particular phenomenon of enumerating objects in Chinese. We have already mentioned it briefly above. In Chinese, the use of Quantity words has some particularities:

3.1. The Quantity words are also used for objects which are countable.

3.2. In most cases, these Quantity words are indispensable.

3.3. Many kinds of objects have their own Quantity words. In Chinese, the number of different Quantity words is greater than one hundred. In our Moon Light language, we have reduced this number to about twenty.

For example, "ge" is one of the most frequently used Quantity words. In fact, our sentence about apple given above was not completely correct in the sense of Chinese. It should be:

This "ge" apple is red "de".

or

This is a "ge" red apple.

4. Auxiliary words

There are three kinds of auxiliary words: the junction words, the temporal words, and the mood words.

4.1. Junction words

4.1.1. "de1", for connecting an adjective with a noun. For an example see what we have said in 2.

4.1.2. "di", for connecting an adverb with a verb or an adjective.

Here are the examples (in the Chinese sentence order):

The result is very "di1" good.

He very loudly "di1" laughs.

4.1.3. "de2" (another "de"), for connecting a verb with an adverb.

Note that the order of the verb "laugh" and the adverb "loudly" in the following example is the reversed one than that in the example above.

He laughs "de2" very loudly.

4.2. Temporal words

See the words "le", "zhuo" and "guo" in 1.1 above.

3.2.2 Syntactic Construction

Unlike the phrase structure of most western languages, the natural Chinese language has its own characteristics of syntactic structure. Experts in Chinese Linguistics have summarized different kinds of basic Chinese language structures. However, different Chinese linguistics experts often have different opinions on the definition and selection of basic syntactic constructions. One can convince oneself about this conclusion if one would have a look at the huge amount of text books and monographs written on this problem. Thus we have defined and selected our own principles of Chinese language constructions in Moon Light

1. Subject-Predicate Construction (SP Construction)
   It means the direct concatenation of a subject and a predicate (S+P). For example,
   Tree very high. # S = Tree, P = very high, Meaning: The tree is very high #
   Leslie draw beautiful picture. # S = Leslie, P = draw beautiful picture #
   are both legal sentences.
   Here the term predicate means actually the predicate-object construction, see below.

2. Verb-Object Construction (VO Construction)
   This is actually a verb phrase (V+O). For example:
   Eat lunch. # V = eat, O = lunch, Meaning: Having a lunch #
   Watch television.

3. Predicate-Complement Construction (PC Construction)
   There is a language construct for complementing the meaning of a predicate with the help of the junction word "de2" (P+de2"+C).
   Walk "de2" very fast. # P = walk, C = very fast, Meaning: walk very fast #
   Eat "de2" happily.
   (Note: "del2" means "manner")
   The PC construction can be extended to POC construction if the simple predicate P (verb) is replaced by a PO construction. There are two syntactic forms for POC:
   3.1. Book read "de2" very fast
   3.2. Read book read "de2" very fast

4. Endocentric Construction (EC Construction)
   There are two kinds of such construction:
   4.1. Nominal Endocentric Construction (NEC Construction)
   It consists of a noun preceded by some modification (M+N). For example:
   My mother "de1" house. # M = my mother "de1", N = house,
   Meaning: my mother's house #
   Young men "de1" viewpoint.
   (Note: "del1" means possessive case.)
   4.2. Verbal Endocentric Construction (VEC Construction)
   It consists of a verb preceded by some modification (M+V). For example:
   Sincerely welcome. # M = sincerely, V = welcome #
   Morning get up. # M = morning, V = get up, Meaning: get up in the morning #

5. Centrifugal Construction (CF Construction)
It consists of a noun (or a numeral with or without a quantity word) followed by some spatial, or temporal description (N+D). It is actually the noun (or the numeral) which plays the role of a modificator. This noun (the numeral) specifies the referential coordinates of the corresponding spatial or temporal description.
   5.1. Spatial Centrifugal Construction (SCF Construction)
      House in front of # N = house, D = in front of, Meaning: In front of the house #
      10 Kilograms above # N = 10 kilograms, D = above,
         Meaning: above 10 kilograms #
   5.2. Temporal Centrifugal Construction (TCF Construction)
      Lunch before # N = lunch, D = before, Meaning: before the lunch #
      1998 year after # N = 1998 year, D = after, Meaning: After the year 1998 #

6. Repeating Construction (RP Construction)
It means juxtaposition of similar expressions with or without connection words (Cons+Cons). For example:
   Blue sky, white cloud, mild wind.
   "You1" eat, "you1" drink, "you1" sing, "you1" dance.
   (Note: "you1" means "and at the same time")

7. Appositive Construction (AP Construction)
It means juxtaposition of several expressions which have the same denotation (N+N). For example:
   Our friend Kristen Rekdal. # N1 = our friend, N2 = Kristen Rekdal #
   The engineer, painter, and scientist Leonardo Da Vinci.

8. Preposition Construction (PR Construction)
   8.1. Simple Prepositional Construction (SPC)
   A preposition followed by a noun or pronoun, for example:
      To Beijing.
      With pencil
   8.2. Prepositional Endocentric Construction (PEC)
   It consists of a SPC followed by some VO construction, or it is another kind of EC construction. For example:
      To Beijing "de1" way. # The way to Beijing #
      With pencil write letter # write a letter with a pencil #

9. Modification Complement Construction (MC Construction)
One striking difference between Chinese and western languages is that one has to add a "de" after a modificator (M+"de") if they do not precede, but rather follow the noun which is to be modified. For example:
   Flower is red "de". # The flower is red #
   This "zhi" pen is John "de". # This is John's pen #
   This is John "de" pen. # This is John's pen #
   (Note: "zhi" is a quantity word for long and thin objects)

10. Verb Complement Construction (VC Construction)
    It consists of a verb followed by a state description by a "le" (V+State+"le"). This construction means that the action denoted by the verb has been completed and some state has been reached. The general-purpose state words include "guo" (the action was done before), "wan" (the action has been finished) , and "gou" (the action has been done enough). They can be applied to almost all verbs. Most of the state words are special-purpose ones. They can only match those verbs the execution of whose actions will produce the corresponding states. For example:
    Eat "guo" "le" # have already eaten #
    Write "wan" "le" # have finished writing #

11. Sequential Verbal Construction (SV Construction)
    Two or more verbs following each other (V+V). The former ones are premises of the latter ones. They have a sequential character. This phenomenon also exists in English. For example:
    Go swim.
    Have intention write a book. # have the intention to write a book #

12. Concurrent Construction (CC Construction)
    It consists of two sub-constructions: a predicate object construction plus a subject predicate construction (PO+SP). These two sub-constructions overlap partially. For example:
    (My student) ask I give he a hint. # My student asks me to give him a hint #
    Let they go. # Let them go #
    In the first sentence, PO = "ask I" and SP = "I give he a hint", the overlapped part is "I". In the second sentence, PO = "let they", SP = "they go", the overlapped part is "they".

In the Moon Light language, each valid sentence can be parsed according to the constructions listed above.

Example 3.2.1

Let us consider a tiny story:

"The mother of Snow White died. Snow White was very sad. The king has married a new queen. The new queen was very jealous of the beauty of Snow White. She asked a hunter to kill Snow White. The hunter did not kill Snow White and set her free. Snow White went lost in a big forest. She was received by seven kind dwarfs. Snow White lived together with the dwarfs. A magic mirror told the queen that Snow White was still living. The queen disguised herself as a peasant woman. She gave a poisonous apple to Snow White. Snow White ate the apple and died. A prince saw the dead Snow White and rescued her. The prince killed the queen. The prince married Snow White. "

If parsed according to the constructions listed above, the story will be assigned with the following list structure, where the numbers denote the different kinds of construction:

((4.1) 1) , (1 (4.2)), (1 (4.1 (4.1))), ((4.1) 1 (4.2 (4.2 (4.1)))), (1 ((4.1) 10)), (1 (9)), (1 (3 (4.1 (4.1)))), (1 (7 (4.1 (4.1)))), (1 (7)), ((4.1) 2 (2 (1 (4.2)))), (1 (2 (3 (4.1 (4.1))))), (1 (2 (2 (4.1 (4.1))))), (1 (2 (9))), ((4.1) 2 (4.1 (9))), (1 (2)), (1 (2)).

3.2.3 The Syntactic Rules

In the past sections, we have introduced the concepts of words and word constructions in Chinese. What is their relation to sentences? There has been a great Chinese linguist called Zhu Dexi. He was holding the opinion that the basic syntactic units in Chinese are the word constructions, not the sentences. He said that words are components of word constructions, but word constructions are not components of sentences. Furthermore, he claimed that sentences are nothing else than word constructions plus intonation. According to this point of view, the written form of sentences and that of word constructions should have no difference. Since Professor Zhu Dexi had a great influence in China, many textbooks and monographs of Chinese linguistics are written for exploring word constructions, not for exploring syntax of sentences.

We do not think that it is a right way to push the importance of word constructions to their extreme. Although Zhu Dexi has right at least in following two sense:

1. The rich set of word constructions in Chinese and their flexible formation rules constitute a fertile domain of research.
2. Many word constructions are at the same time sentences.

The theory of word constructions in Chinese has a vital significance for the designing of the Moon light syntax .Let us compare the word constructions with the concept of a phrase .In the western languages like English, there are only a few of phrase structures, such as noun phrase, verb phrase, etc. But in the Chomsky's terminology, a phrase structure grammar takes any string of terminals and nonterminals as phrase, provided that this string appears as the right hand of a production. Therefore, it is difficult to take the phrase structure of a western language as the basis for a phrase structure grammar in the sense of Chomsky. In this respect, the situation in Chinese is quite different. Since the linguists have found and defined a lot of word constructions, we have taken them as the grammatical basis for our Moon light language. This way of going ahead has a special reason. The Chinese language is very rich and very complicated, while our limited natural language in SWAN should be a relatively simple and humble one. For designing Moon Light, we follow four basic principles:

1. If there are different ways to express the same meaning, we choose basically only one from them.
2. Among the various possibilities of representing the same meaning, we choose the simplest one.
3. Simpler means straightforward, no redundancy and no ellipsis.

4. Those meanings which are themselves complicated, are not accepted in Moon Light.

In order to save space, we do not write down the whole syntax of the input language in this paper, but only give some hints on its characteristics. Some most important syntactic rules are listed as follows:

<Story> ::= <Sentence>;<Series of Sentences>
<Sentence> ::= <Composed Sentence> | <Simple Sentence>
<Simple Sentence> ::= <Word Construction>
<Composed Sentence> ::= <Conditional Sentence> | <Sequential Sentence>
| <Synchronization Sentence>
<Conditional Sentence> ::= <If> <Simple Sentence> <then> <Simple Sentence>
<Sequential Sentence> ::= <T Relation1>,<Simple Sentence>
<Synchronization Sentence> ::= <T Relation2>,<Simple Sentence>
<T Relation1> ::= <when> <Simple Sentence> <Temporal Relation>
<T Relation2> ::= <During> <Simple Sentence> "de 1" <Moment>
<Word Construction> ::= <SP Construction> | <VO Construction>
| <PC Construction>
| <EC Construction> | <CF Construction> | <RP Construction>
| <AP Construction> | <PR Construction> | <MC Construction>
| <VC Construction> | <SV Construction> | <CC Construction>
| ....
<SP Construction> ::= <Subject> <VO Construction>
| <Subject> <Predicate> [<Temporal Indicator>]
<Temporal Relation> ::= <Before> | <After>
<Before> ::= "Yi Qian"
<After> ::= "Yi Hou"
<Moment> ::= "Shi Hou"
<when> ::= "Zai"
<where> ::= "Zai"
<During> ::= "Dang"
<If> ::= "Ru Guo"
<then> ::= "Ze"
<Temporal Indicator> ::= "le" | "guo" "le" | "wan" "le"
<VO Construction> ::= <Verb> <Object> | "ba" <Object> <Verb> "le"
| <Verb> "guo" <Object> "le"
<PC Construction> ::= <verb> "dez" <completion>
<completion> ::= <Adverb> | <Adverb> <completion>
<POC Construction> ::= [[<Verb>]<Object>]<PC Construction>
<Subject> ::= <EC Construction> | <Pronoun>
<Object> ::= <EC Construction> | <Pronoun>
<Predicate> ::= <Verb> | <Adjective> | <IS> <Adjective> "de1"
| <VEC construction>
<EC Construction> ::= <NEC Construction> | <VEC Construction>
<NEC Construction> ::= <N Modification> "de1" <Noun>

| <A Modification> “de1” <Noun>
| <NEC Construction> “de1” <A Modification> “de1” <Noun>
<VEC Construction> ::= <V Modification> <Predicate>
<V Modification> ::= <Place Modification> | <Time Modification> | <Manner Modification> | .....
<Place Modification> ::= <where> <CF construction>
<Time Modification> ::= <T Relation>
<T Relation> ::= <T Relation1> | <T Relation2>
<N Modification> ::= <Noun> | <NEC Construction> | <SP Construction>
<A Modification> ::= <Adjective> | <Adjective> “de1” <A Modification>
| <Adverb> <A Modification>
<CF Construction> ::= <SCF Construction> | <TCF Construction>
<SCF Construction> ::= <NEC Construction> <Spatial Relation>
<TCF Construction> ::= <NEC Construction> <Temporal Relation>
<Spatial Relation> ::= “de1” <Direction1> “mian”
<Direction1> ::= <front> | <behind> | <left> | <right> | <In> | <Out> | <Above> | <Below>
<front> ::= “Qian”
<behind> ::= “Hou”
<left> ::= “Zuo”
<right> ::= “You”
<In> ::= “Li”
<Out> ::= “Wai”
<Above> ::= “Shang”
<Below> ::= “Xia”
<RP Construction> ::= <Type X RP Construction>
<Type X RP Construction> ::= <Type X Word Construction> , <Type X Word Construction> | <Type X Word Construction> , <Type X RP Construction>
<AP Construction> ::= <NEC Construction> <NEC Construction>
<PR Construction> ::= <NPR Construction> | <VPR Construction>
<NPR Construction> ::= <Preposition> <NEC Construction> “de1”
<NEC Construction>
<VPR Construction> ::= <Preposition> <NEC Construction> <VO Construction>
<MC Construction> ::= <Adjective> “de1” | <NEC Construction> “de1”
<VC construction> ::= <Verb> <Action State> “le”
<Action State> ::= <done> | <finished>
<done> ::= “guo”
<finished> ::= “wan”
<SV construction> ::= <Predicate> <Predicate>
<CC construction> ::= [<Subject>] <verb> <Sentence>

3.3 Commonsense Knowledge Check and Unification Grammar

The validity check of the commonsense knowledge, which we have already mentioned in chapter two, is an important step in animation generation. When analyzing a story written in natural language, SWAN has to check whether the plot described in the story follows the principle of commonsense knowledge. Now we will explain more details.

There are two main reasons for the commonsense knowledge checking. The first one is to keep the movie understandable and thus acceptable by the audience. "Snow White is dead. Snow White is reading a book" is not acceptable by the audience because a dead person can not read a book. This is not possible even in the children stories. The second reason is to filter out those plots which are impossible or very difficult to be represented by a movie. "Snow White has eaten Snow White" is impossible to be shown by a movie.

The commonsense knowledge check is done at the case frames level.

Definition 3.3.1

The types of context free commonsense knowledge errors are:

1. The action (root of the case frame) is inconsistent with the action performer.
2. The action is inconsistent with the action target.
3. The action and action performer are inconsistent with the action Target.
4. The action is inconsistent with other cases of the case frame.
5. The action performer is inconsistent with other cases of the case frame.
6. The different cases are inconsistent with each other.

Example 3.3.1

The following statements containing commonsense errors of corresponding types mentioned above.

1. The lamp is reading a book. # (lamp, reading) mismatch #
2. John is reading some water. # (reading, water) mismatch #
3. John is eating grass. # (human, eating, grass) mismatch #
4. John swims in a bed. # (swim, in bed) mismatch #
5. John is reading books in a piece of wood. # (human, in wood) mismatch #
6. In the night, John reads a book under sunlight. # (night, sun light) mismatch #

In order to check all inadequacies of a natural language sentence with respect to the commonsense knowledge, we need an appropriate form of grammar. We have found that the unification grammar is a good choice for this goal since the unification is a good tool for checking context sensitivity and detecting mismatches between words in a sentence. Let us first explain briefly what is a unification grammar.

Roughly speaking, a unification grammar is a context free grammar with context conditions attached to each of its productions. These conditions include:

Boolean attributes, e.g.
  Transitive verb (yes/no)
  Singular form (yes/no)
Single valued attributes, e.g.
  Word category (noun, pronoun, adjective, verb, adverb, ...)
  Case (nominative, possessive, objective, ...)
  Gender (masculine, feminine, ...)
Others.

Each syntactic unit of a natural language can be represented in a frame of attributes, where all syntactic or semantic properties which are relevant to the parsing of this syntactic unit are listed. We call it an attribute frame.

Example 3.3.2

The pronoun "she" can be represented as the following attribute frame:

```
She : Syntax : Category : pronoun,
        Agreement : Case : nominative,
                  Gender : feminine,
                  Singular : yes.
```

Example 3.3.3

The sentence "she likes him" will be represented as:

```
Sentence : She : Syntax : Category : pronoun,
                Agreement : Case : nominative,
                 Gender : feminine,
                 Singular : yes.
        Likes : Syntax : Category : verb,
                Agreement : Singular : yes,
                      Tense : present,
        Him : Syntax : Category : pronoun,
                Agreement : Case : objective,
                      Gender : masculine,
                      Singular : yes.
```

Example 3.3.4

The syntactic structure "subject-verb-object phrase" can be represented as

```
Phrase : Subject : Syntax : Category : noun or pronoun,
                 Agreement : Case : nominative,
                       Singular : (x),
      Verb : Syntax : Category : verb,
                 Transitive : yes,
                 Agreement : Singular : (x)
      Object : Syntax : Category : noun or pronoun,
                Agreement : Case : objective.
```

The variable name x in parentheses appears two times, once in the syntax of "subject", once in the syntax of "predicate". That means there must be an agreement between the numbers of the subject and that of the predicate. Either both are in singular form, or both in plural form.

From the main characteristics of the Chinese language introduced in section 3.1, we know that many attributes in a unification grammar are not needed in Chinese language parsing, since there is no gender, no tense, even no case differentiation in the Chinese characters. They do not undergo any variation caused by different contexts. But the concept of a unification grammar is useful for commonsense knowledge checks. We will extend its definition to meet the need of defining commonsense knowledge constraints. The essential idea is to include the constraints represented by the commonsense error types of definition 3.4.1 in the unification attribute frame. We call such an extended frame a CS frame.

We divide all (physical and mental) concepts in classes which form a hierarchy. Each node of this hierarchy is assigned a label. Each label is a string of digits, separated by dots. Different kinds of concepts have different digit strings. We call this hierarchy the CS-hierarchy and the digit strings the commonsense codes of the corresponding concepts. A small part of the CS-hierarchy is shown in the following.

1. The individual digits in the digit string of a noun have the meaning:
   1: physical entity, 2. mental entity,
   1.1: solid 1.2: fluid 1.3: gas
   1.1.1: living 1.1.2: not living
   1.1.1.1: animal 1.1.1.2 plant
   1.1.1.1.1: terrestrial animal 1.1.1.1.2: aquatic animal 1.1.1.1.3: bird
   1.1.1.1.1.1: human 1.1.1.1.1.2: domestic animal 1.1.1.1.1.3: wild animal 1.1.1.1.1.4 insect
   1.1.1.1.1.1.1: man 1.1.1.1.1.1.2: woman
   1.1.2.1: organic 1.1.2.2: inorganic 1.1.2.3: dead animal
   1.1.2.1.1: human food 1.1.2.1.2: other animal's food
   1.1.2.2.1: paper 1.1.2.2.2: metal 1.1.2.2.3: wood
   1.1.2.2.1.1: book 1.1.2.2.1.2: newspaper
   ....
   2.1: information 2.2: idea
   2.1.1: written information 2.1.2: voice information

2. The individual digits in the digit string of a verb have the following meaning:
   1: mental action 2: labor action
   1.1: transitive 1.2: intransitive
   1.1.1: message receiving 1.1.2: message processing 1.1.3: message sending
   1.1.1.1 with eyes 1.1.1.2 with ears 1.1.1.3: with nose 1.1.1.4: with tongue 1.1.1.5: with body
   2.1: transitive labor action 2.2: intransitive labor action
   2.1.1: input 2.1.2: output 2.1.3: grasp 2.1.4: touch 2.1.5: wear 2.1.6: elabo rate

2.1.1.1: drink 2.1.1.2: eat 2.1.1.3: smell
2.2.1: terrestrial 2.2.2: aquatic 2.2.3: aerial

3. The individual digits in the digit string of a location have the following meaning:
   1: open space 2: closed space 3: no space
   1.1: infinite space 1.2: finite space
   1.2.1: land 1.2.2: see 1.2.3: sky

4. The individual digits in the digit string of a time have the following meaning:
   1: day time 2: night
   1.1: morning 1.2 noon 1.3 afternoon
   2.1: evening 2.2: midnight

5. The individual digits in the digit string of a natural phenomenon have the following meaning:
   1: any time possible 2: particular season possible 3: particular day time possible
   2.1: spring possible 2.2: summer possible 2.3: autumn possible 2.4: winter possible
   3.1: day time possible 3.2: night possible

Note that this hierarchy is not a tree. The neighboring nodes are not necessarily distinct. They may have non-empty intersections.

Now that we have built up the CS-hierarchy of concepts, we are able to construct commonsense constraint frames based on this hierarchy. A traditional production rule of a grammar checks the syntactic validity of a natural language sentence. A commonsense constraint frame checks its semantic validity with respect to commonsense.

Definition 3.3.2

The syntax of a commonsense constraint frame is defined as follows:

<Commonsense Constraint Frame> ::=
  CS-Frame (<CS-Frame Name>)
    <Sequence of CS-Frame Slots>
<Sequence of CS-Conditions>
  End of (<CS-Frame Name>)
<CS-Frame Slot> ::= <Slot Head> : <Term Value>
<Slot Head> ::= <Key Term> | <Non Key Term>
<Key Term> ::= *<Syntactic Term>
<Non Key Term> ::= <Syntactic Term>
<Syntactic Term> ::= <Syntactic Term in Moon Light Grammar>
<CS-Condition> ::= Predicate Formula
<Term Value> ::= <Commonsense Code> | <Term Value> or <Term Value>
<Commonsense Code> ::= (<Line of Codes>)<Digit String>
<Code> ::= <Variable Name> | <Digit>
<Commonsense Chain> ::= <Sequence of Commonsense Codes>

Note that the name “digit” is used here in an extended sense. Generally speaking, it does not only mean a single digit. We use in this section only a very small piece of our knowledge base. Therefore one single digit is enough to represent one level of the concept hierarchy. In the real knowledge base, where there are often more than ten son nodes of a single father node, the word “digit” should be replaced by “number”.

Definition 3.3.3

The commonsense oriented unification grammar, CSU grammar for short, is defined as follows:

<CSU grammar> ::= (<Root Symbol>, <Set of Non Terminal Symbols>, <Set of Terminal Symbols>, <Set of Productions>)
<Production> ::= <Moon Light Production> {<Sequence of Commonsense Constraint Frames> ,<Rule of Commonsense Code Calculation>}

where (<Root Symbol>, <Set of Non Terminal Symbols>,<Set of Terminal Symbols>, <Set of Moon Light Productions>) is a Moon Light Grammar.

Definition 3.3.4 (More General Commonsense Code)

Commonsense code (CSC) a is more general than CSC b, if:

1. a = b
2. or, there is a CSC c, such that b = a.c ,
3. or, there is a CSC c, such that a = b or c (= c or b)
4. or, a can be transformed in b by replacing some variables in a with digits or other variable names, where same variable names should be replaced with same things and at the same time.
5. or, there is a CSC c, such that a is more general than c, and c is more general than b.

Definition 3.3.5 (Unification of Commonsense Code)

Given two CSC a and b, we say that a and b are unifiable if there is a CSC c, such that both a and b are more general than c. We call c a unifier of a and b. Note that each CSC is more general than itself.

C is called a most general unifier of a and b, if there is no other unifier d of a and b, such that d is more general than c, but the reverse is not true.

Proposition 3.3.1

1. If unif(x, y) exists, then there exists also mgu(x, y), where unif means the unification operation, mdu means the most general unifier.
2. If mgu(x, y) exists, then it is unique but a renaming of variables.
3. Commutativity : mgu(x, y) = mgu(y, x)
4. Associativity : mgu(x, mgu(y, z)) = mgu(mgu(x, y), z)

Definition 3.3.6

Two CSC are said to conform to each other, if they have a mgu.

Definition 3.3.7 (More General Commonsense Chains)

A commonsense chain (CCH) a is said to be more general than commonsense chain b, if the first CSC of a is more general than that of b, and after value propagation (if in the procedure of unification of the two first CSC's some variables are instantiated, then this instantiation should be propagated to the whole commonsense chain) :

1. the remaining part of a is more general than that of b,
2. or the remaining part of a becomes empty.

The concepts of unification, unifier, most general unifier of commonsense chains can be defined similarly as those of commonsense codes.

Definition 3.3.8

Combine the CSC's of all term of a CS-frame together in a CCH, where the order of the CSC's is kept unchanged. The result is called the CCH of the CS-frame.

Definition 3.3.9

Given a CS-frame and its CCH. Change all CSC's of this CCH, which correspond to non-key terms, in a simple variable name, where all variable names are different. The result is called the key CCH (KCCH) of the CS-frame.

Definition 3.3.10

Given a CS-frame with its KCCH. Change all CSC's but one of this KCCH, which correspond to key terms, in a simple variable name, where all variable names should be kept different. The result is called a single key CCH (SKCCH) of the CS-frame with respect to the single exception key.

Algorithm 3.3.1

1. Given a Moon Light grammar and a set of commonsense constraint frames.
2. When parsing a sentence, do the following:
   2.1. Use the conventional parsing procedure to parse this sentence with productions of the Moon Light grammar.
   2.2. Each time when a reduction is made (say with the production rule P), use algorithm 3.4.2 to check the current sentence handle with the set C of commonsense constraint frames attached to P.
3. If at least one frame of C is violated, then the parsing fails due to commonsense errors.
4. Otherwise, use the rule of commonsense code calculation to calculate a CSC for the non-terminal symbol to be produced in this reduction step.
5. Go on to parse the next sentence until all sentences are successfully parsed.

End of Algorithm

Algorithm 3.3.2

1. Given a set C of n commonsense constraint frames (CS-frames) of the production rule P, and the commonsense chain cc of the sentence handle to be checked.
2. Let i=1.
3. Let the CCH of the i-th CS-frame be dd.
4. If the i-th CS-frame contains only key terms, then go to 13.
5. If the KCCH of the i-th frame is not unifiable with cc, then go to 8.
6. If the i-th CS-frame contains non syntactic terms (conditions), then go to 11.
7. If the CCH of the i-th frame is not unifiable with cc, then stop algorithm, commonsense check failed.
8. i := i + 1.
9. If i > n, then commonsense check is successful, algorithm finished.
10.Otherwise, go to 4.
11.Use commonsense knowledge base to check the conditions.
12.If successful, go to 8, otherwise stop algorithm, commonsense check failed.
13.If non of the SKCCH is unifiable with cc, then go to 8.
14.If the KCCH of the i-th is unifiable with cc, then go to 8.
15.Stop algorithm, commonsense check failed.

End of Algorithm

Note that the working mechanism of the commonsense constraint frames is opposite to that of the Moon Light grammar. The parsing process of a sentence is successful if there exits at least one parsing tree of this sentence, while the commonsense check is failed if there is at least one commonsense constraint frame which is violated by the sentence.

We pick a small example to demonstrate the use of CSU grammar in commonsense validity checking. First we list a piece of the Moon Light grammar (Note, this is not an English grammar), where the details are omitted:

1. <Sentence> ::= <Subject> <VEC Construction>
2. <VEC Construction> ::= <Modification> <Predicate>
3. <Modification> ::= <Time>|<Location>|<Time> <phenomenon>|<Empty>
4. <Predicate> ::= <Verb> [<Object>]

Let us consider the erroneous statements once again. To detect their errors, we need the following commonsense constraint frames:

Attached to production rule number 1:
(a) CS-Constraint (human-food input)
*Subject (1.1.1.1.1.1) # Human beings eat only human food #
*Verb (2.1.1.2)
Object (1.1.2.11)
End of (human-food input);
(b) CS-Constraint (subject-written message input)
*Subject (1.1.1.1) # Only animals can sense information with eyes #

*Verb (1.1.1.1)
End of (subject-written message input);
(c) CS-Constraint: (subject-place)
*Subject (1.1) # Solid things need space #
Location (1 or 2)
End of (subject-place);

Attached to production number 2:
CS-Constraint : (location-action)
*Location : (1.2.z) # Action type and action location agreement #
*Predicate : (2.2.z)
End of (location-action);
Code = code (<Modification>), code (<Predicate>)

Attached to production number 3:
CS-Constraint : (time-phenomenon)
Time : (x) # Natural phenomenon appears only at right time #
*Phenomenon : (3.x)
End of (time-phenomenon);
Code = code (<Time>), code (<Phenomenon>)

Attached to production number 4:
CS-Constraint : (written material processing)
*Verb (1.1.1.1) # Only written material can be read #
Object (1.1.2.2.1)
End of (written material processing);
Code = code (<Verb>), code (<Object>)

Example 3.3.5

Now we parse the six sentences. Note that our parser runs on Chinese texts. The Chinese grammar is very different from that of English one. Therefore both the grammar and the sentences take only roughly the form presented in this section. The reader should only get a rough idea about how it is working and forget the details. In the following examples we use non-standard English which is more similar to Chinese.

1. Lamp read book.
   Its commonsense chain is (1.1.2.2), (1.1.1.1), (1.1.2.2.1.1). After the parser obtains the sentence handle <Subject> <Predicate>, it finds that ((1.1.2.2), (1.1.1.1)) violates the second CS-Constraint of production rule 1.
2. John read water.
   Its commonsense code is (1.1.1.1.1.1.1), (1.1.1.1), (1.2). After the parser obtains the sentence handle <Verb> <Object>, it finds that ((1.1.1.1), (1.2)) violates the CS-Constraint of production rule 4.
3. John eat grass.
   Its commonsense code is (1.1.1.1.1.1.1), (2.1.1.2), (1.1.1.2). After the parser obtains the sentence handle <Subject> <VEC Construction>, it finds that

((1.1.1.1.1.1.1), (2.1.1.2), (1.1.1.2)) violates the first CS-Constraint of production rule 1.

4. John in wood swim.
   Its commonsense code is (1.1.1.1.1.1.1), (1.2.1), (2.2.2). After the parser obtains the sentence handle <Modification> <Predicate>, it finds that ((1.2.1), (2.2.2)) violates the CS-Constraint of production rule 2.
5. John in wood read book.
   Its commonsense code is (1.1.1.1.1.1.1), (3), (1.1.1.1), (1.1.2.2.1.1). After the parser obtains the sentence handle <Subject> < VEC Construction >, it finds that ((1.1.1.1.1.1.1), (3)) violates the third CS-Constraint of production rule 1.
6. John in night under sun light read book.
   Its commonsense code is (1.1.1.1.1.1.1), (2), (3.1), (1.1.1.1), (1.1.2.2.1.1). After the parser obtains the sentence handle <Time> <Phenomenon>, it finds that ((2), (3.1)) violates the CS-Constraint of production rule 3.

At last, we would like to give a note about the completeness of commonsense check. Since the commonsense knowledge is very vast, very fuzzy and vague, there is no sense to talk about its completeness in general. There is only a relative completeness with respect to our commonsense knowledge base which is being enriched and refined further and further. No matter how long this process will go, one point is worthwhile to mention, all algorithms above are independent of the content of the knowledge base. That is, we do not need to revise our algorithms in the process of knowledge base construction, unless its architecture and representation would be changed.

3.4 Semantic Disambiguation Based on Commonsense Knowledge

In natural language understanding, one of the most important and most difficult problems is that of resolving the semantic ambiguities. The experts of linguistics have developed a lot of theories and techniques to deal with this difficulty. Nevertheless, the problem of disambiguation of natural language understanding is still very far from being solved. There are at least two reasons for explaining this situation. The first reason is the totally irregular feature of any existing natural language and the lack of a formal theory which can cover all phenomena of such a language. Not to mention the steady variation and evolution of the language itself. The second reason is the open character of any real natural language. The meaning of a sentence or other language constructs can not be understood by relying upon the theory of linguistics only. In fact, the natural language understanding should be supported by a broad range of knowledge which has been accumulated by human-beings since thousands of years. It is at least supported by those knowledge items which are shared by the language producers and the language receivers.

People differentiate between syntactic ambiguities and semantic ambiguities. A well-known example of syntactic ambiguity is the following:

John watches the woman with a telescope.

Such kinds of ambiguities can be largely reduced by designing a delicate syntax of limited natural language. In this section, we are mainly interested in discussing techniques of solving semantic ambiguities. A rather narrow view of this problem is to limit it to the pronoun replacement technique. That is, one looks for the nouns which are denoted by some pronouns in a text and to replace the pronouns by the corresponding nouns. This is the so-called problem of anaphora. If the wanted nouns are not before, but after the corresponding pronouns, then the problem is called cataphora. Most of the linguistics researches devoted to semantic ambiguity resolution belong to the area of anaphora or cataphora resolving.

However, the SWAN technique is not only interested in natural language understanding in general, but also in story understanding in special. There are some aspects of a language text, which might be uninteresting in pure natural language understanding, but may have a vital importance in story understanding and automatic animation generation. For example, when doing machine translation, it is enough to translate the English word "several" to "quelque" in French or to "einige" in German. One does not need to make oneself clear about the exact number (how many) the word "several" denotes. But in order to transform the story to animation, the computer should at least have an estimation of this number, otherwise it would be impossible to design a reasonable screen image.

We call such kinds of problems the problem of expressibility, i.e. the possibility of expressing the content of a story written in text form by an animation. We will defer its discussion to chapter six and concentrate us in this section on the anaphora and cataphora problem only. We will illustrate the ubiquity of such problems and the importance of using commonsense knowledge for settling them by a set of examples. In each of the examples, there are three sentences. The first one shows the context (background) of this example. The second and third one are sentences with pronouns to be replaced. They have different solutions which can only be obtained with help of commonsense knowledge.

1. With respect to people's sentiment
   Zhang has broken the expensive glass of Li.
   (a) He feels very sorry. (b) He gets very angry.
2. With respect to people's physical state
   Zhang is sick and lives in the hospital.
   Li takes care of Zhang the whole night.
   (a) He has got a good rest. (b) He gets very tired.
3. With respect to people's social characteristics
   Zhang is sick and visits Dr. Li.
   (a) He describes what is wrong with him.
   (b) He prescribes a receipt for him.
4. With respect to the weather phenomena
   Zhang is waiting for Li at home. It rains outdoor very strongly.

(a) He is cleaning the rain drops on the window.
(b) He returns with his body all over wet.

One of the basic pillars of our SWAN technique is the use of commonsense knowledge. In SWAN, the commonsense knowledge is also used to resolve the ambiguities arising during natural language understanding. In fact, we have established a large scale commonsense knowledge base which not only includes commonsense knowledge in the natural world, but also that in the social relationships between humans which is according to our opinion even more important than the knowledge about the natural domain when analyzing a children story. We will see this in an example below. Our commonsense knowledge base, called Pan Gu (A giant in the ancient Chinese legend, who has separated the sky from the earth and thus created the world from a pure chaos), consists of a large set of agents and agent classes. Each agent or agent class models a concept of the real world. For example, it includes such concepts as a king, a queen, a prince, a princess, a country, a palace, etc. Each agent contains commonsense knowledge about itself as much as possible. This knowledge includes rules as "Each prince is the son of a king", "A dead person can do nothing", etc. Each agent has some intelligence and can do inference based on its knowledge or on the knowledge inherited from its parent nodes (agent classes). This inference is done either separately or in cooperation among several agents. For a detailed introduction to this commonsense knowledge base and its working mechanisms the reader may refer to chapter ten.

Given that the linguistic theory and the commonsense knowledge can both be used to settle the anaphora problem, and given that there are many aspects of commonsense knowledge, which may play a role in the process of problem solving, we should take all of this into consideration. In SWAN, the key technique of disambiguation is to let the various reasons of anaphora resolution compete with each other in every concrete case. The outcome of this competition is the final result. In order to do that, we use the idea of a multi-agent system.

However, the knowledge based inference of disambiguation is a very complicated task. We differentiate between shallow and deep commonsense reasoning for semantic disambiguation. In shallow commonsense reasoning, only direct mismatches between two language constructs in a same sentence are detected. It is what we can do in this section. On the other hand, in deep commonsense reasoning, complicated inference mechanisms, in particular, the mental activities of human-beings, are involved. We will discuss about this technique only in chapter five, in the context of story analysis.

Therefore, in SWAN, the performance of the disambiguation task is divided in two steps. In the first step, we will only use pure linguistic knowledge and shallow commonsense reasoning to solve semantic ambiguities as much as we can. The remaining ambiguities will be resolved by deep commonsense reasoning in chapter five.

The following algorithm is a pure linguistic one with respect to personal pronouns. It deals only with the so-called anaphorical problem, because the cataphorical problem appears very rarely in simple children stories.

Algorithm 3.4.1 (Anaphora Resolving based on Linguistic Knowledge Only)

1. Given a story text S. Scan this text sequentially in the original order and write down all nouns and constructions which relate to nouns (endocentric constructions, appositive constructions, etc.). Note that all nouns contained in these constructions should be considered. Write down also all personal pronouns (third person pronouns).
2. For all nouns and pronouns, write down their attributes (general-purpose nouns or special-purpose nouns, their sexes and their numbers. Note that in Chinese there is no difference between cases, such as nominative cases or objective cases, etc. Usually, one can see the implied cases of nouns or pronouns only at the different positions they take in a sentence and with help of prepositions).
3. For the remaining first pronoun in the story, we collect all nouns of the text, which appear before this pronoun as candidates for replacing it.
4. Assign a weight to all candidates in this set in the following order:
   4.1. those nouns whose attributes of number, sex and person do not match the current pronoun get a weight -1.
   4.2. those nouns, whose attributes of number, sex and person match the current pronoun, and which are in the same sentence as the current pronoun and which are not reflexive pronouns, get a weight 1 if there is only one such noun in this sentence, otherwise zero.
   4.3. those nouns n[i], which have the same attributes (of number, sex and person) as the current pronoun, and which are the subjects in the sentences where they are, get a weight 1 + 1/(distance1 between n[i] and the current sentence) .
   4.4. those nouns n[i], which have the same attributes (of number, sex and person) as the current pronoun, and which are not the subjects of the sentences where they are, get a weight 1 + 1/ (distance1 between n[i] and the current pronoun + distance2 between n[i] and the current sentence/ c)
   where c is a constant which is not less than the number of words in the whole story, distance1 is calculated in unit of sentences, whereas distance2 is calculated in unit of words. Note that the principal sentence and the subordinate sentence of a compound sentence will be considered as two sentences when applying the principles above.
5. That candidate, if any, with the largest weight greater than zero will be chosen to replace the current pronoun.
6. If there is no pronoun any more, then stop the algorithm. Otherwise go to 3.

End of Algorithm

Note if some noun appears more than once in the same candidate set, then only that one which is most close to the current pronoun is chosen. Note also that the reason of processing the candidates mentioned above should be recorded, so that we may change the decision later using a knowledge based inference if necessary.

Example 3.4.1

Assume c = 100.

1. For 4.1 (of algorithm 3.4.1):
   The professor is giving a talk. They like the talk very much.
   My father ordered a rich meal. She has eaten all of it.
   Zhang is leaving. We come to the airport to see them off.
   (Professor, father and Zhang all get the weight -1. That means, they are not valid candidates)

2. For 4.2: Snow White in this year is no more the same as she in last year. (Snow White gets the weight 1. That means, Snow White will be chosen as candidate for replacing the pronoun "she" only then, if all noun candidates in the sentences before the current one fail to match the pronoun. In fact, this is a meaningful sentence.)

3. For 4.3 and 4.4: The peasant woman saw Snow White dancing. She got angry.
   (Peasant woman gets the weight 1 + 1/1 = 2, and Snow White gets the weight 1 + 1/ (1 + 0.02) = 2.02/1.02. Therefore, it is the noun "peasant woman" rather than "Snow White", which will be chosen)

4. For 4.3: The peasant gave a poisonous apple to Snow White. She ate it. She died.
   (For the first "she", Snow White is the only candidate, she gets the weight 1 + 1/1 = 2. After the first "she" is replaced by "Snow White", this "Snow White" becomes a candidate for the second "she". Its weight is also 2.)

Proposition 3.4.1

According to algorithm 3.4.1 (only) we have: there is at most one candidate which has the largest weight greater than zero, and can be chosen to replace a personal pronoun.

Definition 3.4.1

If we have chosen that candidate which has the largest positive weight to replace the pronoun, then:

1. If the noun we have chosen, x, is the only noun with a weight greater than zero in the story text, which is in a sentence before the pronoun y to be replaced, or which is in the same sentence as the pronoun, then we say that x fulfils the "uniqueness principle".
2. Otherwise, if x is the noun we have chosen and is the subject of some preceding sentence or the current sentence, then we say that x fulfils the "subject principle".
3. Otherwise, if x is the noun we have chosen and is not the subject of some preceding sentence or the current sentence, then we say that x fulfils the "position principle".

Our next algorithm deals with shallow commonsense reasoning:

Algorithm 3.4.2 (Anaphora Resolving based on Shallow Commonsense Knowledge)

1. Given a story text S, which has been preprocessed by algorithm 3.4.1.
2. For the first (original) remaining pronoun, reconsider all candidates with their (original) weights calculated.
3. The following members of the candidate set of the pronoun get an extra weight -3:
   3.1. those which do not match the current pronoun in the sense of (subject, predicate) pair.
   3.2. those which do not match the current pronoun in the sense of (predicate, object) pair.
   3.3. those which do not match the current pronoun in the sense of (modification, noun) pair.
   3.4. those which do not match the current pronoun in the sense of (predicate, complement) pair.
4. That candidate, if any, with the largest weight greater than zero will be chosen to replace the current pronoun.
5. If there is no pronoun any more, then stop the algorithm. Otherwise go to 2.

End of Algorithm

In chapter five the reader will see the reason why we have chosen the weight –3 for those candidates who violate the shallow commonsense knowledge.

Example 3.4.2

Cows and tigers in the following sentences get an extra weight –3.

1. For 3.1(of algorithm 3.4.2): There is a cow in the field. It flies very fast.
2. For 3.2: There is a cow in the field. It is eating a chicken.
3. For 3.3: There is a tiger in the field. Its horns are very sharp.
4. For 3.4: There is a tiger in the field. It looks at me from the sky.

Proposition 3.4.2

1. The condition that the attributes of the candidates should match those of the pronouns to be replaced, is absolute. That means it has the veto if it would not be fulfilled
2. The shallow commonsense knowledge has the veto, if it would be violated.
3. Otherwise, candidates who are in sentences before the current sentence always have priority as compared with candidates in the same sentence as the pronoun is.
4. Otherwise, candidates who are in a sentence which has a smaller (sentence) distance from the current sentence have always the priority as compared with those who are in another sentence which has a greater (sentence) distance.

5. Otherwise, candidate who is a subject has always the priority as compared with a candidate who is not a subject, if these two candidates are in the same sentence before the current sentence.
6. Otherwise, if both candidates are not subjects and they are in the same sentence before the current sentence, then that one who has a smaller (word) distance from the pronoun has the priority as compared with the another one.

We have given two algorithms above, containing two kinds of rules: the positive ones and the negative ones. The positive rules suggest principles for determining who might be legal candidates for replacing pronouns. They get positive weights. The negative rules suggest principles for filtering illegal candidates. They get negative or zero weights. The priority criterion of their application is specified in the following algorithm.

Proposition 3.4.3

There is at most one candidate which is selected in algorithm 3.4.2.

Now let us use these algorithms to analyze our tiny story about Snow White. Instead of analyzing the original story as it was given above, we will try to analyze an "anaphoric version" of the Snow White story. This version keeps only the first occurrence for each role in the story. All subsequent occurrences of the same role are replaced by the corresponding pronouns. We mark each pronoun with a number to denote the special occurrence. We will see if we can recover all nouns from their pronouns based on linguistic theory and commonsense knowledge. The new version of story is as follows:

"The mother of Princess Snow White died. She (1) was very sad. The king married a new queen. The magic mirror told her (2) that she (3) is more beautiful than her (4). She (5) was very jealous . She (6) let a hunter kill her (7). He (8) set her (9) free. Seven dwarfs accepted her (10). It (11) told this to her (12). She (13) became a peasant woman. She (14) gave a poisonous apple to her (15). She (16) ate it (17) and died. The prince came and saw her (18) dead. He (19) rescued her (20). He (21) killed her (22). He (23) married her (24). "

In this story, there are four male roles: the king, the hunter, the prince and the seven dwarfs. The dwarfs are considered as one role only, since they do not appear separately in the story. Further, there are four female roles: Snow White, the mother of Snow White, the new queen and the peasant woman. At last, there are two roles which are not human-beings. They are the magic mirror and the poisonous apple. Thus we have ten roles.

On the other hand, there are 24 occurrences of pronouns. All personal pronouns are marked with numbers which denote the order of their occurring. Note that the sex attribute of each role is fetched from the knowledge base.

Now we give the result of voting according to algorithm 3.4.1 and algorithm 3.4.2. Assume still that c = 100.

Table 3.4.1 Candidate Selection in Snow White

Pronoun	Candidate1	Candidate2	Candidate3	Winner
She (1):[1] [2]	Mother of Snow White: – 2,	Snow White: 2.02/1.02,		Snow White
Her (2):	New queen: 2.05/1.05,	Snow White: 3/2,		New queen
She (3):	New queen: 2.02/1.02,	Snow White: 4/3,		New queen
Her (4):	New queen: 1,	Snow White: 4/3,		Snow White
She (5):	New queen: 2,	Snow White: 2.01/ 1.01,		New queen
She (6):	New queen: 2,	Snow White: 3.07/2.07,		New queen
Her (7):	New queen: 1,	Snow White: 3.14/2.14,		Snow White
He (8):	King: 6/5,	Hunter: 2.03/1.03,		Hunter
Her (9):	New queen: 2,	Snow White: 2.04/1.04,		New queen
Her (10):	New queen: 2.05/1.05,	Snow White: 3.11/2.11,		New queen
It (11):	Magic mirror: 7/6,			Magic mirror
Her (12):	New Queen: 2.05/1.05,	Snow White: 4.2/3.2,		New Queen
She (13): [3]	New Queen: 2.01/1.01,	Snow White: 5.23/4.23,		New Queen
She (14):	Peasant woman: 2.01/1.01,	Snow White: 6.3/5.3,		Peasant woman
Her (15):	peasant woman: 1,	Snow White: 6.38/5.38,		Snow White
She (16):[4]	peasant woman: 2,	Snow White: 2.01/1.01,		Peasant woman
It (17):	Magic mirror: 4/3,	Poisonous apple: 2.07/1.07,		Poisonous apple
Her (18):[5]	Mother of Snow White: 14/13,	Peasant woman: 2,		Peasant woman
He (19):	King: 13/12,	Hunter: 8/7,	Prince: 2,	Prince
Her (20):[6]	Peasant woman: 2.05/1.05,	Snow White: 4.22/3.22,		Peasant woman
He (21):	King: 14/13,	Hunter: 9/8,	Prince: 2,	Prince
Her (22):[7]	Peasant woman: 2.04/1.04,	Snow White: 5.28/4.28,		Peasant woman
He (23):	King: 15/14,	Hunter: 10/9,	Prince: 2,	Prince
Her (24): [8]	Peasant woman: - 1.08/1.04,	Snow White: 6.34/5.34,		Snow White

Notes in the above table:

[1] Shallow commonsense knowledge: dead persons do not have any sentiment.
[2] In the following, we deactivate "mother of Snow White". She enters the dead state.
[3] In the following, we deactivate "the new queen".
[4] In the following, we deactivate " Peasant woman". She enters the dead state.
[5] At this moment, only the mother of Snow White and the peasant woman are dead.
[6] In the following, we activate " Peasant woman". She enters the live state.
[7] In the following, we deactivate " Peasant woman". She enters the dead state.
[8] Shallow commonsense knowledge: one can not marry a dead person.

We summarize the result as follows:

She (1) = her (4) = her (7) = her (15) = her (24) = Snow White.
Her (2) = her (3) = she (5) = she (6) = her (9) = her (10) = her (12) = she (13) = the new queen.
She (14) = she (16) = her (18) = her (20) = her (22) = the peasant woman.
He (8) = the hunter.
He (19) = he (21) = he (23) = the prince.
It (11) = the magic mirror.
It (17) = the poisonous apple.

We thus get a very strange story as follows which is quite different from the original one and is unreasonable in many aspects.

"The mother of Princess Snow White died. Snow White was very sad. The king married a new queen. The magic mirror told the new queen that the new queen is more beautiful than Snow White. The new queen was very jealous. The new queen let a hunter kill Snow White. The hunter set the new queen free. Seven dwarfs accepted the new queen. The magic mirror told this to the new queen. The new queen became a peasant woman. The peasant woman gave a poisonous apple to Snow White. The peasant woman ate the poisonous apple and died. The prince came and saw the peasant woman dead. The prince rescued the peasant woman. The prince killed the peasant woman. The prince married Snow White."

In order to get a better effect, the shallow commonsense reasoning is not enough. We need a more powerful tool: the deep commonsense reasoning, which will be introduced in chapter five.

4 Story Understanding: The Theory

Natural language understanding is an important, and also a very difficult domain in AI. Early in the 1950's and 1960's, people attempted to work on sentence understanding. Research on story understanding began in 1970's, whose difficulty and complexity are much larger than those of sentence understanding. A survey of research on story understanding was already given in chapter one of this book. Up to now, scientists have not found any mature and effective theories or techniques to analyse and understand stories. Research on story understanding remains in an exploratory status.

We propose a new approach for story understanding in this chapter. The so–called Story Parsing Grammar (SPG) is used to represent the story abstracting processes with different degrees in story understanding. Syntax, semantics and pragmatics are represented unifiedly and explicitly in the productions in SPG. The story understanding process is converted to the story recognizing process done by the syntactic parser of SPG. We call this kind of story understanding story parsing.

Our study on story parsing is based on sentence understanding in natural language understanding, thus story is not represented in natural language any more. In section 4.1 of this chapter, the so–called Case Frame Forest (CFF) is proposed to represent the superficial meaning of story. CFF is the concatenation of trees by structure, while in respect of semantic representation, each tree of CFF, called Case Frame Tree (CFT), represents the understanding of the corresponding sentence in the story.

Concerning the story representation, SPG would not be simply a type of string grammar anymore. Its productions should possess high–dimensional structure, and it should not be context–free. In this regard, a new type of high–dimensional grammar, Forest Grammar (FG), is defined in section 4.2. Both left and right parts of the production in FG are concatenations of tree structures.

General FG is not suitable for story parsing. In section 4.3, SPG is defined as a suclass of context–sensitive FG. Productions in SPG represent not only replacement relations between forest structures but also semantic and pragmatic information. Derivation by productions in SPG does not simply mean the generation of some forest structure. In fact, it is the step–by–step generation of the story from abstract meaning to concrete story. A type of

R. Lu and S. Zhang: Automatic Generation of Computer Animation, LNAI 2160, pp. 93-122, 2002.

context–sensitive derivation is defined in the definition of SPG due to the fact that stories have high context–sensitivities.

In section 4.4, for a subclass of SPG, called weak precedence SPG, we study and implement its syntactic parsing algorithm, a kind of story parsing process. And data are given and analysed about the runtime efficiency of the algorithm.

We augment SPG with attributes and attribute rules in section 4.5 as a way to strengthen SPG's representation ability without imposing more restrictions on its strcuture.

Lastly in section 4.6, our SPG approach is analysed compared with other related studies in story understanding. Moreover, the significance of our work is discussed.

4.1 Story Representation and Parsing

A sentence is composed of words, several related sentences form the primary or secondary plot, and plots form the story. Based on the analysis of sentence syntax and semantics in natural language understanding, story understanding becomes a profound understanding of pragmatics and internal developing clue of the story. Research on story representation is the basis of this kind of story understanding. We propose Case Frame Forest (CFF) to represent the superficial meaning of a story. Moreover, story parsing process based on CFF is studied.

4.1.1 Case Frame Forest

We would only discuss stories in forward narrative order without flashbacks, where each sentence describes an action which could be physical or mental action, or some state. Those containing comments, explanations, deductions, analyses, etc., are not considered.

One of the important techniques for sentence understanding in natural language processing is the case frame model proposed by Fillmore in 1968 [Fillmore, 1968]. This model takes the verb of a sentence as the heart for parsing and other components as rhetorics for the verb. Every rhetorical component is called a case. CFF is proposed to be a story representation structure based on such sentence understanding. CFF is formed in the way that every sentence in a story is represented by a CFT, then these CFTs are concatenated to form a CFF in order of narration of the story.

In a CFT, the center is the verb and the rhetorical case of the verb could be a sentence component, the profound meaning of the sentence or profound relation between sentences obtained by understanding and pragmatic analysing, such as cause–and–effect relation, goal relation, condition relation, temporal relation, etc. In a CFT, the verb must have at east one rhetorical case and the subject of the verb must be included. A CFT could probably include *and* node, *or* node and *not* node to represent the set of cases, the *or* relation between cases, and negation of the verb, respectively. A CFT could include function node to represent function name and value, and its subtrees whose roots are the successor nodes of the function node (this type of subtree is called direct subtree) represent the function parameters. Furthermore, a CFT could include noun phrase node as well whose right-most direct subtree represents the noun and other direct subtrees represent the rhetorics of the noun.

Every node in CFT has at least two markings, indentifier and attribute. They are the name and characteristic of what the node represents. let $attr(a)$ represent the attribute of node a. All possible attributes of nodes in CFT are listed below.

1) $attr(a) =$ 'kp', meaning that node a is an action identifier and has a third marking, called tree key which marks the action one CFT corresponds to uniquely. The attribute of the root of every CFT is 'kp'.

2) $attr(a) =$ 'p', meaning that node a is an action identifier.

3) $attr(a) =$ 'f', meaning that node a is a function identifier.

4) $attr(a) =$ 'nhp', meaning that node a is a noun phrase identifier.

5) $attr(a) =$ 'r', meaning that node a is a case relation identifier.

6) $attr(a) =$ 'and', meaning that node a is an *and* identifier.

7) $attr(a) =$ 'or', meaning that node a is an *or* identifier.

8) $attr(a) =$ 'x', meaning that node a is a leaf node identifier.

If the attribute of a node is *nph*, *and* or *or*, then the identifier is the same as the attribute.

The leaf node of a CFT could probably be the root marking of another CFT. This is called extendible node. It is thus clear that the attribute of a leaf node of CFT could only be 'x' or 'kp'.

BNF is adopted in the following to define CFF and CFT, where $[< Q >]$ denotes that $< Q >$ can be chosen freely, $\{< Q >\}$ denotes that $< Q >$ can appear 0 or more than 0 times, $(< Q > \mid < Q' >)$ denotes alternativeness, " " denotes terminals, and $\cdots$ denotes omission.

$< CFF > ::= < CFT > \{< CFT >\}$

$< CFT > ::= < tree\ key >< action\ identifier >< case\ relation\ set >$

$< tree\ key > ::= < string >$

$< case\ relatin\ set > ::= \text{“}sub\text{''} < node >< case\ relation >< node >$
$\{< case\ relation >< node >\}$

$< node > ::= < action\ identifier >< case\ relation\ set > \mid$
$< leaf\ node > \mid < function\ node > \mid$
$< noun\ phrase\ node > \mid < and\ node > \mid < or\ node >$

$< leaf\ node > := < string > \mid < negation > \mid < tree\ key >$
$< action\ identifier >$

$< negation > ::= \text{“}\neg\text{''}$

$< functinon\ node > ::= < function\ identifier >< node > \{< node >\}$

$< function\,identifier >::=< string >$
$< noun\,pharse\,node >::= \text{“}nph'' < node >< node > \{< node >\}$
$< and\,node >::= \text{“}and'' < node >< node > \{< node >\}$
$< or\,node >::= \text{“}or'' < node >< node > \{< node >\}$
$< caserealtion >::=< timecaserelation > | < pragmaticcaserelation > |$
$\quad < sentence\,component\,case\,relation >$
$< time\,case\,relation >::= \text{“}before''|\text{“}equal''| \cdots$
$< pragmaticcaserelation >::= \text{“}cause\text{–}and\text{–}effect''|\text{“}goal''|\text{“}condition''$
$< sentence\,component\,case\,relation >::= \text{“}dobj''|\text{“}iobj''|\text{“}tool''| \cdots$

“sub” is also a kind of sentence component case relation denoting initiative relatiion. “dobj” denotes direct object relation, while “iobj” denotes indirect object relation, and “tool” denotes tool relation.

4.1.2 An Example of Story and Its Representation

The following is a story.

“Snow White was more beautiful than Queen. Because of envy Queen ordered somebody to kill Snow White. Queen also ordered Snow White to eat a poisonous apple. Snow White had to eat the poisonous apple. Later, Snow White was saved while Queen died suddenly.”

It is obvious that this story has forward narrative structure. CFTs are constructed to represent corresponding actions in the story and the CFF is formd as shown in figure 4.1.1, where $k_i, 1 \leq i \leq 6$, denotes the tree key and

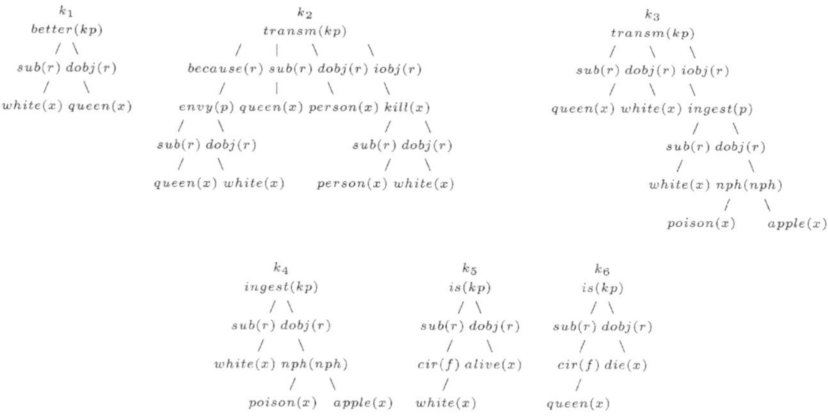

Figure 4.1.1 The CFF Representation of a Story

the string in the parentheses after a node identifier denotes the attribute of the node.

4.1.3 Story Parsing Process

Based on the idea of syntactic parsing in formal language and the story representation discussed above, a new story understanding approach is proposed, in which the role character, developing plot, summary, etc. of the story are analysed according to SPG which represents the transformation from high to low abstraction levels of a story. In SPG, the highest abstraction level is some parsing goal, such as obtaining the summary, while the lowest abstracting leverl is the story itself.

As shown in figure 4.1.2, being aimed at some kind of stories and some parsing goal, an SPG and its syntactic parser are given, and for any given story, if it is proved by the parser that this story belongs to the language generated by the SPG, then it is known that this story could be abstracted to the parsing goal of this SPG. SPG represents semantics and pragmatics explicitly. The syntactic parsing process according to SPG is actually the semantic and pragmatic analysing process as well.

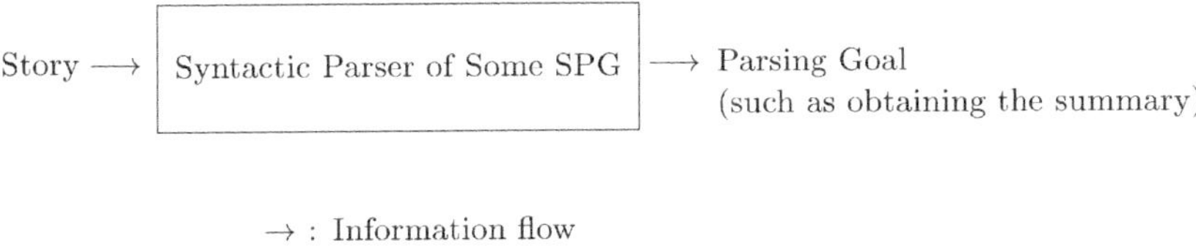

Figure 4.1.2 Story Parsing Process

In order to represent semantics and pragmatics of a story, the context–free string grammar is no longer enough which is universally adopted to represent syntax of programming languages. High–dimensional grammar and context–sensitive grammar must be introduced to represent the profound meaning of a story and the internal connections among story plots respectively. For this purpose, a new high–dimensional grammar, Forest Grammar (FG), is proposed in the next section. Afterwards, a subclass of FG, Story Parsing Grammar (SPG), is defined and used to represent story parsing.

4.2 Forest Grammar

4.2.1 A General Introduction to Forest Grammar

Generally speaking, a grammar G is a 4–tuple , (N, Σ, P, S), where N and Σ are nonempty and finite sets of symbols satisfying $N \cap \Sigma = \Phi$, called nonterminal vocabulary and terminal vocabulary of G, respectively, and elements in N and Σ called nonterminals and terminals of G, respectively; P is the finite set of productions of G while productions take the form $\alpha \rightarrow \beta$ where both α and β are strings of symbols belonging to $N \cup \Sigma$ and α includes at least one nonterminal; S is a specified nonterminal, serving as the starting symbol of G.

According to properties of produtions, grammars can be classified into four types: type 0 grammars, also called phrase structure grammars; type 1 grammars, also called context–sensitive grammars; type 2 grammars , also called context –free grammars; and type 3 grammars, also called regular grammars.

The language produced by a grammar, whose elements are called sentences, is the set of strings of finite terminals that can be produced from the starting symbol through applications of productions. Study on such languages mainly includes two aspects: production and recognition, the former being how to produce sentences of some formal language by a grammar, and the latter how to decide whether an arbitrary string belongs to the language of a grammar or not.

Grammars studied in the formal language domain are string ones, based on which high–dimensional grammars are proposed as being more general and used in pattern recognition [Fu, 1977] [Fu, 1982][Gonzalez and Thomason, 1977]. Compared with string grammars which are one–dimensional, high–dimensional grammars have more complicated structures and objectives being processed. As structural or syntactic methods in pattern recognition, high–dimensional grammars mainly include tree, web, shape grammars, etc.

In this section, a new type of high–dimensional grammar, forest grammar (FG), is proposed, while the tree grammar in syntactic pattern recognition is one of its subclasses. A classification of FG is studied, especially the context–sensitive FG, a subclass of FG.

4.2.2 Definiton of Forest Grammar

First we introduce definitions of tree and forest, then define FG, and finally define the derivation of FG, the language produced by FG, etc.

Definition 4.2.1
A nonempty set of symbols is called a vocabulary.

Definition 4.2.2
A tree T is a finite set which includes one or more elements, called nodes, and satisfies

(i) there exists a unique node specified as the root; and

(ii) other nodes are divided from left to right into m sets, every two of which do not intersect with each other: $T_1, T_2, \cdots, T_m$, where $m \geq 0$ and every set is a tree.

In tree T, a node in T_i, where $1 \leq i \leq m$, is called a descendant node of the root of T, and the root of T_i is called a son node of the root of T.

That a node in T is called node a denotes that symbol a is a marking of this node. In tree T, a tree is called a subtree of T if it takes a node of T, say a, as its root while a is not the root of T, and takes all the decendant nodes of a and a to form its set of nodes. Such a tree is also called the subtree of T at a.

If tree T' is a subtree of T and the root of T' is a son node of a node in T, saya, then T' is called a direct subtree of a. In tree T, the number of direct subtrees of node a is called the rank of a, and while it equals 0, node a is called a leaf of T.

let node (T) denote the number of nodes in T.

Definition 4.2.3
Tree T and tree U are identical , denoted by $T = U$, if and only if

(i) the root of T and the root of U have the identical marking; and

(ii) if all the direct subtrees of the root of T from left to right are $T_1, T_2, \cdots$, and T_m where $m \geq 0$, and all the direct subtrees of the roof of U from left to right are $U_1, U_2, \cdots$, and U_n where $n \geq 0$, then $n = m$ and for every $i, 1 \leq i \leq n$, $T_i = U_i$ holds.

Definition 4.2.4
Let V be a vocabulary, $N \subset V$ and $N \neq \Phi$. T_V denotes the set of such trees that every of their nodes is marked by symbols in V. $T_V^{[N]} \subset T_V$ holds and for every tree in $T_V^{[N]}$, there exists at least one node which is marked by symbols in N.

For any positive natural number n and any $t_1, \cdots, t_n \in T_V$, the string $t_1 \cdots t_n$ formed by concatenating $t_1, \cdots, t_n$ is called a forest on T_V, and n is called the length of this forest, denoted by $|t_1 \cdots t_n|$. If $n = 0$, then $t_1 \cdots t_n$ is called null forest, denoted by ε, which does not include any tree. For any i and j satisfying $1 \leq i \leq j \leq n, t_i \cdots t_j$ is called a subforest of $t_1 \cdots t_n$. T_V^* and T_V^+ denote the following sets, respectively:

$$T^* = \{\alpha | \alpha \text{ is a forest on } T_V\},$$

$$T_V^+ = \{\alpha | \alpha \text{ is a forest on } T_V \text{ and } \alpha \neq \varepsilon \text{ holds } \}.$$

Definition 4.2.5

Let N and Σ be finite vocabularies and $N \cap \Sigma = \Phi$. Let $V = N \cup \Sigma$. An FG G_f is a 4–tuple, $(N, \Sigma P, S)$, where N is the nonterminal vocabulary of G_f, whose elements are called nonterminals; Σ is the terminal vocabulary of G_f, whose elements are called termials; P is the finite set of productions of G_f taking the form

$$\alpha\nu\omega \rightarrow \beta,$$

where $\alpha \in T_V^*$, $\nu \in T_V^{[N]}$, $\omega \in T_V^*$, and $\beta \in T_V^*$ hold; $S \in T_V^{[N]}$, serving as the starting tree of G_f.

From the above definitions, we know the FG has high–dimensional structure. Therefore the derivation in FG includes not only the replacement of forest, similar to those in ordinary string grammars, but also the replacement of subtree of tree as well.

Definition 4.2.6

Suppose FG $G_f = (N, \Sigma, P, S)$. Let $V = N \cup \Sigma$, $\alpha, \beta, \alpha_0, \beta_0, \nu_1, \nu_2 \in T_V^*$, $t_1, T \in T_V^{[N]}$, $t_2, T_2 \in T_V$. We say that α directly produces β or produces β in one step, denoted by $\alpha \Longrightarrow \beta$, which is also called a direct derivation, if and only if the following (i) or (ii) holds.

(i) There exists production $\alpha_0 \rightarrow \beta_0$ in P, and $\alpha = \nu_1\alpha_0\nu_2$ and $\beta = \nu_1\beta_0\nu_2$ hold. Now we say that α string–produces β. This is also called a string derivation.

(ii) There exists production $t_1 \rightarrow t_2$ in P, $\alpha = \nu_1 T_1 \nu_2$ holds where there exists node $a \in T_1$ such that t_1 is the subtree of T at a, $\beta = \nu_1 T_2 \nu_2$ holds, and T_2 is produced by using t_2 to replace t_1 at node a in T_1. Now we say that α tree–produces β, and that T_2 is directly produced by T_1 at node a. This is also called a tree derivation.

For any $\alpha_1, \alpha_2, \cdots, \alpha_n \in T_V^*$ where $n \geq 1$, if $\alpha_1 \Longrightarrow \alpha_2 \Longrightarrow \cdots \Longrightarrow \alpha_n$ holds, then this chain is called a derivation with $(n-1)$ steps from α_1 to α_n, or we say that α_1 can produce α_n in $n-1$ steps, denoted by $\alpha_1 \overset{n-1}{\Longrightarrow} \alpha_n$.

Let $\alpha_1 \overset{+}{\Longrightarrow} \alpha_n$ denote the derivation with no less than 1 step from α_1 to α_n.

Let $\alpha_1 \overset{*}{\Longrightarrow} \alpha_n$ denote that $\alpha_1 \Longrightarrow \alpha_n$ or $\alpha_1 \overset{+}{\Longrightarrow} \alpha_n$ holds.

Definition 4.2.7

Suppose FG $G_f = (N, \Sigma, P, S)$. Let $V = N \cup \Sigma$. For any $\alpha \in T_V^*$, if $S \overset{*}{\Longrightarrow} \alpha$ holds, then α is called a tree sentential form of G_f. For any $w \in T_\Sigma^*$, if $S \overset{*}{\Longrightarrow} \omega$ holds, then ω is called a tree sentence of G_f. All the tree sentences of G_f compose the language of G_f, denoted by $L(G_f)$; that is to say,

$$L(G_f) = \{\omega | \omega \in T_\Sigma^* \text{ and } S \overset{*}{\Longrightarrow} \omega \text{ hold } \}.$$

4.2.3 A Classification of Forest Grammars

We classify FGs by placing different restrictions on their productions.

Definition 4.2.8
Suppose FG $G_f = (N, \Sigma, P, S)$. Let $V = N \cup \Sigma$.

(i) If no restrictions are placed on productions in P, then G_f is called a type 0 FG.

(ii) If every production $\alpha \to \beta$ in P satisfies

$$|\alpha| \leq |\beta|,$$

then G_f is called a type 1 or context–sensitive FG, denoted by csfg.

(iii) If every production in P takes the form

$$A \to \beta,$$

where $A \in N$ and $\beta \in T_V^+$ hold, then G_f is called a type 2 or context–free FG, denoted by cffg.

(iv) If every production in P takes the form

$$A \to T \quad \text{or} \quad A \to tB,$$

where $A, B \in N$ and $t \in T_\Sigma$ hold, then G_f is called a type 3 or regular FG, denoted by rfg.

Obviously, a type 3 FG must be a type 2 one, a context–free FG must be a context–sensitive one, and a type 1 FG must be a type 0 FG.

Definition 4.2.9
Suppose FG $G_f = (N, \Sigma, P, S)$. Let $V = N \cap \Sigma$. If every production $\alpha \to \beta$ in P takes the from

$$T \to t,$$

where $T \in T_V^{[N]}$ and $t \in T_V$, then G_f is called a tree grammar.

Obviously, tree grammar is a kind of context–sensitive FG, and its tree sentential forms and tree sentences are trees.

Definition 4.2.10
Suppose tree Grammar $G_t = (N, \Sigma, P, S)$. Let $V = N \cup \Sigma$.

(i) If every production $T \to t$ in P satisfies

$$node(T) \leq node(t),$$

then G_t is called a context–sensitive tree grammar.

(ii) If every production $T \to t$ in P is of the form

$$A \to t,$$

where $A \in N$ and $t \in T_V$ hold, then G_t is called a context–free tree grammar.

Obviously, a context–free tree grammar must be a context–sensitive one, and a context–free FG as well.

4.3 Story Parsing Grammar

4.3.1 Definition of Story Parsing Grammar

Definition 4.3.1
Suppose csfg $G_f = (N, \Sigma, P, S)$. Let $V = N \cup \Sigma$. If production $\alpha \to \beta$ in P takes the form

$$T \to \nu,$$

where $T \in T_V^{[N]}$ and $\nu \in T_V^*$, then $\alpha \to \beta$ is called a single left production . G_f is called a single left context–sensitive FG, denoed by slcsfg, if and only if its every production is a single left one.

Definition 4.3.2
Suppose slcsfg $G_s = (N, \Sigma, P, S)$ and $V = N \cup \Sigma$. Let $N_1, IDE, CAP, TKEY, DIS$ be different finite nonempty domains, where DIS includes only one element and $N_1, IDE, CAP, TKEY$ and DIS do not intersect two by two. In G_s, N is the nonterminal set and $N = \{S\} \cup N_1 \cup \{r, x, p, f\} \times CAP \cup \{kp\} \times CAP \times TKEY \cup DIS \times CAP \cup CAP$, while Σ is the terminal set and $\Sigma = \{nph\} \times \{nph\} \cup \{and\} \times \{and\} \cup \{or\} \times \{or\} \cup \{r, x, p, f\} \times IDE \cup \{kp\} \times IDE \times TKEY$. S is the initial nonterminal. P is the finite set of productions which have the following form.

$$t \to \alpha, \quad t \in T_V^{[N]}, \quad \alpha \in T_V^*.$$

G_s is called SPG if and only if every condition in the following holds.

(i) For any $S_1 \in N_1, S_1$ never exists in the right part of the production whose left part is not equal to S. Moreover, if S_1 exists in the left part of some produciton $t \to \alpha$, where $t \in T_V^{[N]}$ and $\alpha \in T_V^*$, then $t = S_1$ holds.

(ii) For any $S_1, S_2 \in N_1$ and any $\beta_1, \beta_1 \in T_\Sigma^+$, if $S_1 \neq S_2$, $S_1 \stackrel{+}{\Longrightarrow} \beta_1$, and $S_2 \stackrel{+}{\Longrightarrow} \beta_2$, then $\beta_1 \neq \beta_2$ holds.

(iii) For any produciton $t \to \alpha, t \in T_V^{[N]}, \alpha \in T_V^*$,

(iii-1) if $t = S$, then $\alpha \in N_1$;

(iii-2) if $t \in N_1$, then $|\alpha| \geq 1$, and for any tree T in α where $T \in T_V$, node $(T) > 1$ holds;

and

(iii-3) if $t \neq S$, $t \notin N_1$ and $\alpha \neq \varepsilon$, then one of the following holds.

(iii-3.1) If $t \in N$, then $\alpha \in T_\Sigma$.

(iii-3.2) If $t \notin N$, then $|\alpha| \geq 1$, and for every tree T in α where $T \in T_V$, $node(T) > 1$ holds. And for any $X \in N$, if X is a subtree of t, then there exists tree U, $U \in T_V$, in α such that X is a subtree of U.

(iv) For any $\omega \in L(G_s)$, let $\omega = t_1 \cdots t_n$, $n \geq 1, t_1, \cdots, t_n \in T_\Sigma$, and every $t_i, 1 \leq i \leq n$, is a CFT.

(v) For any $t, u \in PRT(G_s)$, if $t \neq u$ and the roots of t and u are 3–tuples (tp, A, k_1) and (kp, B, k_2) respectively, where $A, B \in IDE \cup CAP$, $k_1, k_2 \in TKEY$, then $k_1 \neq k_2$.

(vi) The derivation of G_s is context–free derivation. For any given derivation $S \stackrel{+}{\Longrightarrow} \beta$ where $\beta \in T_{\Sigma}^{+}$, while production $t \rightarrow \alpha$ is used in the derivation where $t \in T_V^{[N]}$ and $\alpha \in T_V^{+}$, if $t \neq S$, and $t \in N_1$ when $t \in N$, then for any $X \in N$, if X is a subtree of some tree in α, there exists a context–free derivation as follows.

$$\alpha \stackrel{*}{\Longrightarrow} \alpha_1, \quad \alpha_1 \Longrightarrow \alpha_2\alpha_1, \; \alpha_2 \in T_V^{+},$$

where $\alpha_1 \Longrightarrow \alpha_2$ is the replacement of the subtree X of some tree in α_1 through adopting the produciton $X \rightarrow u$, $u \in T_{\Sigma}$. Now u is called an instantiation of X.

(vii) For any given derivation $S \stackrel{+}{\Longrightarrow} \beta$ in G_s, $\beta \in T_{\Sigma}^{+}$, it is the context–sensitive derivation as follows.

(vii-1) Suppose the production $t \rightarrow \alpha(t \in T_V^{[N]}, \alpha \in T_V^{+})$ is adopted in the derivation, for any $X \in N$ which has no value in DIS, if X exists in more than 2 places as a subtree of some tree in α, then only such context–free derivation is permitted that these X_s have different instantiations.

(vii-2) Suppose the production $t \rightarrow \alpha(t \in T_V^{[N]}, \alpha \in T_V^{+})$, is adopted in the derivation, for any $X, Y \in N$ which have no values in DIS , if $X \neq Y$, and X and Y are stutrees of trees in α, then only such context–free derivation is permitted that X and Y have different instantiations.

(vii-3) Suppose the production $t \rightarrow \alpha(t \in T_V^{[N]}, \alpha \in T_V^{+})$, is adopted in the derivation, for any$X, Y \in N$ which have no values in DIS, if X and Y are subtrees of trees in α, then the instantiations of X and Y are permitted to be either the same or different.

Context–sensitiveity of context–sensitive FG lies in that the replacement through production can be made to the subtree structure of a tree. SPG has stronger context–sensitiveity due to the fact that not only can its replacement be made to the subtree structure of a tree, but its derivation is a type of context–sensitive derivation as well.

In order to understand SPG better, a few explanations of its definition are given in the following.

1) Instead of being symbols only, nonterminals and terminals could probably be 2–tuples or 3–tuples of symbols. IDE and CAP could be taken as the set of names of terminals and the set of names of nonterminals in producitons of G_s respectively. $(IDE \cup CAP)$ is called the identifier set of G_s, where elements in IDE are called terminal identifiers, while those in CAP are nonterminal identifiers. N_1 could be taken as a set including a group of special nonterminal identifiers, wholse every element could only be the right part of the production with S as the left part, or be the left part of any production. S could be taken as the initial nonterminal identifier. Taken as the set of tree keys used to mark trees uniquely, $TKEY$ is called the tree key set of G_s. $\{kp, p, f, r, x, and, or, nph\}$ could be considered as the set of attributes of nodes in trees in productions. In DIS, there is only one element

used to distinguish different instantiation demands of different elements in CAP. Every node of trees in producitons of G_s has at least an identifier, and could either have value in DIS or not. Nodes marked by terminal identifiers must have attributes, while those marked by nonterminal identifiers could probably have no attributes. Nodes with the attribute 'kp' must have tree keys, and vice versa. Nodes marked by elements in $\{S\} \cup N_1$ only have identifiers.

2) It can be concluded from the definition of SPG that the tree sentence in language of SPG is CFF and that what SPG generates eventually is the CFF set. Actually, in G_s, IDE, $\{kp, p, f, r, x, andor, nph\}$ and $TKEY$ are the set of identifiers of nodes in CFTs, the set of attributes of nodes in CFTs and the set of tree keys of CFTs, respectively.

3) Empty productions are permitted in SPG because of the possible default of some cases and case relations in CFTs.

4) SPG actually represents syntax, semantics and pragmatics explicitly. The syntactic and semantic representation by SPG mainly lies in the markings of nodes in trees of productions and relations among these markings, while the pragmatic representation by SPG mainly lies in the replacement relation between the left part and the right part of production. The initial nontermainal S of SPG could be taken as standing for the story parsing goal, such as obtaining the summary, etc. Production with the form $S \to S_1, S_1 \in N_1$, could be considered as standing for the meaning of the story parsing goal, and different elements in N_1 stand for different meanings of the parsing goal. From the definition of SPG, it is clear that stories (CFFs) derived from different meanings of the parsing goal are different.

4.3.2 An Example of Story Parsing Grammar

An example of SPG will be given below. Its parsing goal is to get the story's summary. It is concerned with stories whose summaries are that mercy results in happiness and evil brings about bad retribution. Its productions represent the following meanings.

1) If Y is cruel, X is kind and X defeats Y, then the summary is obtained that mercy results in happiness and evil brings about bad retribution.

2) If X is alive and Y is dead, then one can get the conclusion that X defeats Y.

3) If X is better than Y and therefore Y hates or kills X, then one can say that Y is cruel.

4) If Y orders X to eat Z and X does not act accordingly, then one can say that X is kind.

5) If Y orders Z to kill X, then Y kills X.

Suppose slcsfg $G_{exm} = (N, \Sigma, P, S)$, which satisfies that $N_1 = \{S_1\}$; $DIS = \{'d\}$; $IDE = \{cruel, kind, transm, ingest, better, hate, envy, kill, because, cir, alive, die, sub, dobj, iobj, nph\} \cup IDD$, IDD is the set of letter strings whose lengths are less than or equal to 6, obviously IDD is finite;

$CAP = \{CHAR, WIN, DOHARMTO, X, Y, Z, B\}$;
$TKEY = \{k_1, k_2, k_3, k_4, k_5, k_6, k_7, K_1, K_2, K_3, K_4\}$;
$N = \{S, S_1, (kp, CHAR, K_1), (kp, CHAR, K_2), (kp, WIN, K_3),$
$(kp, DOHARMTO, K_4), (p, DOHARMTO), X, Y, Z, B\}$;
$\Sigma = \{(kp, is, k_5), (kp, is, k_6), (kp, better, k_1), (kp, transm, k_3),$
$(kp, ingest, k_4), (kp, transm, k_2), (kp, kill, k_7), (p, kill), (p, ingest),$
$(p, hate), (p, envy), (f, cir), (r, sub), (r, dobj), (r, iobj), (r, because),$
$(x, die), (x, alive), (x, cruel), (x, kind), (nph, nph)\}$.

P is the set of the following productions, where $P_i, 1 \leq i \leq 19$, is the serial number of the production. String in the parentheses after the node indentifier is the node attribute, and that in the sqare brackets is the tree key.

$P_{14}, P_{15}, P_{16}, P_{17}, P_{18}$ and P_{19} represent different finite groups of productions. From definition 4.3.2 one can get the conclusion that G_{exm} is an SPG.

G_{exm} shows how an SPG represents semantics and pragmatics. Take production P_6 as an example. The semantics of P_6 are that Y is cruel and that X is better then Y thus Y does harm to X. P_6 itself tells that if Y does harm to X because X is better than Y then one can say that Y is curel, which is just the pragmatics P_6 represents,and which obviously could not be obtained only through the semantics of P_6.

4.4 Weak Precedence Story Parsing Grammar (WPSPG)

4.4.1 Definition of WPSPG

Let every FG G_f discussed here, where $G_f = (N, \Sigma, P, S)$ and suppose $V = N \cup \Sigma$, satisfy all the following conditions.

(1) There does not exist cyclic derivation $\alpha \stackrel{+}{\Longrightarrow} \alpha$ for any $\alpha \in T_V^*$.

(2) S never exists in the right part of any production.

(3) For any production $t \rightarrow \alpha$ where $t \in T_V$ and $\alpha \in T_V^*$, it must be useful, meaning that there exist $\beta_1, \beta_2 \in T_\Sigma^*$, $r \in T_\Sigma^*$, $u \in T_V$ and $\gamma_1 \in T_\Sigma$, so that one of the following conditions holds.

(3.1) $S \stackrel{*}{\Longrightarrow} \beta_1 t \beta_2$ and $\alpha \stackrel{+}{\Longrightarrow} \gamma$.

(3.2) $|\alpha| = 1$ and $S \stackrel{*}{\Longrightarrow} \beta_1 u \beta_2$, and t is a subtree of u and $\alpha \stackrel{+}{\Longrightarrow} \gamma_1$.

(4) For any $A \in N$, A must be useful, meaning that there exist $\alpha, \beta \in T_\Sigma^*$, $\gamma \in T_\Sigma^*$ and $t \in T_V^{[\{A\}]}$, so that $S \stackrel{*}{\Longrightarrow} \alpha t \beta$ and $t \stackrel{+}{\Longrightarrow} \gamma$ hold.

Definition 4.4.1
Suppose slcsfg $G_f = (N, \Sigma, P, S)$. The set of all trees in left and right part forests of all productions in G_f is called the production tree set of G_f, denoted by $PRT(G_f)$, whose every element is called a production tree of G_f.

```
P1 :   S ⟶ S1
P2 :   S1 ⟶   CHAR(kp)[K1]          CHAR(kp)[K2]          WIN(kp)[K3]
                /      \              /      \              /      \
             sub(r)  dobj(r)       sub(r)  dobj(r)       sub(r)  dobj(r)
               /        \            /        \            /        \
              Y      cruel(x)       X       kind(x)       X          Y

P3 :   S1 ⟶   CHAR(kp)[K2]          CHAR(kp)[K1]          WIN(kp)[K3]
                /      \              /      \              /      \
             sub(r)  dobj(r)       sub(r)  dobj(r)       sub(r)  dobj(r)
               /        \            /        \            /        \
              Y      kind(x)        X      cruel(x)       X          Y

P4 :   WIN(kp)[K3] ⟶        is(kp)[k5]              is(kp)[k6]
         /      \             /      \                /      \
      sub(r)  dobj(r)      sub(r)  dobj(r)         sub(r)  dobj(r)
        /        \           /        \              /        \
       X          Y       cir(f)    alive(x)      cir(f)     die(x)
                            /                       /
                           X                       X

P5 :   WIN(kp)[K3] ⟶        is(kp)[k6]              is(kp)[k5]
         /      \             /      \                /      \
      sub(r)  dobj(r)      sub(r)  dobj(r)         sub(r)  dobj(r)
        /        \           /        \              /        \
       X          Y       cir(f)     die(x)       cir(f)    alive(x)
                            /                       /
                           X                       X

P6 :   CHAR(kp)[K1] ⟶       better(kp)[k1]          DOHARMTO(kp)[K4]
         /      \             /      \              /      |       \
      sub(r)  dobj(r)      sub(r)  dobj(r)         B    sub(r)   dobj(r)
        /        \           /        \           / \      |        \
       Y      cruel(x)      X          Y         Y   X     Y         X

P7 :   CHAR(kp)[K2] ⟶       transm(kp)[k3]          ingest(kp)[k4]
         /      \           /      |      \           /      \
      sub(r)  dobj(r)    sub(r) dobj(r)  iobj(r)   sub(r)  dobj(r)
        /        \         /      |        \         /        \
       X       kind(x)    Y       X     ingest(p)   X          Z
                                          /    \
                                       sub(r)  dobj(r)
                                         /        \
                                        X          Z

P8 :   DOHARMTO(kp)[K4] ⟶          transm(kp)[k2]
        /      |       \         /      /       \        \
       B    sub(r)   dobj(r)    B    sub(r)   dobj(r)   iobj(r)
      / \      |        \      / \     /        /          \
     Y   X     Y         X    Y   X   Y        Z       DOHARMTO(p)
                                                         /     \
                                                      sub(r)  dobj(r)
                                                        /        \
                                                       Z          X

P9 :   DOHARMTO(kp)[K4] ⟶       kill(kp)[k7]
        /      |       \         /     |      \
       B    sub(r)   dobj(r)    B   sub(r)   dobj(r)
      / \      |        \      / \     |        \
     Y   X     Y         X    Y   X    Y         X

P10 :  DOHARMTO(p) ⟶             kill(p)                 P11 :   B ⟶ ε
         /      \                /      \                       / \
      sub(r)  dobj(r)         sub(r)  dobj(r)                  Y   X
        /        \              /        \
       Z          X            Z          X

P12 :   B ⟶       because(r)        P13 :   B ⟶       because(r)
       / \            |                    / \            |
      Y   X        envy(p)                Y   X        hate(p)
                   /     \                             /     \
                sub(r)  dobj(r)                     sub(r)  dobj(r)
                  /        \                          /        \
                 Y          X                        Y          X

P14 :  X ⟶ idf          P15 :  Y ⟶ idf          P16 :  Z ⟶ idf       idf traverses {x} × IDE
P17 :  X ⟶ nph(nph)     P18 :  Y ⟶ nph(nph)     P19 :  Z ⟶ nph(nph)
            /  \                    /  \                    /  \
          idf  idf                idf  idf                idf  idf
```

Definition 4.4.2

Suppose slcsfg $G_f = (N, \Sigma, P, S)$. Let $V = N \cup \Sigma$ and $t \in T_V$. t is called an operand tree of G_f if and only if in P there exists prodution $t \to \beta$ where $\beta \in T_V^*$. $NOTS(G_f)$ denotes the set of all operand trees of G_f, written as:

$$NOTS(G_f) = \{t| \text{ There exists } \ t \to \beta \text{ where } t \in T_V^{[N]} \text{ and } \beta \in T_V^* \text{ in } G_f\}.$$

Definition 4.4.3
Suppose slcsfg $G_f = (N, \Sigma, P, S)$. Let $V = N \cup \Sigma$ and $t \in T_V$. t is called an operator tree of G_f if and only if the following (1) and (2) hold.

(1) There exists $T \rightarrow \gamma_1 t \gamma_2$ in P where $T \in T_V^{[N]}$, and $\gamma_1, \gamma_2 \in T_V^*$.

(2) There does not exist such production as $t \rightarrow \beta$ where $\beta \in T_V^*$ in P.

$OTS(G_f)$ denotes the set of all operator trees of G_f, written as:

$OTS(G_f) = \{t | t \notin NOTS(G_f)$ and there exists $T \rightarrow \gamma_1 t \gamma_2$ where $t \in T_V, T \in T_V^{[N]}, \gamma_1$ and $\gamma_2 \in T_V^*$ in $G_f\}$.

Since the production set of G_f is finite, production tree set, operand tree set and operator tree set of G_f are all finite. Moreover, the following theorem holds.

Theorem 4.4.1
Suppose slcsfg $G_f = (N, \Sigma, P, S)$. The following hold.

(1) $NOTS(G_f) \cap OTS(G_f) = \Phi$;

(2) $PRT(G_f) = NOTS(G_f) \cup OTS(G_f)$.

Definition 4.4.4
Suppose slcsfg $G_f = (N, \Sigma, P, S)$. Let $V = N \cup \Sigma$ and $t \in PRT(G_f)$. The tree derivation set of t, denoted as $DERIV(t)$, includes all the trees of tree derivable from t in 0 or more than 0 steps, written as :

$DERIV(t) = \{u | t \overset{*}{\Longrightarrow} u$ where every direct derivation is a tree derivation$\}$.

From the above definition, it is known that if $t \in T_\Sigma$ then $DERIV(t) = \{t\}$.

Definition 4.4.5
Suppose slcsfg $G_f = (N, \Sigma, P, S)$ and $V = N \cup \Sigma$. Let $t, u \in PRT(G_f), T, U, U_1 \in T_V^{[N]}$, and $\alpha_1, \alpha_2, \beta_1, \beta_2 \in T_V^*$. The precedence relation between production trees t and u exists if and only if one of the following conditions holds.

(1) $t \doteq u$ if and only if there exists $T \rightarrow \alpha_1 t u \alpha_2$ in P.

(2) $t \lessdot u$ if and only if there exists $T \rightarrow \alpha_1 t U \alpha_2$ in P, and $U \overset{+}{\Longrightarrow} u\beta_1$ where every direct derivation is a string derivation.

(3) $t \gtrdot u$ if and only if there exists $T \rightarrow \alpha_1 U U_1 \alpha_2$ in P, and $U \overset{+}{\Longrightarrow} \beta_1 t$ and $U_1 \overset{*}{\Longrightarrow} u\beta_2$ where every direct derivation in these two derivations is a string derivation.

Definition 4.4.6
Suppose slcsfg $G_f = (N, \Sigma, P, S)$ and $V = N \cup \Sigma$. Let $t, u \in T_V$ and there is at least one of t and u which is not a production tree. If one of the following conditions holds,

(1) $t \in PRT(G_f), u \notin PRT(G_f)$ and there exists $u_1 \in PRT(G_f)$ so that $u \in DERIV(u_1)$. Now let $T = t$ and $U = u_1$.

(2) $u \in PRT(G_f), t \notin PRT(G_f)$ and there exists $t_1 \in PRT(G_f)$ so that $t \in DERIV(t_1)$. Now let $T = t_1, U = u$.

(3) $t \notin PRT(G_f)$ and there exists $t_1 \in PRT(G_f)$ so that $t \in DERIV(t_1)$, while $u \notin PRT(G_f)$ and there exists $u_1 \in PRT(G_f)$ so that $u \in DERIV(u_1)$. Now let $T = t_1$ and $U = u_1$.

Then the precedence relation between t and u exists if and only if one of the following conditions holds:

(1) if $T \eqcirc U$ then $t \eqcirc u$;

(2) if $T \lessdot U$ then $t \lessdot u$;

(3) if $T \gtrdot U$ then $t \gtrdot u$.

Definition 4.4.7

Suppose slcsfg $G_f = (N, \Sigma, P, S)$ and $V = N \cup \Sigma$. For any $t, u \in T_V$, $t \lessdot \eqcirc u$ if and only if $t \eqcirc u$ or $t \lessdot u$.

Definition 4.4.8

Suppose slcsfg $G_f = (N, \Sigma, P, S)$. Let $V = N \cup \Sigma$ and $t \in PRT(G_s)$. t is called a tree production tree if and only if for any $\alpha \in T_V^*$ (let $\alpha = t_1 \cdots t_n$ where $n \geq 1$ and $t_1, \cdots, t_n \in T_V$), if $S \stackrel{*}{\Longrightarrow} \alpha$, then for any i where $1 \leq i \leq n$, the following holds.

$$t \neq t_i.$$

$TPRT(G_f)$ denotes the set of all tree production trees in $PRT(G_f)$. If there exists $t \rightarrow u$ where $u \in PRT(G_f)$ in P, then this production is called a tree production.

Obviously $TPRT(G_f) \subset PRT(G_f)$ and the following theorem holds.

Theorem 4.4.2

Suppose slcsfg $G_f = (N, \Sigma, P, S)$. Let $V = N \cup \Sigma$ and $t \in PRT(G_f)$. If there exists $T \rightarrow t$ where $t \in TPRT(G_f)$ in P, then $T \in TPRT(G_f)$.

From the limitation that productions must be useful, the following theorem holds.

Theorem 4.4.3

Suppose slcsfg $G_f = (N, \Sigma, P, S)$ and $V = N \cup \Sigma$. If $t \in TPRT(G_f)$, then there exist $u \in T_V$, and $\gamma_1, \gamma_2 \in T_\Sigma^*$ so that $S \stackrel{*}{\Longrightarrow} \gamma_1 u \gamma_2$ and t is a subtree of u.

From the definitions and theorems given above, it is known that in G_f, instead of being a tree of the forests deriving from S, a tree production tree could only be a subtree of a tree of those forests. Furthemore, in the derivation starting from the initial tree, a tree production tree could only be adopted to replace a subtree instead of a tree of a forest. From the limitation that productions must be useful, the following theorem is obtained.

Theorem 4.4.4
Suppose slcsfg $G_f = (N, \Sigma, P, S)$ and $V = N \cup \Sigma$. For any $t \in PRT(G_f)$, if $t \in TPRT(G_f)$, then for any $u \in PRT(G_f)$, there do not exist any precedence relations between t and u and between u and t. That is to say, the following does not hold.

$$t \lessdot \doteq u \text{ or } t \lessdot u \text{ or } t \gtrdot u \text{ or } u \doteq t \text{ or } u \lessdot t \text{ or } u \gtrdot t.$$

Suppose SPG $G_s = (N, \Sigma, P, S)$ and $V = N \cup \Sigma$. Here are two functions: att: $V \to \{kp, p, f, r, x, .\ and, or, nph\}$ and id: $V \to IDE \cup CAP \cup \{and, or, nph\} \cup \{S\} \cup N_1$. For any $a \in V$, let a be (a_1, a_2, a_3) if a is a 3–tuple; let a be (a_0, a_2) or (a_1, a_2) if a is a 2–tuple; and let a be a_2 if a is a symbol, where $a_0 \in DIS$, $a_1 \in \{kp, p, f, r, x, and, or, nph\}$, $a_2 \in IDE \cup CAP \cup \{and, or, nph\} \cup \{S\} \cup N_1$ and $a_3 \in TKEY$. Thus $att(a) = a_1$ and $id(a) = a_2$ hold.

Definition 4.4.9
Suppose SPG $G_s = (N, \Sigma, P, S)$ and $V = N \cup \Sigma$. G_s is called WPSPG if and only if the following conditions are all satisfied.

(i) For any empty production $t \to \varepsilon$ where $t \in T_V^{[N]}$ in P,

(i-1) $t \to \varepsilon$ is a tree production and $t \notin N$;

(i-2) there exists $t \to u$ where $u \in T_V$ in P;

(i-3) there exist $T \in PRT(G_s)$ and node a in T such that t is a direct subtree of a and $att(a) \in \{k, kp\}$;

(i-4) for any $U \in T_V$, if $U \in PRT(G_s)$, or there exists $U_1 \in PRT(G_s)$ such that $U \in DERIV(U_1)$ and there exists node a in U so that t is a direct subtree of a, then $att(a) \in \{k, kp\}$; and

(i-5) for any $u_1 \in T_V$, $u_1 \stackrel{+}{\Longrightarrow} \varepsilon$ holds if and only if there exists $u_1 \to \varepsilon$ in P.

(ii) For any $t \in T_V$, let a be a node in t and all the successor nodes of a from left to right are $a_1, a_2, \cdots$, and $a_n (n \geq 1)$. If $att(a) \in \{k, kp\}$, then $t \in PRT(G_s)$ or there exists $T \in PRT(G_s)$ such that $t \in DERIV(T)$, then $id(a_1), id(a_2), \cdots, id(a_n)$ are not identical two by two.

(iii) For any two productions in P, if their right parts are identical, then they are both tree productions.

(iv) For any $t, u \in PRT(G_s)$, if $DERIV(t) \cap DERIV(u) \neq \Phi$ and $t \neq u$, then $t \in TRPT(G_s)$ or $u \in TPRT(G_s)$.

(v) For any production in P, if it has the form $T \to t$, $T \in T_V^{[N]}$, $t \in T_V$, then $node(T) \leq node(t)$.

(vi) For any $t, u \in PRT(G_s)$, if $t, u \notin TPRT(G_s)$, then at most one of the following precedence relations exists between t and u

$$t \lessdot \doteq u, \quad t \gtrdot u.$$

(vii) Let $T, U, U_1 \in T_V$, and $\alpha, \beta \in T_V^*$. If there exist $T \rightarrow \alpha U \beta$ and $U_1 \rightarrow \beta$ in P, then $U \lessdot\!\doteq U_1$ does not exist.

From definitions 4.4.6, 4.4.7 and 4.4.9, the following theorem can be proved.

Theorem 4.4.5
Suppose $G_f = (N, \Sigma, P, S)$ and $V = N \cup \Sigma$. For any $t, u \in T_V$, at most one of the following precedence relations exists between t and u.

$$t \lessdot\!\doteq u, \quad t \gtrdot u.$$

4.4.2 Syntactic Parsing Algorithm of WPSPG

The syntactic parsing algorithm of WPSPG is about the way to decide whether a given Case Frame Forest (CFT), representing a story, belongs to the language generated by a given WPSPG or not. The syntactic parsing process of SPG is actually the semantic and pragmatic analysing process as well. Therefore, the syntactic parsing algorithm of WPSPG is actually a kind of story parsing process. WPSPG being a type of context–sensitive high–dimensional grammar, the structure and syntactic parsing process of WPSPG are more complicated than those of weak precedence string grammar. In this section, the precedence relation table of WPSPG is discussed first. Then an algorithm is given deciding whether a tree belongs to the tree derivation set of some productioin tree or not. This algorithm is called the tree decision algorithm of the tree derivation set of production tree. Finally, the parsing algorithm of WPSPG is designed and given.

4.4.2.1 Precedence Relation Table

Suppose WPSPG $G_f = (N, \Sigma, P, S)$ and $V = N \cup \Sigma$. The precedence relation table of G_f is a 2–dimensional matrix $pret(T, U)$ where $T, U \in PRT(G_f) \cup \{\#\}$ and $T, U \notin TPRT(G_s)$, '#' $\notin V$ and is a special symbol used as the end mark of the input forest. '#' is taken as a production tree of G_f. It is specified that for any $t \in PRT(G_f) \cup \{\#\}$, $t \gtrdot \#$ holds. For any $T, U \in PRT(G_f) \cup \{\#\}$, the value of $pret(T, U)$ could only be $\lessdot\!\doteq$, $>$ or bland character denoting that there exist no precedence relations between T and U. According to definition 4.4.9, it is known that $pret(T, U)$ has one and only one value. From theorem 4.4.4, it is known that there exist no precedence relations between any production tree and any tree production tree or between any tree production tree and any production tree of WPSPG. Therefore the precedence relation table of WPSPG does not include any tree production trees.

4.4.2.2 Tree Decision Algorithm of the Tree Derivation Set of Production Tree

Suppose WPSPG $G_s = (N, \Sigma, P, S)$ and $V = N \cup \Sigma$. The tree decision algorithm of the tree derivation set of production tree, 'trderiv', will be given in the following. It has two subroutines, 'subderiv' and 'checkinstan'. Let $t \in PRT(G_s)$ and $u \in T_V$. If $u \in DERIV(t)$, then 'trderiv (t, u)' returns 'success', otherwise returns 'fail'. 'subderiv (t_i, u_j) ' decides whether u_j, a direct subtree of the root of u, is derivable from t_i, a direct subtree of the root of t, and returns 'success" or 'fail' correspondingly. 'checkinstan (t, u)' checks whether the derivation from t to u is the context–sensitive derivation defined in SPG or not, and returns 'success' and 'fail' respectively. if 'checkinstan (t, u)' returns 'fail' then $u \notin DERIV(t)$ holds.

Let $t \in PRT(G_s)$ and all the direct subtrees of t from left to right are $t_1, \cdots, t_n (n \geq 0)$. Let $u \in T_V$ and all the direct subtrees of u from left to right are $u_1, \cdots, u_m (m \geq 0)$. root (T) denotes the root marking of T. 'trderiv (t, u)', 'subderiv (t_i, u_j)' and 'checkinstan (t, u)' are given one by one in the following.

Algorithm 4.4.1

```
trderiv(t, u)
BEGIN
    IF t = u THEN RETURN (success);
    IF t ∈ T_Σ AND t ≠ u THEN RETURN (fail);
    IF n = 0 AND t ≠ u THEN RETURN (fail);
    IF m > n THEN RETURN (fail);
    IF root(t) ≠ root(u) THEN RETURN (fail);
    M := n;
    j := 1;
    FOR i := 1 TO n
    BEGIN
        IF i > m AND t_i → ε does not exist THEN RETURN (fail);
        IF subderiv (t_i, u_j) = fail
        THEN IF t_i → ε exists
              THEN BEGIN j := j − 1;
                         M := M − 1;
                         IF m > M THEN RETURN (fail);
                END;
              ELSE RETURN (fail);
        j := j + 1;
    END;
    RETURN (checkinstan (t, u));
END
```

```
subderiv(t_i, u_j)
BEGIN
    IF t_i = u_j THEN RETUREN (success);
    IF t_i → u_j exists THEN RETURN (success);
    IF t_i ∈ N AND t_i → u_j does not exist THEN RETURN (fail);
    FOR every t_i → t'_i AND t'_i ≠ ε AND t'_i ∈ T_V
        IF subderiv (t'_i, u_j) = success
        THEN RETURN (success);
    FOR every tree derivation t_i ⟹ t''_i where t''_i ∈ T_V
        IF subderiv (t''_i, u_j) = success
        THEN RETURN (success);
    RETURN (fail);
END

checkinstan(t, u)
BEGIN
    IF t = u THEN RETURN (success);
    FOR every T → U, where T,U ∈ T_V , adopted in every tree deriva-
tion in t ⟹+ u
      FOR every two X,Y ∈ N which have no values in DIS and are
subtrees of u
        BEING
            IF X = Y AND X and Y have different instantiations
            THEN RETURN (fail);
            IF X ≠ Y AND X and Y have the same instantiation
            THEN RETURN (fail);
        END;
    FOR every two X,Y ∈ N which have no values in DIS and are
subtrees of t
        BEGIN
            IF X = Y AND X and Y have different instantiations
            THEN RETURN (fail);
            IF X ≠ Y AND X and Y have the same instantiation
            THEN RETUREN (fail);
        END;
    FOR every X ∈ N which has no value in DIS and is a subtree of t
    INSTAN (X, t → u) := instantiation of X;
    RETURN (success);
END
```

End of Algorithm

A few explanations are given in the following about the above algorithm.

1) The algorithm is based on the fact that if $u \in DERIV(t)$, then the roots of u and t have the same marking, and that every direct subtree of the root of u from left to right is derivable from the direct subtree at the corresponding place of the root of t. If empty forest is derivable from some direct subtree of the root of t, then it is possible that the direct subtree of the root of u at the corresponding place does not exist.

2) The following theorem makes it possible that the ambiguity problem need not be concerned within the algorithm while searching for the direct subtree t_i of the root of t corresponding to the direct subtree u_j of the root of u, so that $t_i \stackrel{*}{\Longrightarrow} u_j$ holds.

Theorem 4.4.6

Suppose WPSPG $G_s = (N, \Sigma, P, S)$ and $V = N \cup \Sigma$. Let $t \in PRT(G_s)$ and $u \in T_V$. If $u \in DERIV(t)$, all the direct subtrees of the root of t from left to right are $t_1, \cdots$ and $t_n (n \geq 1)$, there exists k where $1 \leq k \leq n$ such that $t_k \rightarrow \varepsilon$ exists, and all the direct subtrees of the root of u fromleft to right are $u_1, \cdots$, and $u_m (m \geq 1)$, then for any u_j where $1 \leq j \leq m$, there exists a unique t_i where $1 \leq i \leq n$ so that $t_i \stackrel{*}{\Longrightarrow} u_j$.

3) From definition 4.4.9, it is known that for any tree $t' \in T_V$, $t' \stackrel{+}{\Longrightarrow} \varepsilon$ holds if and only if $t' \rightarrow \varepsilon$ exists. Therefore in order to decide whether empty forest is derivable from some tree, the algorithm only needs to decide whether there exists the corresponding empty production.

4) In 'checkinstan', the assignment to $INSTAN(X, t \rightarrow u)$ is for storing the instantiations in $t \Longrightarrow u$ of the subtrees of t which belong to N and have no values in DIS. These instantiations will be used in the syntactic parsing algorithm of WPSPG given later.

4.4.2.3 Syntactic Parsing Algorithm

Generally speaking, the syntactic parsing algorithm of string grammar scans every input symbol from left to right, parses while scanning, and reduces whenever it is possible, which is the inverse process of derivation, until reaching the initial symbol, meaning that the input symbol string belongs to the language generated by the grammar. In the syntactic parsing algorithm of weak precedence string grammar, the so–called handle is reduced according to the precedence relation between symbols in the aplhabet, while in the syntactic parsing algorithm of WPSPG, the concept called tree handle is introduced and reduced.

Definition 4.4.10

Suppose WPSPG $G_s = (N, \Sigma, P, S)$ and $V = N \cup \Sigma$. Let $\alpha_1, \alpha_2, \cdots, \alpha_n \in T_V^*$ where $n \geq 2$. If there exist $\alpha_1 \Longrightarrow \alpha_2, \cdots, \alpha_{n-1} \Longrightarrow \alpha_n$ where every direct derivation $\alpha_i \Longrightarrow \alpha_{i+1}(1 \leq i \leq n-1)$ is a string derivation and it is the leftmost (rightmost) operand tree of α_i that is replaced, then the derivation from α_1 to α_n is called a leftmost (rightmost) derivation, and the sequence $\alpha_n, \alpha_{n-1}, \cdots, \alpha_1$ is called a rightmost (leftmost) reduction. The inverse process of leftmost derivation is rightmost reduction, while the inverse process of rightmost derivation is leftmost reduction.

Definition 4.4.11
Suppose WPSPG $G_s = (N, \Sigma, P, S)$ and $V = N \cup \Sigma$. Let $\alpha_1, \alpha_2, \cdots, \alpha_n \in T_V^*$ where $n \geq 2$. If there exist $\alpha_1 \Longrightarrow \alpha_2, \cdots, \alpha_{n-1} \Longrightarrow \alpha_n$ where every direct derivation is a tree derivation, then the sequence $\alpha_n, \alpha_{n-1}, \cdots, \alpha_1$ is called a tree reduction.

Definition 4.4.12
Suppose WPSPG $G_s = (N, \Sigma, P, S)$ and $V = N \cup \Sigma$. Let $\alpha_1, \alpha_2, \alpha, \beta \in T_V^*$, $T \in T_V$. If

(1) $S \overset{*}{\Longrightarrow} \alpha_1 T \alpha_2$ holds;

(2) $T \Longrightarrow \alpha$ holds and it is a string derivation; and

(3) $\alpha \overset{*}{\Longrightarrow} \beta$ holds where every direct derivation is a tree derivation,

then β is called the direct tree phrase of the so–called tree sentential form $\alpha_1 \beta \alpha_2$ related to the production $T \to \alpha$. The leftmost direct tree phrase of a tree sentential form is called the tree handle of this tree sentential form.

In the syntactic parsing process of WPSPG, the tree handle (e.g. β) of the current tree sentential form (e.g. $\alpha_1 \beta \alpha_2$) is obtained according to the precedence relation between trees which are production trees and trees in the tree derivartion sets of production trees, then the tree, then the tree handle (β) is reduced to an operand tree (e.g. T) according to some production (e.g. $T \to \alpha$), until some initial tree is reached. This kind of reduction is actually the merge of tree reduction (e.g. reducing β to α) and leftmost reduction (e.g. reductin α to T).

Suppose WPSPG $G_s = (N, \Sigma, P, S)$ and $V = N \cup \Sigma$. Let '#' be the end mark of the input forest. Stack ST is used to store forest, and every element of ST stores a tree. For every tree T in ST, if $T \notin T_\Sigma$, then for any $X \in N$ which has no value in DIS and is a subtree of T, when $T \to \alpha$ where $\alpha \in T_V^+$ is used to reduce to T, the instantiation of X, $INSTAN(X, T \to \alpha)$, is stored in ST together with T as an element of ST. The subscripts of ST bottom element and ST top element are 1 and $k(k \geq 1$ and is a positive integer) respectively. The initial value of ST is empty.

Before the parsing algorithm of WPSPG is given, a related subroutine 'reduction (G_s, ST, k)' is constructed. 'reduction (G_s, ST, k)' tries to match the forest $ST(1) \cdots ST(k)$ with the right part of every production in G_s. If all the matching processes fail, it tries to match the forest $ST(2) \cdots ST(k)$ with the right part of every production, and so on, until the first successfully matched production is obtained. Then it returns the left part tree of this production. If all the matching attempts between the forest $ST(k)$ and the right part of every production in G_s fail, then 'reduction (G_s, ST, k)' returns 'fail'. Let $\alpha = t_1 \cdots t_n,\ n \geq 1, \beta = u_1 \cdots u_m,\ m \geq 1, t_1, \cdots, t_n,\ u_1, \cdots, u_m \in T_V$. Forest α is matched successfully with the right part β of some production $T \rightarrow \beta$ if and only if (1) $T \notin TPRT(G_s)$ holds and for any u_i where $1 \leq i \leq m,\ u_i \notin TPRT(G_s)$ holds; and (2) $n = m$ holds and for any t_i where $1 \leq i \leq n,\ t_i = u_i$ or $t_i \in DERIV(u_i)$ holds.

'reduction' includes a subroutine as well, called 'contrad', to check whether the instantiation of the subtree which belongs to N and has no value in DIS of some tree in the right part of productin satisfies the definition of context-sensitive derivation of SPG or not, and it returns 'success' or 'fail' accordingly. 'reduction (G_s, ST, k)' is given in the following, where $k \geq 1$ and k is the subscript of ST top element.

```
reduction(G_s, ST, k)
BEGIN
  FOR l := k TO 1
  FOR every T → t_1 ··· t_n and n = l and T ∉ TPRT(G_s) and t_1, ···, t_n ∈
TPRT(G_s)
    BEGIN
      Y := 0;
      FOR i := 1 TO l
        IF ST(k − l + i) ≠ t_i AND trderiv(t_i, ST(k − l + i)) = fail
        THEN BEGIN Y := 1; i := l + 1; END;
      IF Y = 0
      THEN IF contrad(G_s, T → t_1 ··· t_l, ST(k − l + 1) ··· ST(k)) =
success
        THEN RETURN (T and the instantiations of its subtrees which
belong to
                              N and have no values in DIS)
        ELSE RETURN (fail);
    END;
  RETURN (fail);
END
```

'contrad $(G_s, T \rightarrow t_1 \cdots t_n,\ u_1 \cdots u_n)$' is given in the following, where $u_1 \cdots u_n$ is the forest in ST or the right subforest of the forest in ST.

```
contrad (G_s, T → t_1 ··· t_n, u_1 ··· u_n)
BEGIN
    FOR i := 1 TO n − 1
    FOR j := 2 TO n
    FOR every X ∈ N which has no value in DIS and is a subtree of t_i
    FOR every Y ∈ N which has no value in DIS and is a subtree of t_j
```

```
BEGIN
    IF t_i = u_i
    THEN t := INSTAN(X, u_i → α_i);
      /* INSTAN(X, u_i → α_i) is stored together with u_i in ST */
    ELSE t := INSTAN(X, t_i → u_i);
      /* INSTAN(X, t → u_i) is assigned in trderiv(t_i, u_i) */
    IF t_j = u_j
    THEN u := INSTAN(Y, u_j → α_j)
      /* INSTAN(Y, u_j → α_j) is stored together with u_j in ST */
    ELSE u := INSTAN(Y, t_j → u_j);
      /* INSTAN(Y, t_j → u_j) is assigned in trderiv(t_j, u_j) */
    IF X = Y AND t ≠ u THEN RETURN (fail);
    IF X ≠ Y AND t = u THEN RETURN (fail);
  END;
  FOR i := 1 TO n
  FOR every X ∈ N which has no value in DIS and is a subtree of t_i
  IF X is a subtree of T
  THEN IF t_i = u_i THEN INSTAN(X, T → t_1 ··· t_n) :=
                                              INSTAN(X, u_i → α_i);
    /* INSTAN(X, u_i → α_i) is stored together with u_i in ST */
    ELSE INSTAN (X, T → t_1 ··· t_n) := INSTAN(X, t_i → u_i);
    /* INSTAN(X, t_i → u_i) is assigned in trderiv(t_i, u_i) */
  RETURN (success);
END
```

The syntactic parsing algorithm of WPSPG is as follows.

Algorithm 4.4.2

Step 1. Read an input tree $t \in T_\Sigma$ into stack ST.

Step 2. Check the precedence relation between ST top tree and the next input tree.

1)If there are not any precedence relations, then output that the parsing fails, and the algorithm stops.

2) If ST top tree $\lessdot\!=$ the next input tree, then go to Step 1.

3) If ST top tree $\gtrdot$ the next input tree, then call 'reduction'. If it succeeds and returns the left part of some production, then replace the successfully matched forest at the top of ST with this left part forest, and go to Step 2. If 'reduction' returns 'fail', then output that the parsing succeeds if and only if the forest in ST is equal to S and the next input tree is '#', otherwise output that the parsing fails. The algorithm stops.

End of Algorithm

For this algorithm, there are two conclusins in the following.

Theorem 4.4.7
Suppose WPSPG $G_s = (N, \Sigma, P, S)$ and $V = N \cup \Sigma$. For any $\beta \in T_{\Sigma}^{+}$, if according to G_s algorithm 4.4.2 succeeds, then opposite to this reduction, the derivation from S to β satisfies the definition of context–sensitive derivation of SPG.

Theorem 4.4.8
Suppose WPSGP $G_s = (N, \Sigma, P, S)$ and $V = N \cup \Sigma$. For any $\beta \in L(G_s)$, algorithm 4.4.2 according to G_s can parse β correctly and unambiguously.

4.4.3 An Example of Story Parsing

Parsing an example story according to an example of WPSPG will be shown in this section. The example of SPG, G_{exm}, in section 4.3.2 is taken here as the grammar for story parsing. According to the definition of G_{exm}, the following holds.

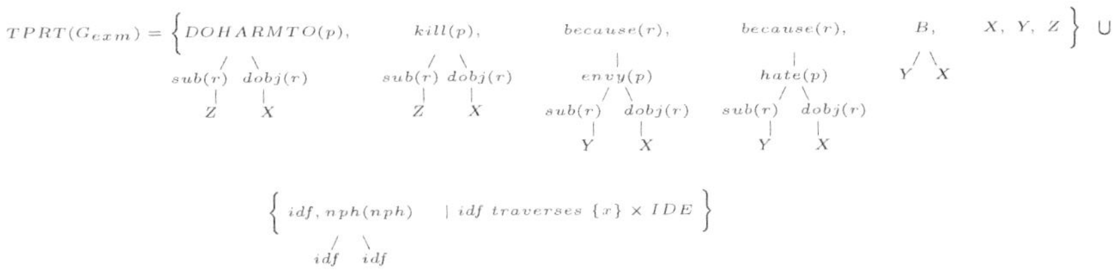

```
TPRT(Gexm) = { DOHARMTO(p),      kill(p),           because(r),          because(r),          B,      X, Y, Z } ∪
                 /    \            /    \                |                    |                / \
            sub(r)  dobj(r)   sub(r)  dobj(r)         envy(p)              hate(p)           Y   X
              |       |         |       |              /   \                /   \
              Z       X         Z       X         sub(r)  dobj(r)      sub(r)  dobj(r)
                                                    |       |            |       |
                                                    Y       X            Y       X

             { idf, nph(nph)   | idf traverses {x} × IDE }
                    /   \
                  idf   idf
```

For the production trees of G_{exm} which do not belong to $TPRT(G_{exm})$, the precedence relation table is constructed as shown in table 4.4.1.

From the precedence relation table of G_{exm} and definition 4.4.9, it is known that G_{exm} is a WPSPG.

As for the story to be parsed, we take the example of story in section 4.1.2. Let $k_1k_2k_3k_4k_5k_6\#$ stands for the input CFF. For every CFT k_i where $1 \leq i \leq 6$, call 'trderiv' and 'subderiv' to obtain its unique corresponding production tree which does not belong to $TPRT(G_{exm})$ and from which the k_i is derivable and the derivation is the context–sensitive derivation defined in SPG. The results are shown in the following.

$$k_1 \in DERIV(T_8) \qquad k_2 \in DERIV(T_{10}) \qquad k_3 \in DERIV(T_8)$$

$$k_4 \in DERIV(T_9) \qquad k_5 \in DERIV(T_4) \qquad k_6 \in DERIV(T_5)$$

Therefore the precedence relation within the tree pair could be obtained. The parsing process of CFF $k_1k_2k_3k_4k_5k_6\#$ using algorithm 4.4.2 according to WPSPG G_{exm} is shown in table 4.4.2, where the tree key $K_i(1 \leq i \leq 4)$

Table 4.4.1 The Precedence Relation Table of G_{exm}

	S	S_1	T_1	T_2	T_3	T_4	T_5	T_6	T_7	T_8	T_9	T_{10}	T_{11}	$\sharp$
S													$\gtrdot$	
S_1													$\gtrdot$	
T_1													$\gtrdot$	
T_2													$\gtrdot$	
T_3													$\gtrdot$	
T_4													$\gtrdot$	
T_5													$\gtrdot$	
T_6											$\lessdot\doteq$	$\lessdot\doteq$	$\gtrdot$	
T_7				$\gtrdot$	$\gtrdot$	$\gtrdot$	$\gtrdot$			$\gtrdot$				$\gtrdot$
T_8													$\gtrdot$	
T_9			$\gtrdot$		$\gtrdot$	$\gtrdot$	$\gtrdot$	$\gtrdot$						$\gtrdot$
T_{10}				$\gtrdot$	$\gtrdot$	$\gtrdot$	$\gtrdot$			$\gtrdot$				$\gtrdot$
T_{11}				$\gtrdot$	$\gtrdot$	$\gtrdot$	$\gtrdot$			$\gtrdot$				$\gtrdot$
$\sharp$														

```
T1 = CHAR(kp)[K1]
      / \
sub(r)  dobj(r)
  /        \
 Y      cruel(x)

T2 = CHAR(kp)[K2]
      / \
sub(r)  dobj(r)
  /        \
 X      kind(x)

T3 = WIN(kp)[K3]
      / \
sub(r)  dobj(r)
  /        \
 X          Y

T4 = is(kp)[k5]
      / \
sub(r)  dobj(r)
  /        \
cir(f)   alive(x)
 /
X

T5 = is(kp)[k6]
      / \
sub(r)  dobj(r)
  /        \
cir(f)    die(x)
 /
Y

T6 = better(kp)[k1]
      / \
sub(r)  dobj(r)
  /        \
 X          Y

T7 = DOHARMTO(kp)[K4]
     /    |     \
    B  sub(r)  dobj(r)
   / \    |       \
  Y   X   Y        X

T8 = transm(kp)[k3]
     /       |       \
sub(r)   dobj(r)   iobj(r)
  /          |         \
 Y           X      ingest(p)
                      / \
                 sub(r)  dobj(r)
                   /        \
                  X          Z

T9 = ingest(kp)[k4]
      / \
sub(r)  dobj(r)
  /        \
 X          Z

T10 = transm(kp)[k2]
     /     /        \         \
    B   sub(r)   dobj(r)   iobj(r)
   / \    /         /          \
  Y   X  Y         Z       DOHARMTO(p)
                              / \
                         sub(r)  dobj(r)
                           /        \
                          Z          X

T11 = kill(kp)[k7]
     /    |     \
    B  sub(r)  dobj(r)
   / \    |       \
  Y   X   Y        X
```

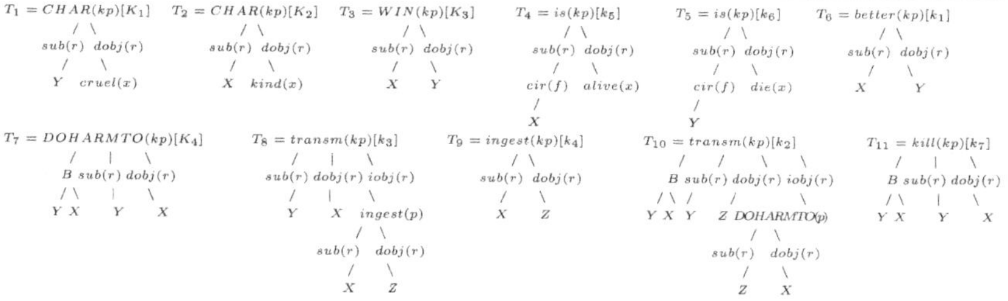

stands for the production tree reduced to in the parsing. From the result of parsing, it is known that the summary of the example story is that mercy results in happiness while evil brings about bad retribution.

4.4.4 Data about Runtime Efficiency of the Syntactic Parsing of WPSPG

A syntactic parser of WPSPG has been implemented on micriocomputer in order to analyse the runtime efficiency of this parser. CFF SA, SB, SC, SD and SE have been parsed according to SPG Ga, Gb and Gc respectively.

Data about the corresponding runtime efficiency ar shown in table 4.4.3. One can see that for the same SPG, parsing time is in proportion to CFF (story) length, while for different SPGs, with the increase in the number

Table 4.4.2 A Story Parsing Process

Step	Stack	Input CFF	Parsing Action	Pre. Rel. betw. Stack Top Tree and Next Inp. Tree
0		$k_1k_2k_3k_4k_5k_6\sharp$		
1	k_1	$k_2k_3k_4k_5k_6\sharp$	Read an Input Tree	$k_1 \Leftarrow k_2$
2	k_1k_2	$k_3k_4k_5k_6\sharp$	Read an Input Tree	$k_2 > k_3$
3	k_1K_4	$k_3k_4k_5k_6\sharp$	Reduce using P_8	$K_4 > k_3$
4	K_1	$k_3k_4k_5k_6\sharp$	Reduce using P_6	$K_1 \Leftarrow k_3$
5	K_1k_3	$k_4k_5k_6\sharp$	Read an Input Tree	$k_3 \Leftarrow k_4$
6	$K_1k_3k_4$	$k_5k_6\sharp$	Read an Input Tree	$k_4 > k_5$
7	K_1K_2	$k_5k_6\sharp$	Reduce using P_7	$K_2 \Leftarrow k_5$
8	$K_1K_2k_5$	$k_6\sharp$	Read an Input Tree	$k_5 \Leftarrow k_6$
9	$K_1K_2k_5k_6$	$\sharp$	Read an Input Tree	$k_6 > \sharp$
10	$K_1K_2K_3$	$\sharp$	Reduce using P_4	$K_3 > \sharp$
11	S_1	$\sharp$	Reduce using P_2	$S_1 > \sharp$
12	S	$\sharp$	Reduce using P_1	$S > \sharp$
13	S	$\sharp$	Reduction fails, parsing succeeds	$S > \sharp$

Table 4.4.3 Data about Runtime Efficiency of the Syntactic Parser of WPSPG

Length of Input CFF	Depth of Input CFT	Complexity of Grammar (Production Number)	Parsing Time(ms)	Time /CFF
SA: 6	5	Ga: 19	160	26.7
SB: 11	9	19	165	15
SC: 13	9	19	190	14.5
SD: 20	9	19	270	13.5
SE: 35	9	19	485	13.8
SA: 6	5	Gb: 48	225	37.5
SB: 11	9	48	875	79.5
SC: 13	9	48	1020	78.5
SD: 20	9	48	1540	77
SE: 35	9	48	2640	75.4
SA: 6	5	Gc: 60	230	38.3
SB: 11	9	60	1025	93.1
SC: 13	9	60	1165	91.1
SD: 20	9	60	1765	88.2
SE: 35	9	60	3030	86.5

of SPG productions, parsing time of the same CFF (story) increases a lot. Nevertheless it is acceptable in regard of the parsing time itself.

4.5 Story Parsing Grammar with Attributes

Although more powerful than Rumelhart's story grammar [Rumelhart, 1975], SPG lacks the effective mechanisms for processing more useful commensense knowledge for story understanding, e.g., it is not very convenient to represent the computation, nor the global variable. So we augment SPG with attribute mechanism so as to strengthen its representation ability in computation, global variable, etc. We also call such a SPG attribute SPG.

The attribute grammar was proposed by Kunth in the 1960's to specify the semantics of programming languages, and it is probably the most widely applied semantic formalism [Knuth, 1968][Deransart and Jourdan, 1990][Paakki, 1995]. Generally, the attribute grammar is a context–free grammar augmented with attributes and sematic rules.

Definition 4.5.1
An attribute SPG is a 3–tuple $< G, A, R >$, where,

(i) G is a SPG, $G = (N, \Sigma, P, S)$, $N \cap \Sigma = \Phi$, N is a finite nonterminal set and Σ finite terminal set, $S \in N$, is the starting nonterminal, P is the production set, and its production p takes the form $T_0 \rightarrow T_1 \cdots T_n (n \geq 0)$ where $T_0, T_1, \cdots$, and T_n are all trees whose nodes are marked by elements in $(N \cup \Sigma)$, and in T_0, there exists at least one node marked by nonterminal in N. Let:

$tree(p) = \{T | T = T_i$, or T is a subtree of $T_i, 0 \leq i \leq n\}$

(ii) Let T satisfy

(ii-1) there is a $p \in P$ such that $T \in tree(p)$, or

(ii-2) there is $T\prime$ and $p \in P$ such that $T\prime \in tree(p)$ and T is one value of an attribute of $T\prime$.

Then $A(T)$ is a finite set of attributes of T. Let $A = \bigcup A(T)$.

(iii) A production $p: \ T_0 \rightarrow T_1 \cdots T_n (n \geq 0) \in P$ has an attribute occurrence $T.a$ if $a \in A(T)$, and $T \in tree(p)$ or T is one value of an attribute of a $T\prime \in tree(p)$. R_p is a finite set of attribute rules associated with p taking the form $T.a = f(\nu_1, \cdots, \nu_k), k \geq 0$, where

(iii-1) $T \in tree(p)$ or T is one value of an attribute of a $T\prime \in tree(p)$,

(iii-2) every $\nu_i, 1 \leq i \leq k$, is an attribute occurrence in p, and

(iii-3) f is a function maps the values of $\nu_1, \cdots, \nu_k$ to the value of $T.a$. Let $R = \bigcup R_p$.

SPG is a context–sensitive grammar representing syntax, semantics and pragmatics uniformly, so attributes in attribute SPG are actually pragmatic attributes, and the attribute rule serves as a more effective way for specifying some special types of pragmatic knowledge.

4.6 Conclusions

4.6.1 Story Parsing Grammar and Rumelhart's Story Grammar

Grammar formalism is one of the earliest approaches for story understanding in natural language processing. Rumelhart in 1975 proposed the story grammar theory, aiming at describing and analysing the overall syntactic structure and semantic connections of the story. It failed to be an effective approach due to the fact that the grammar is context–free and syntax–oriented. Moreover, the knowledge representation schema in the rules of the grammar adopts such a large granularity that it ignores the syntax and semantics of every sentence in the story which are very informative and generally essential for understanding. The story grammar formalism was once critized as being unsuccessful because of very limited and ineffective representation schema.

The difficulty of story understanding lies in the close context–sensitivity of story and the understanding of story's profound meaning. Being a kind of grammar for story understanding, Story Parsing Grammar differs from Rumelhart's story grammar in its context–sensitiveity, which lies in the replacement of subtree structure by production of SPG and the context–sensitive derivation in SPG. And it is oriented towards the semantics and pragmatics of story, since story parsing is based on CFF which represents the semantics and pragmatics of the story. These advantages make it possible for SPG to be used to understand stories more deeply and widely than Rumelhart's story grammar.

Compared with Rumelhart's story grammar, SPG is more powerful in representation. But it has drawbacks as well. Its context–sensitivity brings about the exponential complexity of its syntactic parsing algorithm. Nevertheless this is not very serious since the exponential complexity is mainly relevant to the depth of the trees in Case Frame Forest representing the story. The main problem of SPG is its low flexibility, for the knowledge in SPG is pre–defined and the productions are pre–constructed to meet the definition of SPG, they cannot be changed dynamically. Actually this problem is shared by many to–down approaches for story understanding.

4.6.2 From SPG to SPG with Attributes

Attribute grammar is a formalism for specifying semantcis of the context–free grammar. We adopt this attribute mechanism in SPG by augmenting a group of pragmatic attributes and the associated attribute rules. This augmentation has widened the representation scope of SPG. We have pointed out while analysing the drawbacks of SPG that its main problem is the low flexiblity, partly because all the knowledge is represented in productions which must meet the definition of SPG, this acctually to some extent restricts the representation scope of SPG. The augmentation of attributes and rules does not influence the structure of productions, thus it is not only an effective way to specify some special type of knowledge, but also makes SPG to be more powerful without imposing more restrictions on the production structure. In another word, one could write attrbute rules ignoring the definition of SPG. What need to be executed additionally is the attribute evaluation while the syntatic parser of SPG parsing the story.

Nevertheless, attribute SPG does not get rid of the disadvantage of low flexibility completely due to the fact that it remains to be a top–down formalism, all productions and attribute rules are pre-constructed.Attribute SPG is still incapable of dealing with the huge amount of various commonsense knowledge, which is necessary for intelligent story understanding. Therefore our future work will still focus on the improvement of the flexibility of SPG apporach.

4.6.3 Significance

A new story understanding approach is proposed and studied in this chapter, whose significance mainly lies in that

1) instead of being aimed at understanding stories with specific topics, SPG approach has a relatively wide application domain;

2) SPG approach combines syntax, semantics and pragmatics in one knowledge representation schema. The syntactic parsing process of story is actually the semantic and pragmatic analysing process as well;

3) study on a new high–dimensional grammar, Forest Grammar, has developed the research on formal language and compiling theory; and

4) deepgoing research has been done on the special structure and characteristics of the high–dimensional grammar applied to story parsing.

Research on story understanding remains to be a long and diffcult exploratory process.

5 Story Understanding: The Practice

5.1 Goal of Story Understanding

Why does the project of automatic generation of computer animation need story understanding? Why is it important for us? The reason is that the computer has to play the role of a script adapter and a movie director. A script adapter needs to read and to understand a story thoroughly in order to adapt it to a script. A movie director has to read and analyze the script thoroughly in order to design the plots, the roles, the cameras, etc., appropriately. The goal of story understanding in our project is to mimic this process.

The following topics are of interest for us.

1. The theme of the story. It means: what does the writer of the story want to tell to the children by this story? This is the most important point of which both the movie adapter and movie director should be aware. Most of the children stories have a salient theme, such as "Good people will eventually get good results, bad people will eventually get bad results", "People should unite themselves in the struggle against evil things", "kind-hearted people should be able to differentiate between true and false friends", etc.
2. The main plots of the story. It is a common experience that when a novel is adapted to a script in order to be made into a movie, the content of the novel has to be reduced largely, because the amount of plots which can be included in a movie is far less than that included in the original novel. It is thus the job of the adapter to find out the most central part of the plots contained in the novel. In our project, this is also the job of the computer.
3. The development threads of the story. Every story is represented by a text. Each text is a sequence of sentences (characters). Thus the events of the story are described in a linear way. But in reality, they happen concurrently and should be represented as a tree structure which represents in turn the development threads of the story and is very useful in the process of story adapting.
4. Leading roles and minor roles. Every script adapter and movie director will agree that more attention should be paid to the leading roles when working out the plots and designing the camera techniques used for shooting these plots. Thus given a story, techniques have to be found to find out who are the leading roles and who are the minor ones.

R. Lu and S. Zhang: Automatic Generation of Computer Animation, LNAI 2160, pp. 123-172, 2002.

5. Main characters of the roles. There is no novel or story in which all the roles have the same character and the same behavior (kind, cruel, lively, serious, sly, honest, etc.). In the literature, differences and conflicts of human characters and human behaviors are the soul of each successful novel. They are not only the basis for designing the detailed plots, but also the basis for molding the portrays of these roles. Furthermore, the determination of role character and role behavior is also necessary for the computer to decide about the attitudes of the animation director towards these roles (like, dislike, sympathize, detest, etc.).

6. Outlook of the roles. In order to determine roles' outlook (figures), it is important to clarify the social position of a role (noble person, such as emperor, king, queen, or common person, such as citizen, soldier, or lowly person, such as beggar, prisoner, etc.), and the role's age (very old, old, middle-aged, young, child, baby, etc.). Although the social position can not determine the outlook of a role completely, it often provides a lot of information for that.

7. Mental activities of the roles. The characters of a role are relatively stable. They do not change frequently. These characters include both the internal character and the external behavior. The mental activities of a role (belief, desire, intention, sentiment, ...) are rather different in this aspect. They are not stable and change steadily with the development of the story. Among them, the sentiment of roles (happy, sorrow, angry, surprised, astonished, lonely, excited, ...) is a particularly important mental activity. A mental activity does not need to be detectable by other persons based on the behavior of the subject. Sometimes it has to be detected by an inference based on social knowledge about human-beings and on the history and context of the story.
   For the purpose of making an animation, it is sometimes appropriate to design and insert special plots to expose the mental activity of a role to the audience. Take the sentence: "the queen is jealous of the beauty of Snow White" for an example.

8. The Environment of the story. Every story will be finally shown to the audience in form of a movie. Everything the director wants to show must be visible to the audience or inferable by the audience from the visible scenes. An environment includes many things: the location (indoor, outdoor, field, street, valley, mountain, lake,....), the time (morning, afternoon, evening, night,....), the weather (sunny, rainy, foggy, rainstorm, snowstorm, ...), etc.

9. The intention of the writer. The theme of the story certainly belongs to the intention of the writer. Of course we do not consider such cases where the writer is not aware of his/her implied intention or where the reader has another understanding about the theme of the story than the writer who has written it. On the other hand, in many cases the theme is not the only thing which the writer cares. S/he may have some other information to tell to the reader. Take the theme "Good people will eventually get good results, bad people will eventually get bad results" as an example. The writer may want to tell the reader also that "Good people should not wait until good results for them appear. They

should strive for getting good results" or "Bad people will always do whatever they can, in order to prevent themselves from getting bad results". It is the job of the computer to dig out the intention of the writer completely and to find a way to present it to the audience faithfully.

As it was mentioned in the first chapter, there are different approaches for understanding a story. Some of them are syntax based and are thus at the shallow level, as the experts of computer linguistics like to call them. Others are semantics based and are thus at the deep level. The syntax based approaches are in general less powerful than the semantics based ones. But from the point of view of implementation, the syntax based approaches are usually more easy to implement. Therefore, in order to make experiments, to compare and study different approaches, and to develop a story understanding software quickly, we have studied and used both kinds of approaches in the process of generating animation movies from a natural language story in our SWAN project.

The tasks of understanding a story can be explained from two points of view. The first point of view is the pure artificial intelligence one. Let us imagine the situation that a teacher of literature is giving a lecture in front of a group of students. Assume in the current class hour, he should explain to the students the content of a story written by a famous writer. What should he do? He should tell the students the title of the story, its theme, its division into episodes, its main roles and minor roles, the development of its plots, its outcome, the style of writing of the author, the metaphors used by the author, etc. To let a computer understand a story is the same as to let the computer mimic this teacher in explaining a story to the students.

The second point of view is application based. More precisely, in the process of transforming a natural language story to an animated movie, the procedure of understanding the story will produce a lot of information which will be used in the following steps: plot and act planning, director planning, camera planning, light planning and color planning, etc. Among them, the most important task of this chapter is to provide information for the plot planning module in chapter six and the director's planning module in chapter seven.

This information includes three aspects. The first aspect includes time, location and environment of event happening in the story. We call it "hard information", because it is basically determined by the story itself. In this chapter, we mainly use keyword based technique to get such information. For example, with the keyword "king" we guess the location should be in the palace, etc. This technique is relatively simple and we will not discuss it in detail. Note also we do not "inference" such information in this chapter. For example, we do not inference from the description "everywhere is blossom" that the season is spring. This task will be done in chapter seven.

The second aspect includes main roles, main minor roles, main plot, main development threads, etc. This kind of information can be obtained roughly by using the syntactic method only. Our syntactic method is based on the analysis of story graphs. Section 5.2 is devoted to this topic.

The third aspect involves semantic issues which are very difficult to obtain by syntactic methods only. These issues include characteristics and characters of roles, feelings, sentiment, belief, intention, desire, goal, etc. The basic tools are the Young Pine grammars. In order to let it meet the need of story analysis better, we have generalized it to temporal grammars. This is the content of the section 5.3.

The fourth and also last aspect is the global estimation of the story. Problems such as the global structure of a story, its basic paradigm and basic rhythms, etc. belong to this area. This kind of information will be used by the director's planning module to determine the keynote of the future movie.

5.2 Story Graph: The Shallow Approach

One technique which has been established and tested by us in our SWAN project was the graph based technique of story analysis. In another word, it is a relation based technique, since the nodes of the story graph denote some basic elements of the story, and its arcs represent the relations among these basic elements. For different basic elements and different relations we get different story graphs. Therefore, the concept "story graph" is realized in a family of different story graph types. First we will define the connection graph.

Definition 5.2.1 (Connection Graph)

A connection graph is a undirected hypergraph which has a finite set of elements, called connection set, on each of its arcs, and a finite set of elements, called appearance set, on each of its nodes. As a hypergraph, self-loops (arcs with only one end point) are allowed. Besides, each arc and each node has an identifier.

Definition 5.2.2 (Simple Graph)

A connection graph is called a simple graph, if the following three additional limitations are satisfied.

1. No two nodes have the same identifier.
2. The connection set of an arc is the set intersection of all (1 or 2) nodes at the ends of this arc.
3. The appearance set of a node is the set union of the connection sets of all arcs which are incident with this node.

Definition 5.2.3 (Role Graph)

A simple graph G can be interpreted as a role graph of a story S if

1. Each role of S is represented by the node identifier of a node in G, called role identifier.
2. Each statement of S is represented by a positive integer, denoting its order in the story.

3. The appearance set of a node in G is the set of numbers of all statements in S where the corresponding role appears.
4. Two nodes of G are connected by an arc A if and only if their node identifiers represent roles appearing in at least one same statement of S. The connection set of A is the set of numbers of all these statements.

The connection set of a self-loop A is the difference of the appearance set of the node n, which is the unique end point of A, minus the union of all connection sets of arcs other than A, which are incident to n.

Algorithm 5.2.1 (Constructing a Role Graph)

1. Consider the series CF of the case frames cf(i) of the story.
2. Construct an empty graph RG. Let i := 1.
3. Take the i-th case frame cf(i) from CF.
4. For all roles r in cf(i) do
   4.1. If RG does not include r, then add r to RG as a new node with the appearnce set {i}. Otherwise, add the integer i to the appearance set of r.
   4.2. If r is the only role in cf(i), then
   (if in RG there is no arc from r to r, then add an arc from r to r with the connection set {i}. Otherwise, add the integer i to the connection set of this arc.)
   4.3. If there are other roles (nodes) r' of cf(i), which are already in RG, then for all these r' do
   (if in RG there is no arc between r and r', then add such an arc to RG with the connection set {i}.
   Otherwise, add the integer i to the connection set of this arc.)
5. i:=i+1.
6. If cf(i) does not exist, then algorithm finished.
7. Go to 3.

End of Algorithm

In the following algorithm, we call the cardinal number of the appearance set of a node the weight of this node. Correspondingly, we call the cardinal number of the connection set of an arc the weight of this arc.

Algorithm 5.2.2 (Find a Largest Component)

1. Given a Role Graph RG. Let its connected components be RG1, RG2, ..., RGn.
2. Find the maximal connected components according to one of the following principles.
   2.1. with the maximal number of nodes, or
   2.2. with the maximal weighted number of nodes, where the weight of a node is defined as the cardinal number of its appearance set, or
   2.3. with the maximal number of arcs, or
   2.4. with the maximal weighted number of arcs, where the weight of an arc is defined as the cardinal number of its connection set, or
   2.5. with the node with maximal weighted incident arcs.

2.6. with the sum of the five numbers listed in 2.1 to 2.5.

End of Algorithm

Definition 5.2.4 (Main Role)

The main role of a story is that one which is represented by a node of the largest component (of the story graph) and can be determined according to one of the following principles

1. it has the maximal weighted incident arcs, or
2. its appearance set has the maximal cardinal number.

Definition 5.2.5 (Main Minor Roles)

The main minor roles of a story are those which are different from the main role and are included in the largest component (of the role graph) , which can be determined according to one of the following principles:

1. the arcs connecting them with the main role have weights whose values are above some threshold values, or
2. their weighted incidence numbers of arcs are above some threshold values, or
3. the cardinal numbers of their appearance sets are above some threshold values.

Example 5.2.1

We try to determine the main role and main minor roles of a new Snow White story. Each sentence is marked with a series number.

"(1) The old queen died. (2) The king was very sad. (3) The king's mother let the king to get married once again. (4) A server of the king told this to a witch. (5) The witch became a beautiful princess Mary. (6) The king married Mary. (7) Princess Snow White was more beautiful than the new queen. (8) The new queen gave a poisonous apple to Snow White. (9) Snow White ate the poisonous apple and died. (10) A prince took out the poisonous apple and rescued Snow White. (11) The prince married Snow White. (12) The prince killed the new queen."

The role graph of this story is shown in figure 5.2.1. There are in total three connected sub-graphs: A, B and C. Let us have a look at the result of analysis, where we use the symbols f1, f2, f3, f4, f5 and f6 to represent the weight numbers to be calculated in the steps 2.1, 2.2, 2.3, 2.4, 2.5 and 2.6 of algorithm 5.2.2.

The weight numbers of the sub-graphs:

1. f1(A) = 4, f1 (B) = 5, f1 (C) = 1.
2. f4(A) = 14, f4 (B) = 9, f4 (C) = 1.
3. f3(A) = 6, f3 (B) = 5, f3 (C) = 1.
4. f2(A) = 10, f2 (B) = 5, f2 (C) = 1.
5. f5(A) = 7, f5 (B) = 4, f5 (C) = 2.
6. f6(A) = 41, f6 (B) = 28, f6 (C) = 6.

Therefore it is easy to decide about the largest component. It is the sub-graph A. The next step is to decide the main role and main minor roles, where we use the symbols f7 and f8 to represent the weight numbers to be calculated in step 1 and 2 of definition 5.2.4.

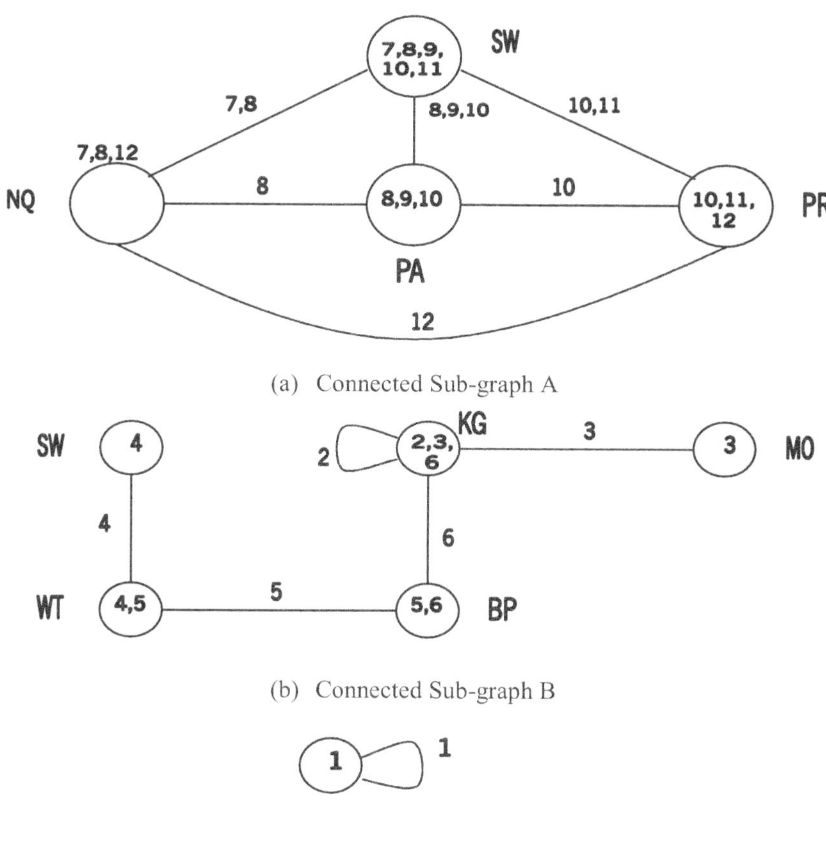

(a) Connected Sub-graph A

(b) Connected Sub-graph B

(c) Connected Sub-graph C

Figure 5.2.1 Find Maximal Sub-graph

1. The main role is Snow White because f7 (SW) = max {f7 (x) | x is a node of A} = 7.
2. The main role is also Snow White because f8 (SW) = max {f8 (x) | x is a node of A} = 5.

For the main minor roles, we see that among the three roles (new queen, prince and poisonous apple) the poisonous apple is the main minor role in this simple story, is the thread hold value is appropriately set.

Definition 5.2.6 (Main Plot)

The main plot of a story can be determined according to one of the following principles:

1. The set of events, whose statement numbers are included in the appearance sets of nodes in the maximal connected graph, form the main plot of the story.
2. The set of events, whose statement numbers are included in the appearance set of the main role, form the main plot of the story.
3. The set of events, whose statement numbers are included in the appearance sets of the main role and the main minor roles, form the main plot of the story.

Example 5.2.2

Determine the main plot of figure 5.2.1, according to definition 5.2.6.

1. main plot is {7,8,9,10,11,12}
2. main plot is {7,8,9,10,11}
3. main plot is {7,8,9,10,11}

Usually, all sentences in a story should be connected in some sense. Since otherwise there is no reason to include this sentence in the story. But why is the role graph not always connected? Isn't it a contradiction? A closer look at this problem reveals the real cause. It is because the role graph is at the syntactic level. Two different roles may be semantically equivalent. But this semantic equivalence often remains implicit. For example, if we change the first sentence of the above story to "The mother of Snow White died" and the sixth sentence to "Mary became the new queen", then there will be only one connected graph. This fact means that the core part of the story may be a union of several components of the role graph.

We are interested in dividing the story into a group of series of important events. We call each of such series a development thread or a process. Here we lose the limitation we made at the beginning of this book that the set of all events in a story must form a linear thread as represented by the sequence of the statements. Rather, we allow that they form a partial order according to the time when they happen.

Definition 5.2.7 (Event Graph)

A directed a cyclic graph is called an event graph, if

1. Each node represents an (occurrence of an) event.
2. Each node has a set of role identifiers who participate in the event represented by this node. This set is called the relevance set of this node. Each role (identifier) of this set is called relevant to this node and to each path going through it.

3. Each arc represents a time ordering. If an event a happens after another event b, then there is a path going from a to b.

In a natural language, there are many ways for describing the partial order of event occurrence. In order to simplify the matter, we introduce in the section only three temporal delimiters: "before", "after" and "now". Their semantics is as follows:

1. "Before e1, ..." means that the time pointer moves back to the point before e1.
2. "After e1, ..." means that the time pointer moves back to the point after e1.
3. "Now" means that the time pointer moves forward until after the most recent event.

For the sake of simplicity, in the algorithm below, sometimes we do not differentiate a sentence from its corresponding node.

Algorithm 5.2.3 (Construction of an Event Graph)

1. Given a story S.
2. Let n = 1, T:=empty.
3. Establish a new node N with S, Call it the current node, N is also a recent node.
4. If S contains a temporal delimiter, then there is an error, stop the algorithm.
5. If the story is finished , then
   - 5.1. For all pairs of nodes (N_1,N_2), if there is an arc A from N_1 to N_2, and a different path from N_1 to N_2, then delete A.(Note: an arc is also a path).
   - 5.2. Algorithm finished.
6. n:=n+1.Establish a new node N with Sn.
7. If Sn does not contain any temporal delimiter, then go to 13.
8. If the node mentioned in the temporal delimiter does not exist, or is N itself, then there is an error, stop the algorithm.
9. If the temporal delimiter is "before S_j", then
   - 9.1. If T:= before S_k", then construct an arc from the current node to S_k
   - 9.2. T:= before S_j
   - 9.3. The current node becomes N
   - 9.4. If S_n is the last sentence, then construct an arc from N to S_j. T:=empty.
10. If the temporal delimiter is "after S_j", then
    - 10.1. Construct an arc from S_j to N.
    - 10.2. If T= before T_h and Sj is not the current node, then construct an arc from the current node to T_h, T:=empty.
    - 10.3. The current node becomes N.
    - 10.4. N is also a recent node
    - 10.5. S_j is no more a recent node (if it was a recent node)
11. If the temporal delimiter is "now", then
    - 11.1. If T:= before S_k, then construct an arc from the current node to the node corresponding to S_k

11.2. T:=empty.
11.3. For each recent node Nc, Construct an arc from Nc to N.
11.4. N is the current node and also a recent node. All other nodes are no more current nodes, nor recent nodes.

12. Go to 5.
13. Construct an arc from the current node C to N. N becomes the current node.
14. If C is a recent node, then C isn't it any more, but N is a recent node.
15. Go to 5.

End of Algorithm

Definition 5.2.8

Each node of an event graph, which has no incoming arcs, is a start node. Those nodes without outgoing arcs are end nodes.

Definition 5.2.9 (Development Threads)

In the event graph of a story S, each path from the start node to the end node is a development thread of S. The number of occurrences of a role on such a path is called the relevant number of this role with respect to this development thread.

Definition 5.2.10 (Main Development Thread)

The main development thread of S could be defined as:

1. The development thread where the main role has its largest relevant number.
2. The development thread where the sum of the relevant numbers of all roles is the largest.
3. The development thread with the maximal length (= number of nodes – 1)

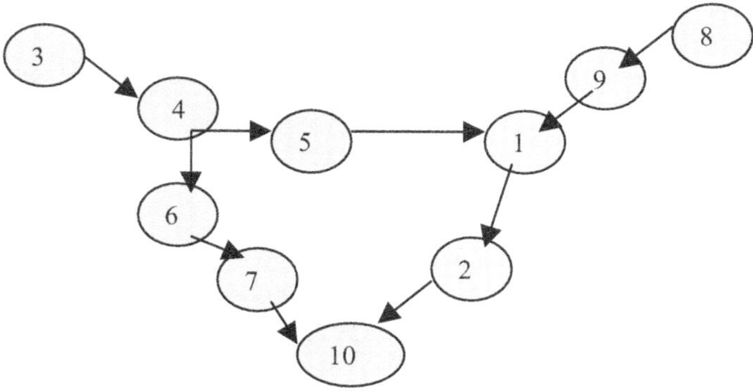

Figure 5.2.2 An Event Graph.

Example 5.2.2

Assume the following story is given.

1. The king fell in love with Marry
2. He married Mary as the new queen
3. Before (1) Elisabeth was the queen.
4. Elisabeth was seriously ill.
5. Elisabeth died unfortunately.
6. After (4) a witch came.
7. The witch put some poison in Elisabeth's glass.
8. Before (1) the king has looked for a new queen
9. Finally the king found Elisabeth.
10. Now the king and the new queen live together.

We construct the event graph of it, which is shown in figure 5.2.2.

There are three development threads in this graph:

1. (3,4,6,7,10)
2. (3,4,5,1,2,10)
3. (8,9,1,2,10)

It is easy to decide that the king is the main role and the third development thread is the main development thread.

Note that events on different threads are generally concurrent, possibly synchronized at some later node. These events leave room to the story adapters for designing an appropriate time order. An often used technique in movie direction is to make contrasts, including contrasts of two roles, two roles' behaviors, two events, two environments, two atmospheres, two development threads, etc. Once the director has seized a good topic of contrasting, he/she can use the technique of parallel Montage to display it in the movie.

One may argue that in figure 5.2.2, node 5 should be placed after node 7. But with this method it is impossible. Note that the graph approach presented here is a syntactic approach. To get a more precise graph, one has to resort to semantics.

When we analysis a story, we often find that there are development threads which are assigned to particular roles. We call these development threads the role specific ones. Generally speaking, the main development thread of a story can be considered as the role specific development thread of the main role. with the following definition it is possible to assign development threads to other roles, where the story is limited to a sequential one.

Definition 5.2.11 (Role Specific Development Threads)

1. Given two main roles, or one main role and one main minor role A and B.
2. Given the threshold values : $0 < v < 1$, $1/2 < u < 1$, $0 < w < 1$, $1/2 < p < 1$.
3. Count the number n (A) of events at which the role A participates.
   Count the number n (B) of events at which the role B participates.

Count the number m (A) of events at which only the role A, but not the role B participates.
Count the number m (B) of events at which only the role B, but not the role A participates.
Count the number k (A,B) of events at which both A and B participates.

4. Calculate :
   P (x) = n (x) / (n (x) + n (y) - k (x, y)),
   Q (x) = m (x) / (n (x) + n (y) - k (x, y)),
   R (x) = m (x) / (m (x) + m (y)),
   S (x) = m (x) / n (x),
   For (x, y) = (A, B) and (x, y)=(B, A).
5. If S (A) > v and/or S (B) > v, then there is a role specific development thread for A (SDT (A) for short) and/or one for B ((SDT B) for short), where SDT (A) consists of the n (A) events in which A participates, SDT (B) consists of the n (B) events in which B participates. Otherwise, there is no separate thread. We have only story development threads.
6. If SDT (A) and SDT (B) both exist, then we call SDT (A) the main SDT, if R (A) > u. Otherwise SDT (B) the main SDT, if R (B) > u, otherwise there are only two parallel SDT, but no main SDT.
7. SDT (A) is called a strong SDT, if Q (A) > w, otherwise a weak one. The same for SDT (B).
8. Redefine the main role as follows: A is called the main role, if P (A) > P (B). Otherwise B is called the main role, if P (B) > P (A). Otherwise both A and B are main roles.

Example 5.2.3

Given the following story:

" (1) The new queen wanted to kill Snow White. (2) Snow White escaped from the palace. (3) Snow White lost her way in a big forest. (4) Seven Dwarfs discovered Snow White. (5) The seven dwarfs received Snow White as their guest. (6) The new queen asked the magic mirror where Snow White now was. (7) The magic mirror told the new queen that Snow White is now in the forest. (8) The new queen went to the forest to seek Snow White. (9) A rabbit told this to Snow White. (10) Snow White was surprised and did not know what to do. (11) The new queen saw Snow White. (12) The new queen apologized to Snow White for having treated her badly. (13) The new queen gave a poisonous apple to Snow White. (14) Snow White ate the apple. (15) Snow White died. (16) The new queen laughed loudly. (17) The new queen went away. "

Transforming this story into an event graph, we obtain the graph as it is shown in figure 5.2.2, where we have separated the story development thread in three lines. On the left is the SDT of Snow White. On the right is the SDT of the new queen. In the middle is their common part. We list the weight numbers calculated as follows:

1. n (Snow White) = 11, n (new queen) = 9, m (Snow White) = 8, m (new queen) = 6.
2. P (Snow White) = 11/17, P (new queen) = 9/17.
3. Q (Snow White) = 8/17, Q (new queen) = 6/17.
4. R (Snow White) = 4/7, R (new queen) = 3/7.
5. S (Snow White) = 8/11, S (new queen) = 2/3.

Let u = v = w = p = 1/2, then:

1. Both Snow White and the new queen have their own role specific development threads.
2. SDT (Snow White) is the main SDT. SDT (new queen) is not.
3. Both SDT (Snow White) and SDT (new queen) are weak SDT.
4. Snow White is redefined as the main role, new queen the main minor role.

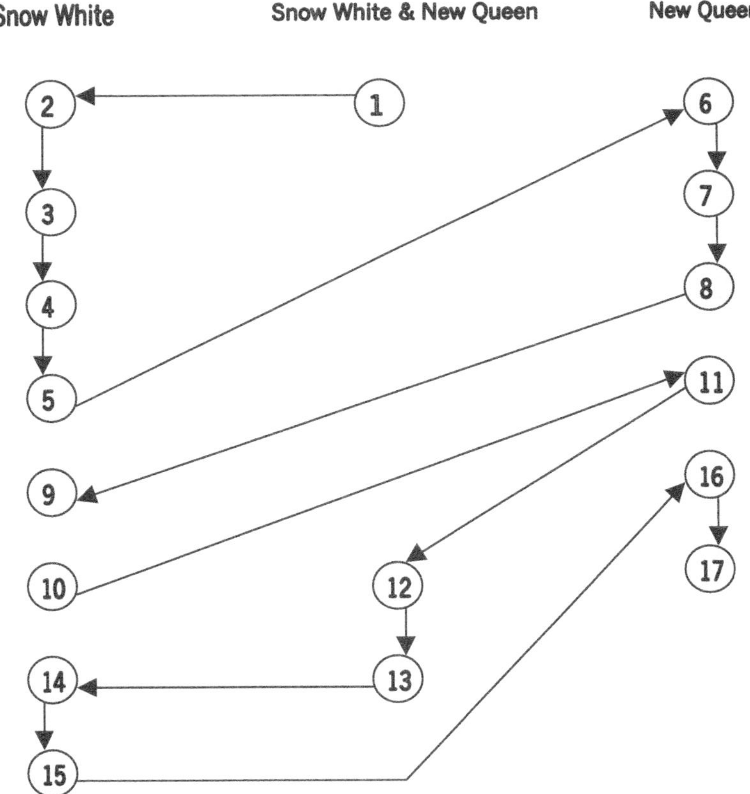

Figure 5.2.2 Role Specific Threads

5.3 The Temporal Grammar Approach

5.3.1 Deficiency of the Traditional Approaches

With the conventional context free grammar, the recognition of a language is based on a reduction process of the text string. Each time a sentential form consisting of a string of terminal and non-terminal symbols will be reduced to a non-terminal symbol, until finally the root symbol is obtained.

In our forest grammar and story parsing grammar, we have basically followed this tradition. Only the reduction process is not based on symbol strings, but on tree strings, i.e. forests. The variables of different syntactic terms in the same production are connected by synchronic replacements. That means, they are context sensitive. This kind of grammar is suitable for parsing stories written in natural languages.

In the practical use of traditional grammars, we have found some of their insufficiencies, which we list as follows:

1. When reducing a sentential form, only a contingent (continuous) string of symbols can be reduced (to a nonterminal symbol). Symbol strings with distance among the symbols can not be reduced.
2. No symbol can be neglected.
3. No symbol can be used more than once.
4. No specification of time relations between symbols.

We will use examples to explain these points.

Example 5.3.1

Given the following productions:

A: fortune (x) → diligent (x), enough_food (x)

B: Misfortune (x) → lazy (x), hungry (x)

C: more_diligent (x, y) → diligent (x), lazy (y)

D: god_like_diligence → more_diligent (x, y), fortune (x), misfortune (y)

Given the following story:

1. Ant and cicadae are both insects.
2. Ant works diligently.
3. Cicadae is lazy.
4. Ant has enough food.
5. Cicadae is hungry.

The reduction process will be:

1,2 – (C) → more_diligent (ant, cicadae) (5)

1,3 – (A) → fortune (ant), (6)

2,4 – (B) → fortune (cicadae), (7)

5,6,7 – (D) → god_like_diligence

Note three phenomena in this reduction process:

First, the reduction is not always based on a continuous string of symbols. In each of the reduction step3 (6), (7), one of the original symbols is skipped. Second, each of the symbols 1 and 2 has been applied two times. Third, the symbol 0 has not been used at all and is simply ignored.

Parsing: It is impossible to parse this story by using the two rules above. But if we are allowed to skip some sentences while parsing, then the following parsing mode is possible:

"work_hard (Wang), skip, great_achievement (Wang)" reduced to success (Wang),
"lazy (Li), skip, no_achievement (Li)" reduced to fail (Li).

In each reduction, one sentence is skipped. The result is:
success (Wang) & fail (Li)

Example 5.3.2

A small story:

1. Once upon a time, there was a crocodile and a monkey.
2. The crocodile told the monkey that he would bring it to the other bank of the river, so that the monkey could eat the bananas over there.
3. The monkey believed it and jumped onto the back of the crocodile.
4. In the middle of the river, the crocodile sank suddenly into the water and let the monkey be submerged for a while.
5. The monkey was astonished and asked for help.
6. The crocodile told the monkey that he wanted to kill the monkey to get monkey's heart as a medicine for curing the sickness of crocodile's mother.
7. The monkey told the crocodile that he has left his heart on the river bank.
8. The crocodile believed that and brought the monkey back for its heart.
9. After arriving at the river bank, the monkey climbed to the top of a tree and begun to throw stones against the crocodile's head.
10. The crocodile knew now that he was fooled and swam away disappointedly.

In this story, the monkey understood that the crocodile cheated him only when the crocodile told his true intention to monkey: to kill the monkey to get his heart for crocodile's mother. Similarly, the crocodile understood that the monkey cheated him only when monkey jumped on the river bank and ran away. Since the intention "cheating" is not explicitly stated at the beginning, the parsing module is unable to reduce the sentence 2 to "cheating" until the sentence 6 is parsed. But there are lots of other events between sentence 2 and sentence 6. The situation is similar for sentence 7 and 9. The parser has to skip these "useless" events to reach the wanted conclusion.

Note that this phenomenon is different from the group keywords in programming languages. For example, the keywords "if", "then", "else", "fi", which denote a conditional clause, are also separated by strings of other symbols. But one can recognize the beginning of a conditional clause at the keyword "if" and its end at the keyword "fi". This is not difficult. The grammar remains to be context free. But in case of a story parsing grammar, it is impossible for the parser to recognize the beginning of a cheating process by only parsing the sentence.

Before we explain the design of a new kind of grammar and grammar parsing mechanism, we have first to solve the problem of describing time relations between events. How can we specify them in the syntax and their evolution during the process of parsing? The first idea is to use the time relations of Allen.

Remember that in Allen's definition there are thirteen possible time relations between two events. Assume x and y are events with time intervals [a, b] and [c, d] with $a< b$, $c < d$, where a and c are start points, then the following relations, together with their reversed ones, are defined.

x precede y if $b < c$,
x meet y if $b = c$,
x overlap y if $a < c < b < d$
x contain y if $a < c < d < b$
x begin y if $a = c$ and $b < d$,
x end y if $c < a$ and $b = d$,
x coincide with y if $a = c$ and $b = d$.

But the Allen time relations are in fact not enough for the purpose of describing rules of commonsense.

Example 5.3.3

Consider the following two stories:

Story 1: X swears at y. Y swears at x.

Story 2: X swears at y. Y tells that to his mother. Mother says you should swear back. The next day y swears at x.

These two stories tell the same thing: there happens a dispute between x and y. But the time relations between the two swear events are different. So we would have different rules for the same thing in the two stories:

Dispute (x, y) → (1) swear (x, y), (2) swear (y, x). (1) meet (2)
Dispute (x, y) → (1) swear (x, y), (2) swear (y, x). (1) precede (2)

With this example we can see that the time relations of Allen are not enough for our goal. In the example above, there is no single Allen time relation corresponding to (precede or meet). In this sense, the time relation of Freksa may be useful. Let us make a short review.

Freksa has developed a semi interval time representation parallel to the full interval representation of Allen. He called it a coarse sized representation as compared with the fine sized one of Allen.

Definition 5.3.1 (Partial Order of Temporal Relations)

Given a finite set S of concrete actions and a finite set T of Allen temporal constraints on the members of S. Let x, y be two members of S. We use the notation x (begin) and y (begin) to denote the start time of the events x and y, and the notation x (end) and y (end) to denote their finish time.

1. Define "<" as a transitive, non symmetric, non reflexive relation.
2. For each temporal constraint x op y in T, where op is an Allen operator, x and y are events, x may equal to y or not equal to y, do the following:
    - 2.1. For x precede y we write x (end) < y (begin)
    - 2.2. For x meet y we write x (end) = y (begin)
    - 2.3. For x overlap y we write x (begin) < y (begin) < x (end) < y (end)
    - 2.4. For x contain y we write x (begin) < y (begin) < y (end) < x (end)
    - 2.5. For x begin y we write x (begin) = y (begin) < x (end) < y (end)
    - 2.6. For x end y we write y (begin) < x (begin) < x (end) = y (end)
    - 2.7. For x coincide with y we write x (begin) = y (begin) and x (end) = y (end)
    - 2.8. We do also the same thing for the reverse operators.
3. For each event x, let x (begin) < x (end)

Definition 5.3.2 (Semi Interval Time Relation of Freksa)

Assume x (begin) = a, x (end) = b, y (begin) = c, y (end) = d, then

x is older than y if a < c,
x is same old as y if a = c,
x dies latter than y if b > d,
x dies at the same time as y if d = b,
x dies before y is born if b < c,
x and y are contemporaries if the intersection of [a, b] and [c, d] is not empty,
x is born before y dies if a < d,

etc.

Definition 5.3.3 (Neighboring Time Relations)

Two time relations t and t' are called neighboring time relations if t can be turned into t' continuously by a linear transformation on the time axis without going through a third time relation.

Example 5.3.4 (Combining Neighboring Time Relations)

Precede and meet are neighboring time relations. Based on this idea, one may define a new time relation by combining some existing neighboring ones. Thus the precede and meet relations can be combined to form a new relation called, say, pre-meet which means precede or meet. In the above example, the rule may be written as:

Dispute (x, y) → (1) swear (x, y), (2) swear (y, x). (1) pre-meet (2)

But this is not yet enough. Let's consider the following situation.

Example 5.3.5 (Not Neighboring Time Relations)

Assume somebody x has got the job to move two heavy things A and B from one place to another. Then in real life there are two possibilities for x: move (A) precedes move (B) or move (B) precedes move (A). The relation "move (A) meets move (B)" is impossible because after having moved (A) he has first to come back to the start place to get (B). It is impossible to use neighboring relations to summarize these two in one relation only. Though in a movie it is possible to arrange "move (A) meet move (B)" or its reverse, the four possible relations are also not neighboring.

5.3.2 Introduction to Temporal Models

We need to loose the constraints of Allen and Freksa to allow combinations of not neighboring time relations. To this end, we have to introduce new frameworks of defining time relation. The first one introduced in this section is called CTR (Combined Time Relation).

Definition 5.3.4 (Syntax of CTR)

1. Each event t is attached with a time marking [a, b], where a and b are integers (later will be generalized to rational numbers), called begin point and end point of the time interval [a, b], denoted with t (begin) = a, t (end) = b. It must be a < b.
2. For any two events x and y , the four expressions:
   x (begin) op y (begin), x (begin) op y (end), x (end) op y (begin), x (end) op y (end)
   are all well-formed temporal formulas (WFTF), where op may be one of "precede", "equal" or "follow".
3. True and False are WFTF.
4. If t1 and t2 are well-formed temporal formulas, then the four expressions:
   t1 and t2, t1 or t2, t1 imply t2, not t1
   are all well-formed temporal formulas.
5. CTR consists of all WFTF defined above.

Definition 5.3.5 (Semantics of CTR)

Given events x, y and their time markings [a, b], [c, d].

1. x (begin) precede y (begin) is true if and only if a < c.
   x (begin) follow y (begin) is true if and only if a > c.
   x (begin) equal y (begin) is true if and only if a = c
   Similar definitions for x (begin) op y (end), x (end) op y (begin), x (end) op y (end).
2. The semantics of the four operators "and", "or", "imply" and "not" are the same as in the classical predicate calculus.

Definition 5.3.6 (Temporal Closure and Temporal Abstract)

Given a set E of events and a set T(E) of WFTF describing the temporal relations between some events of E. The set of all WFTF based on T(E) is called the temporal closure of T(E) (or of E), and is denoted with TC(T(E)) (or TC(E)).

T(E) is a temporal abstract of TC(T(E))

Definition 5.3.7 (Temporal Model)

A temporal closure without the element fake is a temporal model. The elements of a temporal model are said to be consistent with each other.

In the following, we use also the notation x (u) < y (v), x (u) = y (v) and x (u) > y (v) instead of x (u) precede y (v), x (u) equal y (v) and x (u) follow y (v) , where u and v may be begin or end.

Definition 5.3.8 (Temporal Product)

Given two sets T_1, T_2 of WFTF. The temporal product of T_1, T_2 is defined as

$$TC\ (T_1 \cup T_2)$$

Example 5.3.6

E = {x, y, z}, T(E) = {end (x) < begin (y), begin (z) < end (y)}, then
TC(T(E)) = {begin (x) < end (x) < begin (y) < end (y), begin (z) < end (z), begin (z) < end (y)}
Note that we have need a non-standard representation for the WFTF in TC(T(E)).

TC(T(E)) is a temporal model.

Example 5.3.7

E1 = {x, y}, T(E1) = {end (x) < begin (y)}

E2 = {y, z}, T(E2) = {end (y) < begin (z)}

E3 = {z, x}, T(E3) = {end (z) < begin (x)}

Then each of TC(T(E1) ∪ T(E2)), TC(T(E2) ∪ T(E3)), TC(T(E1) ∪ T(E3)) is a temporal model. But TC(T(E1) ∪ T(E2) ∪ T(E3)) is not a temporal model.

Example 5.3.8

Given three event groups {x, y}, {z, w}, {s, t}, then:

1. From ({x (begin), y (begin)} < z (begin) and (z (begin) < s (begin), w (begin) < t (begin)) follows
   TC ({x, y}, {s, t}) ⊇ ({x (begin), y (begin)} < s (begin)).
2. From (x overlap z, y precede w) and (s precede z, w overlap t) follows
   TC ({x, y}, {s, t}) ⊇ {s (end) < x (end), y precede t}

Example 5.3.9

Given three event groups with internal time relations {x, y | x contain y}, {z, w | z follow w}, {s, t | s precede t}, then

1. From ({x, y} precede z) and (z precede s, w precede t) follows
   TC ({x, y}, {s, t}) ⊇ ({x, y} precede s)
2. From (x overlap z, y precede w) and (s begin w, w overlap t) follows
   TC ({x, y}, {s, t}) ⊇ {x contain s, x (begin) < t (begin) < x (end)}

Proposition 5.3.1

The temporal product is commutative and associative.

Note: the commutativity should be understood in the sense that to calculate the temporal relation TC (G1, G2) is the same as to calculate TC (G2, G1). The associativity should be understood in the sense that

TC(TC (G1, G2) , G3) = TC (G1, TC (G2, G3))

In order to analyze a story, we need still the following:

Definition 5.3.9 (Temporal Relation between Groups)

1. Assume G = {x, y, z, ...} is a group of events.
   We call the element x as a leading event of G, if for any other element y, x (begin) ≤ y (begin), and the element z as a tailing element of G, if for any other element y, y (end) ≤ z (end).
2. Given two groups G1 and G2 of events. We define:
   2.1. G1 precede G2 if for a tailing event x of G1 and a leading event y of G2, x (end) < y (begin).
   2.2. G1 overlap G2 if there are leading elements x of G1 and y of G2, and tailing elements z of G1 and w of G2, such that the following relations are valid:
   x (begin) < y (begin) , z (end) < w (end)
   2.3. G1 contain G2 if there are leading elements x of G1 and y of G2, and tailing elements z of G1 and w of G2, such that the following relations are valid:
   x (begin) < y (begin) , w (end) < z (end)
   2.4. G1 begin G2 if there are leading elements x of G1 and y of G2, and tailing elements z of G1 and w of G2, such that the following relations are valid:
   x (begin) = y (begin) , z (end) < w (end)
   2.5. G1 end G2 if there are leading elements x of G1 and y of G2, and tailing elements z of G1 and w of G2, such that the following relations are valid:
   y (begin) < x (begin) , z (end) = w (end)
   2.6. G1 coincide with G2 if there are leading elements x of G1 and y of G2, and tailing elements z of G1 and w of G2, such that the following relations are valid:
   x (begin) = y (begin) , z (end) = w (end)

The other definitions can be given accordingly.

Definition 5.3.10 (Full Time Relation)

The combined time relation extended with group time relation defined above is called full time relation, FTR for short.

Definition 5.3.11 (Temporal Implication)

Given two WFTF r1 and r2. If r1 is implied by r2, then we denote this implication with

$$r1 \leq r2$$

r1 and r2 are called equivalent iff r1 $\leq$ r2 and r2 $\leq$ r1 are valid.

Example 5.3.10

Assume:

r1 = x is older than y

r2 = x precede y

In this case r1 is implied by r2 because x is always older than y if x precede y.

The reverse conclusion is not true.

Proposition 5.3.2

The temporal implication is reflexive and transitive, but not symmetric. It forms a partial order.

Definition 5.3.12 (Temporal Unification)

Given two WFTF r1 and r2. To be found is a third WFTF r3 such that r1 and r2 are both implied by r3. The WFTF r3, if it exists, is called a temporal unifier of r1 and r2.

If there is no other temporal unifier r4 of r1 and r2, such that r4$\neq$r3, and r4 is implied by r3, then r3 is called a most general temporal unifier of r1 and r2, mgtu for short.

Definition 5.3.13 (Implication of Temporal Models)

Given two temporal models M1 and M2. If every WFTF of M1 is implied by M2, then we say that M1 is implied by M2, and denote it with M1 $\subseteq$ M2. M1 and M2 are called equivalent iff M1 $\subseteq$ M2 and M2 $\subseteq$ M1 are valid.

Example 5.3.11

Assume:

M1 = TC({x is older than y, y die before z})

M2 = TC({x contain y, z contain x})

In this case M1 is implied by M2.

Proposition 5.3.3

The implication of temporal models is reflexive and transitive, but not symmetric. It forms a partial order.

Definition 5.3.14 (Temporal Model Unification)

Given two temporal models M1 and M2. To be found is a third model M3, such that M1 and M2 are both implied by M3 which, if found, is called a temporal unifier of M1 and M2.

If there is no other temporal unifier M4 of M1 and M2, such that M4≠M3, and M4 is implied by M3, then M3 is called a most general temporal unifier of M1 and M2, mgtu for short.

Definition 5.3.15 (The Temporal Limits)

Given a temporal model M. We consider M as a graph G(M), called a temporaler graph, where the events in M are considered as nodes, and the WFTF in M are considered as sets of arcs. Two nodes e1 and e2 are connected, iff (begin(e1) and/or end(e1)) and (begin(e2) and/or end(e2)) appear in the same WFTF. M is called a connected temporal model, if G(M) is a connected graph.

An Event x in M is called an early starting limit of M, if there is no other event y in M, such that y (begin) < x (begin); x is called an early ending limit of M, if there us no other event y in M with y (end) < x (end); x is called a late starting limit, if there is no other event y in M with x (begin) < y (begin); x is called a late ending limit, if there is no other event y in M with x (end) < y (end). In the following, we use esl(M), eel(M), lsl(M) and lel(M) to denote these four kinds of limits.

Definition 5.3.16 (Model Considered as Event)

Given a connected temporal model M. We define:

M (begin) = min {x (begin) | x is an esl(M)}

M (lbegin) = max {x (begin) | x is an lsl(M)}

M (end) = max {x (end) | x is an lel(M)}

M (eend) = min {x (end) | x is an eel(M)}

With M (begin) and M (end), we can treat the model M as a single event.

5.3.3 The Heuristic Temporal Forest Grammar

Definition 5.3.7 (STSPG)

Given a story parsing grammar G = (N, D, P, R). Change the form of the production in P in the following way: the (left and right) trees of each production do not form a sequence, but a set. This set has at least two elements (trees). And with each production is attached a connected temporal model M, where the temporal relations between the trees are specified. M should cover all trees of this set. The following four assumptions are always valid:

1. We always assume that the left hand tree T of each production p "contain" all its right hand trees in the sense of Allen, if T is not mentioned in the temporal model of p.
2. If no M is specified, then the right hand trees of the tree set get the default temporal relation of "T_i precede T_{i+1}" for each i in the order the trees are written.
3. Some (not all) productions may have empty left hand trees.
4. If there are multiple copies of a same tree in a same production, then each tree should have a different mark.

Such a grammar is called a stochastic temporal story parsing grammar (STSPG). We use the notation

$$T \rightarrow \{ T1, T2, \ldots, Tn \mid M(T, T1, T2, \ldots, Tn) \}$$

To denote a production, where T's are trees and M is a connected temporal model. Note that T may be empty.

Definition 5.3.18 (HTSPG)

A STSPG is called a heuristic temporal story parsing grammar (HTSPG) if all productions with empty left hand trees are attached with environment conditions. That means each such production has the form

$$(T1, T2) \rightarrow \{ T3, T4, \ldots, Tn \mid M(T1, T2, \ldots, Tn) \}$$

Where T1 and T2 are trees, too, and are called left, resp., right environment of the empty left hand tree.

Algorithm 5.3.1 (Story Derivation)

A sentence of a temporal grammar will be derived in the following way:

1. Take the root tree as the current sentential form F, with an empty set TR of WFTF.
2. Repeat the following process until there are no nonterminal trees anymore in F:
   2.1 Select a nonterminal tree from the current sentential form F, let's say N; Or select a place in F and take the empty tree, call it also N.
   2.2. Select a production rule R with N as its left hand side, replace that N of F with the right hand side RH of R; Or insert RH at the selected place if N is an empty tree. In case of an empty N, the left and right environment of the place selected in F should match the corresponding environments of the environment specification of R.
   2.3. If RH contains trees which equal to some trees of F (before replacement), then for each such tree, give it a special mark such that in the new F no two trees are equal.
   2.4. Delete all WFTF involving N from TR.
   2.5. Calculate $TC((F - N) \cup RH)$ as the new model TR.

End of Algorithm

Note that there is a basic assumption implied in the above algorithm: for each nonterminal tree N there is at least one way of derivation which starts from the root tree R and produces a set of terminal trees with a connected temporal model, which contains N as one of its nodes. Without this assumption the algorithm would fail at some place, or the node N would not be able to participate at any process of story generation. A HTSPG satisfying this assumption is called a normal HTSPG.

Algorithm 5.3.2 (Story Recognition)

A story of a heuristic temporal story parsing grammar will be recognized in the following way:

1. Given a set S of temporal trees with a connected temporal model TR of WFTF between these terminal trees of S.
2. If there are multiple copies of the same tree T in S, then we denote them with T[1], T[2], etc., such that all trees in S are different.
3. Mark all trees of S as unused and as level 0.
4. Let i := 0, j :=0.
5. Find a subset Q of S , where the elements (trees) of Q form the right hand side of a production rule p, each element x of Q has a level k(x) with $j \leq k(x) \leq i$, and at least one tree of Q is unused and at level j, and the set of WFTF in TR has a temporal unifier with the model M attached to p. Furthermore, if the left hand tree N of p is an empty tree, then the environment of p and Q should coincide at the place N.
6. If the step 5 is not successful then
    6.1. For each relation a op b in each WFTF of TR, where a or b is G(begin) or G(end), where G is a tree of j-th level, replace a op b with true.
    6.2. j := j+1.
    6.3. If j > i then
        6.3.1. If the root tree belongs to S, then algorithm finished.
        6.3.2. Otherwise, algorithm failed.
        Otherwise go to 5.
7. If the step 5 is successful then
    7.1. Mark all elements of Q as used.
    7.2. Mark N as unused tree of level h+1, where h is the highest level of trees in Q.
    7.3. Add the tree N to S.
    7.4. i := max {level of tree x | x belongs to S}.
    7.5. If there is another N (or other Ns) already in S, then give a special mark to N, such that the new N is different from all old Ns in S.
    7.6. TR := mgtu {TR, M}.
    7.7. For each relation a op b in each WFTF of TR, where op is defined in definition 5.3.4, and where a or b is N(begin) or N(end), where N is not an empty tree, replace a op b with true.

7.8. If the set U of all trees of the j-th level are marked as used, then go to 6.1. Otherwise, go to 5.

End of Algorithm

Note that if some tree T of Q matches a corresponding tree T' in a production rule p, and if there are multiple copies of T in Q, then only those copies will be marked as used which are needed by p, because Q may include more copies of the same tree than it is needed by p.

Proposition 5.3.4

The algorithm 5.3.2 terminates for any given finite story (story with finitely many initial trees) if the number of right hand side trees of each production is no less than 2.

Proof. There are three different loops in this algorithm: step 5 → step 6 → step 5; step 5 →step 7 → step 6 → step 5; step 5 → step 7 → step 5. In the first two loops, the value of j will be increased by 1. In the third loop, the value of i will be increased by 1. Since j must not be greater than i, it is enough to prove that the value of i is always bounded. Note that i will be increased only in the third loop. Each time we enter this loop, at least one unused tree will be marked as used. At the same time, one new unused tree (at a higher level) will be produced. If we can prove that more unused trees will be marked as used than the number of new produced unused trees, then we will prove that in finitely many steps all unused trees will be exhausted and thus the third loop will not be entered anymore. This equals to the assertion that the growth of i is bounded.

We consider the behavior of our algorithm at any level j of trees. Each successful reduction must consume at least one unused tree. We differentiate between two cases:

Case 1. All trees of level j are used. There are two subcases.

Case 1.1. All reductions made at this level do not involve trees from levels lower than j. Then the first reduction at this level consumes at least two unused trees.

Case 1.2. At least one reduction made at this level involves a tree from a level lower than j. Then the first one among these reductions consumes at least two unused trees.

Case 2. At least one tree of this level remains unused until the processing of level j is finished.

It follows from each of these cases that the completion of processing of level j for each j reduces the number if unused trees at least by 1. That means, the number of unused trees will be reduced to zero after finitely many loops.

The termination of algorithm 5.3.2 is thus proved.

Proposition 5.3.5 (Derivation Lattice)

If the derivation in algorithm 5.3.1 or recognition in algorithm 5.3.2 is successful, then the derivation resp. recognition procedure can be represented as a semi lattice as follows:

1. For each derivation using the rule A → M1, M2, ..., Mn, let A' < {M1', M2', ..., Mn'}, where A' is a copy of A, which is produced in the past. M1', M2', ..., Mn' are new copies of M1, M2, ..., Mn, which are produced in this derivation step.
2. For each recognition using the rule M1, M2, ..., Mn → A, let {M1', M2', ..., Mn'} < A', where M1', M2', ..., Mn' are copies of M1, M2, ..., Mn, which are produced in the past. A' is a new copy of A, which is produced in this recognition step.

Note that the symbol "<" does not mean any time relation. It just means the order of derivation or recognition. It is transitive, anti reflexive and anti symmetric. It is easy to see that in the case of derivation, the root tree is the smallest element of the semi lattice, and in the case of recognition, the root tree is the largest element of the semi lattice. We call such a semi lattice a derivation lattice.

The reader may compare this conclusion with the derivation and recognition procedure of conventional grammars, where the procedure is represented as a tree. This shows the essential difference between the two approaches.

Example 5.3.12

Assume we have the following rule set:

→ once_there_were (x)
→ appear (x)
keep_promise (x) → (1) promise_help (x), (2) helpful (x). (1) ≤ (2)
break_promise (x) → (1) promise_help (x), (2) not_helpful (x). (1) ≤ (2)
helpful (x) → (1) ask_help (y, x), (2) help (x, y). (1) ≤ (2)
not_helpful (x) → (1) ask_help (y, x), (2) not_help (x, y). (1) ≤ (2)
faithful (x) → (1) keep_promise (x), (2) keep_promise (x).
slippery (x) → (1) break_promise (x), (2) break_promise (x).
good_attitude (x) → (1) faithful (x), (2) keep_promise (x).
bad_attitude (x) → (1) slippery (x), (2) break_promise (x).
good_luck (x) → (1) wish_to_be (x, y), (2) make_to_be (x, y). (1) ≤ (2)
bad_luck (x) → (1) wish_to_be (x, y), (2) make_to_be_not (x, y). (1) ≤ (2)
good_attitude_awarded (x)→(1) good_attitude(x), (2) good_luck(x)(1)≤ (2)
bad_attitude_punished (x) → (1) bad_attitude (x), (2) bad_luck (x) (1) ≤ (2)
story → (1) good_attitude_awarded (x), (2) bad_attitude_punished (x)
where ≤ is a short notation for (before or meet).

Assume we have the story (where the sentences are numbered):

[1] Once upon a time there were two sisters.
[2] The elder sister wished to be beautiful.

[3] The younger sister wished to be beautiful, too.
[4] The elder sister promised to always help other people.
[5] The younger sister promised to always help other people, too.
[6] An old woman is thirsty and asked for some water.
[7] The elder sister refused to give her water.
[8] The younger sister gave her some water for drink.
[9] A rabbit chased by a wolf sought for protection.
[10] The elder sister refused to protect the rabbit.
[11] The younger sister hid the rabbit under her skirt.
[12] An old apple tree complained on carrying too many heavy apples.
[13] The elder sister did nothing to help the tree.
[14] The younger sister picked away many apples to easy the burden of the tree.
[15] Suddenly, a fairy appeared in front of them.
[16] The fairy made the elder sister an awful girl.
[17] The fairy made the younger sister a beautiful girl.

Now we list the recognition procedure:

[1] reduced to empty.
[6] and [7] reduced to [18] : not_helpful (elder sister) , level = 1.
[4] and [18] reduced to [19] : break_promise (elder sister), level = 2.
[6] and [8] reduced to [20] : helpful (younger sister) , level = 1.
[5] and [20] reduced to [21] : keep_promise (younger sister), level = 2.
[9] and [10] reduced to [22] : not_helpful (elder sister) , level = 1.
[4] and [22] reduced to [23] : break_promise (elder sister) , level = 2.
[19] and [23] reduced to [24] : slippery (elder sister) , level = 3.
[9] and [11] reduced to [25] : helpful (younger sister) , level = 1.
[5] and [26] reduced to [26] : keep_promise (younger sister) , level = 2.
[21] and [26] reduced to [27] : faithful (younger sister) , level = 3.
[12] and [13] reduced to [28] : not_helpful (elder sister) , level = 1.
[4] and [28] reduced to [29] : break_promise (elder sister) , level = 2.
[12] and [14] reduced to [30] : helpful (younger sister) , level = 1.
[5] and [30] reduced to [31] : keep_promise (younger sister) , level = 2.
[24] and [29] reduced to [32] : bad_attitude (elder sister) , level = 4.
[27] and [31] reduced to [33] : good_attitude (younger sister) , level = 4.
[15] reduced to empty.
[2] and [16] reduced to [34] : bad_luck (elder sister), level = 1.
[3] and [17] reduced to [35] : good_luck (younger sister), level = 1.
[32] and [34] reduced to [36] : bad_attitude_punished (elder sister), level = 5.
[33] and [35] reduced to [37] : good_attitude_awarded (younger sister), level = 5.
[36] and [37] reduced to [38] : story, level = 6.

The recognition procedure presented above is at the same time a representation of the derivation lattice with story as the largest element. We see that in this procedure all four disadvantages mentioned at the beginning of this section have been overwhelmed to some degree. Firstly, grammatical symbols have been skipped during parsing. Secondly, useless actions are filtered out. Third, many symbols are used more than once. Fourth, there are time specifications attached to some productions.

Now a few discussions. There are some points which make the algorithm 5.3.2 non-deterministic and heuristic. First, if at some moment, more than one reduction with different production rules can be made, the choice is still free. Second, it is allowed that some (terminal or nonterminal) trees remain unused in the recognition process and will be thus skipped by the algorithm. The information these trees carry will get lost. Third, there may be more than one root tree in the set S after the algorithm stops.

For the first kind of non-determinism, we may impose some principles of decision making on the recognition process while selecting the set Q in step 5. But there are many possible principles which may serve as candidates. It is difficult to explain why take this principle but not that one. So the principles are also heuristic themselves. We consider the whole set Q which is a connected temporal model as if it were a single event with the time marking Q (begin) and Q (end) (See definition 5.3.15). We define:

1. If Q1 contain Q2, then Q1 has priority.
2. If Q1 precede Q2 or Q1 meet Q2, then Q1 has priority.
3. If Q1 overlap Q2, then Q1 has priority.
4. If Q1 begin Q2 or Q1 end Q2, then Q1 has priority.
5. If Q1 coincide with Q2 and Q1 includes more elements (trees) than Q2 does, then Q1 has priority.

More detailed principles can be added. But as we have said before, it is difficult to explain the reason of taking these principles due to the heuristic nature of story understanding.

For the second kind of non-determinism, we could use context sensitive production rules (see definition 5.3.17) with empty left hand tree (but non-empty environments) to limit the possibility of skipping. Only those trees in S, which match the environment conditions can be skipped. This method would not help much since there are too many variations in a story so that it is difficult to cover all of them with a fixed number of production rules.

As for the third kind of non-determinism, we may consider the existence of multiple root trees as multiple possibilities of analyzing a story.

5.4 Abstract Representation: The Deep Approach

5.4.1 The Main Idea

In the last chapter, we have presented a formal grammar approach of story understanding. We have introduced a family of two dimensional context sensitive grammars which are called Young Pine grammars. They are of the kind of forest grammars. We have studied the Chomsky hierarchy of forest grammars and proved their important properties. We have given algorithms for parsing a subtype of forest grammars: the week precedence context sensitive forest grammars and proved their correctness. Further, we have defined a practical variation of forest grammars: the story parsing grammars with their parsing algorithms. Using a set of examples we have shown how useful this new kind of grammar is for parsing a story written in natural language texts.

In the last section, we have introduced the heuristic temporal story parsing grammar to extend the story parsing capabilities of story parsing grammars. However, if the story analysis module of SWAN were to start from Adam and Eva when it is used to parse a great lot of stories, then the quantity of grammar rules we need would be enormously large such that the grammar itself and the inference mechanism would be too complex and totally out of control, because it involves a huge set of commonsense knowledge which is very difficult to be formalized and represented by a finite set of grammar rules of a reasonable size.

On the other hand, there are a great lot of different approaches for analyzing a story, its content, its theme, its main roles, etc. Each of these approaches can be implemented in the production form of our forest grammars. It would be a very long and even endless procedure to program all these approaches in grammar form. Even if it were possible, it is also hard to image how we can run an effective inference mechanism on such a huge production base.

So, the huge multiplicity of commonsense and the great variety of different approaches form the two main difficulties for a practical story analysis. A way out of these difficulties is to normalize the process of story parsing. If we could define an abstract representation language which is quite small and contains only a few most important concepts for event and character description, then this language can serve as a core of our story analysis in the way that the story parsing module first uses a story analysis grammar to translate the story written in natural language to an abstract version of this story, and then uses a abstract parser to analyze this abstract version. This way of going ahead would easy our task and avoid the development of a too big knowledge base of production rules.

Another technique we have adopted to easy the burden of the grammar is to develop a large sized commonsense knowledge base called Pangu. We have already mentioned it in chapter two. Pangu consists of a large set of agents and ontology bodies. Both the agents and the ontology bodies are organized in inheritance hierarchies. With the help of Pangu we have separated a great part of commonsense knowledge from the set of grammar rules to reduce its size. For example, if we are writing down a commonsense rule which involves money,

buy (x, y) → pay (x, money), get (x, y)

then this rule should be valid for any kind of money: Chinese Yuan, American Dollars, German Mark, etc. We do not need to write a rule for each kind of money, because the commonsense knowledge base tells us that all these are different kinds of money.

5.4.2 Silver Beach: The Abstract Representation Language

This abstract language has been designed by us and is called Silver Beach. In order to keep simplicity, we do not incorporate the Allen or Freksa temporal relations in this language. We just assume that all events happen in a sequential way. Thus the language Silver Beach is sequential.. First we list its syntax as follows.

Definition 5.4.1 (Syntax of Silver Beach)

```
<Abstract Story> ::= <Sequence of Exps>
<Exp> ::= Nil | <W-Exp> | <B-Exp> | <P-Exp> | <D-Exp> | <H-Exp>
        | <S-Exp> | <A-Exp> | <M-Exp> | <I-Exp> | <L-Exp> | <R-Exp>
        | Repeat: <Sequence of Exps> End of Repeat
# Intention Group#
<W-Exp> ::= <Role> want <Intention> | <Role> do not want <Intention>
        | <Role> like <Intention> | <Role> dislike <Intention>
        | <Role> should <Intention> | <Role> should not <Intention>
        | <Role> must <Intention> | <Role> must not <Intention>
        | <Role> decide <Intension>
#Belief Group#
<B-Exp> ::= <Role> believe <Inf> | <Role> do not believe <Inf>
#Performance Group#
<P-Exp> ::= <Role><Perform>[<Validity>]action [of<Action>][according to<Interest>of <Role>]
      | <Role><Perform>[<Validity>] action [of<Action>] [against the <Interest> of <Role>]
#Attitude Group#
<D-Exp> ::= <Role> damage <Role> [<In the Way>] | <Role> do not damage <Role>
<H-Exp> ::= <Role> help <Role> [<In the Way>] | <Role> do not help <Role>
<C-Exp> ::= <Role> cooperate [<In the Way>]
        <Role> do not cooperate [<In the Way>]
<M-Exp> ::= <Role> has good moral | <Role> has bad moral | <Role> has defects
#Situation Group#
<T-Exp> ::= <T-Sit> due to <Reason>
<T-sit> ::= <Role> have got trouble | <Role> have no trouble | <Role> have solved trouble
      | <Role> is [not] lucky | <Role> is damaged | <Role> become <Role> | <Role> succeed
| <Role> fail
#Sentiment Group#
<S-Exp> ::= <Role> is happy [due to <Reason>] | <Role> is unhappy [due to <Reason>]
<A-Exp> ::= <Role> like <Role > [due to <Exp>] | <Role> dislike <Role> [due to <Exp>]
```

#Communication Group#
<I- Exp> ::= <Role> give [<Role>] [<Quality>] information [by telling <information>]
<G-Exp> ::= <Role> get [<Quality>] information [of <Exp>]
#Interest Group#
<L-Exp> ::= <Role> have common interest [of <Exp>]
| <Role> have interest [of <Exp>] [against the interest of <Role>]
<R-Exp> ::= <Role> succeed [in <Intention>][<In the Way>]
| <Role> fail [in <Intention>][due to<Reason>]
<In the Way> ::= by doing <Event> | by telling <Information> | by <Exp> | by solving the trouble
<Reason> ::= <Exp> | <Event> | <Information>
<Interest> ::= interest | intention | plan
<Validity> ::= right | wrong
<Quality>::= good | bad | <Validity>
<Perform> ::= do | have done | will do
<Information> ::= <Exp> | <Atom>
<Inf> ::= [<Validity>] <Information>
<Intention > ::= <Exp> | <Atom>
<Event> ::= <Atom>
<Action> ::= <Atom>
<Role> ::= <positive role> | <negative role> | <defective role> | <somebody>
<positive role> ::= <Role name> | positive role
<negative role> ::= <Role name> | negative role
<defective role> ::= <Role name> | defective role
<somebody> ::= <Role name> | somebody | main role
<Atom> ::= <A Name>

Let us use Silver Beach to analyze the small story we have mentioned in examples 5.3.2. This time we translate it in Silver Beach form. Note that the square brackets in concrete Silver Beach representation (as it is given below) has different meaning than those appearing in the Silver Beach grammar. While the former denote nested structures of Silver Beach sentences, the latter denote optional parts in the Silver Beach grammar. The representation used below follows the Silver Beach grammar. It does not follow the standard English.

Example 5.4.1

Monkey and Crocodile

1. Text:
   Once upon a time, there was a crocodile and a monkey.
   SB representation:
   Nil.
2. Text:
   The crocodile told the monkey that he would bring it to the other bank of the river, so that the monkey can eat the bananas over there.
   SB representation:

Crocodile give monkey wrong information by telling [crocodile want [crocodile help monkey]].

3. Text:
   The monkey believed it and jumped onto the back of the crocodile.
   SB representation:
   Monkey believe [crocodile want [crocodile help monkey]].
4. Text:
   In the middle of the river, the crocodile sank suddenly into the water and let the monkey be submerged for a while.
   SB representation:
   Crocodile damage monkey.
5. Text:
   The monkey was astonished and asked for help.
   SB representation:
   Monkey is unhappy.
   Monkey give information by telling [monkey want [somebody help monkey]].
6. Text:
   The crocodile told the monkey that he wanted kill the monkey to get monkey's heart as a medicine for curing the sickness of crocodile's mother.

   SB representation:
   Crocodile give monkey information by telling [crocodile want [crocodile damage monkey]].
7. Text:
   The monkey told the crocodile that he has left his heart on the river bank.
   SB representation:
   Monkey give crocodile wrong information by telling [crocodile should [crocodile help monkey]].
8. Text:
   The crocodile believed that and brought the monkey back for its heart.
   SB representation:
   Crocodile believe [crocodile should [crocodile help monkey]].
   Crocodile help monkey.
9. Text:
   After arriving at the river bank, the monkey climbed to the top of a tree and begun to throw stones against the crocodile's head.
   SB representation:
   Monkey damage crocodile.
10. Text:
   The crocodile knew now that he was fooled and swam away disappointedly.
   SB representation:
   Crocodile fail.
   Crocodile is unhappy.

Example 5.4.2 (Wolf and the Bush)

Consider another children story which was contributed by Pat Hayes and Lokendra Shastri on the internet as one of the commonsense problems seeking solutions.

1. Text:
   A small girl is walking through a forest to visit her grandmother.
   SB representation:
   Girl want [Girl help grandmother by doing E2].
2. Text:
   The girl passes a bush behind which a wolf is hiding.
   SB representation:
   Nil.
3. Text:
   The wolf plans to pounce out and to eat the girl.
   SB representation:
   Wolf want [wolf damage girl by doing E3 and E4]
4. Text:
   The girl gets close to the wolf.
   SB representation:
   Nil.
5. Text:
   The wolf hears the singing of the woodcutters as they start work nearby.
   SB representation:
   Wolf get information of [Wolf must not [Wolf damage girl]].
6. Text:
   The wolf decides to stay hidden and not pounce on the girl after all.
   SB representation:
   Wolf decide [wolf do not damage girl].

We make a note here. The translation from story text to SB representation can not be always made sentence by sentence, since the intention or influence of some action done by an agent is often opaque at the beginning and will become clear only later. For example, the conclusion "crocodile give monkey wrong information" in the second statement of example 5.4.1 can not be deduced from the second story sentence only. The crocodile's intention becomes clear only later in the sixth sentence.

5.4.3 Determine Story Patterns

Based on the abstract representation of a story represented above, we will go a step further to summarize the "abstract scripts" of story patterns. In this way we can classify the stories in different types. And this classification will again help us to obtain necessary information which is needed by the animation director but which is still missing until now in our discussion. Since this analysis is based on analyzing contradictions and conflicts among roles of a story, we call the abstract representation of a story as a CC-chain and call a "standard" CC-chain as a story pattern. The word CC-chain means Contradiction-Conflict chains. In the following, we list a few story patterns which are at the same time modes of development threads, where a pseudo-programming language format is used. Contents within a pair of square brackets are optional. We use labels to denote expressions sometimes to keep simplicity. Note that this list is by no means complete. We also take some stories for example. For the sake of saving space, we do not include the details of these stories in this book. The interested readers may refer to a children story book for getting a rough impression of them.

1. Mode A:
   Main roles: one positive plus one negative.
   CC-chain: [L: The positive role is lucky.
   Negative role is unhappy due to L.]
   Repeat: Negative role [want negative role] damage positive role.
   Somebody help positive role by somebody do action against the interest of negative role.
   Negative role fail.
   End of Repeat.
   Negative role is damaged.
   Examples: Snow White, the little red hat.
2. Mode B:
   Main roles: one positive plus one negative.
   CC-chain: [L: Positive role is lucky.
   Negative role is unhappy due to L.]
   Repeat: Negative role [want negative role] damage positive role.
   Positive role succeed due to positive role have solved trouble.
   Negative role fail.
   End of Repeat.
   [Negative role is unhappy.]
   Examples: The white snake, the monkey and the crocodile
3. Mode C:
   Main Roles: one positive role.
   CC-chain: [Positive role is unhappy due to positive role is not lucky.]
   Positive role want positive role is lucky.
   Repeat: Positive role is unhappy due to positive role have got trouble.
   Positive role is happy due to positive role have solved trouble.
   End of Repeat.
   Positive role is happy due to positive role succeed.
   Examples: The little Mock.
4. Mode D:
   Main roles: one positive role, one negative role.
   CC-chain: [Positive role is unhappy due to positive role is not lucky .
   Negative role is happy due to negative role is lucky.]
   Repeat: Positive role help somebody.
   Negative role do not help somebody

End of Repeat.
Positive role is happy due to positive role is lucky.
Negative role is unhappy due to negative role is not lucky.
Examples: The fairy.

5. Mode E:
Main roles: one defective role, some other roles.
CC-chain: [Positive role has defects.]
Repeat: L: Defective role do a wrong action.
Somebody give defective role right information by telling defective role have done wrong action.
Defective role get right information.
End of Repeat.
[Defective role become positive role].
Examples: The little black hen, the toad.

6. Mode F:
Main roles: one main role
CC-chain: main role is unhappy due to main role is not lucky.
Repeat: main role do right action.
Main role succeed.
End of Repeat.
Main role is happy due to main role is lucky.
Examples: The cat wearing boots.

7. Mode G:
Main roles: one or two positive roles, some other roles.
CC-chain: [L: Somebody is unhappy due to somebody is not lucky.
Positive role is unhappy due to L.]
Repeat: M: Positive role help somebody.
Somebody is happy due to M.
[Positive role is damaged due to M]
End of Repeat.
Examples: The happy prince, the daughter of the see.

8. Mode H:
Main roles: one positive role, one negative role, some other role.
CC-chain: [Negative role B have got trouble.]
Repeat: [Negative role B is unhappy.]
L: Positive role A help negative role B.
Negative role B is happy due to L.
End of Repeat.
[Negative role B want] negative role B damage positive role A.
Negative role B fail.
[Negative role B is damaged].
Examples: The young man with a flute, the tiger learns from the cat, the Zhongshan wolf.

9. Mode I:
Main roles: One positive role and some other roles.

CC-chain: Repeat : Somebody is unhappy due to somebody have got trouble.
L: Positive role A help somebody.
Somebody is happy due to L.
End of Repeat.
Positive role A is happy.
Examples: The kind little girl.

10.Mode J:
Main roles: one positive role, some other roles.
CC-chain: Positive role is unhappy due to positive role have got trouble.
Repeat: Positive role want positive role is lucky.
Positive role fail.
End of Repeat.
Positive role is damaged.
Examples : the little girl selling matches.

11.Mode K :
Main Roles : one positive role B and some other roles
Repeat :
Defective role B do not want somebody is lucky.
[[Defective role B want] defective role B damage somebody.]
End of Repeat
[Defective role B is damaged.]
Defective role B get information of defective role B have done wrong action.
Defective role B become positive role B.
[Positive role B is lucky.]
Examples : the rabbit learns from the bock.

5.4.4 Use Story Patterns to Determine Global Information

Together with the determination of the pattern of a story, as it is presented above, we have also obtained a method of determining other global information of the story at the same time. This global information includes the theme of a story, the basic plot development threads of the story, the paradigm and rhythms of a story, etc. All of these are needed by the director's planning module in chapter seven. The generation of this global information is supported by our knowledge base.

5.4.4.1 Determine Themes of the Story

Following is a list of possible themes of the story modes introduced above.

1. Mode A: Good people will have good fortune. Bad people who do harm to good people, will eventually fail and will be punished.
2. Mode B: Good people will succeed in defending their own fortune if they know how to struggle against the sabotage of bad people.

3. Mode C: One will succeed if one always face and overcome the difficulties bravely.
4. Mode D: Good people have good results, bad people have bad results.
5. Mode E: People will recognize their weakness in practice and improve themselves by overcoming their weakness.
6. Mode F: One will have one's desire realized if one does not cease one's effort to realize it.
7. Mode G: Good people sacrifice themselves to help other people.
8. Mode H: Do not help the evil people because these people will requite kindness with enmity.
9. Mode I: One should always help other people.
10. Mode J: One should not forget the pain of other people and should help them.
11. Mode K: One should correct one's behavior of treating the other people badly.

For their better use as story modules, it is better to have a classification of these modes. This classification could be considered as their type definitions. Each story pattern will be classified according to its characteristic plot. We will give a short, but characteristic notation to each of these modes. These notations are organized in an inheritance hierarchy. For example, we could define:

Happy Pattern
  Success Pattern (Mode F)
    Bravo Child Pattern (Mode F)
  Kindness Pattern (I)
Unhappy Pattern
  Fail Pattern (Mode J)
  Sacrifice Pattern (Mode G)
  Pain and Poor Pattern (Mode J)
Wrong Action Pattern
  Behavior Improvement Pattern (Mode E, Mode K)
Right Action Pattern
  Hero Pattern (Mode G)
Contrast Pattern
  Good and Bad People Pattern (Mode A)
  Right and Wrong Action Pattern (Mode E, Mode K)

5.4.4.2 Determine Director's Attitude of Story Adaptation

One of the most important factors of director planning is the director's attitude. Unlike other factors which have an influence on the animation planning (theme, plot, roles, season, weather, daytime, etc.), this one is only partly objective, but largely subjective. It depends on the personal experience and flavor of making a movie. We have a plan to establish an expert knowledge base of director techniques, where the different styles of many world famous movie directors are collected and represented in applicable forms. For the moment, we are satisfied in having rather simple rules for determining the director's intention. This section prepares necessary information needed by the director planning module in chapter seven.

In the current SWAN version, the director's intention includes three aspects: the basic paradigm, the basic rhythms and their attitudes towards roles in the movie. For a more detailed syntax please see chapter seven, section 7.3.3.

Mode A: paradigm = realistic
Director's attitude: negative role (critique or sneer), positive role (sympathizing)
Plot Threads: thread1 (negative role's sabotage)
thread2 (positive role's experience)
Mode B: paradigm = realistic or terrifying
Director's attitude: negative role (critique or sneer), positive role (appreciating)
Plot Threads: thread1 (negative role's sabotage)
thread2 (positive role's experience)
Mode C: paradigm = realistic or heavy
Director's attitude: positive role (extolling)
Plot Threads: thread1 (positive role meets difficulty)
thread2 (positive role's effort to overwhelm the difficulty)
Mode D: paradigm = realistic or romantic
Director's attitude: positive and negative role (contrasting)
Plot Threads: thread1 (positive role's good moral)
thread2 (negative role's bad moral)

Mode E: paradigm = realistic or romantic
Director's attitude: defective role (depreciating)
Plot Threads: thread1 (defective role does wrong action)
thread2 (other people's critique)
Mode F: paradigm = realistic
Director's attitude: positive role (introducing and appreciating)
Plot Threads: thread1 (positive role meets difficulty)
thread2 (positive role's effort to overwhelm the difficulty)
Mode G: paradigm = heavy or sorrow
Director's attitude: positive role (appreciating and sympathizing, or extolling and sympathizing)
Plot Threads: thread1 (positive role's sacrifice and suffering)
thread2 (other people's happiness or indifference)
Mode H: paradigm = realistic
Director's attitude: positive role (sympathizing), negative role (critique)
Plot Threads: thread1 (positive role's selfless help)
thread2 (negative role's sham thankfulness)
Mode I: paradigm = realistic or terrifying
Director's attitude: positive role (extolling)
Plot Threads: thread1 (positive role's selfless help)
thread2 (other people's happiness and thankfulness)

Mode J: paradigm = heavy
Director's attitude: positive role (sympathizing)
Plot Threads: thread1 (positive role's dream for a better fate)
thread1 (positive role fails to have a better fate and suffers from pain)
thread2 (other people's happiness or indifference)
Mode K : Paradigm = realistic
Director's attitude: defective role (critique and encouraging)
Thread1 (defective role's bad behavior)
Thread2 (Other people's generosity)

5.4.5 Construct New Patterns

5.4.5.1 The C Calculus

In the last section, we have used the concept of CC-chains to define story patterns (modes of development threads). We have also explained how to use them to analyze a story for obtaining useful information. This approach seems to be promising if the final CC-chain we got from the story exists also in our knowledge base.

But in fact it is impossible to exhaust all possible CC-chains of children stories. That means it is impossible to establish a complete knowledge base of story patterns. In order to be able to analyze as many stories as possible, we introduce the idea of going ahead in the following way. First we collect a basic set of most typical CC-chains. Then we use some operations to construct new CC-chains , like the following ones. Note that to allow the construction of new story patterns does not mean we might do everything wantonly and willfully. There are limitations for each operation.

Definition 5.4.2 (Construction of New Story Patterns)

1. Concatenation: CC-chain 1 + CC-chain 2
Condition : the output of the first CC-chain should be equal to the input of the second one.
Or, the roles in the two CC-chains are not identical.
By "output" we mean the outcome of the main roles at the end of the CC-chain and by "input" we mean the initial specification of the main roles.
2. Refinement: One or more CC-chain 1 sentences are refined in a complete CC-chain 2.
By "refinement" we mean replacing an abstract statement of one CC-chain by the "Repeat …
End of Repeat" part of another CC-chain
The replacement stated above is either in semantic sense or in pragmatic sense.
2.1. It may be done in a sense of semantic equivalence, like:
"Role x is happy" may be replaced by a "happy story pattern"
"Role x is unhappy" may be replaced by a "unhappy story pattern"

"Role x succeed" may be replaced by a "success story pattern"
"Role x fail" may be replaced by a "fail story pattern"
"Role x do right action" may be replaced by a "right action story pattern"
"Role x do wrong action" may be replaced by a "wrong action story pattern"

2.2. It may also be done in a sense of pragmatic equivalence, like:
"Role x is lucky" may be replaced by a "success story pattern"
"Role x is not lucky" may be replaced by a "fail story pattern"
"Role x is happy" may be replaced by a "success story pattern"
"Role x is unhappy" may be replaced by a "fail story pattern"

3. Fusion: CC-chain 1 and CC-chain 2 will be mixed.
Condition : The input of the first CC-chain should be equal to that of the second CC-chain.
By "fusion" we mean the interleaving of copies of repeat bodies (a repeat body is that part of a CC-chain, which is between "Repeat" and "End of Repeat") of the two CC-chains. Note that each of the copies will be kept as an integrated whole and will not be decomposed.
Sub-cases of fusion :
3.1. Insert : By "insert" we mean the insertion of the whole "Repeat ... End of Repeat" part of one CC-chain into two copies of the repeat body of another CC-chain.
3.2. Overlap : By "overlap" we mean for each copy x of the repeat body of the first CC-chain there is at least one copy y of that of the second CC-chain, which is after x.
3.3. Contain : By "contain" we mean for each copy x of the repeat body of the second CC-chain there are at least two copies y and z of that of the first CC-chain, such that y is before x and z is after x.

4. Fill up: One CC-chain + details
Insert Nil statements at some places of a CC-chain.

We call the algebraic closure of the operations above the C calculus.

One will soon ask at least three questions. The first question is the usability of the newly constructed CC-chains. In most cases, they will be no more typical for representing development threads of children stories. One will hardly find children stories which match the new CC-chains well. The second question is whether the new CC-chain can still be assigned a meaningful theme, as we have done for the original CC-chains. The third question is: if it is possible to assign a new theme to the new CC-chain, is it possible to construct this new theme from the old ones? Does there exist a feasible algorithm which allows us to "compose" the new theme in this way?

All these questions can be answered with one reason. In fact, when we designed our story patterns above, we have oversimplified the structure of a story. It is rather rare that a story has only one simple structure. It is much more frequently that a (long) story has to be decomposed in several episodes, of which each has a different structure, a different theme, a different paradigm and different rhythms, etc. In order to parse such stories, one needs to construct new CC-chains to understand this complicated structure.

5.4.5.2 Use Incomplete Matching

If the existing story patterns do not match the current story, we may use our C calculus presented in the last section to construct new story patterns by using the reconstruction operators. But what can we do if this approach (the C calculus) fails, too? In this section, we introduce another way of utilizing the CC-chain concept. Taking in account that the contradiction and conflicts information presented in a story may be (and in fact, it is often so) incomplete, we allow imperfect matching between the patterns and the real CC-chains. Based on a similar idea of the conceptual dependency theory of Schank, we may use it as a tool to dig out the potential contradictions and conflicts information which is implied in the story, but which is not stated explicitly by the author, and then to use this information to complete the story in plot and act planning (see chapter six).

Definition 5.4.3

A story pattern P is said to match the CC-chain S of a story completely if P and S can be made identical by performing the following operations.

1. Delete the role description of P.
2. Instantiate each loop sentence (Repeat) in P to a finite sequence of repeated SB sentences.

Definition 5.4.4

A story pattern P is said to match the CC-chain S of a story strongly if P and S can be made identical by performing the following operations:

1. All operations mentioned in definition 5.4.2.
2. Delete some or all Nil sentences in P and S.

Definition 5.4.5

A story pattern P is said to match the CC-chain S of a story weakly if P and S can be made identical by performing the following operations.

1. All operations mentioned in definition 5.4.3.
2. Delete all SB sentences from P and S, which can be derived from the remaining SB sentences of P and S.

Let us take the crocodile and monkey story as an example. It can be seen easily that in the range of the eleven modes given above, the best match happens between the story and mode B. Using mode B to develop the abstract of the story, we get (the new SB representation without the original text):

1. L1: Crocodile give monkey wrong information by telling [crocodile want [crocodile help monkey by doing E1]].

2. L2: Monkey believe [crocodile want [crocodile help monkey by doing E1]].
   Monkey is happy due to L2.
   L3: Crocodile succeed due to L2.
   Crocodile is happy due to L3.
3. Crocodile damage monkey by doing E3.
4. Monkey is unhappy due to E3.
5. Crocodile give monkey right information by telling [crocodile want [crocodile damage monkey by doing E4]].
   Monkey is unhappy due to [crocodile want [crocodile damage monkey by doing E4]].
6. Monkey want [monkey help monkey by L4]
   L4: Monkey give crocodile wrong information by telling I1.
7. L5: Crocodile believe [monkey want [monkey help crocodile by telling I1]].
   L6: Crocodile do wrong action E4.
   Monkey succeed due to L4.
8. L7: Monkey damage crocodile by doing E4.
   Crocodile is unhappy due to L7.
9. Crocodile fail due to E5.
   Monkey succeed due to E5.

5.5 Semantic Disambiguation Based on Deep Commonsense Reasoning

5.5.1 The Anaphora Problem Revisited

In chapter three, section 3.5, we have engaged in resolving the anaphora problem of our Snow White story. We could not be sure of the correctness of the solution we obtained there, because in section 3.5 we could only use pure linguistic knowledge and shallow commonsense reasoning. After that we have introduced techniques for analyzing a story in chapter four and the preceding sections of this chapter, we are now able to do some deep commonsense reasoning for solving this problem at a higher level. The key for completing this task is to rely on the mental activities of roles in the story.

Definition 5.5.1

For each role x of a story, any sentence of this story, which mentions x, provides a behavioral item of this role. We say also that it provides a behavioral item of the agent corresponding to this role. This behavioral item can be

1. An action performed by x.
2. An action performed upon x by somebody else.
3. A state of x.

The sequence of behavioral items of x (arranged according to its time order) in the whole story is called the behavior of x. In case that we have a role specific development thread d for x, all information about x's behavior is contained in d.

We simulate each role in a story with an agent and will use multi agent techniques to analyze each agent's behavior. We sketch the basic idea of the algorithm as follows:

Algorithm 5.5.1

1. While parsing a story (by using the conventional natural language understanding techniques), assign an agent to each noun (called noun agent) and to each occurrence of every pronoun (called pronoun agent).
2. Record the behavior of each agent. All behavioral items are marked with time scale.
3. At the end of story parsing (without solving the anaphora problem), fetch the corresponding commonsense knowledge (see chapter ten) from the knowledge base, including
   3.1. those commonsense agents which correspond to the noun agents constructed from the story.
   3.2. those commonsense agents which contain knowledge about the concepts which occur in agents description of the story, and which are useful when solving the anaphora problem.
4. Combine the commonsense agents fetched from the knowledge base with the corresponding noun agents in the story respectively. The noun agents with this additional commonsense knowledge are called enriched noun agents.
5. For each pronoun agent, the anaphora solver invites bids from all other agents which are now newly produced enriched agents and represent nouns. We call them enriched agents. Each bid protocol is attached with a specification of the pronoun's characteristics.
6. Each enriched agent makes use of linguistic theory and/or commonsense knowledge to decide whether it should submit a bid with corresponding reasons.
7. The anaphora solver compares and analyzes the reasons of the bidder. It makes also a commonsense based inference to decide about which enriched agent the current pronoun agent denotes.
8. The anaphora solver combines the current pronoun agent with the enriched agent it denotes. It obtains thus a new enriched agent (to replace the old one).
9. The anaphora solver uses the result of this step to modify all other enriched agents and the remaining pronoun agents.
10. Perform the above steps further until there is no pronoun agent remaining anymore.

End of Algorithm

Let us consider the anaphora problem of the Snow White story once again. We copy both the anaphorical version (with pronouns) and the hypothetical version (with the pronouns replaced by nouns, based on linguistic knowledge and shallow commonsense knowledge only) in the following. We will attack this problem once again and try to get a better solution by inferring a new hypothetical version, based on deep commonsense reasoning.

First we copy the anaphorical version of the story as follows.

"The mother of Princess Snow White died. She (1) was very sad. The king married a new queen. The magic mirror told her (2) that she (3) is more beautiful than her (4). She (5) was very jealous . She (6) let a hunter kill her (7). He (8) set her (9) free. Seven dwarfs accepted her (10). It (11) told this to her (12). She (13) became a peasant woman. She (14) gave a poisonous apple to her (15). She (16) ate it (17) and died. The prince came and saw her (18) dead. He (19) rescued her (20). He (21) killed her (22). He (23) married her (24)."

Then we reproduce the hypothetical version. We list also the weights of the winner candidates and other competitors which were calculated in chapter three, where we omit all negative weights because they have the veto and can not become positive by adding some possible deep commonsense knowledge to it.

The mother of Princess Snow White died. Snow White (2.02/1.02) was very sad. The king married a new queen. The magic mirror told the new queen (2.05/1.05, Snow White: 3/2) that the new queen (2.02/1.02, Snow White: 4/3) is more beautiful than Snow White (4/3, new queen: 1) . The new queen (2, Snow White: 2.01/1.01) was very jealous. The new queen (2, Snow White: 3.07/2.07) let a hunter kill Snow White (3.14/2.14, new queen: 1) . The hunter (2.03/1.03, king: 6/5) set the new queen (2, Snow White: 2.04/1.04) free. Seven dwarfs accepted the new queen (2.05/1.05, Snow White: 3.11/2.11) . The magic mirror (7/6) told this to the new queen (2.05/1.05, 4.2/3.2) . The new queen (2.01/1.01, Snow White: 5.23/4.23) became a peasant woman. The peasant woman (2.01/1.01, Snow White: 6.3/5.3) gave a poisonous apple to Snow White (6.38/5.38, peasant woman: 1). The peasant woman (2, Snow White: 2.01/1.01) ate the poisonous apple (2.07/1.07, magic mirror: 4/3) and died. The prince came and saw the peasant woman (2, mother of Snow White: 14/13) dead. The prince (2, king: 13/12, hunter: 8/7) rescued the peasant woman (2.05/1.05, Snow White: 4.22/3.22). The prince (2, king: 14/13, hunter: 9/8) killed the peasant woman (2.04/1.04, Snow White: 5.28/4.28). The prince (2, king: 15/14, hunter: 10/9) married Snow White (6.34/5.34).

5.5.2 A Solution Based on Deep Commonsense Knowledge

In the anaphorical version of the above story, most of the role occurrences appear in form of pronouns. Since the equivalence between the different occurrences of pronouns is yet unclear, the number of apparent roles (= 24) is too much and thus the information about roles' behavior is distributed to this large set of apparent roles. This situation makes our job much more difficult. It is understandable that the commonsense knowledge used to analyze this story is quite massive. It would be too much to list all rules in their exact Young Pine grammar form or temporal grammar form. We will rather state them in some quasi natural language format.

The rules which we will list below for solving our anaphora problem, in addition to the shallow commonsense knowledge mentioned in chapter three, are of the nature of deep commonsense knowledge. The power of deep commonsense knowledge in decision making is not bigger than that of shallow commonsense knowledge as its name might suppose. In fact, the shallow commonsense knowledge forms "hard" rules for resolving semantic ambiguity, while the deep commonsense knowledge forms only "soft" rules for doing the same job. The reason is that most of the deep commonsense knowledge rules are only heuristic rules. In many cases, they are quite plausible and can be used to inference a conclusion with high certainty. But they are not, as the shallow commonsense knowledge rules do, so powerful that they can not be violated in people's daily life (In the fantastic world of children stories, all rules of commonsense may be violated). For every deep commonsense rule, we may have exceptions.

We have mentioned the plan based speech understanding approach of Cohen and Perrault in chapter one. Here we will borrow some idea from their approach and from the speech-act theory. It is easy to see the following insufficiencies of the Cohen-Perrault approach for our purpose of story understanding:

1. It deals only with pure predicates, not making use of any knowledge outside of the predicate calculus. Therefore, its power is limited. For example, the proposition "one should eat in order to live" is not an axiom nor a result of inference in the axiom system of Cohen and Perrault.
2. It follows the honesty principle of the speech-act theory of Searle. For example, the axiom W3 says that if you want somebody believe something then you should yourself believe it. This limitation excludes many complex phenomena in conventional stories, for example cheating.
3. It describes only the static states of human believes and human desires. It fails to describe the transformation of these states.
4. It does not involve the description and processing of human sentiment which is very important in understanding a story.

Based on this analysis, we have proposed a new approach which is aiming at including the mental factors of story analysis which have been neglected by other researchers. They are given in form of axioms. There are two kinds of axioms: the conditional axioms and the default axioms. A default axiom DA means: DA is valid unless some adverse situation is stated. For example, a default axiom says that every person is a good person. Once a person commits some crimes, this person becomes a bad person. We have introduced such kind of axioms in order to avoid the well known negation problem. And this is a partial solution to the closed world assumption. The axioms are formulated with a few keywords, where BELIEVE, WANT and FEEL are the most essential keywords. Keywords can be nested. There are two kinds of keywords: the state keywords and the action keywords (both called operators) whose meaning can be roughly explained as follows:

State1 → State2: State2 can be inferred from State1.
State1 → Action1: Action1 may happen under State1.

Action1 → State1: Action1 produces State1 and deletes any state contradicting State1.
Action1 → Action2: The result of Action1 includes that of Action2.

BELIEVE, WANT and FEEL are all system keywords. These axioms are useful but not complete. Some of them are included with the particular care of the example story above. Some of the axioms are of second order.

Meta Axioms:
M1: ANY OPERATOR (x, y) => BELIEVE (x, ANY OPERATOR (x, y))
M2: ANY OPERATOR (x, y) <=> not (not (ANY OPERATOR (x, y))
M3: ANY OPERATOR (x, y) or ANY OPERATOR (x, z) => ANY OPERATOR (x, (y or z))
M4: ANY OPERATOR (x, y) and ANY OPERATOR (x, z) => ANY OPERATOR (x, (y and z))

The BELIEVE Axioms :
B1: BELIEVE (x, all true statements of the predicate calculus)
B2: BELIEVE (x, all true statements derived from the Pangu knowledge base)
B3: inform (x, y, z) => BELIEVE (y, z)

The WANT Axioms:
W1: is-good-for (x, y) => WANT (y, x)
W2: has (x, y) => not (WANT (z, give (z, x, y)))
W3: BELIEVE (z, BELIEVE (x, y))=> not (WANT (z, inform (z, x, y)))

The Ability Axioms:
A1: more-powerful (x, y) => more-possible (let (x, z, do (z, w)), let (y, z, do (z, w)))
A2: disabled (x) => not (enabled (x))
A3: disabled (x) => ~ there exists y, and action X, X (x, y)
A4: disabled (x) => ~ there exist y, z and action X, X (x, y, z)

The Need Axioms:
N1: is-necessary (y, x) => need (x, y)
N2: WANT (x, do-harm (x, y)), more-powerful (x, y) => need (y, help)

The Axioms of Feelings and Sentiment:
F1: FEEL (a, x) => BELIEVE (b, FEEL (a, x))
F2: get (x, y), is-good-for (y, x) => FEEL (x, happy)
F3: lose (x, y), is-good-for (y, x) => FEEL (x, unhappy)
F4: get (x, y), is-bad-for (y, x) => FEEL (x, unhappy)
F5: lose (x, y), is-bad-for (y, x) => FEEL (x, happy)
F6: more-x (y, z), is-good-for (x, z) => FEEL (z, unhappy)

The Existence Axioms:
E1: is-born (x) => enabled (x)
E2: died (x) => disabled (x)
E3: become (x, y) => not-exist (x), exist (y)

E4: Default: person (x) => enabled (x)
E5: enabled (x) => not (disabled (x))
E6: exist (x) => enabled (x)
E7: not-exist (x) => disabled (x)

The Relation Axioms:
R1: good relation (x, y) => good relation (y, x)
R2: relative (x, y) => good relation (x, y)
R3: good relation (x, y) => friendly (x, y)

The Object Passing Axioms:
O1: give (x, y, z) => is-possessed -by (z, y)
O2: is-possessed-by (z, y) <=> possess (y, z)
O3: not (is-possessed-by (x, x))

The Good and Bad Axioms:
G1: good-for (x, y) => not (is-bad-for (x, y))
G2: good relation (x, y) => is-good-for (x, y)
G3: useful things (x), person (y) => is-good-for (x, y)
G4: Default: person (x) => good person (x)

The Comparison Axioms:
C1: more-x (y, z) => not (more-x (z, y))
C2: not (more-x (y, y))

The Help Axioms:
H1: friendly (x, y), in-danger (y) => liberate (x, y)
H2: friendly (x, y) => help (x, y)
H3: good person (x), good person (y), need (y, help) => help (x, y)
H4: good person (x), good person (y), in-danger (y) => liberate (x, y)
H5: help (x, y) => BELIEVE (x, help (x, y))
H6: help (x, y) => BELIEVE (y, help (x, y))
H7: disabled (x) => there is y, liberate (y, x)
H8: disabled (x), liberate (y, x) => enabled (x)
H9: help (x, y) => not (do-harm (x, y))

The Axioms of Contradictions:
CT1: BELIEF (x, more-y (z, x)), is-good-for (y, x) => dislike (x, z)
CT2: BELIEF (x, do-harm(y, x)) => dislike (x, y)
CT3: dislike (x, y) => not (friendly (x, y))
CT4: bad relation (x, y) => not (friendly (x, y))
CT5: do-harm (x, y) => BELIEVE (x, do-harm (x, y))
CT6: do-harm (x, y) => BELIEVE (y, do-harm (x, y))

The Axioms of Conflicts:
CF1: not (friendly (x, y)) => do-harm (x, y)
CF2: Default: not (do-harm (x, x))
CF3: let (x, y, do-harm (y, z)) => do-harm (x, z)
CF4: do-harm (x, y) => in-danger (y)

CF5: liberate (x, y) => in-safety (y)
CF6: in-danger (x) => not (in-safety (x))
CF7: is-dangerous-thing (x), give (y, z, x) => do-harm (y, z)

Commonsense Facts:

1. Beautiful, kind, strong, wise, clever, ...are good for every one.
2. Awful, ill, weak, ... are bad for every one.
3. Jealous, sad, angry, ... are unhappy feelings.
4. Satisfied, ... are happy feeling.
5. Father, mother, husband, wife, son, daughter, etc. are relatives.
6. Emperor, king, queen, prince, princess, ... are royal members.
7. Worker, peasant, hunter, ... are common persons.
8. Apple, orange, bread, ..., are food.
9. Food, house, cloth, ... are good things and needed by everybody.
10. Poisonous food, dirty food, snake, ..., are dangerous things.
11. To kill, beat, hit, abuse, ... somebody, is to do harm to this person.
12. To set free, rescue, ... somebody, is to liberate this person.
13. To liberate, accept, receive, ...somebody, is to help this person.
14. To eat, drink, beat, burn, ... something, is to process it.
15. More-powerful (royal member, common person)

Now we build the agents, one for each role and one for each occurrence of pronouns. Thus, we obtain in total 34 agents. Since we have deliberately created as many pronouns as we can, too many agents are produced. At the beginning of the parsing, there is very little to say about each agent.

1. The mother of Snow White is a family member of Snow White. According to the FEEL axioms it is reasonable that Snow White feels sad due to her mother's death. Therefore Snow White obtains an extra weight of +1 in the bidding for the quality of replacing her (1).
2. Since the magic mirror told her (2) the information that she (3) is more beautiful than her (4), according to the BELIEF axioms it is to conclude that her (2) now knows this information.
3. According to the FEEL axioms, if her (4) knows this information, her (4) would be jealous.
4. Now she (5) is very jealous. So it is plausible to believe that she (5) is equal to her (4), if one has reason to prove that she (5) knows this information.
5. If we assume that her (2) is equal to her (4), then we get a reasonable (partial) solution: Her (2) = her (4) = she (5).
6. According to the comparison axioms, it is impossible that x is more beautiful than x, therefore she (3) is not equal to her (4).
7. According to the axioms of contradictions and conflicts, it is reasonable to conclude that she (6) = she (5), since these axioms suggest she (6) = she (5) and her (7) = she (3).
8. It is not plausible that she (6) is equal to her (7) according to the conflicts axioms.

9. He (8) may be the king or the hunter according to the relation axioms. As a result of competition, the hunter wins the bid because the sentence where he appears is more close to her (9) than that sentence where the king appears.
10. Her (9) is not equal to she (6), because "set free" is a liberate action. According to the context, she (6) is not in danger and does not need a liberation. That person who is in danger is her (7).
11. Therefore, her (9) must be equal to her (7), because there are only two women.
12. No new information provided by deep commonsense knowledge. Her (10) is equal to her (9) according to the linguistic knowledge and shallow commonsense rules in chapter three..
13. It (11) = magic mirror. This is the only possible solution.
14. Her (12) is not equal to her (10). Reason: In the sentence "It (11) told this to her (12)" the meaning of the word "this" is not exactly specified. But according to the linguistic knowledge stored in our knowledge base, it includes at least the content of the previous sentence: "Seven dwarfs accepted her (10)". But her (10) knows it already according to the help axioms, note that "accept" is a kind of help. The magic mirror does not need to tell this to her (10) according to the want axioms. Therefore, we have her (12) = she (6).
15. There is no hint from the commonsense knowledge to solve the anaphora of she (13). We can only use linguistic knowledge to assume that she (13) = her (12), because the position of her (12) in the text is most close to she (13).
16. Beginning from this point, we may assume that the woman who is denoted by she (13) (= her (12) = she (6) = she (5) = her (4) = her (2)) disappears and a new woman, the peasant woman, appears according to the existence axioms.
17. She (14) = the peasant woman, based on the linguistic knowledge, because this is the woman whose position in the text is most close to she (14).
18. Her (15) is not equal to she (14), because "poisonous apple" is a dangerous thing, which nobody will give to him/her self according to the conflict axioms.
19. Therefore, her (15) = her (10).
20. Two non-living things: the magic mirror and the poisonous apple, compete for the pronoun "it (17)". The apple is the winner, because one can not eat a mirror according to commonsense knowledge.
21. Thus, she (16) = her (15) according to the object passing axioms.

    Another reason for she (16) = her (15) is that her (15) is the woman most close to she (16).
22. Two women: the mother of Snow White and she (16) compete for the pronoun "her (18)". She (16) is the winner of the bid because this is the woman whose position in the text is most close to her (18).
23. He (19) = the prince, because prince is the man whose position in the text is most close to he (19).
24. According to existence axioms and help axioms, her (20) = she (16), who is now enabled again.
25. He (23) = he (21) = he (19), because the distance between he (21) and he (19), and that between he (23) = he (21) are the shortest ones.

26. Her (22) is not equal to her (20), because there is no reason that the prince first rescues somebody and then kills her right away according to the help axioms.
27. Therefore, her (22) = her (14) = peasant woman.
28. According to the existence axioms, her (24) is not equal to the peasant woman, neither is she equal to the mother of Snow White, because both of them are now dead, and thus disabled.
29. Therefore, her (24) = Snow White, the only remaining woman.
30. On the other hand, her (24) is assumed to be equal to her (20), i.e. that woman, whose position in the text is most close to her (24) among all female pronouns who are still living.

As a result the anaphora problem is solved in the following way:

She (1) = her (3) = her (7) = her (9) = her (10) = her (15) = she (16) = her (18) = her (20) = her (24) = Snow White.
Her (2) = her (4) = she (5) = she (6) = her (12) = she (13) = the new queen.
She (14) = her (22) = the peasant woman.
He (8) = the hunter.
He (19) = he (21) = he (23) = the prince.
It (11) = the magic mirror.
It (17) = the poisonous apple.

We have recovered the story as follows:

"The mother of Princess Snow White died. Snow White was very sad. The king married a new queen. The magic mirror told the new queen that Snow White is more beautiful than the new queen. The new queen was very jealous . The new queen let a hunter kill Snow White. The hunter set Snow White free. Seven dwarfs accepted Snow White. The magic mirror told this to the new queen. The new queen became a peasant woman. The peasant woman gave a poisonous apple to Snow White. Snow White ate the poisonous apple and died. The prince came and saw Snow White dead. The prince rescued Snow White. The prince killed the peasant woman. The prince married Snow White."

The thus recovered story is a little bit different than the original one in that the prince kills the peasant woman rather than the new queen. This is understandable, since it is not stated in the story that the peasant woman has been turned back into the new queen again. At that moment, the new queen does not exist anymore. So the woman the prince kills can only be the peasant woman. Apart from that, the recovered story is equal to the original one. Note also that we have not exhausted all possibilities of using commonsense knowledge in the analysis of this story. To use more commonsense knowledge, we should have much more strong axioms.

6 Plot Planning and Act Planning

A story is not a script ready for shooting. To make a film, one has to adapt the story into a script. In order to transform a story into a script, the first thing the script adapter has to do is to grasp the main idea of the story as the basis of the film to be produced. In chapter four, and especially in chapter five, we have shown how SWAN tries to perform this task as good as it can.

The second thing a film adapter has to do is the design of a general framework of the film he wants to shoot. In doing this, he has to play the role of a filter which selects only the most important parts of the story to be incorporated in the film. He has to reconfigure these selected parts to an integrated form suitable for film presentation. For the computer, this is a very difficult task. We have not yet implemented it in the current version of SWAN. For the present, we assume that every event contained in the story is important and should be accepted to the script.

The third thing a film adapter has to do is to produce the script itself. There are different opinions about the definition of the script concept. While the cameraman defines a script as consisting of a series of camera shoots, we define it as consisting of a series of scenes. In this chapter we only do the first step towards the production of a script. Namely, we produce only a series of acts. We call it act planning. For the difference between an act and a scene see below. The production of a complete script is the task of the film director and will be described in chapters seven, eight and nine.

What is an act? Roughly speaking, an act is a continuous piece of plot presentation, continuous both in the sense of time and space. For example, that part of a wedding which has happened in some church forms an act. Another part of this wedding which happened later on the street forms another act. There may be a second wedding on the same day and in the same church. It is then again another act of our script.

In act planning, all the events, which appear in the original story and may seem to be abstract, have to be instantiated to concrete ones. Let us take the word "married" in the sentence "The prince married Snow White" as an example. The event "marry" is an abstract one, since it does not say anything about the procedure of the wedding, which may have a great deal of different forms. A cartoon is unable to show an abstract "wedding" event to the audience. It is thus a job of the SWAN system to produce an implementation for each of such abstract events. On the other hand, an "event" in a story can also be just a state description. For example: "The new queen is very jealous" is a description of the mental state of the new queen. But in order to let the audience be able to observe it, one often has to find some action to make this mental state visible to the audience. In this way, we are

R. Lu and S. Zhang: Automatic Generation of Computer Animation, LNAI 2160, pp. 173-228, 2002.

also transforming an abstract event into a concrete one. We call these transformations the plot planning.

It is easy to see that, from the point of view of the implementation, the plot planning mentioned above should precede the act planning, because the sequence of acts can only be determined after the abstract events are instantiated. Therefore we start from plot planning. After that all events are turned into concrete ones, we will be able to do the second task: divide the series of concrete events into acts.

6.1 A Knowledge Base of Dramas and Plots

Before going into details, let us clarify some important concepts once again to avoid ambiguities of understanding.

Definition 6.1.1

1. Event: A concrete action, abstract action or a state described by a GF2 action statement, henceforth called a frame statement (for a detailed meaning of a frame statement see definition 6.1.5).
2. Action: The same as an event.
3. Concrete Action: An action whose implementation can be found in the action library (chapter ten). It is also called a macro action.
4. Abstract action: An action which does not have an implementation in the action library and, in order to be implemented, must be replaced by a set of other abstract or concrete actions.
5. Plot Agent: An agent of the SWAN commonsense knowledge base whose presentation part consists of a set of concrete actions and is an implementation of some abstract action.
6. Drama Agent (Drama Plan): An agent of the SWAN commonsense knowledge base whose presentation part is an implementation of some abstract action and consists of a set of calls to drama agents and/or plot agents.
7. Movie Agent: drama agent or plot agent.
8. Act: A set of concrete actions which form the plot specification part of a scene. The temporal relations among them are qualitatively determined. These actions are continuous in time and happen in the same space.
9. Plot: The content of an act.
10. Scene: A program module of the Rainbow language, which roughly consists of a plot specification (i.e. act) plus a camera plan and a light plan. Let us make a metaphor: an act is that which we see from a drama in a theatre. A scene is that which we see from a movie in a cinema.
11. Shot: A unit of a camera plan, together with the concrete actions this unit of camera plan is made for. The result of its shooting will be a shot in the sense of a traditional movie.
12. Script: A sequence of scenes which is the result of implementing a story.
13. Plot Planning: Transform a story (consisting of a set of concrete and/or abstract actions) into a set consisting of concrete actions only.

14.Act Planning: After the plot planning is done, group the concrete actions into a set of acts.
15.Scene Planning: Act planning plus camera planning and light planning.

6.1.1 A Hierarchy of Drama Agents and Plot Agents

Generally speaking, a movie agent represents a basic unit of a story. For example, a wedding, a funeral, a ball, a meeting, a tour, etc. each of these may form the content of a movie agent in our sense. The movie agents are organized in a knowledge base, called movie base, which is a part of our general commonsense knowledge base (see chapter ten). There are movie classes and movie instances. They form a hierarchy in the knowledge base. The leaf nodes of the hierarchy are movie instances, others are movie classes. Each movie instance or movie class, which is not the root of the hierarchy, inherits attributes and values from its ancestors. A set of selection rules are used when there are more than one movie agent corresponding to the same "abstract action". Of course human interference should also be possible at this point.

The background of this representation is the theory of conceptual dependency and that of scripts developed by Schank which originally belongs to the research area of natural language understanding. The intended use of these theories was to make the job of understanding natural language texts (more specially, that of understanding story texts) by computers easier. In our case, we let the things go in another direction. We use these theories to develop a technique, by which the computers can write stories themselves based on a given abstract of the story. That means, the computer may "imagine a story". We have used the idea of Schank in SWAN to animate those actions in a story, which are not atomic and some times abstract.

Example 6.1.1

For the event "wedding" we have the following tree of wedding classes:

#wedding
  #wedding in western
    #wedding in ancient western
      #wedding of royal family members
      #wedding of other people
        #wedding of very rich people
        #wedding of citizens living in a city
        #wedding of peasants
    #wedding in modern western
      #wedding of citizens living in a city
      #wedding of peasants
  #wedding in China
    ....

6.1.2 Generalized Case Frames and Basic Plot Representation

Though the concept "agent" is used everywhere in our SWAN system, its structure is different depending on the role it plays in different parts of SWAN. In this plot planning module, the internal structure of each movie agent is organized as follows: first the head of the agent, then the identifier of the father agent (class), then the list of conditional child agents, which represent the refinements of the plot. The degree of the richness of the content of the future animation depends on the degree of refinement of the movie classes. A conditional child name consists of a condition followed by the name of a child class or a child instance. (For example, if the current agent is "wedding", then its refinements may be: is the bridegroom a rich Arabian salesman? (rich Arabian salesman wedding) Is the bride a Moslem? (Moslem wedding). Is this an ancient time wedding? Etc.) . The core of a movie agent is the movie declaration which consists of a series of action statements and control statements.

There are two kinds of movie agents in our plot planning module. Agents of the first kind, called drama agents, contain knowledge at drama level. It specifies the composition of a drama (abstract event) from a set of other dramas (abstract events). Agents of the second kind, called plot agents, contain knowledge at concrete action level. It specifies the composition of a drama (abstract event) from a set of concrete actions. These two kinds of agents have many aspects in common, but also have some important differences. For example, the drama agents do not need to contain background specification, because each such drama contains multiple calls to different other dramas which may need different backgrounds.

Definition 6.1.2 (Simplified Syntax of Drama Agents and Plot Agents)

```
<Movie Agent> ::=
DRAMA AGENT ( <Agent Name> ):
    Father :  < Father >
    Child : <Child>
    Drama Description Begin:
        [<Drama Specification Part>]
    Drama Description End
    [T-Specification : <Sequence of Temporal Constraints> ]
    [Candidate:  [Object : < Sequence of Objects >]
            [Role : < Sequence of Roles > ]
            [Action: <Sequence of Action Names>]]
END (<Agent Name>)

| PLOT AGENT ( <Agent Name> ):
    Father :  < Father >
    Child : < Child >
    Plot Description Begin:
        [<Plot Specification Part>]
    Plot Description End
    [T-Specification : <Sequence of Temporal Constraints>]
```

```
   [Candidate: [Background: <Sequence of Backgrounds>]
          [Object : < Sequence of Objects >]
          [Role : < Sequence of Roles >]
          [Action: <Sequence of Action Names>]]
END (<Agent Name>)
  <Father> ::= <Father Name> | None
  <Child> ::= < Sequence of Guarded Childs > | None
  <Drama Specification Part> ::= [Object : < Sequence of Objects >]
                    [Role : < Sequence of Roles > ]
            [Presentation : < First Kind Sequence of Generalized Case Frames >]
  <Plot Specification Part> ::=  [Background : < Environment >]
                    [Object : < Sequence of Objects >]
                    [Role : < Sequence of Roles > ]
         [Presentation : < Second Kind Sequence of Generalized Case Frames >]

  <Guarded Child> ::= <Guard> → <Child Agent Name>
  <Guard> ::= <Group of Guard Elements>
  <Guard Element> ::= <Type> = <Attribute Value>
            | Type (<Type>) = <Type> | Value (<Type>) = <Attribute Value>
            | <Logic Formula>
  <Environment> ::= <Background Name> | <Time Name> | <Weather Name>
            | <Background> | <other Name>
  <Type> ::= <Role Type> | <Object Type> | <Environment Type>
  <Environment Type> ::= <Background Type> | <Time Type>
            | <Weather Type> | ...
  <Role Type> ::= Human | Man | Woman | ...
  <Object Type> ::= Tree | Table | Car | ...
  <Background Type> ::= Street | Room | Building | ...
  <Time Type> ::= Time | Times | Season | ...
  <Weather Type> ::= Weather
  <Attribute Value> ::= <Role Name> | <Object Name> | <Other Name>
  <Role> ::= <Role Type> (<Role Content>) | <Role Descriptor>
  <Object> ::= <Object Type> (<Object Content>) | <Object Descriptor>
  < Role Descriptor > ::= <Fuzzy Descriptor> . <Role Type>
  <Fuzzy Descriptor> ::= Some | Few | Many ......
  <Background> ::= <Background Type> (<Background Content>)
           | <Background Descriptor>
  <Background Descriptor> ::= <Fuzzy Descriptor> . <Background Type>
  <Background Content> ::= <Background Variable Name>
           | <Background Name>
  < Object Descriptor > ::= <Fuzzy Descriptor> . <Object Type>
  <Role Content> ::= <Role Variable Name> | <Role Name>
  <Object Content> ::= <Object Variable Name> | <Object Name>
  <Temporal Constraint> ::= <WFTF>
```

The Background, Roles and Objects are attributes of an agent. They are also called parameters of the agent since they behave like formal parameters when the agent is called for by other agents. The variable names in the same agent are unique. Repeating definitions are not allowed.

The T-Specification specifies the temporal relations between generalized case frames of an agent or of father and son agents. Having a time denotation is the main difference between them and the conventional case frame series. For the definition of WFTF see chapter five. Static consistency checks are needed to prevent it from temporal contradictions.

The definition of a drama or plot agent is used for unfolding an abstract action represented by this agent, together with its candidate part which is used to test the legality of merging some information of a given story with this agent. In another word, it tests the compatibility of a piece of information from the story with the information contained in the agent. For example, if the candidate part of the agent "wedding ceremony" does not contain any animal as its possible role, then any statement of a wedding story, which refers to a dog, will be considered as irrelevant to "wedding ceremony" and will be rejected to be included in the finally developed "wedding ceremony" plot. The exact meaning and use of the candidate part will be described in section 6.2.2.

Although we have not yet introduced the concrete syntax of generalized case frame statements, we will give examples at this place to easy the reading of the above syntax of drama and plot agent. The examples are very simple in that we do not use variables.

Example 6.1.2

```
DRAMA AGENT (Revolution) :
                    ......
 Drama Description Begin :
   Presentation :
                      ......
   (10)  Call (Demonstration; (3) : Number (People) = Many ),
   (11)  Call ( Abdicate; (1912) : Speed = Slowly ),
   (12)  Call (Cheers; (7) : Number (People) =  Many)
  Drama Description End
END (Revolution)
```

This is a drama of revolution, saying that after a demonstration of many people, the Last Emperor leaves his palace (see next example), followed by cheers of the people. The drama presentation consists of three call statements. Each of them calls a plot agent or another drama agent. The first call statement means: add a parameter "Number (People) = Marry" to the statement with label (3) in the agent "Demonstration" when calling it. The meanings of other call statements are similar. There is no T-Specification. That means the default: the three calls are temporally sequential.

Example 6.1.3

PLOT AGENT (Abdicate):
  Father: Moving
  Child: None
  Plot Description Begin:
    Background : Building (Forbidden City)
    Object : Vehicle (Dragon Car)
    Role : Human (Last Emperor)
    Presentation :
      ......
    (1912) Walk (Last Emperor, start = in-front-of (gate(Forbidden City)),
      end = by-side-of (Dragon Car))
      ......
  Plot Description End
END (Leave)

It says that the Last Emperor is leaving the Forbidden City in the way that he walks from the gate of the Forbidden City to his carriage.

Both examples have no variables. This simplification limits their use in plot and act planning. Below we will introduce agents with variables.

The job of an agent is multifold. First, it can be called for by the drama and plot planning module of SWAN directly, on the basis that the content of this agent matches the semantics of some abstract action in the story text. Second, it can be called for by some other agent which is not a child or a father of this agent, in a form similar to a macro expansion. The expansion mechanism will be described in algorithms 6.2.1, 6.2.2, 6.2.3 and 6.2.4. Thus, the presentation part of an agent may contain or even consist of a series of calls to other agents. This is an appropriate way of modularizing the organization of knowledge about plots. Third, its content may be inherited by some child agent. The way of inheritance will be described in algorithm 6.2.2 and 6.2.3. Fourth, it may serve as the start point of refinement, in any or all of the following sense: refinement of parameters, that of the presentation part and that of the temporal constraints.

At this place, some words should be said about the semantics of the transition process from father agents to child agents. If, during the drama planning, some agent X is selected, then, in most of the cases, both the parameters and the drama (or plot) presentation of X should be refined. This is implemented by forking into the child agents. In order to do that, the guards of all guarded child names will be tested as the basis for selecting a child. The principles are summarized in definition 6.1.3 and algorithm 6.2.4. Roughly speaking, the conditions (guards) in child selection are not indispensable for some child to be selected. Rather, they give priorities to those children who meet the conditions exactly, and prevent the selection of children who contradict the information provided by the story.

Definition 6.1.3 (Mechanism of Child Selection)

1. All children whose guards meet the real information of the story have the first priority. By "meet the real information" we mean the "best meet". That is, the

information contained in the agent should not be broader neither narrow than that provided by the story.
2. All children whose guards do not contradict the real information of the story have the second priority.
3. Any child all whose guards contradict the real information of the story can not be accepted as a candidate.

A precise definition of the child selecting procedure based on above mechanism will be given in algorithm 6.2.4.

In order to get information from a story to be compared with the guards, we need rules consisting of commonsense knowledge. The general purpose rules are stored in a commonsense knowledge base as described in last chapter and in chapter ten. The special purpose rules (related to the current agent) have similar forms as the general purpose ones, but are stored in the local knowledge base of each relevant agent.

Example 6.1.4

Assume the guarded children are:

Bridegroom = Chinese → wedding 1,
Bridegroom = Asian → wedding 2,
Bridegroom = European → wedding 3,
Bridegroom = Arabian → wedding 4

If the story says that the bridegroom is a Chinese, then wedding 2, 3 and 4 will not be selected, notwithstanding that a Chinese is also an Asian. Only wedding 1 is possible. On the other hand, if the story says only that the bridegroom is an Asian, then wedding 1, 3 and 4 will not be selected. If the story says that the bridegroom is a German, then wedding 3 will be selected. If the story says that the bridegroom is an American, then the procedure fails. No child can be selected. But if the story says nothing about the bridegroom, then all four wedding forms can be selected. In section 6.2.2 below, we will see other mechanisms of selecting children.

As it is shown in the structure of the drama agent above, the Presentation of a drama class or drama instance consists of a set of generalized case frames. Following is the static syntax and semantics of generalized case frames:

Definition 6.1.4 (Generalized Case Frames)

1. Each generalized case frame is either a frame statement or a frame variable.
2. Each generalized case frame is attached with a label, which has the form of a natural number.

<First Kind Sequence of Generalized Case Frames> ::=
<Sequence of Generalized Case Frames without Action Statements>
<Second Kind Sequence of Generalized Case Frames> ::=
<Sequence of Generalized Case Frames without Call Statements>
<Generalized Case Frame> ::= (<Label>) <GCF Without label>
<Label> ::= <Natural Number>

<GCF without label> ::= <Frame Variable> | <Frame Statement>
<Frame Variable> ::= FR <Frame Variable Name>

3. In each drama or plot presentation, the labels are unique. That means, no two frame statements, or two frame variables, or a frame statement and a frame variable, may have the same label.
4. If a frame statement S of a plot or drama agent ag which is not a root agent is not a replace statement, nor an enrich statement, then it must be mentioned by some replace statement. That is, there must be a replace statement:
   Replace anc(n) with (m)
   Where m is the label of S, or is the label of another statement containing S.
5. No root agent contains a replace statement or an enrich statement.

Definition 6.1.5 (Frame Statements)

There are eight types of different frame statements:

<Frame Statement> ::= <Action Statement> | <Enrich Statement>
| <Call Statement>
<Conditional Statement> | <Case Statement> | <Loop Statement>
<Bloc Statement> | <Replace Statement>

We list the syntax and semantics of each kind of frame statements in the following:

1. Action Statement, which denotes a concrete action, has the following form:

<Action Statement> ::= <Action Name> (<Sequence of A-Parameters>)
<A-Parameter> ::= <A-Parameter Expression> | <Direct Speech>
| <Cluster of Simple A-Parameters>
<Simple A-Parameter> ::= <Role or Object Variable Name>
| <Role or Object Name>
<A-Parameter Expression> ::= <A-Parameter Type> = <A-Parameter Value>
<A-Parameter Type> ::= <A-Parameter Name>
| <A-Parameter name> (<A-Parameter Type>)
<A-Parameter Value> ::= <ROB-Parameter> | <Modifier>
<ROB Parameter> ::= <ROB-Variable> | <Attribute> (<ROB-Parameter>)
| <ROB-Name>
<Attribute> ::= <Noun Attribute> | <Other Attribute>
<Noun Attribute> ::= gate | window | surface | top | cloth | hat | hair ......
<Other Attribute> ::= in-front-of | behind | above | below | left-to
| right-to ......
<ROB-Variable> ::= <Variable Name>
<Modifier> ::= slowly | quickly | repeatedly | loudly | slightly ......
<Direct Speech> ::= "<Queue of English Sentences>"

Note that a ROB-Variable denotes a role, an object or a background, which has been specified at the beginning of the drama (plot) description of an agent. These variables will be instantiated when plot agent is called for. Within a ROB-Parameter, the attributes may be nested. For example, in-front-of (gate (X)) means in front of the gate of X, where X may be a building, a house, a park, etc. Here, both "in-front-of" and "gate" are attributes. The string of dots at the end of a BNF formula means that many items may follow which are too many to be all listed there.

Now we will consider plot agents with variables:

Example 6.1.5

```
PLOT AGENT (Leave):
   Father: Moving
   Child: Time = daytime --> Leave 1,
       Time = night --> Leave 2
   Plot Description Begin:
        Background : Building (Y)
        Object : Vehicle (Z)
        Role : Human (X)
        Presentation :
                     ......
              (15) Walk (X, start = in-front-of (gate(Y)), end = by-side-of (Z))
                     ......
   Plot Description End
END (Leave)
```

This agent has two sons: Leave 1 and Leave 2, representing refinements of the Leave agent in case of daytime and night.

2. Enrich Statement:

<Enrich Statement> ::= Enrich (<Ancestor Agent> [; <GA-Parameter>])
<Ancestor Agent> ::= <Name of Some Ancestor Agent >
<GA-Parameter> ::= (<Label>) : <Sequence of A-Parameter Expressions>

An Enrich statement adds more information to the parameters and statements of the <Ancestor Agent> while inheriting it. The result of executing an Enrich statement has the following effect: merge its GA-Parameter with the A-Parameters of the statements headed by <Label> in the ancestor agent. All of this is done at the beginning of the inheritance. Note that no new statement could be created by any Enrich statement.

Example 6.1.6

```
PLOT AGENT (Leave 1):
  Father: Leave
  Child : None
  Plot Description Begin :
    Presentation :
             ......
    (1) Enrich ( Leave;  (15) : Speed = quickly )
             ......
    Plot Description End
END (Leave 1)
```

is an enrichment to the example statement in the father agent. As result we get:

(15) Walk (X, Start = In-front-of (Gate(Y)), End = By-side-of (Z),
Speed = quickly)

3. Call Statement (simple statement of type 2), denoting an abstract action which should be further instantiated by another drama agent or plot agent, has the following form:

<Call Statement> ::= Call (<Agent Name>[; <Sequence of C-Parameters>]
[; <Series of GA-Parameters>])
<C-Parameter> ::= Type (<Attribute Name1>) = <Attribute Name2>
| Value (<Attribute Name>) = <Attribute Value>

A call statement is a macro call to the relevant agent denoted by <Agent Name>, possibly with a set of C-Parameters and GA-Parameters. Each C-Parameter binds an attribute class to a subclass (e.g. binds a Building to a Palace) or an attribute class to an instance (e.g. binds a Palace to the Forbidden City), or instantiates a guard and selects a child agent. Each GA-Parameter contains a list of A-Parameter enrichments to some statement (with <Label> as its label) of the called agent. The meaning of enrichment here is similar to that of Enrich Statements above. For details see the next section.

Note that it is not allowed to call an ancestor agent or a child agent. This limitation is meaningful because the agent knowledge base is not organized as a big tree, but as a forest consisting of a large amount of small trees.

Example 6.1.7

Assume we have the sentence "Next morning, Qin Shihuang (first emperor of the Qin dynasty) started the inspection of his land". Further we assume the planning module has found several dramas for representing this sentence. Since the time of inspection is morning, and morning is a value of daytime, the planning module selects the drama agent Emperor's Inspection1, whose value of Time is daytime:

```
DRAMA AGENT (Emperor's Inspection1):
        ......
 Drama Description Begin :
      Role : Emperor (X)
      Presentation :
    .......
      Call ( Leave; Type (Human) = Emperor, Type (Building) = Palace,
         Type (Vehicle) = Carriage; Value(Time) = daytime)
    ......
  Drama Description End
END (Emperor's Inspection1)
```

The planning module replaces the X parameter with Qin Shihuang, transforming the call statement into:

Call (Leave; Type (Human) = Emperor, Value (Human) = Qin Shihuang,
Type (Building) = Palace, Type (Vehicle) = Carriage, Value (Time) = daytime)

Note that the value "Qin Shihuang" does not come from the knowledge base, but from the story text itself. As the result of performing the Call statement above, the drama description of this agent will be expanded into the plot description of Leave which contains a Walk statement. The types of Building, Vehicle and Human are instantiated to sub-types Palace, Carriage and Emperor. The value of Emperor is further instantiated to Qin Shihuang. Since there are no values provided for Palace and Carriage, the default values any palace and any carriage are used. Since the value of Time is daytime, the plot agent Leave goes one step down to its son agent Leave 1, which performs an enrich statement to enrich the Walk statement with a speed parameter. Thus the final result is:

Plot Description Begin:
Background : Palace (any palace)
Object : Carriage (any carriage)
Role : Emperor (Qin Shihuang)
Presentation :
......
(15) Walk (Qin Shihuang, Start = In-front-of (Gate(any palace)),
End = By-side-of (any carriage), Speed = quickly)
......
Plot Description End

4. Conditional Statement

<Conditional Statement> ::= If <Guard> Then <GCF Without Label>
[Else <Intern Generalized Case Frame>] Fi
<Intern Generalized Case Frame> ::= <Conditional Statement>
| <GCF Without Label>

A conditional statement is a macro definition which will be expanded during planning time. If the <Guard> is fulfilled by the story, then the <GCF Without Label> is chosen. Otherwise, the <Intern Generalized Case Frame> is chosen. In case that the <Guard> is not fulfilled, but the Else part is missing, the conditional statement is equal to an empty clause.

Example 6.1.8

If Type (Human) = Emperor Then Enrich (Leave, (15) : Type (Z) = Carriage)
Else If Type (Human) = Major Then Enrich (Leave, (15) : Type (Z) = Car)
Else If Type (Human) = President Then Enrich (Leave, (15) : Type (Z) =
Airplane) Fi

5. Case Statement, which has the form:

<Case Statement> ::= Case <Sequence of Guarded Commands> Esac
<Guarded Command> ::= <Labeled Guard> --> <GCF Without Label>
<Labeled Guard> ::= (<Label>) <Guard>

A case statement is a macro definition which will be expanded during planning time. The principle of selecting a generalized case frame using guards here is similar to that of selecting a child agent explained above.

Example 6.1.9

```
Case
(1)Type (Human) = Emperor --> Bloc (3) Enrich ( Leave, (15) :
                Type (Z) = Carriage),
                    (4) Enrich (Leave, (16) : Color (flag) = yellow)
                  Colb,
(2)Type (Human) = Salesman --> Bloc (5) Enrich ( Leave, (15) :
                Type (Z) = Car),
                    (6) Enrich (Leave, (16) : Color (flag) = pink)
                  Colb
Esac
```

Please be sure to distinguish the different uses of guarded commands in case statements and in child selection at the beginning of an agent specification.

6. Bloc statement, which has the form:

<Bloc Statement> ::= Bloc <Sequence of Generalized Case Frames> Colb

A Bloc statement is a macro definition which will be expanded during planning time. The Bloc statements are used to bracket a set of generalized case frames to be included or referred in statements of type 4, 5 and 8.
Typical Example: see example above.

7. Loop Statement, which has three alternative forms:

```
<Loop Statement> ::= Until <Event> Do <Sequence of Action Statements> Od
     | While <State> Do <Sequence of Action Statements> Od
     | Repeat <Sequence of Action Statements> For <Natural Number> Times
<Event> ::= start (<Sequence of Labels>) | end (<Sequence of Labels>)
     | all-start (<Sequence of Labels>) | all-end (<Sequence of Labels>)
<State> ::= active (<Sequence of Labels>) | sleep (<Sequence of Labels>)
     | all-active (<Sequence of Labels>) | all-sleep (<Sequence of Labels>)
```

A Loop statement specifies how long some action sequence should repeat. The Until statement says that the action sequence between Do and Od should be iterated until the <Event> happens. The While statement says that the action sequence should be repeated as long as the <State> is not changed. Note that both a Until statement and a While statement may stop in the middle of an action sequence, whenever the event happens or the state changes. They guarantee only that no loop statement will stop in the middle of a single action. The Repeat statement specifies the exact number of times an action should be done.

An <Event> happens when at least one of the statements headed by a label in the <Sequence of Labels> of a "start" specification has started, or any statement of an "end" specification has finished. An <Event> also happens when all statements headed by a label in the <Sequence of Labels> of an "all-start" specification have started, or all statements of an "all-end" specification have finished.

A <State> is valid when at least one of the statements headed by a label in the <Sequence of Labels> of an "active" specification is still being performed, or there is any statement of the "sleep" specification, which is not being performed. A <State> is also valid when all statements headed by a label in the <Sequence of Labels> of an "all-active" specification are being performed, or none of the statements of an "all-sleep" specification is being performed.

Example 6.1.10

(19) Until start (20) Do
Walk (King, Start = door, End = window, Speed = quickly),
Walk (King, Start = window, End = door, Speed = quickly)
Od
(20) Until start (21) Do Knock-Door (Server, gently) Od
(21) Speak (King, "Come in!")

The semantics of the loop statements is not as simple as one might suppose. There are at least two questions to be discussed.

First, the test of the terminating condition does not only take place at the end of each cycle of the loop. Rather, the loop may terminate at any time, as soon as the terminating condition is fulfilled. This property distinguishes its semantics from that of loop statements in conventional programming languages, where the body of a loop will be always executed as a whole. In the case above, the king may stop walking between the door and the window when the server knocks.

Second, each Loop statement implies a temporal relation between statements. In the example above, it is implied that (19) meet (20) and (20) meet (21). There are also other types of frame statements which imply temporal relations, see below. These implied temporal relations will be added to the T-Specification of the agent.

There is yet a third question, which does not relate to the semantics of loop statements, but to the general connection of statement semantics. In the example above, one may notice that there is no statement after each walk statement in the loop body, describing how the king turns back his body in order to be able to go in the opposite direction. This problem is a general one and will be solved generally in our low level action planning module. The principle is to detect any "default" action which is missing in the plot description but which has to be added to make the plot complete.

In section 6.3, we will define the exact meaning of time relation between two actions (see table 6.3.1). But the definition given there is only applicable to temporal relations between two single actions, not including the repetition of the same action which is implemented by Loop statements.

8. Replace Statement, which has the form:
<Replace Statement> ::= Replace <Ancestor Agent> (<Label1>)
With (<Label2>)

This statement replaces a frame variable of some ancestor agent by a frame statement of its offspring agent which contains this replace statement. Note that in case <Label2> is heading a Bloc statement, the statement headed by <Label1> will be replaced by a set of statements.

Example 6.1.11

```
DRAMA AGENT (Holiday) :
 ..........................
 (10) FR  Relaxation,
 ...........................
END (Holiday)
DRAMA AGENT (Man's Holiday) :
Father : Holiday
 ...............................
 (15) Replace Holiday(10)  with (16),
 (16) Call (Play Golf, ......),
 ................................
END (Man's Holiday)
DRAMA AGENT (Woman's Holiday) :
Father : Holiday
 .................................
 (21) Replace Holiday(10)  with  (22),
 (22) Call (Shopping, ......),
 ..................................
END (Woman's Holiday)
```

At this place, it would be appropriate to note three points about the use of replace statements: First, the replacement takes place only when the agent containing the frame variable is being inherited by the agent containing the replace statement. Second, any frame variable which has not been replaced during the inheritance procedure is equal to an empty statement. Third, if agent AA is an ancestor of BB which is in turn an ancestor of CC, and if BB and CC both replace the same frame variable of AA, then the replace statement of BB has no influence on CC. That means, the replacement of CC pre-empts that of BB.

Note that the types 4, 5, 6, 7, 8 of frame statements are structured. Within a structured frame statement, each intern frame statement or frame variable also has its own label. The layers of a structured frame statement form a tree structure. Those frame statements and frame variables which are not within any structured statement form the layer zero.

The labels are unique with respect to individual agents. That means all labels in the presentation part of any agent are different from each other.

A sequence of generalized case frames not containing action statements is called a first kind sequence. Those not containing call statements are called second kind sequences. They belong to drama agents and plot agents, respectively.

Example 6.1.12 (Drama Agents and Plot Agents)

```
DRAMA AGENT (Birthday Congratulation):
  Father Class:  Visit
  Child : None
  Drama Description Begin :
     Presentation :
     (1) Replace Visit (1) with (2)
     (2) Call (Prepare Birthday Felicitation; Value (Client) =
         X, Value (Clerk) = ? any, Value (Receiver) = Y, Value (Ware) = ? Z)
     (3) Replace Visit (4) with (4),
     (4) Call (Offer Birthday Gift; Value (Giver) = X, Value (Receiver) = Y,
         Value (Gift) = ? Z)
  Drama Description End
 END (Birthday Congratulation)

 DRAMA AGENT (Visit):
  Father Class:  None
  Child : True → Birthday Congratulation
  Drama Description Begin:
      Role: Guest (X),
            Host (Y)
      Object : Gift (Z)
      Presentation :
      (1) FR Preparation,
      (2) Call (Drive; Value (Driver) = X, Value (Car) =? any),
      (3) Call (Enter Home; Value (Human) = X),
      (4) FR Gift_Offering
  Drama Description End
 END (Visit)

 DRAMA AGENT (Prepare Birthday Felicitation):
  Father Class:  Shopping
  Child :  None
  Drama Description Begin:
      Role : Receiver (R)
      Presentation :
      (1) Replace Shopping (2) with (2),
      (2) Case
      Type (Receiver) = Man → Call (Buy; Value (Client) = x,
                          Value (Clerk) = Y, Value (Ware) = {Book, Whiskey})
     Type (Receiver) = Woman → Call (Buy; Value (Client) = x,
                          Value (Clerk) = Y, Value (Ware) = {Lipstick, Perfume})
     Type (Receiver) = Child → Call (Buy; Value (Client) = x,
                          Value (Clerk) = Y, Value (Ware) = {Toy, Chocolate})
         Esac
  Drama Description End
```

```
END (Prepare Birthday Felicitation)
DRAMA AGENT (Shopping):
 Father Class: None
 Child : Goal = Birthday Congratulation → Prepare Birthday Felicitation,
      Goal = Daily Consumption → Supermarket Visiting
 Drama Description Begin :
      Role : Client (X),
           Clerk (Y)
      Object : Ware (Z)
      Presentation :
       (1) Call (Enter Shop; Value (Human) = X),
       (2) FR Buy_Things
 Drama Description End
END (Shopping)

PLOT AGENT (Buy):
 Father Class: None
 Child : None
 Plot Description Begin :
      Background : shop_intern
      Role : Client (X),
           Clerk (Y)
      Object : Ware (Z)
      Presentation :
       (1) Give (Y, X, Z),
       (2) Give (X, Y, Money)
 Plot Description End
END (Buy)

PLOT AGENT (Offer Birthday Gift):
 Father Class: None
 Child : None
 Plot Description Begin :
      Background : room_1
      Role : Giver (X),
           Receiver (Y)
      Object : Gift (Z)
      Presentation :
       (1) Give (X, Y, Z),
       (2) Speak (X, Y, "happy birthday to you"),
       (3) Speak (Y, X, "thank you")
 Plot Description End
END (Offer Birthday Gift)

PLOT AGENT (Enter Shop):
 Father Class: Enter
 Child : None
```

```
  Plot Description Begin :
      Background : street_1
      Presentation :
       (1) Enrich (Enter, (1) : Type (house) = shop)
  Plot Description End
END (Enter Shop)

PLOT AGENT (Enter Home):
  Father Class:  Enter
  Child :  None
  Plot Description Begin :
      Background : street_2
      Presentation :
       (1) Enrich (Enter, (1) : Type (house) = home)
  Plot Description End
END (Enter Home)

PLOT AGENT (Enter):
  Father Class:  None
  Child :  Goal = Shopping → Enter Shop,
      Goal = Visit → Enter Home
  Plot Description Begin :
      Role : Human (X)
      Presentation :
       (1) Enter (X, house)
  Plot Description End
END (Enter)

PLOT AGENT (Drive):
  Father Class:  None
  Plot Description Begin :
      Background : street_3
      Role : Driver (X)
      Object : Car (Y)
      Presentation :
       (1) Drive (X, Y, building_1, building_2)
  Plot Description End
END (Drive)
```

Note that the T-Specification in all agents is not mentioned in the above examples, because all actions are sequentially arranged. This is the default specification.

6.2 Skeletal Plot Planning

The skeletal plot planning is not a simple and straightforward procedure. It involves different techniques which may be used under different situations for solving different problems. The main points of the content of section 6.2.1 have been mentioned roughly in the last section. They will be made more formal in section 6.2.1. Further techniques for enhancing the multiplicity of generated plots will be presented in sections 6.2.2, 6.2.3 and 6.2.4.

6.2.1 Plot Planning through Inheritance and Instantiation

In this section, we will summarize some definitions and algorithms which have the job of formalizing the working mechanism of our drama agents and plot agents defined in section 6.1.2.

Algorithm 6.2.1 (Unfold an Abstract Action)

1. Given a GF2 statement c of the GF2 statement series of a story which represents an abstract action, find a drama (or plot) agent ag, whose name is equal to the root name of c. The algorithm fails if there is no such agent.
2. If there are child agents of ag, which meet the situation of c (determined by other cases in the same case frame) and the context condition CON (this data structure collects all information gathered by unfolding abstract actions), then select one of them according to algorithm 6.2.4, call it again ag.
3. Repeat step 2 to select a child for the new ag, until no appropriate child agent can be found. Store all newly obtained information in CON.
4. Consider the original case frame c as a virtual call statement call (ag, … …). Apply algorithm 6.2.3 to ag with information contained in this virtual call statement to instantiate the variables of ag.
5. Let ag inherit information from all its ancestors according to algorithm 6.2.2
6. If ag is a drama agent, then
   Until ag contains no call statement
   DO Perform a call statement according to algorithm 6.2.3
   OD
7. While there is a statement in ag with variables which can be instantiated with information in CON and in the specification part of ag
   DO Instantiate the variables of this statement
   OD
8. If there are still statements with variables, then algorithm fails (to instantiate ag).
9. Otherwise, algorithm finished successfully.

End of Algorithm

In our hierarchy of agents, on the same inheritance path, the same role or object may be defined several times, each new definition preempts all old ones. So we need an exact notation for that definition which is currently the valid one.

Algorithm 6.2.2 (Inheritance)

1. Assume ah is that agent which is going to inherit all properties of its ancestors. Make a copy of ah, called ag.
2. Assume there are n ancestor agents of ag. Take them in the order ag_1 , ag_2 , ……, until ag_n , where ag_1 is the top agent. For each i, a_i is the ancestor of a_{i+1}.
3. For i = 2, …, n , do the local inheritance of ag_i from ag_{i-1}, and ag from ag_n . By local inheritance we mean an agent inherits from its nearest ancestor. It includes the following steps 4 to 12, where we use the unified name ag for the inheritor.
4. If ag has a background, then any background of its ancestor will be ignored.
5. Otherwise, ag inherits the background of its ancestor, if there is any.
6. Each object b of its ancestor will be inherited by ag, except that there were an identical object b' in ag, such that both the attribute names and attribute values of b and b' are equal.
7. Do the same for all roles.
8. Make a copy ca of the presentation part of the ancestor agent. For each replace statement of ag, do the following: replace the frame variable or frame statement preceded by < father label > in ca, say x, by the frame statement preceded by < label > in the current agent.
9. Delete from ag all replace statements and statements used for replacing.
10. For each Enrich statement of ag, add its new content to the corresponding statement in ca to be enriched.
11. Delete from ag all Enrich statements.
12. Let x inherit all statements (possibly modified by replacements and/or enrich statements) of ca, where all inherited statements should be headed by the name of the ancestor agent they belong to.

End of Algorithm

Algorithm 6.2.3 (Instantiation of Call Statements)

1. Let the call statement s be call (hg; x_1, $x_{2,\ldots,}$ x_n ; y_1, y_2, …, y_m), where hg is the name of another agent, x_1, x_2 ,…, x_n are the C-Parameters, y_1, y_2, …, y_m are the GA-Parameters. Assume s belongs to the agent cag.
2. If there are child agents of hg, which meet the situation as given in the story and in CON (see algorithm 6.2.1), then select one of them according to algorithm 6.2.4, call it hg again, and store the decision information in CON.
3. Repeat step 2 to select a child for the new ag, while considering the information CON contained in the decisions made in the previous steps of child selection, until no appropriate child agent can be found.
4. If s is not called by other call statements, then establish an enpty context set S. Put s, all father agents of s, hg, all father agents of hg in S. If s is called by some other call statements, then check if hg is in S. If yes, then the algorithm fails, because a recursive call of agents is forbidden. Otherwise put hg and all its father agents in S.
5. Make a copy of the agent hg. Call this copy chg1.

6. Do the steps 1 to 7 of algorithm 6.2.2 to let chg1 inherit all roles, objects and backgrounds of its ancestors.
7. For each x_i, i = 1, …, n, do the following:
   7.1 If x_i is Type (<Attribute Name1>) = <Attribute Name2>, then change Attribute Name1 (which is a Role Type, Object Type or Background Type) of the specification part of chg1 to Attribute Name2 (which is a sub-type).
   7.2. If x_i is Value (<Attribute Name>) = <Attribute Value>, then replace the parameter of the Attribute Name with the Attribute Value.
8. For each y_i, i = 1, …, m, do the following:
   If y_i is (<Label>) <Sequence of GA-Parameters>, then for each GA-Parameter gp do:
   Take gp as an A-Parameter and add it to the <Sequence of A-Parameters> of the generalized case frame headed by (<Label>) in chg1.
9. We call the procedure of step 6 and 7 as value instantiation. Propagate the information obtained in value instantiation:
   9.1 To all statements in chg1 and those in all its ancestors.
   9.2 To the specification part and statements of cag.
10. Expand all conditional statements, case statements and bloc statements in chg1.
11. Let chg1 inherit all statements of its ancestors according to steps 9 to 12 of algorithm 6.2.2. We get thus a new version of chg1 and call it still chg1.
12. For each Attribute Name (which is a Role Type, Object Type or Background Type) of chg1, which does not yet have a value (i.e. whose argument is still a variable), assign a default value to it. Call the result chg2.
13. Replace the call statement s in cag with chg2 (which has now no variable anymore).
14. For all variables v_i which are shared by s and cag – s at the beginning of this algorithm, let their occurrences in cag – s have the same values which are obtained by their occurrences in s (now in chg2) during above steps.

End of Algorithm

Definition 6.2.1 (Partial Ordering of Propositions)

1. Let S = {P[1], P[2], …P[n]} be n propositions which form the set of all guards in the Child part of an agent. For each i and j, we say that P[i] ≤ P[j], if P[j] can be inferred from P[i]. We say that P[i] = P[j] if both P[i] ≤ P[j] and P[j] ≤ P[i] are valid. We get a partial order of all g in this way.
2. A proposition P from S is called a specialization of P[j], if P ≤ P[j], but P ≠ P[j]. The specialization is called least, if there is no P[i] such that P is a specialization of P[i], and P[i] is a specialization of P[j].
3. A proposition P from S is called a generalization of P[j], if P [j] ≤ P, but P [j] ≠ P. The generalization is called least, if there is no P[i] such that P is a generalization of P[i], and P[i] is a generalization of P[j].

End of Algorithm

Proposition 6.2.1

1. If guard g has a specialization, then it has a least specialization. Similarly, if g has a generalization, then it has a least generalization.
2. If g is a least specialization of f, then f is a least generalization of g, and vice versa.

Algorithm 6.2.4 (Selecting Children)

We consider each guard as a proposition. Test all guards with information obtained from the story. Let the form of a guard g be Parameter = Parameter Value. Let there be n different ROB-Parameters rob[1], rob[2], …, rob[n] in the current agent. Denote the set of guards of this agent be G = {g[1], g[2], …, g[m]}. Each guard is represented in the form (rob[i] = a, rob[j] = b, …, rob[k] = c). Collect all information about the n attributes from the story together and represent it as g[m+1].

1. If there is at least one g[i], such that g[i] = g[m+1], then choose a child in a non-deterministic way which corresponds to such a g[i]. Algorithm finished.
2. If at least one g[i] is a specialization of g[m+1], then choose a child in a non-deterministic way , which corresponds to a least specialization g[i]. Algorithm finished.
3. If at least one g[i] is a generalization of g[m+1], then choose a child in a non-deterministic way , which corresponds to a least generalization g[i]. Algorithm finished.
4. If there is at least one g[i], which does not imply ┐(g[m+1]) (means the negation of g[m+1]), then choose a child in a non-deterministic way which corresponds to such a g[i]. Algorithm finished.
5. No child can be selected. Stop the algorithm.

End of Algorithm

Example 6.2.1

In the group {Bride is a Pekinese, Bride is a Chinese, Bride is a Japanese, Bride is an Asian}, "Bride is a Chinese" is a least specialization of "Bride is an Asian", and at the same time a least generalization of "Bride is a Pekinese". On the other hand, "Bride is a Japanese", which has no least specialization, is itself another least specialization of "Bride is an Asian".

Example 6.2.2

We reconsider the set of agents in example 6.1.12 and use them to develop a plot plan for the sentence:

Ms. Wang congratulates Mr. Li on his birthday.

1. Find the drama agent "birthday congratulation". No child can be selected.
2. Find its father agent "Visit" and first inherit from it the parameters. Now the agent "birthday congratulation" looks like :

Role: Guest (X),
Host (Y)
Object : Gift (Z)
(1) Replace Visit (1) with (2)
(2) Call (Prepare Birthday Felicitation; Value (Client) = X,
Value (Clerk) = ? any, Value (Receiver) = Y, Value (Ware) = ? Z),
(3) Replace Visit (4) with (4),

(4) Call (Offer Birthday Gift; Value (Giver) = X, Value (Receiver) = Y,
Value (Gift) = ? Z)

3. The original sentence is equal to "call (birthday congratulation; Type (Guest) = Woman, Value (Guest) = Wang, Type (Host) = Man, Value (Host) = Li, Value (Gift) = ? Z)", where the value of Z is yet to be determined.
4. Instantiate the types and values of parameters (Guest, Host, Gift) with the parameter types and values of the calling statement in 2 and propagate them to the statements, get

Role: Woman (Wang),
Man (Li)
Object : Gift (Z)
(1) Replace Visit (1) with (2)
(2) Call (Prepare Birthday Felicitation; Type (Client) = Woman,
Value (Client) = Wang, Value (Clerk) = ? any, Value (Ware) = ? Z,
Type (Receiver) = Man, Value (Receiver) = Li),
(3) Replace Visit (4) with (4),
(4) Call (Offer Birthday Gift; Type (Giver) = Woman,
Value (Giver) = Wang, Type (Receiver) = Man,
Value (Receiver) = Li, Value (Gift) = ? Z)

5. Propagate the instantiation of types and values of roles and object back to the statements of "visit", transform them to:

(1) FR Preparation,
(2) Call (Drive; Type (Driver) = Woman, Value (Driver) = Wang,
Value (Car) = ? any),
(3) Call (Enter Home; Type (Human) = Woman, Value (Human) =
Wang),
(4) FR Gift_Offering

6. Perform the two Replace statements in "birthday congratulation", replace the two frame variables of "visit" with corresponding statements, inherit the statements of "visit", obtain:

Woman (Wang)
Man (Li)
Gift (Z)
(1) Call (Prepare Birthday Felicitation; Type (Client) = Woman,
Value (Client) = Wang, Value (Clerk) = ? any, Value (Ware) = ? Z,
Type (Receiver) = Man, Value (Receiver) = Li),
(2) Call (Drive; Type (Driver) = Woman, Value (Driver) = Wang,
Value (Car) = ? any),

(3) Call (Enter Home; Type (Human) = Woman, Value (Human) = Wang),
(4) Call (Offer Birthday Gift; Type (Giver) = Woman, Value (Giver) = Wang, Type (Receiver) = Man, Value (Receiver) = Li, Value (Gift) = ? Z)

7. Start to perform the first call statement above.
8. Let the agent "prepare birthday felicitation" inherit all parameters from its father "shopping", get:

Role : Client (X),
Clerk (Y)
Receiver (R)
Object : Ware (Z)
(1) Replace Shopping (2) with (2),
(2) Case
Type (Receiver) = Man → Call (Buy; Value (Client) = x, Value (Clerk) = Y, Value (Ware) = {Book, Whiskey})
Type (Receiver) = Woman → Call (Buy; Value (Client) = x, Value (Clerk) = Y, Value (Ware) = {Lipstick, Perfume})
Type (Receiver) = Child → Call (Buy; Value (Client) = x, Value (Clerk) = Y, Value (Ware) = {Toy, Chocolate})
Esac

9. Instantiate its parameters in specification part and also in presentation part with type and value information from the calling statement, get:

Role : Woman (Wang),
Clerk (Y)
Man (Li)
Object : Ware (Z)
(1) Replace Shopping (2) with (2),
(2) Case
Type (Man) = Man → Call (Buy; Type (Client) = Woman, Value (Client) = Wang, Value (Clerk) = Y, Value (Ware) = {Book, Whiskey}),
Type (Man) = Woman → Call (Buy; Type (Client) = Woman, Value (Client) = Wang, Value (Clerk) = Y, Value (Ware) = {Lipstick, Perfume}),
Type (Man) = Child → Call (Buy; Type (Client) = Woman, Value (Client) = Wang, Value (Clerk) = Y, Value (Ware) = {Toy, Chocolate})
Esac

10. Propagate the above instantiated types and values of parameters back to the father agent "shopping" to instantiate its statements, get

(1) Call (Enter Shop; Type (Human) = Woman, Value (Human) = Wang),
(2) FR Buy_Things

11.Perform the case statement of "prepare birthday felicitation" to make a choice and propagate the ware parameter value of the call statement (first alternative of the case statement) to the object specification part, get:

Role : Woman (Wang),
Clerk (Y)
Man (Li)
Object : Ware ({Book, Whiskey})
(1) Replace Shopping (2) with (2),
(1) Call (Buy; Type (Client) = Woman, Value (Client) = Wang,
Value (Clerk) = Y, Value (Ware) = {Book, Whiskey})

12.Perform the replace statement, transform the presentation part of "shopping" to:

(1) Call (Enter Shop; Type (Human) = Woman, Value (Human) = Wang),
(2) Call (Buy; Type (Client) = Woman, Value (Client) = Wang,
Value (Clerk) = Y, Value (Ware) = {Book, Whiskey})

13.Inherit the statements from "shopping", the agent "prepare birthday felicitation" becomes:

(1) Call (Enter Shop; Type (Human) = Woman, Value (Human) = Wang),
(2) Call (Buy; Type (Client) = Woman, Value (Client) = Wang,
Value (Clerk) = Y, Value (Ware) = {Book, Whiskey})

14.Propagate the value instantiation in the second call of 13 back to 6, instantiate the last variable of the fourth call and change it to:

(4) Call (Offer Birthday Gift; Type (Giver) = Woman, Value (Giver) = Wang, Type (Receiver) = Man, Value (Receiver) = Li, Value (Gift) = {Book, Whiskey})

15.Start to perform the first call statement in 13, find the agent "enter shop".

16.Find the father "enter" of "enter shop", inherit from it the specification part. "enter shop" becomes:

Role : Human (X)
(1) Enrich (Enter, (1) : Type (house) = shop)

17.Instantiate it with information from the call statement in 13, get:

Role : Woman (Wang)
(1) Enrich (Enter, (1) : Type (house) = shop)

18.Propagate the value instantiation back to "enter" and perform the Enrich statement, transform the presentation part of "enter" to:

(1) Enter (Wang, house, Type (house) = shop)

19.Inherit this statement from "enter", "enter shop" becomes:

Background: street_1
Role : Woman (Wang)
(1) Enter (Wang, house, Type (house) = shop)

20.Start to perform the second call statement in 13, find the agent "buy". There is no ancestor.

21.Instantiate it with information from the call statement, get:

Background : shop_intern
Role : Woman (Wang),
Clerk (Y)

Object : Ware ({Book, Whiskey})
(1) Give (Y, Wang, {Book, Whiskey}),
(2) Give (Wang, Y, Money)

22.Since there is no information for Clerk, assign a random value Any clerk to it and return the following two statements:
(1) Give (Any clerk, Wang, {Book, Whiskey}),
(2) Give (Wang, Any clerk, Money)

23.Now that the first call in 6 is finished, we start to perform its second call and find the agent "drive". Instantiate it with information from the call statement, get:
Background : street_3
Role : Woman (Wang)
Object : Car (Y)
Presentation :
(1) Drive (Wang, Y, building_1, building_2)

24.Since there is no information for Car, assign a random value Any car to it and return the following statement:
(1) Drive (Wang, Any car, building_1, building_2)

25.Start to perform the third call in 6, find the agent "enter home".

26.Find the father "enter" of "enter home", inherit from it the specification part. "enter home" becomes:
Role : Human (X)
(1) Enrich (Enter, (1) : Type (house) = home)

27.Instantiate it with information from the call statement, get:
Role : Woman (Wang)
(1) Enrich (Enter, (1) : Type (house) = home)

28.Propagate the value instantiation back to "enter" and perform the Enrich statement, transform the presentation part of "enter" to:
(1) Enter (Wang, house, Type (house) = home)

29.Inherit this statement from "enter", "enter shop" becomes:
Background : street_2
Role : Woman (Wang)
(1) Enter (Wang, house, Type (house) = home)

30.Start to perform the fourth call in 6, find the agent "offer birthday gift". Instantiate it with information from the call statement, get:
Background : room_1
Role : Woman (Wang),
Man (Li)
Object : Gift ({Book, Whiskey})
(1) Give (Wang, Li, {Book, Whiskey}),
(2) Speak (Wang, Li, "happy birthday to you"),
(3) Speak (Li, Wang, "thank you")

31.Collect the results together by renumbering the statements (of concrete actions) and sorting the temporal relations, we have:
Role : Woman (Wang),

Man (Li),
Clerk (Any clerk)
Object : Car (Any car),
Gift ({Book, Whiskey})
Presentation : Background : street_1
(1) Enter (Wang, house, Type (house) = shop)
Background : shop_intern
(2) Give (Any clerk, Wang, {Book, Whiskey}),
(3) Give (Wang, Any clerk, Money)
Background : street_3

(4) Drive (Wang, Any car, building_1, building_2)
Background : street_2
Enter (Wang, house, Type (house) = home)
Background : room_1
(5) Give (Wang, Li, {Whiskey, Book}),
(6) Speak (Wang, Li, "happy birthday to you"),
(7) Speak (Li, Wang, "thank you")

Thus, the plot planning for the "birthday congratulation" sentence is done, of course in a very much simplified way. Note that this is the result of unfolding an abstract action. Its representation does not follow the syntax of agents.

In the following, we will introduce time markings for the event, in order to prepare for the qualitative temporal planning in section 6.3.

Algorithm 6.2.5 (Time Marking for Events)

1. Given a finite set S of concrete actions and a finite set T of WFTF constraints on the members of S.
2. Calculate the closure of these relations.
3. If for a pair of time points x (alpha) and y (beta), where event x may equal or not equal to event y, alpha and beta denote begin or end, more than one of the three following relations is valid:
4. x (alpha) < y (beta) x (alpha) = y (beta) y (alpha) < x (beta)
5. Then we have an inconsistency in T, algorithm fails.
6. Otherwise, the time points x (alpha) form a partial order with respect to "<", where x means any event and alpha means begin or end.
7. Use a topological sort to get a total order of all x (alpha).
8. If, after the sort, there are m elements (note that some x (alpha) may coincide), then assign the numbers 1, 2, …, m to these elements.
9. Each element, which is assigned the number i, get the time mark t_i.
10. In this way, each event x obtains a time marking $[t_{i.}, t_k]$, where $i < k$.

End of Algorithm

Calculation of time markings is the basis for qualitative temporal planning. If we consider a story as a melody, then the time markings are the "beats" of this melody. Now that we have a time marking (time interval) for each event and the relative time ordering for all events in a story, we will be able to define the "length" of a time interval by quantitative planning to complete the whole melody.

6.2.2 Plot Planning through Crossover and Mutation

We use the terms crossover and mutation which originate from the theory of genetic algorithms to denote two techniques of plot planning which may enhance the multiplicity of generated animation. The crossover technique makes use of extra information of the story and merges it with the content of the drama or plot agent to develop an abstract action into details which are different than if we were to use the content of the agent only. The mutation technique modifies parts of the agent actions to produce a rich variety of different versions of plot planning. There are now three possibilities to do the mutation. First, we design different son (drama or plot) agents with the guard "true". That means, the son (drama or plot) agents may be chosen on a random basis. Second, we design different case choices with guard "true" in the case statements. That means, the different cases may be chosen on a random basis. Third, we use the technique of partial presentation of plots and their combinations to realize the mutation. This technique will be described in detail in section 6.2.3.

Let us start from the crossover technique. It originates from a problem we have not considered yet. Namely, the influence of (maybe partial) information contained in the story on the details of an abstract agent.

Example 6.2.3

Assume we have the following drama:

```
    DRAMA AGENT (TM Marriage):
    Father : Chinese Marriage
    Child : None
    Drama Description Begin:
        Presentation :
            ...............
            Call (Shopping, ......);
            ................
    Drama Description End.
    Candidate: Action: Health Consultation.
  END (TM Marriage)
```

Let us consider the following stories about marriage:

Story A: Guiwen and Wenyan got married.

Story B: Guiwen and Wenyan got married. Before the wedding ceremony, they went to a big shop to do shopping.

Story C: Guiwen and Wenyan got married. Before the registration, they went to a hospital to receive health consultation.

Story D: Guiwen and Wenyan got married. Guiwen rented an helicopter as an ushering traffic tool to guide Wenyan to his home.

What are the differences of these four stories? Story A contains no detail about the marriage. The plot planning module needs only to make use of the drama agent "TM Marriage". Story B contains a detail "shopping". But the action "shopping" is already contained in the presentation part of the agent "TM Marriage". The planning module has nothing else to do other than just ignore this detailed information of the story. Story C contains another detail "health consultation". It is not contained in the presentation part of the "TM Marriage" agent, but contained in its candidate part. So it is harmless to combine this detail with that agent to form a plot plan different to that given in the agent. Story D contains a unusual detail "helicopter" which is not contained in this agent in any sense. So the planning module has to think about how to merge this information with the "standard" presentation of the "TM Marriage" agent without producing contradiction.

The problem will become more complicated if the drama contains much more details and the story itself is a long one. See the following example:

Example 6.2.4

Assume we have the following plot agent:

PLOT AGENT (Wedding Ceremony in Church)
Father : None
Plot Description Begin
Role : Pastor (Z), Bride(Y), Bridegroom(X),
Father (F), Mother (M), Friend (F1), Friend (F2)
Object : Ring (R)
Presentation :
(1) Walk-together ({ X, Y }, gate (church), tribune)
(2) Stand (Z, tribune, in-front-of ({X, Y}))
(3) Sitting ({F, M, F1, F2}, banks (church), facing(tribune)),
(4) Watch ({F, M, F1, F2}, {X, Y}),
(5) applaud ({F1, F2}),
(6) Ask (Z, X, "Do you want Y as your wife?"),
(7) Talk (X, Z, "Yes, I want Y as my wife"),
(8) Ask (Z, Y, "Do you want X as your husband?"),
(9) Talk (Y, Z, "Yes, I want X as my husband"),
(10) Talk (Z, (X, Y), "I declare you to be married"),
(11) Turn-to (X, Y),
(12) Turn-to (Y, X),
(13) Put (X, R, finger2 (Y)),
(14) Talk (Z, {X, Y}, "God bless you!").
(15) applaud ({F, M, F1, F2}),
(16) Walk-together ({ X, Y }, tribune, gate (church))
Plot Description End.
T-Specification : 2 = 3, 1 = 5, 1 begin 4, 2 contain {4, 15}, 16 begin 15,
5 < 6 < 7 < 8 < 9 < 10 < 11 < 12 < 13 < 14 < 15
END (Wedding Ceremony in Church)

If we use this plot agent to develop the following story (the statements are numbered), what will happen?

Story:

1. The wedding ceremony of A and B is held in a church.
2. Before this wedding, A and B have asked their parents for permission.
3. Among the parents, only A's father was present at the wedding ceremony.
4. An old friend of A came and brought a bunch of flowers to A and B.
5. A and B stood in front of the pastor.
6. The pastor asked A whether he wants to marry B.
7. A says yes to the pastor.
8. The pastor asked B whether she wants to marry A.
9. Two policemen dashed in, declared that A, the bridegroom, was a criminal
10. The policemen arrested A and took him away.
11. All participants of the ceremony were surprised.
12. The bride said nothing.
13. The bride started to cry.
14. In the police office, people started to interrogate A.
15. A said: "I have done all of that because I love my wife very much".
16. A sits in a room of the prison.

If we were to develop a plot plan for each sentence separately as we usually do, then we would meet a lot of troubles. Assume the result we get is Res.

Trouble 1. Sentence 2 should appear before sentence 1. But in Res it is after sentence 1.

Trouble 2. Some events (friend coming, policemen arrested A) should happen during the ceremony. But in Res they happen after the wedding ceremony.

Trouble 3. The role "mother" of the plot agent does not exist in the story.

Trouble 4. The old friend of A and the policemen of the story are missing in the plot.

Trouble 5. The statements 11, 12, 13, 14, 16 in the plot agent are impossible, because the role A has already been arrested.

Trouble 6. The statements 9 and 15 in the plot agent are unreasonable.

Trouble 7. The statements 9, 10, 11, 12, 13 of the story do not exist in the plot agent

In order to get rid of these troubles, we have to solve at least three problems:

Problem 1. Which part of the plot agent should be deleted to conform to the story?

Problem 2. Which part of the story should be added to the plot?

Problem 3. Where to insert the new content mentioned in problem 2?

Generally speaking, these problems are very difficult to solve. Some limitations on them are unavoidable. Based on the current situation of SWAN development, we have set three principles to guide the solution procedure:

Principle 1. There must be some "hook" in the story to hook the additional content of the story to the drama agent or plot agent. More precisely, there must be some keywords in the story sentences, which remind of the relevance of these sentences to the drama agent or plot agent.

Principle 2. This "hook" has a second job of pointing to the place in the plot agent where the new content should be inserted.

Principle 3. There must be some "hook detacher" in the story to show the boarder (end) of the new content. To define a hook detacher is more difficult than to define the hook itself.

In order to easy the task of planning, we need two further principles:

Principle 4. The sentence containing a hook must follow the abstract action immediately.

Principle 5. There should be only one hook and one hook detacher. In particular, there should be no new hook after a hook detacher.

What kind of information can serve as a hook? We allow the following:

1. An event which is critical for the current plot plan is a hook. (which events may be considered as critical, should be defined separately)
2. A hook plus a temporal delimiter "after", "during", "before" is also a hook.

These principles are implemented in the following algorithm, where we assume that all actions are sequential, to make the matter simple.

Algorithm 6.2.6

1. For each abstract action ab, after using the plot agent pa to develop a plot plan pp for it, consider the part paa of the story, which is after ab.
2. If ab is the last statement of the story, do nothing and terminate the algorithm.
3. Consider the statement ns immediately after ab.
4. If ns does not include any hook, the algorithm finished.
5. Otherwise (ns contains a hook), look forwards to find the first statement hd which reminds of a different location or a different time other than the background of pp.
6. Call the sequence of statements from ns to the statement bhd before hd as SQ.
7. If the hook is the keyword "after ab", then do nothing and the algorithm finished.
8. If the hook is a frame statement fs of pp, then use SQ to replace the statement sequence in pp, from that fs in pp until end of pp. The algorithm finished.
9. If the hook contains a temporal delimiter td, then
    9.1. If td = before s, where s is a statement in pp, then insert SQ before s.
    9.2. If td = after s, where s is a statement in pp, then insert SQ after s.
10. If the hook involves the disappearance or disability of some roles or objects in pp, then:
    10.1. If at least one role is a main role, then delete all statements in pp after SQ.

10.2. Otherwise, delete all statements in pp after SQ, which involve at least one of these roles and objects.

End of Algorithm

Note that this algorithm does not involve the inclusion of temporal constraints among the actions of SQ themselves.

6.2.3 Plot Planning through Abstraction and Partial Presentation

In the last two sections, we have introduced our plot knowledge base and also shown how to produce a fully developed plot, given an abstract event. In this way we may get a complete plot, if the related knowledge is stored in the knowledge base, or nothing, if the needed knowledge does not exist. We have also shown how to get different variations from the stored (standard) plot to avoid over-simplicity and monotony of the produced drama.

But this is not yet enough. It is not a good idea to produce a complete plot each time when an abstract event is given. This way of plot planning does not correspond to the reality of the practice of movie making. Usually, in order to present some event to the audience, besides showing a corresponding complete plot, the movie director may have many other possibilities. Instead of presenting the whole plot with all details, he may only show some part of it, or even some hint or symbol to the audience so that people may obtain necessary information and imagine the procedure of the event themselves.

Following the conventions of human movie directors, SWAN provides similar alternatives in plot planning.

Algorithm 6.2.7 (Planning Partial Plots)

1. Adopt only some part from the complete plot, which is characteristic for the whole plot. For example, exchange of rings between the bride and the bridegroom is characteristic for a wedding. It is enough to take this action as a representative scene for a wedding.
2. Present only the result of the event, instead of presenting the event itself. For example, in order to show that somebody has died, it is enough to show a gravestone with the name of this person inscribed on it.
3. Present only the cause (which is some other event or some phenomenon) , which may serve as a hint that the event mentioned in the story is going to happen. For example, in order to show that somebody is killed by a soldier, it is enough to show that the soldier raised his gun, aiming at this person, and pressed the trigger.
4. Present both the cause and the result of an event, while omitting the procedure of the event itself. For example, in order to display the collision of a car with a truck, it is enough to produce two shoots. The first one shows that the car driver drives the car very fast and suddenly sees a huge truck appearing in front of his car (cause of the collision). The second one shows the dead driver lying on the

street, near the damaged car. A group of policemen are taking photos of him (result of the collision).

5. If the first sentence is the cause and the second sentence is the event itself, then it is enough to produce a presentation for the cause only. Similarly, if the first sentence is the event itself and the second one is the result, then it is enough to produce a presentation for the result only.
6. Let a role in the drama tell somebody else that the mentioned event has already happened. This is the simplest way, of course not necessary the best way, to tell the audience that some event has happened.

End of Algorithm

In order to realize this algorithm, we have extended our definition of agents to provide the planning module with the possibility of selecting only part of the plot.

Definition 6.2.2 (Extended Syntax of Drama Agents and Plot Agents)

```
<Movie Agent> ::=
DRAMA AGENT ( <Agent Name> ):
    Father :  < Father >
    Child : <Child>
    Drama Description Begin:
        [Object : < Series of Marked Objects >]
        [Role : < Sequence of Marked Roles > ]
        [Presentation : < First Kind Sequence of Marked Generalized Case
                Frames >]
    Drama Description End
    [T-Specification : <Sequence of Temporal Constraints> ]
    [Candidate:  [Object : < Sequence of Objects >]
            [Role : < Sequence of Roles > ]
            [Action: <Sequence of Action Names>]]
END (<Agent Name>)

| PLOT AGENT ( <Agent Name> ):
    Father :  < Father >
    Child : < Child >
    Plot Description Begin:
        [Background : < Environment >]
        [Object : < Series of Marked Objects >]
        [Role : < Series of Marked Roles > ]
        [Presentation : < Second Kind Sequence of Marked Generalized Case
                Frames >]
    Plot Description End
    [T-Specification : <Sequence of Temporal Constraints>]
    [Candidate:  [Background: <Sequence of Backgrounds>]
        [Object : < Sequence of Objects >]
        [Role : < Sequence of Roles >]
        [Action: <Sequence of Action Names>]]
END (<Agent Name>)
```

<Marked Object> ::= [<Importance>] <Sequence of Objects>
<Importance> ::= (<Sequence of Labels>) | (*) | (**)
<Marked Role> ::= [(<Sequence of Labels>)] <Sequence of Roles>
<Marked Generalized Case Frame> ::= <Mark> <Generalized Case Frame>
<Mark> ::= * | ** | Cause : | Procedure : | Result : | Step (<Positive Integer>) :

Definition 6.2.3 (Semantics of the Extended Syntax)

1. The <Sequence of Labels> in a marked object (role) means each of these labels requests the existence of the current object (role). In another word, the current object (role) is necessary if any of the statements headed by these labels is selected by the planning module.
2. The mark with one star means the statement (object, role) is important (a key).
3. The mark with double stars means the statement (object, role) is necessary (should not be neglected).
4. The marks with Cause :, Procedure : and Result : have the meaning as said in algorithm 6.2.7
5. If there are many statements marked with Cause : (Procedure :, Result :), then it means one of the marked statement is enough to show the whole cause (procedure, result). Of course it is allowed to accept all statements marked with Cause : (Procedure :, Result :).
6. The mark with Step (<Positive Integer>) : means this statement is the <Positive Integer> th step of the whole action (represented by the current agent).

Example 6.2.5

```
PLOT AGENT ( Car Accident):
Father : Accident
Child : None
Plot Description Begin:
   Background : street_3
   Object : (**) Car (X),
        (**) Car (Y)
   Role : (6) Policeman (Z),
        (1, 3, 4, 7, 8) Driver (X1),
        (2, 7, 9) Driver (Y1)
   Presentation :
                ......
      Cause : (1) Drive (X1, X, speed = very fast),
      Cause : (2) Drive (Y1, Y, speed = very fast),
      Procedure : (3) Bloc
             (4)  See (X1, Y, State = driving, Distance = very short),
            * (5)  Clash (X, Y, Speed = very fast)
             Colb,
      Result : (6) Investigate (Z, X, Y, Time = long, State (X) = damaged,
               State (Y) = damaged),
```

```
        Result : (7) Bloc
                (8) Clinging (X1, steering wheel, State = dead),
                (9) Clinging (Y1, steering wheel, State = dead)
               Colb
                     ......
    Plot Description End
    END (Car Accident)
```

It is easy to see that with this agent there are more than one hundred possibilities to show an event of car accident.

6.3 Qualitative Temporal Planning

In last section, we have avoided to use qualitative time markings for drama agents and plot agents, because the use of time marking will qualitatively determine the relative time order of events and thus limit the multiplicity of scripts these agents may produce. In case of some frequently used drama and plot agents, where the time order is fixed, we use also agents with time markings to improve the efficiency of work of the act planning module. We call act planning without time marking the skeletal plot planning, and act planning with time marking the qualitative plot planning. This section is devoted to the latter.

6.3.1 A Notation for Time Representation in Plots

Before giving details of plot representation with qualitative time marks, we will first clarify the notations we are going to use. The WFTF introduced in chapter five serves as the basis of our time marks. For the purpose of using them for our drama and plot representation, some important modifications are needed to allow a more flexible time representation of events.

Is the semantics of the time relations defined in the literature enough for our purpose? In order to answer this question, we have to note that the time relations presented in this book do not mean those one sees in the real life. Rather, they mean time relations in animation presentation which has at least four characteristics:

1. The presentations of events at different locations are strictly sequential in the sense that no parallelism is possible.
2. All unimportant events between two important events can be neglected. For example, it is possible to neglect all events between the event "wedding" and the event "get baby" in a movie, while this is impossible in real life.
3. Events with a single time point, e.g. [a, a] are not allowed in a movie.
4. In some cases, the real time order can be reversed. For example, when somebody remembers an event in the past, the remembered event can be shown as if it were a current event.

In the current implementation of SWAN, we do not consider the fourth point above. But the first three points should be taken into account. Therefore, we have to redefine the meaning of time relations. For example:

1. "a precede b" means not only that event a should be shown before event b, but also that some other event c must be presented between a and b.
2. "a meet b" means that event b should be shown right after event a is shown.
3. "a overlap b" has complete different meanings for drama presentation and plot presentation. While it means certain concurrency in actions for a plot, it may mean cutting and editing for drama agents.

Table 6.3.1 Semantic Difference of Allen Time Relations for Drama and Plot Presentation

Allen's Time Relation	Meaning for Drama Presentation	Meaning for Plot Presentation
A before B	There is a drama C, such that drama A is shown before drama C, while C is shown before drama B.	In the same plot, there is an action C, such that action A happens first, then action C, then action B
A meet B	Drama A is shown before drama B. No other drama is shown in-between	In the same plot, action B follows immediately action A.
A overlap B	Dramas A and B are both decomposed into pieces and are merged together, such that: 1. The original orders of pieces in A and B are kept unchanged. 2. The first piece of A is before or meet all pieces of B. 3. The first piece of B is before or meet at least one piece of A.	In the same plot, action A has started before action B has started, and action B has started before action A has finished.
A begin B	Undefined	In the same plot, actions A and B started at the same time. Action A finished first.
A end B	Undefined	In the same plot, actions A and B finished at the same time. Action B started first.
A coincide B	Undefined	In the same plot, actions A and B started and finished at the same time.
A contain B	1.The original orders of pieces in A and B are kept unchanged. 2.The first piece of A is before or meet all pieces of B. 3.The last piece of B is before or meet at least one piece of A.	In the same plot, action A started earlier than B's start and finished later than B's end.

We summarize the difference of time relation semantics with respect to plot and drama agents in table 6.3.1 with respect to Allen time relations. The other time relations may be re-interpreted in a similar way.

Now come back to the events “wedding” and “get baby”. How can we define a time relation of these two events in our knowledge base such that it conforms to commonsense on the one hand, and is general enough to be included in any drama on the other hand? The relation “wedding” precede “get baby” conforms to commonsense, but does not cover all possibilities of movie representation. The relation “wedding” meet “get baby” is not enough, either. The correct representation should be “wedding” (precede or meet) “get baby”.

This example reminds us again of the extended time relations FTR we have introduced in chapter five. Fortunately we have extended the Allen and Freksa time relations there and have also introduced group time relations which are very useful for defining a plot plan or drama plan. We will see this point in the next section 6.3.2.

6.3.2 Plot Processing at Qualitative Temporal Level

Note that in each time marking [a, b] both a and b , called also lower and upper limit of the time interval [a, b] respectively, while being integer numbers or variables initially, may be instantiated as rational numbers during run time, which can be represented by pairs of integers. Thus, a may be represented by (m, n), for example, meaning: a is the rational number m/n.

First we explain how to change the syntax of our plot and drama agents to include time markings in their definitions.

Definition 6.3.1 (Agents with Time Marking)

1. A time marking is a pair of positive rational numbers, written as [a, b], with $a < b$.
2. Each generalized case frame has a time marking, with the exceptions of Enrich statement and Replace statement which have no influence on the time relations between statements.
3. If a statement s is used by a replace statement to replace a frame variable of some ancestor agent, then the time marking tm (s) of s has only a local meaning (with respect to its internal statements, if there are any). Tm (s) has no relation with the time markings of other statements.
4. If [a, b] is the time marking of a nested statement, [c, d] is that of one of its internal statements, then it must be always: $a \leq c < d \leq b$.
5. Each internal statement of a conditional or case statement has the default time marking of their external statement.
6. In agents with time markings there is no T-Specification part.

Algorithm 6.3.1 (Dynamic Semantics of Time Markings)

1. When an ancestor agent ag is being inherited by some son agent, all the inherited statements keep their original time markings in ag unchanged.

2. When a replace statement r replaces a frame variable FR with a statement s, do the following:
   2.1. If s is a nested statement, recalculate the time markings of its internal statements according to step 3.
   2.2. Use the time marking of FR as that of s.
   2.3. Replace FR with s. Call the result ss.
   2.4. Algorithm finished.
3. Assume s has the time marking [m, n], FR has the time marking [q, r]. Then ss obtains the time marking [q, r]. If s is a nested statement, then the new time marking [g, h] of each its intern frame statement or frame variable with the old time marking [u, v] will be

$$g = q + (u - m) \times (r - q) / (n - m),$$
$$h = q + (v - m) \times (r - q) / (n - m).$$

End of Algorithm

It is easy to see that for u = m, v = n, the new time marking of ss will be [q, r], as we have prescribed before. Since the rational numbers are closed under four arithmetic operations (where any division by zero is excluded), the run time values of new time markings are also pairs of rational numbers.

We see also that there are two kinds of time markings, the independent ones and the dependent ones. During the time quantification, the independent time markings will be determined or calculated first, then the dependent ones will be calculated with the values of independent time markings as parameters.

Note that the time markings of internal statements of a loop statement have only a static meaning. While the real length of a time marking of other statements is calculated at compile time, the real length of the time markings of a loop statement and its internal statements will only be calculated during run time.

One may wonder why we rather want to do a complicated calculation in step 3 of the algorithm above and do not let the frame variable FR have the same time marking with the statement which is going to replace FR. This method may seem simpler. But it would cause other problems. Since a frame variable may be replaced by more than one statement, this method would prohibit us, for example, from having two different replacing statements with different time markings in different son agents of the same father agent. This is why we need an algorithm to recalculate the time markings of the frame statement for each replacement separately.

In the following we will give some examples to illustrate the dynamic semantics of drama inheritance, especially that of presentation inheritance, where we write the frame statements in simple natural language form. The letter F means father agent, S means a son agent before inheriting, R means this son agent after inheriting. The time markings are represented by using symbols instead of using numbers. It is always assumed that $t_i < t(i+1)$ for each i.

Example 6.3.1

F: (5) x reads a newspaper, [t1, t5]
S: (7) y talks to x, [t2, t3]
R: (5) x reads a newspaper, [t1, t5]
(7) y talks to x, [t2, t3]

Example 6.3.2

F: (5) x reads a newspaper, [t1, t5]
(3) FR , [t8, t9]
S: (7) y talks to x, [t2, t3]
(12) replace F (3) with (7)
R: (5) x reads a newspaper, [t1, t5]
(7) y talks to x, [t8, t9]

Example 6.3.3

F: (5) x gets off, [t1, t2]
(24) Bloc
(9) x is having a breakfast, [t3, t10]
(7) FR , [t3, t5]
(4) x reads a newspaper, [t5, t8]
(15) FR , [t8, t10]
Colb.
(3) FR , [t5, t8]
S: (7) y talks to x, [t2, t3]
(12) Replace F (7) with (7)
(22) Replace F (15) with (7)
(23) Replace F (3) with (7)
R: (5) x gets off, [t1, t2]
(24) Bloc
(9) x is having a breakfast, [t3, t10]
(7) y talks to x, [t3, t5]
(4) x reads a newspaper, [t5, t8]
(15) y talks to x, [t8, t10]
Colb.
(3) y talks to x, [t5, t8]

Example 6.3.4

F: (2) x and y are having a rest, [t5, t10]
(3) FR , [t6, t9]
S: (7) Bloc
(23) y talks to x, [t2, t3]
(24) FR, [t3, t4]
Colb, [t1, t5]
(12) Replace F (3) with (7)
R: (2) x and y are having a rest, [t5, t10]
(7) Bloc

(23) y talks to x, [t6 + (t2 - t1) × (t9 - t6) / (t5 - t1),
t6 + (t3 - t1) × (t9 - t6) / (t5 - t1)]
(24) FR, [t6 + (t3 - t1) × (t9 - t6) / (t5 - t1)
t6 + (t4 - t1) × (t9 - t6) / (t5 - t1)]
Colb, [t6, t9]

6.4 Dividing the Story in a Series of Acts

After that the story is fully developed (in concrete actions) in that way, we will start to divide the chain of actions in a series of acts. The main problem to be solved is to determine the grouping of actions in episodes and to determine the roles, objects and backgrounds in each group. The principles are rather simple and are as follows:

The actions, roles and objects contained in a frame statement are considered as keywords for determining the possible backgrounds of this statement. When grouping the statements in acts, we follow the principle of maximal extension. This procedure of grouping is similar to the physical procedure of crystallization. Those abstract actions which are transformed into concrete ones by plot agents serve as centers of crystallization. Other statements join these centers whenever it is possible. Thus the centers of crystallization grow up and become bigger and bigger acts. A simple algorithm of act crystallization looks as follows:

Algorithm 6.4.1

1. Use drama agents and plot agents to develop all abstract actions into concrete actions.
2. All concrete actions produced by plot agents are marked with backgrounds specified in these plot agents. The concrete actions produced by the same plot agent form a group.
3. The neighboring groups with the same background are merged into a bigger group.
4. Determine the set of possible backgrounds for each remaining concrete action whose key words remind of some typical backgrounds.
5. Choose a background from each set in a way such that if these actions would be grouped in acts according to the next step and algorithm 6.4.2, the number of acts will reach its minimum.
6. Group the frame statements in acts such that:
   6.1 Each frame statement with the same background as that of a neighboring group will be combined with that group;
   6.2. The neighboring frame statements with the same background can be combined into a group, and
   6.3. The neighboring groups with the same background are merged into a bigger group.
7. Each group is called an act.

End of Algorithm

Algorithm 6.4.2

1. Actions with different backgrounds belong to different acts.
2. Actions at different places or different times belong to different acts.
3. If two actions A1and A3, which happen with the same background, and at the same place, have the time intervals [t1, t1'] and [t3, t3'], respectively. A2 is another action with different place or background, which has the time interval [t2, t2']. Assume further t1' <= t2 < t2' <= t3. Then A1 and A3 belong to different acts.

End of Algorithm

At a first glance, these principles may seem too simple and naive. Nevertheless, they are practical.

Example 6.4.1

Assume we have the following story:

"(1) Christian returned to Hamburg from a China tour. (2) He knocked at the door of his home. (3) He was welcome by his wife. (4) He put his overcoat in the wardrobe."

After plot planning, we get a series of concrete actions:
(1.1) An airplane is landing.
(1.2) Christian went out from the airport Hamburg.
(1.3) A car stopped in front of a house.
(1.4) Christian got off the car and approached the house.
(2) Christian knocked at the door of the house.
(3.1) Christian's wife opened the door.
(3.2) Christian's wife kissed Christian.
(4) Christian put his overcoat in the wardrobe.

Use algorithm 6.4.1, we have:

The actions (1.3) and (1.4) combined to one act (act A) according to step 6.2.
The actions (3.1) and (3.2) combined to one act (act B) according to step 6.2.
The action (2) combined with act A according to step 6.1.
The action (4) combined with act B according to step 6.1.

Those actions (statements) which have not been able to be grouped into acts by the above algorithms, will be processed further in chapter seven.

6.5 Solving the Quantification Problem

6.5.1 Introduction

While translating natural language stories to computer animations, it is often a very difficult task of deciding the quantities of various objects in stories and then to use appropriate animation techniques to show these objects. This is a problem which relates to commonsense knowledge and commonsense reasoning. In this section, some of our methods and techniques for solving this problem are presented.

The difficulty of processing the quantity relations in a story has many reasons. Firstly, natural language understanding itself has well known difficulties which have not yet been solved effectively, e.g., the reference problem, which we have mentioned earlier in chapter three of this book. Expressibility in animation is the second problem. Because of the limitations of animation techniques, it is not the case that every sentence or paragraph in the story, which has been clearly understood by SWAN, could be presented through animations. For example, the sentence:

He thinks he is more capable than any other person.

is difficult to present by animation because "thinking" is a process which happens in human's brain and can not be seen by other people. One would argue that one could present this "thinking" process by using some facial expressions. For example, he could show a face of arrogance. But what should we do if there is a second sentence following the above one?

But he has never let other people detect this idea of him.

This sentence forbids the director to use any facial expression to show this person's idea.

The third problem is the difference in information content implied in different media of story representation. Let us compare the information content of an animation and of a story text. It is well known that in some sense, the information contained in a piece of image is usually much richer than any text could describe. Just think at the fact that an image is only one of the 25 frames an animation movie produces each second. On the other hand, each story text is an abstract representation which allows a great multiplicity of detailed representations. It is quite often that different scenes could be imagined and designed for expressing the meaning of the same sentence. Each of them is possible, that is to say, it accords with our commonsense. Therefore it is troublesome to select among these possibilities. In resume, an image or an animation is abound in details, while a story text is abound in possibilities of producing details.

The above three problems become more complicated since we require that SWAN should posses such robustness that given the syntactic rules and lexicon library, the user could write any story conforming to the rules and the library. Then the system should be able to either generate a cartoon appropriately illustrating the plots of the story or indicate the commonsense errors in the story. From the examples shown later in this section, one can say that even if we restricted ourselves to the partial problem of only processing the quantity relations, our task is extremely difficult. We will discuss the commonsense problems relating to these quantity relations, which appear in one sentence or among several sentences in the story. Most of the time, much or less, they are context-sensitive.

Note that stories accepted by SWAN are written in Chinese. Since the problems of expressibility are closely related with Chinese grammar representation, and since the Chinese grammar is very different from that of English, we keep the order of words as it is specified in the Chinese grammar while translating Chinese sentences into English, such that some example sentences below may not follow the English grammar. Moreover, we let the English example sentences be in non-conjugated form because Chinese sentences are not conjugated. In this way, the reader may find it easier to understand the difficulty of understanding Chinese.

6.5.2 Commonsense Problems Relating to the Quantity

It is quite common for commonsense problems relating to the quantity to exist in natural language sentences. So far we have found the following ones.

1. There are no quantity descriptions for characters in the sentence.

Example 6.5.1

Dog chase cat.

In Chinese, one does not distinct singular and plural forms of nouns and verbs, and nouns do not have articles before them. Therefore, for the example sentence, one cannot tell how many dogs chase after how many cats. Obviously, the number of dogs and cats which we should produce in the animation is uncertain.

2. The quantity of the characters in the sentence may be unreasonable.

Example 6.5.2

There are one thousand dogs in the room.

We cannot decide the reasonability of this sentence at once. One can image that there exists a room big enough to hold one thousand dogs. However, it is a commonsense that most of the rooms cannot hold so many dogs, and what is more important is that to generate one thousand dogs and their actions in the animation has very high computational complexity, and is very space - and time-consuming, and it is extremely difficult to do static and dynamic planning. Thus the system should try to avoid such scene in the animation that one thousand dogs are present. In this respect, we have to ask a question: what is the reasonable quantity of dogs in a room, or generally, how many objects y are allowed to exist reasonably in circumstance x?

3. It is not always possible to express in the animation the quantity of characters in the story.

Example 6.5.3

There are 1.2 billion people in China.

This sentence is completely correct, but it is impossible for 1. 2 billion people to appear in the animation scene. What we want to ask here is that even though it were possible to do this, is it really necessary to show 1.2 billion people on the screen? Generally, while using animation to express the meaning of a sentence, must the quantities in the sentence be expressed by the exact number of objects?

4. It is often difficult to show abstract objects in an animation.

Example 6.5.4

There are about two hundred countries in the world.

It is impossible to display a whole country on the screen, needless to say two hundred countries together on the same screen.

5. The characters in the sentence are described by inexact quantity words.

Example 6.5.5

Several dogs chase several cats.

In the example sentence there are more than one dog and one cat. But we still do not know the exact numbers, which have to be known for animation generation. One solution is to define a default number, e.g., whenever the concept "several" is mentioned, replace it with the number 2 or 3. But these quantities are closely related to the character types and their circumstances. If the sentence tells that there are several cats in Jane's handbag, then two cats probably are the most since we believe that Jane's handbag is not big enough to hold more than 2 cats. If the sentence tells that there are several cats in the room, then probably there should be 5 or 6 cats. If the sentence tells that there are several baby cats in Jane's handbag, then it is possible that there are 5 or 6 baby cats. In this regard, default quantities should be, rather than predefined, decided according to the object properties and circumstances.

Furthermore, there are many uncertain quantity words in Chinese which may have different default values. The sentence "there are many cats in the room" should be given different number of cats from the sentence "there are several cats in the room".

6. The quantity of characters in the sentence is described by words difficult to display.

Example 6.5.6

There are two kilograms of apples on the table.

Apples are countable, and once given the exact number, they can be expressed in the animation. "Two kilograms of apples" is exact in weight but not in quantity. We cannot express it in animation since weights cannot be visualized directly. The computer has to know approximately how many apples there are in two kilograms. To solve this problem, it is necessary for computer to have knowledge about relations among weights, quantities and sizes.

There is another situation where it is possible to visualize the measure word but the expression way is not natural according to commonsense and customs, e.g.,

"Tom is carrying a piece of cloth two meters long on shoulder". In the animation expressing this sentence, the cloth is already rolled up, thus "two meters long" is difficult to express. Now the computer needs to know the conversion method of how big is the cloth two meters long after rolled up.

7. Non-unique transformation between different measures

The above examples prompt us that we cannot always express exactly the quantities in animation. Take the apples for example. Even if the computer animation system could compute the approximate quantity of apples in two kilograms based on its knowledge, you can never tell that the quantity is exact. In reality, it is quite possible for two people while buying two kilograms of apples to get the different numbers of apples. It is even more difficult to express how big rolling up a piece of cloth two meters long is. One way out of this difficulty is to determine the average weight of an apple for calculating the number of apples of two kilograms in the first case, or to determine the average radius of a roll of cloth of two meters long in the second case. Every reader would agree that this way of settling the problem is very inefficient and cumbersome. Is there any better method for it?

8. Uncertainty is caused by the multiple identities of one character.

Example 6.5.7

There are two fathers and two sons in the room.

Generally speaking, all characters mentioned in the sentence should be displayed in the animation. In the example sentence, there are four characters, two fathers and two sons. But a person who is the father of somebody must be a son of another person. One person could have multiple identities. In this regard, "two fathers and two sons" can be understood as a grandpa, a father and a son, where only three characters appear in the animation. Furthermore, if we take a father as a man with children, and take a son as a man with parent, then the two fathers mentioned in the above sentence could be understood as fathers of somebody who are not necessary the two sons in the sentence. The two sons are understood similarly. Therefore it is reasonable to display only two men in the animation, whose fathers and sons are beyond the description of this sentence.

9. The references to characters are not clear in the story (general name and proper name).

Example 6.5.8

Dog Jack and Dog Rose are playing in the room.
A dog is dancing.

Who is dancing, Jack or Rose? It is not clear at all. In some sense, this is also a problem of anaphora like that we have mentioned in chapter three. The difference consists in the use of a non-deterministic article instead of a pronoun. But we see clearly that an exact and unique solution is impossible in this case.

10.The references to characters are not clear in the story (general name and general name).

Example 6.5.9

A dog is singing. ...... A dog is dancing.

The story does not tell whether the two sentences refer to the same dog or two different dogs.

11.There is direct contradiction among character quantities in different sentences.

Example 6.5.10

The king has only one son.
The king's elder son likes hunting.
The king's younger son likes reading.

From the latter two sentences one can conclude that the king has at least two sons. This is in contradiction with the first sentence.

6.5.3 Principles of Quantity-Oriented Commonsense Reasoning

The algorithms which have been designed for these problems are rather complicated. In this section, we will only introduce the principles which the SWAN algorithms adopt to solve the above commonsense problems relating to quantity. Actually, the best principle should be context- sensitivity analysis, because people understand and decide the quantities according to the context in one sentence or among several sentences when they are reading a story. The SWAN system, relying upon the Pangu commonsense knowledge base, is able to do some of the context sensitivity analysis. Unfortunately, SWAN's ability is still too weak to analyze so much and so deep context-sensitivity as human beings do. In this respect, SWAN has to use some principles to make decisions when its context-sensitivity analysis is not so informative. These principles should be reasonable and close to commonsense as much as possible.

1. The Default Principle

   When the object quantity is not indicated at all in the story,

   1.1. if no information shows that the object is plural, then the object is taken as being single, in this regard, "dog chase cat" is understood as "a dog chases after a cat";
   1.2. if before the sentence "dog chase cat" there is information in the story showing that there are more than one dog and/or more than one cat, then cat and/or dog is taken as being plural, thus "in room there are three dog and two cat. dog chase cat" is understood as "three dogs chase after two cats";
   1.3. otherwise, take the object as being single.

Besides, for the situation as follows,

A dog is dancing.
A dog is singing.

or

Some people are reading.
Some people are writing.

unless it is otherwise stated, generally they are taken as representing different objects, that is to say, the dancing dog is different from the singing dog, and the people reading are not those writing.

2. The Relativity Principle

The semantics of adjectives representing uncertain quantities such as "many", "few", "whole", etc. have relativity, e. g., in a school composed of 800 students, 300 students could be understood as "many", whereas they are understood as "few" in a school composed of 3000 students.

The membership function on fuzzy set is a rather effective method to represent and process relativity. The method is described in the following.

2.1. If after story analysis the maximum quantity of the characters in a scene is decided as M, then give a membership function to every quantity adjective based on M, as shown in figure 6.5.1 where M= 10. It would be reasonable to let the numbers 0 and 1 belong to "few", if we were to only consider the strict quantity relations. However, according to commonsense, when people talk about "few", they refer to neither 0 nor 1, but a number no less than 2. This is why in figure 6.5.1 the values of the membership function of "few" between 0 and 1 do not equal to 1. The membership function of "many" is given in figure 6.5.1 in this way as well.

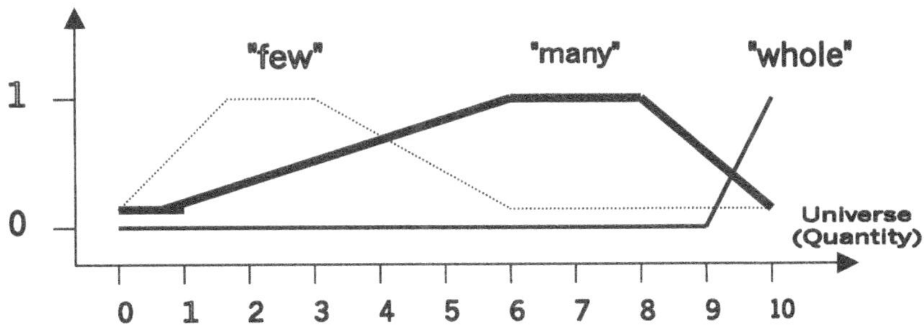

Figure 6.5.1 Membership Functions of Quantity Adjectives

2.2. Otherwise, evaluate M according to the default rules, and then decide the membership functions. Note that M itself is relative either in two aspects. Firstly, the quantity adjectives in the story are usually relative to, instead of the entirety of the characters in the story, the entirety of the characters in the current scene.

Example 6.5.11

There are 10 people in the room.
Many people are talking with each other.
Another 10 people come in.

Now the total number of people is 20, but "many" is relating to 10. Secondly, when the exact value of M is not available, we can only use the default method, where default values are relative either.

Example 6.5.12

There are many people in the room.

In this sentence "many people" actually is just "the whole people" in the room. It is relative to the maximal number of people the room can hold. "Maximal number of people the room can hold" is a membership function as well relating to the size of the room.

3. The Optimization Principle

For every quantity adjective in the story, we obviously select the maximum of its membership function values, which generally equals to 1. Usually the point where the maximum is reached is not unique. There are often several points whose membership function values equal to 1.

Example 6.5.13

There are few people in the room.

In this sentence the "few" values at point 2, point 3 and point 4 all equal to 1. Therefore a uniqueness problem appears as to how many objects, 2, 3 or 4, should be displayed in the animation. But if there is a second sentence

They are playing pokers.

then it is most appropriate to take the point 4, because the number of players of a poker game is generally 4.

Generally speaking, we may take the information obtained from each sentence as a kind of constraint condition, and when there are more than one constraint condition, we consider them as a system of conditions and select the optimized solution. As another example, we consider the two sentences in the following whose membership functions are shown in figure 6.5.2.

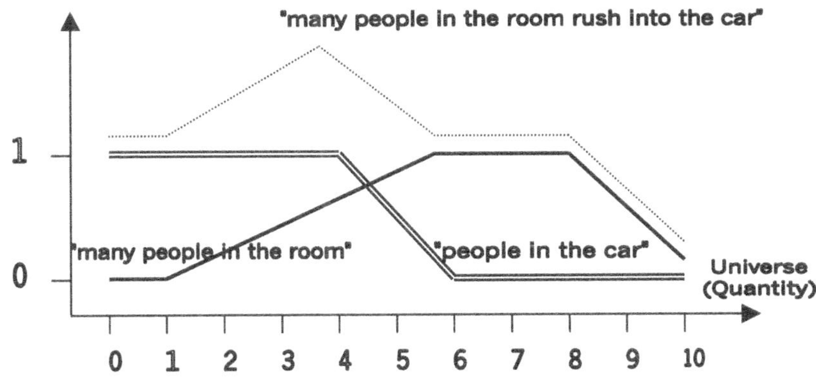

Figure 6.5.2 Optimization Solution under Several Constraint Conditions

Example 6.5.14

> Many people walk out of the room.
> They rush into a car.

There are 3 curves in figure 6.5.2, one representing the "many" concept relative to the normally reasonable quantity of people in the room, another representing the normally reasonable quantity of people in a car, and the third showing the summarization of the former two curves. Points have the maximum value on the third curve indicate the quantities after optimization. Therefore, the optimized quantity should be 4 rather than 6, 7 or 8 obtained by only considering "many people in the room".

Note that if the same quantity adjective appears several times in the story describing the different objects, then the constraint conditions they represent should not be mixed together.

Example 6.5.15

> There are 20 men and 10 women in the room.
> Many men are dressed in blue.
> Many women are dressed in white.

In the above three sentences, the two "many" words have different meanings, thus the constraint conditions they represent should not be mixed together.

The problems mentioned above about how many apples are there in 2 kilograms, etc. could be solved in a similar way.

4. The Simplification Principle

If many solutions are obtained about a quantity problem after commonsense reasoning, the simple ones have priority, where "simple" here means to be simple in commonsense and in animation expression. For the example given above of "two fathers and two sons", the simplest understanding in commonsense is that there are four people in the room, whereas two or three people are special solutions obtained only by special reasoning. Therefore, the solution simple in commonsense refers to the one which ordinary people realize immediately in direct perceiving. For the example that there are many people in the room, without any constraints, the quantity of the people could probably be 6, 7 or 8 according to a curve of membership function in figure 6.5.1. Now the principle of being simple in animation expression should be taken into account, thus the quantity of people in the room is considered as 6.

5. The Non-Contradiction Principle

If the average number of apples per kilogram is, say, 6.45. Then no one would argue if we demonstrate 12 or 13 apples in our animation for the sentence: "There are two kilogram apples". We may even display 11 or 14 apples instead of 12 or 13. We have this freedom because the information about the size or the weight of an apple is missing in the sentence. Thus we are allowed to produce this missing information by deciding the number of apples when transforming the text into image, provided that we do not violate commonsense (e.g. we do not draw 100 apples for the weight of two kilograms). Another example is shown by the following three sentences.

Example 6.5.16

> The king has 100 soldiers.
> Some of the soldiers are dressed in red.
> Some of the soldiers are dressed in green.

For displaying the content of these sentences by image, we are allowed to produce any number x of soldiers dressed in red, and any number y of soldiers dressed in green, provided that the following two conditions are fulfilled:

> Neither x nor y is equal to zero.
> The sum of x and y is equal to 100.

We may do this because the information about the partition of 100 soldiers dressed in red and in green is missing in the original text. Thus we again have the freedom to produce this information when deciding the numbers of these two groups.

Summarizing what we have done for these two examples, and remembering that an image usually contains much more information than the corresponding text, we can form the idea as follows: we may, and we also must produce any information which is missing, but which is necessary, by not contradicting the commonsense.

6. The Abstract Representation Principle

If a quantity is reasonable, e.g., there are 1. 2 billion people in China, but it is impossible or very difficult to directly express it in the animation, the indirect presentation methods should be taken into account. For representing the example sentence about 1.2 billion people given above, we can design an animation scene where many people are walking in a Beijing street and a subtitle tells that China has a population of 1. 2 billion people. Pedestrians hurriedly come and go gives the audience the impression that there are many people, and the subtitle makes the audience know the number 1.2 billion. These two techniques are combined together to express the meaning of the sentence.

Generally speaking, small quantities are always expressible, whereas large ones are not so easy to express. In this regard, we could abstract the concept "many" and conclude the above method with the following two points.

6.1. Use some symbolized means to express "many".
6.2. Use appropriate techniques such as subtitles, asides, etc. to indicate the exact number if necessary.

There are two problems about this principle. The first one involves determining conditions under which quantities in the sentence should be expressed by the exact number of objects, or expressed in an abstract way when the quantity is too large to represent. Is it only related to the boundary of quantities, or some other principles should be adopted to make a decision? The second problem relates to the selection of symbolized means used for presenting the content of the sentence abstractly. In the case of using pedestrians to represent a large amount of population, there is still a third problem as to how many pedestrians appearing is reasonable.

For the first problem, two membership functions of the expressibility in animation and the complexity of animation expressing are used. Other principles could be referred to as well. Let's assume two stories A and B:

Example 6.5.17

The king has 100 soldiers.
The king leads his 100 soldiers to fight.

Example 6.5.18

The king has 100 soldiers.
10 of these 100 soldiers are dressed in red.
10 of these 100 soldiers are dressed in green.

100 soldiers in story A can be expressed by abstraction method, whereas those in story B cannot only be expressed by abstracting due to the requirements of counting the soldiers in different clothes. As for the second problem, it is closely related to the context and plots of the story.

7. The Completion Principle

When there exist contradictions in quantities, the system normally should output error information. Yet this is not always correct for sometimes contradictions are caused by the incompleteness of the story content. If such circumstance appears and is recognized by the act planning module of SWAN, some delicate details may be added to the act automatically to get a new one free of contradiction. We call it the completion principle.

Example 6.5.19

> Mother puts three apples on the table and goes out.
> Jack comes in and sits at the table.
> Mother returns to the room and sees only two apples remaining on the table.

It seems that there is a contradiction about the quantity of apples. The number of apples has been reduced to two while it is not stated at all that somebody has taken away one of the apples. However, when adopting the completion principle, we can reason that adding the sentence "Jack takes an apple from the table and eats it" between the second and third sentence above would eliminate the contradiction.

As for when and how to complete the content of story and how to avoid the contradictions between the added part and the original story are closely related to the context and plots of the story. This is a problem of commonsense. Its realization depends on the size and content of the commonsense knowledge base.

6.5.4 An Algorithm of Quantity Estimation

In this section, the sketch of an algorithm is given for deciding the quantities of objects in a story, based on the seven principles given in the last section. This algorithm is especially useful for determining the rough number of roles and objects in an act (see next chapter).

The following eight classes of objects are called super objects.

<Object Class A>::= <Basic object>;
#Objects without quantity specification, e.g., rabbit #
<Object Class B>::=<Non-quantity adjective> <Basic object> | <Object Class A>;
e.g., big rabbit
<Object Class C> :: = <Numeral> <Object Class B>;
e.g., three big rabbits
<Object Class D> ::= <Quantifier> <Object Class B>
e.g., a basketful of big rabbits
<Object Class E> ::= <Object Class B> <Auxiliary word>
e.g., big rabbit group
<Object Class F> ::= <Reference pronoun> <Object Class B>
e.g., that big rabbit
<Object Class G> ::= <Object Class B> <Proper noun>
e.g., big rabbit Rose
<Object Class H> ::= <Quantity adjective> <Object Class B>
e.g., many big rabbits

Note that in order to calculate the values of membership functions for inexact quantities appearing in a story, which are fuzzy quantity concepts, we need a method to estimate the total number of each kind of objects at each moment of plot development. In this regard, we take every sentence in the story as a group of object operations. Each operation increases, diminishes, or keeps the number of objects. There are three types of such operations classified by their influences on the quantities of objects.

1. operation type I, which increases the quantities of objects, e.g., "three rabbits and a tiger come in"
2. operation type II, which decreases the quantities of objects, e.g., "three rabbits leave"
3. operation type III, which indicates the existence of objects, e.g., "three rabbits are singing"

Algorithm 6.5.1 (Sketch)

1. Merge the eight classes of objects. For example, objects in class A could be taken as those in class B with a null adjective, thus are merged into class B. Moreover, objects in class E "the big rabbits" could be understood as "all big rabbits" where "all" is a quantity adjective. Therefore, objects in class E are merged into class H. Use similar reasoning methods to merge other classes. After these merging, there are four classes left: class B, C, F and H.
2. Use similar techniques as those presented in chapter 3 and chapter 5 to solve the reference problem with respect to objects in the class F. That is, from the position of the object being referred (<reference pronoun> <Object Class B>) in the story, search backwards in the story, once an object is found matching <Object Class B>, then replace the <Object Class B> with this object; otherwise, the system outputs error information.
3. Now there are only classes B, C, and H left. For each kind of objects (for example, rabbits and dogs are two kinds of objects), take all objects of this kind in class B (including those involved in class C and H) to form an inheritance hierarchy according to the compositions of non-quantity adjectives of the objects. An example of such hierarchy (rabbits) is shown in figure 6.5.3, where "big rabbit" is a father object of "red big rabbit", and "rabbit" is a father object of "big rabbit", etc. Note that the son objects of the same father object are not exclusive with each other in this example.
4. Attach a Boolean expression to each node of the hierarchy of each kind of objects to represent the limitation of the quantity of the object corresponding to this node. An example is shown in figure 6.5.4, where n(x) denotes the quantity of x. Initially: there are five rabbits, among them there are two with long ears. There may be some red rabbits and some big rabbits.
5. As the initial state of the hierarchy, denoted with Frame (0), let n(x)=0 for any node x. For i=1, 2,...., m where m is the number of sentences in the story, when sentence i is processed, construct Frame (i) from Frame (i-1) in the way of rearranging the Boolean expressions of nodes in Frame (i-1) and meanwhile updating the Boolean expressions in Frame (0), ..., and Frame (i-1) to make them

more precise. In this way, we get a series of hierarchies Frame (i), i = 1, 2,..., for each kind of objects. Suppose the hierarchy in figure 6.5.4 is Frame (5), and the sixth sentence is "two big rabbits leave". After processing the sixth sentence, Frame (6) is shown in figure 6.5.5, and Frame (5) is updated to be more precise in figure 6.5.6.

6. During the procedure going from Frame (i) to Frame (i+1), several situations may occur as follows.
   6.1. There are unsolvable contradictions, e.g., at the moment there are only four people, but the sentence says five people leave. In that case the system tries to apply the completion principle mentioned above to solve the contradiction. If this principle does not apply to the current situation, the system outputs error information.
   6.2. The quantity is not exact, e.g., the sentence says "many people leave". In that case the system calculates a most reasonable number according to the optimization principle given above.
   6.3. Quantities of objects in some Frame (i) have not been decided even after the last sentence of the story is processed. In this case the system calculates a relatively reasonable number according to the default values and rules in our commonsense knowledge base. We differentiate between two situations:
      6.3.1. There is information contained in the text, which reminds of the possible number of objects, e.g., the only sentence in the story saying "many rabbits are singing in a big room". According to the membership function of the concept "big room", more than 20 rabbits should be present in the animation.
      6.3.2. There is no information which may help us in deciding the exact quantity. For example, the sentence "many rabbits are singing" does not contain information about the place where the rabbits are. In this case the system assumes a small room according to the simplification principle. Then the number of rabbits is estimated to be eight or nine based on the optimization principle.
7. Repeat the steps from 1 to 6, until the last sentence is processed.

End of Algorithm

We have discussed in this section the difficulties in deciding the quantity of objects in a story while generating computer animation directly from natural language texts, and the corresponding solutions by commonsense reasoning. It is well known that natural languages always have ambiguity. However, from analyzing the examples shown in this section, one can see that what we call difficulties in deciding the quantities of objects in natural language stories are not those in natural language understanding itself. For most of those examples, it is not difficult to understand them in natural language processing, e.g., "2 kilograms of apples" is very clear in semantics and easy to understand. But to convert it to animation is not an obviously easy task any more. In this respect, we actually propose a new topic in linguistics, whose contents and significance go beyond those in traditional research on syntax, semantics and pragmatics of natural languages. The decision of the quantity is just one part of this new topic which deserves research. We will go further to study the other parts of this topic apart from quantity decision.

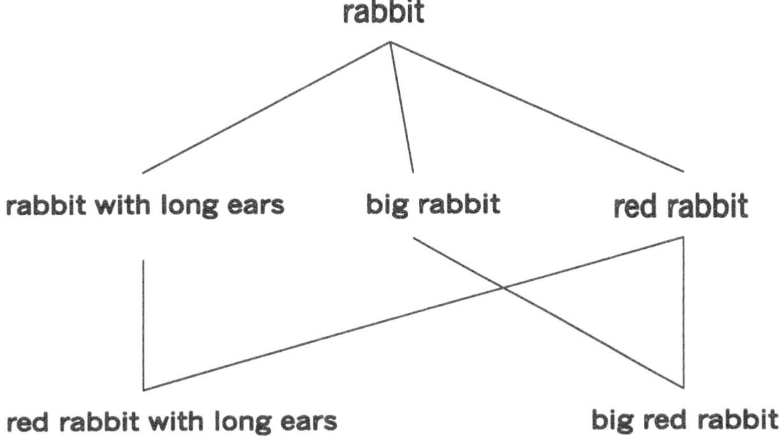

Figure 6.5.3 An Inheritance Hierarchy (in non-Conjugated English)

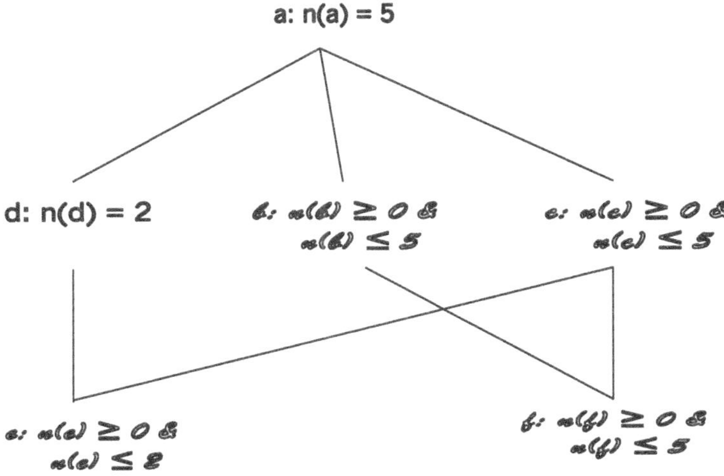

Figure 6.5.4 An Inheritance Hierarchy with Boolean Expressions

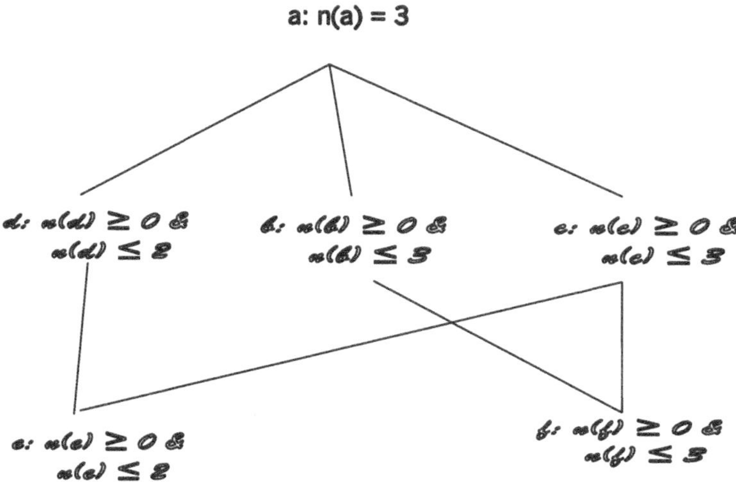

Figure 6.5.5 A Successive Inheritance Hierarchy

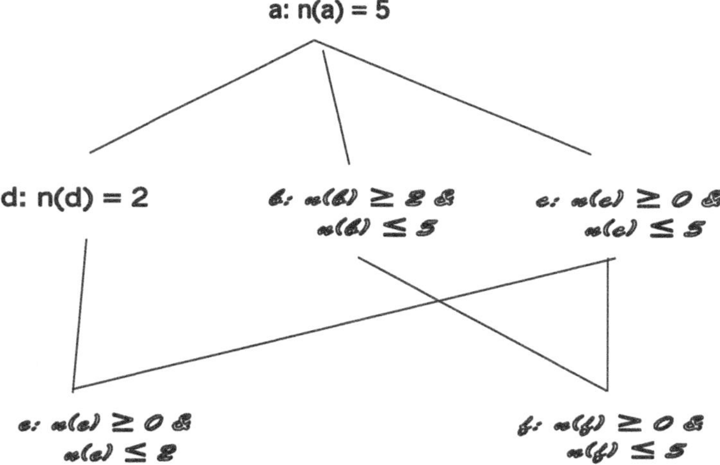

Figure 6.5.6 An Updated Inheritance Hierarchy

7 Director's Planning

7.1 The Mission of an Animation Director in SWAN

This chapter is devoted to the introduction of automatic director's planning in animation generation and to the description of how to produce it. Usually, after a story has been adapted to a script, the director of the movie has to make idea about how to film the shot such that the resulted film will present the story to the audience in the most effective way. This is also valid for making cartoon films. Our computer animation generation system SWAN has to model the designing and working process of a movie director automatically, once the script (already decomposed in a series of scenes) is given.

The mission of a film director is to transform a film script which is represented completely in text form into a synthesized multi-media form which is a combination of audio and video presentations. The creativity of the work of a director usually decides the outcome (success or failure) of a film. As it is generally recognized and practiced, the jobs of a movie director include many aspects.

First, the director has to read the script carefully and to try to grasp the main idea of the script that its author wants to express. This corresponds to the phase of requirement elicitation of software engineering.

Then, the director has to design a general framework of the film to be produced. He has to make a great deal of decisions. This corresponds to the specification and design phase of software engineering. This phase includes various aspects of movie making techniques. We list some of them in the following:

1. Further adaptation and modification of the script, where not to exclude is the modification of the original script and the addition of more details to it.
2. Portraying of the principal roles and important minor roles
3. Design of the use of camera
4. Design of the use of light
5. Design of the use of colors
6. Design of the use of music

This chapter deals with the decision principles of all these technical problems but the last one (we have not yet studied the automation of the use of music in SWAN). The discussion about their implementation is realized by detailed plans of camera and light use and is deferred to next two chapters.

In order to produce decisions about the design issues listed above, the director needs the following information (we call them requirement items):

R. Lu and S. Zhang: Automatic Generation of Computer Animation, LNAI 2160, pp. 229-253, 2002.

1. For the whole story:
   1.1. Characteristics of the times and places where the story happens
   1.2. Main plot and development threads of the story
   1.3. Major and minor roles.
   1.4. Characteristics of the roles
   1.5. Intention of the author who has written the story.
2. For each scene:
   2.1. Natural environment, including seasons, weather and daytime.
   2.2. Background and environment
   2.3. Quantity of roles and their distribution in groups.
   2.4. Layout of the scene (position of roles and objects)
   2.5. Portrait and figures of the roles
   2.6. Sentiment of the roles
   2.7. Attitudes and actions of the roles
   2.8. Relation and atmosphere among the roles
3. Focus of attention:
   3.1. Director's intention
   3.2. Spatial focus of attention
   3.3. Sentimental focus of attention
   3.4. Basic rhythms of plot development

We differentiate three kinds of requirement items:

1. Obligatory

   Those requirement items which are essentially determined by the author of the story. The director has in general little chance to change the original idea or to introduce new ideas. They are mainly the items listed in the first group above.

2. Suggestive

   Those requirement items which are essentially listed in the second group above. They may have been specified in the original story. The original specification may be incomplete or hidden. The director can complement it based on a thorough analysis of the story with techniques mentioned in chapter five and chapter six. The original specification may also not coincide with the point of view of the director. In this case the director can change it according to his/her own design.

3. Selective

   Those requirement items which are essentially listed in the third group above. They are very rarely mentioned in the original story. Their design is mainly a creative work of the director. It depends on different styles of different director schools, the director's own style of film making and the director's own intention of shooting this particular film, also the director's personal attitude toward the roles in the film, and his/her personal creative thinking.

Note that these three aspects are not necessary disjoint. In many situations, some technical condition may belong to more than one aspect. One example is the influence of time. It is possible that the time of the event's happening has been specified in the script, say "early in the morning". This specification is obligatory and will of course influence the effect of camera use. On the other hand, it is also possible that the exact time of some event's happening has not been specified in the script. It is the director who thinks that it would be better to select the "early morning" time for shooting this episode because the early morning's sun light will produce a good effect for creating a harmonic atmosphere. In this case, the condition "early morning" becomes suggestive or selective.

The director's planning module of SWAN includes almost all of the functions of a human director. This chapter deals with the first two aspects of the film director's work. The problems to settle are: how to recognize the inherent general requirement of the original script on the end effect of the movie (first aspect) and how to form the director's intention of shooting the film (following the general requirement on the one hand, and realize the director's own creation on the other hand). This is the second aspect. Finally, the third aspect, namely how to implement the director's intention, will be discussed in the next two chapters.

From another point of view, these requirement items may also be classified in three groups. The first group contains those "abstract" items which can not be represented by themselves, but only be represented by using some "concrete" items. For example, the "roles' sentiment" is an abstract item, which can only be observed by attitudes and actions of the roles. The second group contains "concrete" items which are already determined by the story itself (or by the result of its analysis). For example, the quantity of roles and their distribution in groups. The third group contains items which may be specified by the story partially, but often incomplete. They are frequently used by movie directors to express the "abstract" items, for example using person's attitude and actions to express the sentiment of roles. Note that it is just this classification of "abstract" and "concrete" items which serves as a borderline between the "specification" part and the "implementation" part of directors' intention in this chapter.

7.2 DPRS: A Language for Director Planning

This section introduces the format of requirement specification for the animation director. We need such a language for programming the director's intention, which is called DPRS (Director Planning Requirement Specification). Note that this intention of the director does not belong totally to his/her creation. As we have mentioned above, a large part of it comes from the result of analyzing the original story.

After that the division of the script in a series of scenes is completed, the most important thing for the director's planning is to determine the scenario for each scene, which must belong to one of a set of predefined typical scenarios. A typical scenario consists of two parts: its basic scenario and its additional ingredients.

<DPRS> ::= <Typical Scenario> | <DPRS> ; <Typical Scenario>
<Typical Scenario> ::= <basic scenario> | <typical scenario> ,
<additional ingredient>

7.2.1 Basic Scenarios of the Episodes

A basic scenario is the most important part of a typical scenario. The information contained in a basic scenario is indispensable for the following steps of director planning. In order to establish a knowledge base for movie director's planning, it was our first job to summarize the basic scenarios appearing in movies or computer animations. The essential content of a basic scenario includes the number of principal roles, the spatial distribution of these roles and their essential behaviors with respect to each other.

The number of different basic scenarios would be infinitely many, if we were to classify them in a very detailed way. For the sake of practicability, we will make only a fuzzy classification. Note that the basic scenarios are classified in two levels: the quantity level (how many principal roles) and the quality level (the spatial distribution of these roles and their essential behaviors with respect to each other). The quantity level identifies the number and the layout of groups of people, which we call center of focus (COF). The quality level identifies the relative actions of the different centers of focus.

Now let us summarize the syntax of a DPRS.

<Basic Scenario>::=<Quantity Level Scenario>.<Indexed Quality Level
Scenario><Time Interval>
<Indexed Quality Level Scenario> ::= <Quality Level Scenario> |
<Quality Level Scenario> (<Sequence of Persons>)
<Quantity Level Scenario> ::= Solo | Double | Few | Few_Times_Few | Many
| Few_Plus_Many | Few_Times_Many | Many_Times_Few
<Person> ::= <Role Name>
<Time Interval> ::= [<Begin> , <End>]
<Begin> ::= <Time Mark>
<End> ::= <Time Mark>
<Time Mark> ::= t<Digit String>

We first give the semantics of the quantity level scenarios. They denote roughly the quantity and distribution of people and people groups in the space. This distribution implies also the difference between the main role, main minor role and other roles in this particular scene (it does not necessarily mean the main role with respect to the whole story).

1. Solo : a single person (main role) is the only actor;
2. Double : two persons (two main roles or a main role with a main minor role) act concurrently;
3. Few : more than two and less than, say 10, persons (no main role);

4. Few_Times_Few : two small groups, each is Solo, Double or Few (no main role);
5. Many : a large or huge group of persons (no main role);
6. Few_Plus_Many : a small group (containing the main role and the main minor roles) and a large one;
7. Few_Times_Many : a few large groups (no main role);
8. Many_Times_Few : many small groups (no main role).

The content of quality level scenarios depends largely on the corresponding quantity level scenarios. The different quality level scenarios will be introduced below. On the other hand, each basic scenario must be attached with a time specification in form of a time interval [t1, t2]. The basic scenarios are produced on the basis of the plot description which is always attached with a time specification, which is then inherited by the produced basic scenarios.

It is just for the clarity of presentation that we classify the members of <quality level scenario> in groups in the following syntax according to their membership with respect to the corresponding quantity level scenarios.

<Quality Level Scenario for Solo> ::= No_Action | Body_Action | Moving | ...
<Quality Level Scenario for Double> ::= Talking | Following | Siding
| Collecting | Separating | ...
<Quality Level Scenario for Few> ::= Meeting | Separating | Following
| Collecting | Ceremony | ...
<Quality Level Scenario for Few Times Few> ::= Sensing | Watching | ...
<Quality Level Scenario for Many> ::= Ceremony | Marching | Chaos |
<Quality Level Scenario for Few Plus Many> ::= Centralization | Conferencing
| ...
<Quality Level Scenario for Few Times Many> ::= Confrontation | ...
<Quality Level Scenario for Many Times Few> ::= Distribution | ....

The semantics and examples for some quality level scenarios:

1. No_Action: neither role's place nor role's posture is changed (e.g., thinking, sleeping, etc.)
2. Body_Action: posture change without moving (e.g., singing, eating, etc.)
3. Moving: both posture and place may change (e.g., running, walking, driving, etc.)
4. Talking: two actors face to face (e.g., conversation, game playing, fighting, etc.)
5. Following : several persons one after another in a queue (e.g., stand a queue, run after a thief, etc.)
6. Siding: several persons side by side (e.g., siting, walking, etc.)
7. Collecting : several persons come together (e.g., welcome a guest, rush to catch a thief, come to get in a bus, etc.)
8. Separating : several persons go in different directions (e.g., say goodbye to each other, part after the end of a meeting, get off a bus, etc.)
9. Meeting : a small group of people around a table or something else (e.g., have a group meal, have a discussion, watch TV, etc.)

10.Ceremony : a group of persons cooperating for accomplishing something (e.g., birthday party, wedding, funeral, a piece of theater or office work, etc.)
11.Sensing : People talking face to face, but in a large distance (e.g., girl at a window while boy on the street, etc.)
12.Watching : watch a group's behavior from a distance (e.g., watch a couple dancing, watch a car moving, etc.)
13.Marching : many persons moving to the same direction : (e.g., refuges fleeing, troops moving, car race championship, etc.)
14.Chaos : a lot of persons, each acts independently (e.g., market, restaurant, street passengers, etc.)
15.Centralization : some person or object in middle of an audience (e.g., listen to a talk, surround a building, etc.)
16.Conferencing : some person or object in front of an audience (e.g., chair a conference, teach a class, direct an orchestra, etc.)
17.Confrontation : two groups of persons confront each other (e.g., war, team match, etc.)
18.Distribution : a group of small groups act independently (e.g., dancing, team struggling, etc.)

Note that all possible plots (whose use in composing stories are provided to the users by the SWAN software) are classified into the categories of the previously mentioned basic scenarios. For example, "buying a ticket" is classified into the "Talking" scenario. The two partners "talking" to each other are the ticket buyer and the ticket seller. "Tennis playing" is also classified into the "Talking" scenario. The two partners "talking" to each other are the two tennis players.

To determine a scenario with n persons does not mean that other persons should not appear on the screen. Again take "buying a ticket" as example, there may well be other ticket buyers standing in a queue behind the first buyer. But these people won't have any influence on the determination of the basic situation "Talking" in the director requirement specification, because the principal roles are the current ticket buyer and ticket seller. If the whole staff of a queue is taken as the principal roles, then the scenario will be classified into Few.Following. This illustrates that in each case, the determination of a basic scenario depends mainly on the set of principal roles.

There is no one-one correspondence between a scene and a basic scenario. For example, there may be a meeting of a small group at the beginning of a scene. After a while, the meeting may have finished. All participants but two of them may have left the room. These two persons may remain in the room for a further conversation. Thus the basic scenario may have to change from "Meeting" to "Talking".

Examples 7.2.1

1. The statement "John is standing alone on the top of the hill" will be abstracted to the basic scenario:

   Solo.No_Action (John)

2. The statement "Jack, Thom and Hans are discussing about their travel plan" corresponds to:
   Few.Meeting (Jack, Thom, Hans)
3. The statement "John is giving a talk to the audience" corresponds to:
   Few_Plus_Many.Conferencing (John)

where the time intervals have been omitted in all these examples.

7.2.2 Additional Ingredients

The additional ingredients are used to be combined with basic scenarios to form typical scenarios. They are determined by two essential factors: the situation of the real scenarios (i.e. what is described in the script and what the people should be able to see) and the intention of the director (e.g. the director wants to appreciate some role in the movie or wants to depreciate him/her) The former is basically independent of the director's intention, but must be concerned by the director.

Roughly speaking, the ingredients which could be taken to form a typical scenario are dependent on the basic scenario, though different basic scenarios may also have similar ingredients. On the other hand, the combination of different ingredients is also not arbitrary. It depends first on the commonsense and also on the theory and practice of movie art and camera technique. In the following, we list some of the ingredients which exist now in our knowledge base of director's planning. Each ingredient may be attached with parameters. For example, the ingredient "sympathizing" may have the form sympathizing (no), sympathizing (a little), sympathizing (much), or sympathizing (very much).

We also classify the additional ingredients in groups according to the different types they belong to.

<Additional Ingredient> ::= <Ingredient Class> = <Ingredient Value>
| <Additional Ingredient>(< Modification>)
<Ingredient Class> ::= Weather | Time | Place | Background | Object
| <Role Ingredient> (<Role's Name>) | <Relation Ingredient>
(<Sequence of Role Names>) | Director's Attitude
(<Sequence of Role Names>) | <Director's Intention>
<Role Ingredient> ::= Social Position | Role's Character | Role's Key Action
| Role's Sentiment | Role's Age | Role's Position | Role's Figure
| Figure Change
<Relation Ingredient> ::= Relation | Atmosphere
<Director's Intention> ::= Rhythms | Paradigm | Spatial Focus
| Temporal Focus | Event Focus | Atmosphere Focus
<Modification> ::= <Degree Modification> | <Number Modification>
| <Distance Modification> | <Situation Modification>
| <Background Modification> | <Target Modification>
<Degree Modification> ::= No | A Little | A Few | Quite | Much | Very Much
| Weak | Strong | ...
<Number Modification> ::= No | One | Two | Three | Few | Many | ...

<Distance Modification> ::= Near | Far | Very <Distance Modification> | ...
<Situation Modification> ::= Staying | Moving | Chaos | ...
<Background Modification> ::= Building | Scenery | <Weather> | ...
<Target Modification> ::= <Sequence of Roles' Names>
| <Sequence of Absolute Objects> | ...
<Ingredient Value> ::= # to be listed in the next section 7.2.3 #

The modifications are used to refine the additional ingredients. In fact, their use is context sensitive. We have written the syntax in context free form only because we do not want to introduce too many details and want to have a shorter and simpler grammar form. For example, following is the specification of a typical scenario:

Solo.No_Action (Jack) [t1, t2],
place = open field,
role's sentiment (Jack) = sorrow,
weather = rainstorm (strong)
spatial focus = eyes (Jack),
atmosphere focus = heavy.

7.2.3 Natural Environment

The particular environment where the events of the animation happen plays an important role in background, camera and light planning. The main factors of environment which may have an influence include weather and time:

<ingredient value of environment> ::= < ingredient value of weather> |
< ingredient value of time> | ...

1. The weather phenomena.
   < ingredient value of weather> ::= sunny | cloudy | overcast | rainy | foggy
   | windy | snowing | lightning | thunder | rain storm | snow storm
   | slightly <weather> | ...
2. The time
   <time> ::= <season> | <daytime> | ...
   <season> ::= spring | summer | autumn | winter | ...
   <daytime> ::= morning | noon | afternoon | evening | night | ...

7.2.4 Background

1. The place

   < ingredient value of place> ::= outdoor | indoor | street | open field
   | complex | ...

The place plays a crucial role in the use of camera and light, just as in the case of time specification. Note that a complex place is a mix of several simple places. A complex place occurs often in a long shot where the camera follows the actor by going through different places, for example, from indoor to out door, then again indoor.

2. The background

   < ingredient value of background> ::= mountain | river | forest | street
   | building | …

   In fact, the items here mean just "the main part of the background". It does not exclude things other than mentioned by its name. For example, the background "mountain" does not exclude the existence of a forest on its hillside.

3. The objects

   < Ingredient Value of Object> ::= <Absolute Object> (<Position>)
   <Absolute Object> ::= Tree | Car | Passenger | …
   <Position> ::= <Relative Position> <Ingredient Value of Background>
   | <Position> and <Position>
   <Relative Position> ::= Over | Under | In Front Of | On | Inside | Outside | …

7.2.5 Roles' Characteristics

This is to illustrate the characteristics of roles, especially their qualities. The various aspects of roles' qualities include:

1. Social position:

   <Ingredient Value of Social Position> ::= <Noble Person> | <Common Person>
   | <Lowly Person> | …
   <Noble Person> ::= Emperor | King | President | General | Prince | Princess | …
   <Common Person> ::= Citizen | Soldier | …
   <Lowly Person> ::= Beggar | Prisoner | …

2. Role's characteristics

   < Ingredient Value of Role's Character> ::= Kind | Cruel | Lively | Serious
   | Sly | Honest | …

3. Role's key action

   < Ingredient Value of Role's Key Action> ::= # some transitive or intransitive
   action #

The role's key action is such an action performed by this role that plays a crucial role in the current scene, or for characterizing this role's special character, or for presenting the current sentiment of this role.

4. Role's age

< Ingredient Value of Role's Age> ::= Very Old | Old | Middle-Aged | Young | Child | Baby| …

5. Role's sentiment

<Ingredient Value of Role's Sentiment> ::= General | Happy | Sorrow | Angry | Surprised | Astonished | Lonely | Excited | Moved | Nervous | Mad | Hysterical | Sad | Disappointed | Disturbed | Mental Disorder| Ponder | Very <Role's Sentiment> | <Role's Sentiment> and <Role's Sentiment> |…

6. Role's position

< Ingredient Value of Role's Position> ::= <Position>

7. Role's static figure

<Ingredient Value of Role's Figure> ::= <Role's Basic Figure> [<Body Part Modification>]

<Role's Basic Figure> ::= Beautiful | Awful | Fat | Thin | Tall | Short | Very < Role's Basic Figure > | <Role's Basic Figure> and <Role's Figure> | …

<Body Part Modification> ::= <Body Part Replacement> | <Body Part Addition>

<Body Part Replacement> ::= <Body Part> Replaced by <Replacement>

<Replacement> ::= <Absolute Object> | <Body Part> of <Role's Name> | Empty

<Body Part Addition> ::= Add <Sequence of Absolute Objects> to <Articulate Name>

<Body Part> ::= Head | Left Arm | Right Arm | …

8. Role's changing figure

< Ingredient Value of Figure Change> ::= Morphing <Body Part> to <Replacement> | Recover

The specifications 7 and 8 are mainly used for presenting exotic phenomena in children stories and scientific fantasy stories. For example, to replace a human's head by a lion's head, or to transform a human into a lion by morphing, etc.

7.2.6 Relation and Atmosphere among Roles

1. Relation among people

< Ingredient Value of Relation> ::= Friendly | Hostile | Loving | Hating | Equal | Master-slave | Round Robin | Outstanding | General | Suppressed | Harmonic | Isolate | Confronting | Indifferent | Respecting | Despising | Very < Ingredient Value of Relation> | …

2. Atmosphere of the environment

< Ingredient Value of Atmosphere> ::= Happiness | Sorrow | Lonely
| Mysterious | Tense | Terrifying | Bustling | ...

7.2.7 Director's Intention and Attitude

A director's intention of shooting a movie includes, in the sense of this book, his/her attitudes toward the roles of the story, his/her special point of view on the events happening in the story and his/her own way of presenting everything in the movie.

1. Basic paradigm

< Ingredient Value of Paradigm> ::= Realistic | Romantic | Heavy | Terrifying
| ...

2. Basic rhythms

< Ingredient Value of Rhythms> ::= Fast | Slow | Very <Ingredient Value of Rhythms>

3. Director's attitude toward the roles.

< Ingredient Value of Director's Attitude> ::= Sympathizing | Extolling
| Critique | Sneer | Appreciating | Depreciating | Introducing | Stressing
| Contrasting | ...

where stressing means pushing somebody forwards from a group of people (raise the attention of the audience to this person), and where contrasting means the director wants to contrast two persons (or two groups of persons) of two totally different characteristics (rich and poor, honest and sly, tall and short, fat and thin, beautiful and awful, etc.)

One may think that the director's attitude towards a role x only depends on the character or behavior of x itself. For example, a director will always portray a good figure for some role x, if x is kind and helpful, or always portray a bad figure if x is cruel and fierce. But this over-idealization does not correspond to the reality, because different directors may have different attitudes toward the same role. Even the same director may have different attitudes toward the same kind of role in different movies. Furthermore, even in the same movie, the director may have different attitudes toward the same role in different situations (different episodes of the movie). Therefore, it is reasonable to specify the director's attitude explicitly.

4. Focus of attention

The director who is designing a scene or a shot, bears in mind always some goal of presentation, which s/he intends to implement through underlining some characteristic events or objects. More precisely, the director implements her/his idea by stressing something in the movie and putting it forward, which may be some person, or some object, or some part of some person, or some background, or some atmosphere in this scene or in this shot. The director hopes to give the audience a deep impression by showing these particular things. This is usually called the focus of attention.

< Ingredient Value of Focus of Attention> ::= [<Simple Focus of Attention>]
<Temporal Focus of Attention>)
< Simple Focus of Attention> ::= < Spatial Focus of Attention >
| < Atmosphere Focus of Attention > | <Event Focus>
< Spatial Focus of Attention> ::= (<Sequence of Focus Targets>)
< Focus Target> ::= <Role's Name> | <Absolute Object> | <Body Part> (<Role's Name>)
< Temporal Focus of Attention > ::= (<Sequence of Time Intervals>)
< atmosphere focus of attention > ::= < Ingredient Value of Atmosphere> |
< Ingredient Value of Environment>
<Event Focus> ::= <Event Name>

Note that among all the ingredients, the focus of attention ingredient is the one which is subject to a timely change most frequently. Often the same scenario and the same principal roles allow different focus of attention. Let's take the example of having a class. If some student becomes the (single) principal role of the class scenario, there are several possibilities of focusing on this student. We may focus on his writing down teacher's lesson on his notebook (the students handwriting), we may focus on his careful listening to teacher's talk (the students face) , we may focus on his quick writing (the student's hand or pen), etc. The introduction of focus of attention has both a spatial and a temporal meaning. On the one hand, it specifies the place where the focus should be put on. This is its spatial meaning. On the other hand, it specifies a set of temporal intervals, each of which belongs to a scenario. Within each of these intervals a special focus of attention is given. At each moment, the integrated focus of attention is the union of all focuses of attention which are valid for this moment. This is its temporal meaning.

7.3 The Generation of Global DPRS

In this section, we concentrate on the generation technique of DPRS from a parsed story. We call this procedure of designing DPRS the point-of-view design. In SWAN, the determination of DPRS consists of the following steps: for each shot, determine a set of typical scenarios; for each typical scenario, determine its basic scenario and the associated additional ingredients. In a story, the events develop in a concurrent way. Accordingly, the scenarios should be also concurrent. Since a movie can only be shown in a sequential way, we are forced to use some technique of linearization to produce a sequential description of scenarios. In the procedure of generating a director plan, the views of originally concurrent events will be merged to produce a sequential series of scenes. Therefore, a DPRS for a plot is a sequence of typical scenarios. Their time intervals are arranged in a "one following another" way.

To solve the problem of producing director planning requirement specification, we use both professional knowledge of movie directors and also knowledge of commonsense, which is summarized in our Pangu knowledge base.

Generally speaking, for each given plot description, there are quite many possibilities of letting the audience watch the progress of the movie story, thus quite many possibilities of designing the director's work exist. Apart from that, different movie directors have different styles of adapting a story and shooting a movie. It is impossible to consider all these cases. In the current version of SWAN, we use following five kinds of information to produce DPRS: the type of the plot, the background of the plot, the objects of the plot, the (number and properties of the) roles of the plot, the sentiments of the roles of the plot. All these five types of information can be obtained from the case frame series and agent set provided by the preceding plot design process.

We differentiate between global and local implementation decisions of a director. Decisions relating to the movie as a whole, such as the basic paradigm and the basic rhythms of the movie, are called global decisions, whereas decisions relating to a particular scene, a particular event, a particular atmosphere or a particular person are called local decisions.

7.3.1 Determine the General Style of a Movie

In the circle of famous directors all over the world, there have been many different schools. Each of them has its own style. In order to enable SWAN to generate manifold and colorful products, we need a knowledge base of director styles and their implementation techniques. We need also our own technique of combining different styles of different directors for producing cartoon films which can not be produced by any particular director style alone. This rather ambitious plan has not yet been considered and implemented in our current version of SWAN.

Therefore, in this book, we will be satisfied with a single style of director planning. This is our <basic paradigm> introduced in 7.2.7. There are two possibilities of determining the basic paradigm for a script. The first one is to let the user of SWAN input his/her decision by a user interface. The second one is to use information obtained from the story analysis phase. In this section, we are taking the second approach. Remember we have studied in chapter five how to determine the paradigm of a story according to its story pattern. This information will be now used to make the director planning of SWAN.

The implementation of movie paradigms involves almost every aspect of movie technique. In this section, only the principles of its implementation are mentioned. They are considered as alternatives to be used in SWAN. More detailed implementation techniques will be introduced in next two chapters.

1. Principle of script selection :

In the whole plot planning phase (of chapter six), if there exists more than one possibility (in the Pangu knowledge base) to develop an abstract event, then always try to choose the script which is the closest to the specified paradigm. Here, the closeness of a plot plan to a movie paradigm is calculated as the sum of weights of all paradigm factors of this plot plan.

We take the above mentioned four paradigms as examples:

Paradigm is "realistic" : always choose those plot plans to develop a story which contain more details of daily life. This corresponds to the maximal value of the paradigm factor "length of plot".

Paradigm is "romantic": always choose those plot plans to develop a story which contain more mentally positive and encouraging things. This corresponds to the maximal value of the paradigm factor "positive emotion".

Paradigm is "heavy": always choose those plot plans to develop a story which contain more disappointing, discouraging and even sorrow things. This corresponds to the maximal value of the paradigm factor "tragic atmosphere".

Paradigm is "terrifying": always choose those plot plans to develop a story which contain more shocking, terrible and even catastrophic things. This corresponds to the maximal value of the paradigm factor "terrible atmosphere".

Note that all paradigm factors with their values are recorded in the plot plans of our knowledge base. It follows then, that the determination of basic paradigms should be performed right after the story analysis of chapter five and before the plot design in chapter six. So is it done in SWAN.

2. Principle of background selection:

The first principle relates only to plot plans. If our story consists only of concrete actions, then no plot planning is needed. In this case, the first principle would be useless. The second principle we now introduce relates also to individual concrete actions.

The word "background" in this paragraph is used in a broader sense than before. It includes the (physical) background, the environment, the atmosphere and even the music (not considered in this book). This principle requires that we always select the background which is the closest to the specified paradigm.

For fixed backgrounds, we have built up a background base (see chapter ten), where each background is also attached with paradigm factors. For montage backgrounds, we may choose particular weathers and particular colors of buildings, which are also assigned values of paradigm factors.

For example, assume the paradigm is "heavy", then more cloudy, overcast or rainy weather should be used in background design than sunny ones, whenever possible. For the same reason, cold colors, especially the gray and dark colors, should be used for buildings and streets. In our knowledge base, each color and each weather is also attached with paradigm factors and values.

3. Principle of rhythms control:

   Speed up or lower down the rhythms of plot progressing according to the requirement of paradigms. Using this principle, the problem of paradigm implementation is reduced to that of rhythms implementation.

   For example, a slow rhythms is suitable for implementing a heavy paradigm.

7.3.2 Determine the Basic Rhythms

While the basic paradigm relates generally to the whole story, the concept of basic rhythms relates both to the whole script and to the individual scenes. A movie may have only one basic rhythm. But in most of the cases it may have different rhythms for different scenes.

For determining the basic rhythm of the whole script, we use only very simple rules. It is determined based on the paradigm specification (or paradigm analysis). We have already given an example above. As for the basic rhythms of each scene, remember that we have discussed how to determine the theme for the whole story in chapter five, section 5.4.4.1. By using similar techniques, we can also determine the sub-themes for each story. In SWAN, these sub-themes are used to determine the basic rhythms of the individual scenes. They are also represented by simple rules and are attached to the plot knowledge base. In the following, we list a few of these rules.

sub-theme = catch bus → rhythm = fast
sub-theme = fight → rhythm = very fast
sub-theme = scientific experiment → rhythm = slow
sub-theme = ceremony → rhythm = slow
sub-theme = funeral (a special ceremony) → rhythm = very slow

Here are some heuristics for implementing the basic rhythms:

1. Principle of controlling abstraction levels: The rhythm of a movie depends largely on the level of abstraction. Abstractness means less details. The higher the level of abstraction, the faster is the rhythm of the movie. The key of enhancing the abstractness is to delete more details from the plot plan stored in Pangu knowledge base, each time when using this plot plan to develop an abstract event of the story.

   Remember section 6.3, where we introduced the concept and technique of "plot planning by abstraction". Using that technique, it is enough to produce only a partial presentation for an event. For example, for displaying a wedding ceremony, it is enough to show how the pastor declares the bride and bridegroom to be a married couple, or how the married couple leaves the church and accepts the cheers of their friends and relatives.

2. Principle of abstracting the script: Instead of abstracting the plot plan of the knowledge base, one can also abstract the script (story) itself. Remember that in

chapter five algorithms have been given to extract the main plot from a story by using a story graph. This main plot is in fact an abstract of the story.

In example 5.2.1 of chapter five, there are three abstracts of the story, each at a different level of abstractness. These levels can be represented with the graph components of figure 5.2.1. Level 1 = {sentences 7, 8, 9, 10, 11, 12}, which is the largest component; level 2 = level 1 + {sentences 2, 3, 4, 5, 6}, which is level 1 plus the second largest component; level 3 = level 2 + {sentence 1}, which is the sum of all three components

3. Principle of qualitative time control: With this principle, we do not use special values of ingredients to implement the specified rhythms, but use qualitative modifications (with fuzzy values) to prescribe the rhythms of the scenes. But we do not use this technique very often because a fast rhythm of actions does not always mean a fast rhythm of a movie. Sometimes, we may even reach an effect of caricature which we may not wish to produce.

7.4. The Generation of Local GPRS

7.4.1 Divide the Story into Scenes

If a story only consists of statements which have abstract actions as their predicates, then the division of the story in scenes is easier to do, because naturally each abstract action represents an independent scene or a series of scenes whose backgrounds are in general defined in the knowledge base. But usually the statements with abstract actions (called also abstract events) and those with concrete ones (called also concrete events) are mixed in a story. So there remains a job of grouping the concrete actions into a series of scenes. During this process, the basic scenarios and ingredients of each scene can be determined. We have already discussed this problem in section 6.4. Now we will continue the discussion and give more details.

Definition 7.4.1 (Circumstance of Concrete Statements)

Let CA be a set of concrete actions. The circumstance CU of CA, denoted CU(CA) consists of environmental factors under which the actions of CA happen. The environmental factors help to determine the background (as a direct consequence) and the division of the script in scenes (as an indirect consequence). These factors are: the background, the weather, the season, the daytime, the props and the roles.

Algorithm 7.4.1 (Determine Circumstance)

1. If the values of some environmental factors are given explicitly, then put these values in CU;

2. If the action of the statement (called key action) gives some hints on the values of environmental factors, then take all those hints which do not contradict the already (in CU) existing ones, and add them to CU;
3. If some object mentioned in the statement (called key object) gives some hints on the values of environmental factors, then:
   3.1. If these hints do not contradict each other, then take all those hints which do not contradict the already (in CU) existing ones, and add them to CU;
   3.2. If these hints contradict each other, then use the priority order of environmental factor values provided by the knowledge base to delete the relatively impossible contradicting hints and do the same as above;
4. If some person mentioned in the statement (called key person) gives some hints on the values of environmental factors, then:
   4.1. If the current statement contains the first occurrence of this person, then do the same as step 3.
   4.2. Otherwise, do nothing;
5. If CU is empty, assign the value "any" to it;
6. Finish the algorithm.

End of algorithm

This algorithm follows a priority order: first action, then object, lastly person, because in general a person can appear in any environment (e.g. a king can appear in a beggar's house). Usually there is only one action in a statement. Therefore we do not consider possible contradictions of actions in the same statement. For objects we must consider this possibility. For example, a well reminds of outdoor, while a lamp reminds of indoor. The statement: "John is throwing a lamp into the well" implies a contradiction. Since outdoor has priority with respect to indoor, the background is determined as outdoor. On the other hand, a person with social position (e.g. a king) or some special situation (e.g. being ill) may give a hint on possible backgrounds. But a general person without any specification may remind of nothing, for example: "John is very angry". In this case we use the value "any".

Among all environmental factors used to divide a story into scenes, the background is the most important and most useful one. The following algorithm is based on background differentiation.

Algorithm 7.4.2 (Group the Statements in Scenes)

1. Assume the plot planning (chapter six) of the story S is completed. The absorption of neighboring statements by abstract statements (algorithm 6.4.1) is also done;
2. If there is no concrete statement remaining, then finish the algorithm;
3. Let n := 1, x := empty, y := empty, z := empty;
4. Take the n-th statement ST of S;
5. Determine all possible environments {E} for ST, which must be a concrete statement, according to algorithm 7.4.1,
6. If x is empty, then, assign {E} to x and assign ST to y;
   Otherwise,
   Begin

If the intersection of {E} with x is not empty,
Then: assign this intersection to x and add ST to y;
Otherwise, add the pair (content of x, content of y) to z; x := {E}; y := ST
End;

7. Let n := n + 1,
8. If the story is not yet finished, then go to 4;
9. Otherwise, finish the algorithm.

End of algorithm

After performing this algorithm, z contains a series of (environment, statement) pairs. This is the result of grouping concrete actions.

At this place, the reader may get confused about one point: since the plot plan is already done, the background of each action should be known. But in fact this does not need to be true, because only those concrete actions, which are produced based on plot planning, have well-determined backgrounds. Other concrete actions, which exist already before plot planning, do not have well-determined backgrounds yet. The algorithm above is designed for such concrete actions.

Let us apply algorithm to the following example.

"(1) The mother of Princess Snow White has been ill since long time. (2) The king told Snow White that her mother was dead. (3) The king married a new queen. (4) The magic mirror told the new queen that Snow White was more beautiful than the new queen. (5) The new queen was very jealous. (6) The new queen let a hunter kill Snow White. (7) The hunter brought Snow White into a forest and set her free. (8) Snow White lived in the house of seven dwarfs. (9) The magic mirror told this to the new queen. (10) The new queen became a peasant woman. (11) The peasant woman found Snow White and gave a poisonous apple to her. (12) Snow White ate the poisonous apple and died. (13) A prince came and saw Snow White dead. (14) The prince made Snow White alive. (15) The prince killed the new queen. (16) The prince married Snow White. "

This is a simple example, from which we may get information about the possible backgrounds of the scenes. No other information, such as that about the weather, etc., is available. Use algorithms 7.4.1 and 7.4.2, we get the following result of finding backgrounds for all statements. In this way, we obtain also a way of grouping the statements in scenes. We obtain in total nine scenes, namely the statement groups: (1, 2), (3), (4, 5, 6), (7), (8), (9, 10), (11, 12, 13, 14), (15), (16).

In fact, this division of statements in scenes is not enough. The quantity of persons, the atmosphere of the environment, even the principal roles of a scene may vary drastically during the process of event progressing. Therefore, a more refined division is needed.

Algorithm 7.4.3 (Statements Grouping based on Merging Concurrent Actions)

1. Assume a scene is produced after plot planning;
2. Assume the time interval of the scene is [t_0, t_0']. Consider each action in the scene as a virtual scenario and get a set of virtual scenarios vs [i] with time interval [t_i, t_I'] , i = 1,2,..., n.

Table 7.4.1 Determination of Backgrounds

State-ment Number	Key Action	Action Type	Key Object	Key Person	Hint for Back-ground	Selected Back-ground
1	be ill	Abstract		Mother of Snow White	bed room, hospital	bed room,
2	Tell	Concrete		king, Snow White	palace room, bed room	bed room
3	Marry	Abstract		king, new queen	Church	church
4	Tell	Concrete	mirror	new queen	bed room	bed room
5				new queen	Any	bed room
6	Let kill	Concrete		new queen, hunter	any	bed room
7	set free	Abstract		Hunter, Snow White	Forest	forest
8	Live	Abstract		Snow White, seven dwarfs	House in Forest	house in forest
9	Tell	Concrete	mirror	new queen	bed room	bed room
10	Become	Concrete		new queen peasant	bed room	bed room
11	Find	Concrete		Peasant, Snow White	House in forest	house in forest
12	Die	Abstract		Snow White	House in forest	house in forest
13	come, see	Concrete		Prince,	House in Forest	house in forest
14	make alive	Abstract		Prince, Snow White	House in Forest	house in forest
15	Kill	Abstract		Prince, new queen	Palace	palace
16	Marry	Abstract		Prince, Snow White	Church	church

3. Arrange all t_i and t_i' (i = 0, 1, ..., n) in a total order according to the natural order of integers. We get a sequence of m increasing time points $s_1, s_2, ..., s_m$, where $s_1 = t_0$, $s_m = t_0$'.
4. For each interval [s_i, s_{i+1}], consider all intervals [t_j, t_j'] which have a non-empty intersection with [s_i, s_{i+1}], build a union of all events in these intersections and define it as the events eves [i] of the interval [s_i, s_{i+1}].
5. As a result, we obtain m new "scenes". Note that these scenes are only calculated for director's planning. They do not have independent pragmatics in this movie.

End of Algorithm

A premise of this algorithm is that all actions processed in it should share the background. An example of this algorithm will be seen below.

7.4.2 Determine Principal Roles in Each Scene

Among the factors which may have an influence on the director's decision and the final presentation of the movie, the most important one is the identification of main roles. We have already discussed the concept of main roles in the chapter five of story analysis. But those roles were only principal with respect to the whole story. Each story has a large set of scenes. Each scene consists of a set of shots. Within a scene or a shot, there are also principal roles, who are not necessarily the main roles in the whole story. Similarly we can determine the principal minor roles. There are also critical objects which play a key role in the development of the story. For example, the wolf wanted to tarn itself as the grandmother of the little girl. But it was not able to hide its big tail. So the big tail became a critical object of this scene. In this section, we care only about the principal roles and their basic behaviors.

For determining the principal roles of a scene, we use the following algorithm

Algorithm 7.4.4 (Determine Principal Roles of each Scene)

1. Reconstruct a story graph for each scene based on the new case frame series which has been developed by the plot development algorithm in chapter six and algorithm 7.4.2;
2. Determine the principal roles of this story graph, according to the syntactic principle explained in chapter five;
3. Similarly, determine the principal main roles.

End of Algorithm

7.4.3 Determine the Basic Scenarios

To determine the basic scenario for a scene, we need to have a rough estimation of the number of roles in this scene, their rough distribution in the whole space and the types of actions they are performing. Information about the last point can be obtained from the knowledge base and needs not to be calculated. The main problem is to determine the quantity level scenario of the scene. We will do this in two steps. In the first step, we determine it for each action (the virtual scenario). Then we try to "unite" them together to get a quantity level scenario for the whole scene. This way of going ahead is much easier than trying to do everything at once. Note that the first step is easy and we have already done it in our story analysis phase in chapter five.

As we have mentioned above, a scene may consist of a set of concurrent actions. Each action involves a group of people. To get an overall estimation, we must unite the originally concurrent scenes, which have some time intervals in common, together, to obtain a rough estimation of the quantity of people at any time moment.

Example 7.4.1

Assume we have the following scene:

In the hall there is a ball. [t1, t8].
Tom and Mary are dancing together. [t2, t6]. (*)
John watches the two jealously. [t3, t5].

where there are three events: people dance, Tom and Mary dance, John watches. They represent three virtual scenarios. Using the role graph we know that Tom and Mary are principal roles and John is the main minor role. We have the following new time intervals:

People dance [t1, t2]
People dance, Tom and Mary dance [t2, t3]
People dance, Tom and Mary dance, John watches [t3, t5] (**)
People dance, Tom and Mary dance [t5, t6]
People dance [t6, t8]

The problem is: if we have already transformed the three concurrent events of (*) in the five sequential events in (**) , how can we use the quantity level scenarios of (*) to calculate those of (**)? First we need a heuristic algorithm which is effective in case that not too many concurrent events are merged together. We list only some important rules in the following algorithm to show the idea for saving our space:

Algorithm 7.4.5 (Fuzzy Addition of Quantity Level Scenarios)

1. Solo and Solo = Double;
2. (Solo or Double or Few) + (Double or Few) = Few_times_Few;
3. Few + Many = Few_Plus_Many;
4. (Few_Plus_Many) + ((Few_Plus_Many) or (Few_Times_Many))
   = Few_Times_Many;
5. Many + Many = Few_Times_Many;
6. (Few_Times_Few) + (Many_Times_Few) = Few_Times_Few;
7. (Few_Times_Many) + Many = Few_Times_Many;
8. ((Many_Times_Few) or (Few_Times_Many)) + (Solo respectively Double)
   = Solo respectively Double;
9. ((Many_Times_Few) or (Few_Times_Few)) + Few = Few_Plus_Many;

End of Algorithm

At the first sight, some rules of this algorithm may seem strange. For example, in rule 6 the result is not Many_Times_Few, but Few_Times_Few. In rule 8 the result is neither Few, nor Many, but Solo respectively Double. The reason: this fuzzy addition is not to be considered as a pure addition of fuzzy numbers only. It involves the determination of the attention of focus in the combined scenario. In rule 6, the people representing "Few_Times_Few" become the focus of the combined scene, while the remaining "Many_Times_Few" plays a role of background people only. Similarly, in rule 8, the people repesenting "Solo" respectively "Double" become focus of attention. Other people play the role of background people.

Using this algorithm, we have the following result for the example above:

Many times Few + Double = Double,
with ingredient: background people = Many.
Solo + Double + Many times Few = Few times Few,
with ingredient: background people = Many.

where we use the symbol + to represent the union operation of elements of a set. According to these rules, we may obtain the quantitative level of the basic scenario for each new interval. They are: Many times Few, Double, Few times Few, Double, Many times Few.

7.5 Determine and Implement Abstract Ingredients

7.5.1 The Director's Attitude

Most of the abstract ingredients have been determined during the story analysis phase. An important job left is to determine the director's attitude.

We can classify the values of the director's attitudes in three groups: the positive attitudes (sympathizing, extolling, appreciating), the negative attitudes (critique, sneer, depreciating) and the neutral attitudes (introducing, stressing, contrasting), which can be determined according to the result of our story analysis (see chapter five).

In the current version we do not assume different schools of movie directors. We do not assume director's personal styles, either (though we allow the user to input his/her own decision by a man-machine interface). Therefore, the director's attitude in SWAN depends only on the story itself. There is a special module in the Pangu knowledge base to support this decision. Some simple criteria are listed below to show its flavor.

good moral + bad fate → sympathizing,
good moral + good action + big success → extolling
good moral or good action → appreciating
the first time a person appears → introducing

Let us consider the small example about dance, Tom, John and Mary again. Using script description and Pangu commonsense knowledge base we can calculate the qualitative level of the basic scenarios and the additional ingredients. The final director's planning requirement specification might be the following, where we omit the names of roles if no ambiguity will arise:

Example 7.5.1

Many times Few.Distribution [t1, t2]
  Atmosphere = happy,
Double.Talking (Tom, Mary) [t2, t3]
  Relative position = equal,
  Attitude to each other = harmonic,
  Director's attitude = introduce ,
  Sentiment (Tom, Mary) = happy ,
  Background people = many ,
  Relation to background people = harmonic,
Few times Few.Watching (John, {Tom, Marry}) [t3, t5]
  Director's attitude = introduce ,
  Sentiment (John) = angry ,
  Spatial Focus = face (John),
Double.Talking (Tom, Mary) [t5, t6]
  Relative position = equal ,
  Attitude to each other = harmonic ,
  Sentiment (Tom, Mary) = happy ,
  Background people = many ,
  Relation to background people = harmonic ,
Many times Few.Distribution [t6, t8]
  Atmosphere = happy.

The three basic scenarios have a nested time relation. They are temporally not separable. Each scenario A which is in the inside of another scenario B is a modification to B during the time interval of A. Thus the scenario A plays both a role of spatial modification and a role of temporal modification to B. This does not mean that B does not have any influence on A. In fact, when implementing this scenario, an often used technique is taken to divide the time interval of B and to let small pieces of A appear in the middle of B to produce an impression of cross attention. We will see this point later.

7.5.2 Implement Abstract Ingredients

All abstract ingredients, including those of the director's decision, must be implemented through concrete ones. There are three ways to implement them: by using special plots, props, environments or natural phenomena; by camera planning; and by light and color planning. The last two will be discussed in the next two chapters. For the moment, we are only interested in the first aspect. It is the professional skill of a movie director to design a typical scene for displaying some typical sentiment of a role or some typical atmosphere in the script, if such a typical scene is not already provided by the script itself.

The problem is that there are too many possible ingredients which can be used to refine a typical scenario. It is not easy to design a typical scene for each combination of such ingredients under all possible circumstances.

1. Use typical props
   Cigarettes are very often used as typical props, e.g.
   1.1. To show some person is pondering deeply and has difficulty to make a decision:
        Show that this person just smokes cigarettes one after another and says nothing. His/her face is very serious.
   1.2. To show some person has worked the whole night through:
        Show that there are lots of smoked cigarettes scattered in an ashtray on the desk.
   1.3. To show some person has just made an important decision to do something after a long process of thinking or waiting:
        Show that this person suddenly presses his cigarette with force and throws it away.
2. Use typical weather phenomena
   In section 7.2.3, we have given a list of typical weather phenomena. Apart from their normal use (i.e. when the corresponding weather condition is already prescribed in the given script), each of them has some particular use for displaying some typical sentiment of roles or typical atmosphere. For example, lightning or thunder is such a typical weather phenomenon.
   2.1. To show a sharp conflict between two persons, during which at least one of the two partners of the conflict feels very sorrow:
        Show that somebody (mostly a woman) is crying near a window, where the water drops are flowing down along the window glass. Outside is a strong thunder and lightning.
   2.2. To show a feeling of despair after receiving a heavy strike:
        The same as above, except that it shows somebody staring into the distance through the window, instead of showing his/her crying.
   2.3. To show a terrifying and mysterious atmosphere. Something terrible is going to happen:
        Show a strong thunder and lightning in the deep night. Nobody is to be seen. One can only watch the shadow of tree branches shaking here and there on the ground.
3. Use typical season phenomena
   The scenery of spring is often used as a typical season phenomenon:
   3.1. To show that somebody gets good emotion again after having experienced some bad events or having overwhelmed some big difficulties:
        Show that the thick ice of a previously frozen river starts to melt.
   3.2. To show that the situation (atmosphere) has started to change from bad to good:
        The same as above.
   3.3. To show a couple of young people falls in love with each other:
        Show that the trees start to blossom.

One will ask how SWAN is able to get always the right presentation for the abstract ingredients to be implemented. It is based on the organization of knowledge in Pangu. We use mainly two forms of knowledge representation: the agents and the ontology. The abstract ingredients are represented as ontology bodies, while the concrete ones are represented as agents. In each such agent, there are pointers pointing to the ontology bodies this agent belongs to. That menas: this agent may play a role in that ontology, for example, the agent "cigarette" has a pointer to the ontology body "thinking". On the other hand, each ontology body has intern structures to represent the use of agents in it. This structure is a special form of semantic networks. For example, the ontology body "thinking" has at least three semantic networks to represent the three sub-cases a), b) and c) of case 1, i.e. long time thinking, long time thinking without decision, and long time thinking with a sudden decision. This combined representation has an advantage that the basic units of knowledge (agents) and the connections between knowledge units (ontology body) are separately organized.

Another advantage of this representation is the inheritance hierarchy of both agents and ontology bodies. The language and plots used in a story may be very rich. But a huge and comprehensive knowledge base can not be built up at once or within very short time. A hierarchy of agents and hierarchy of ontology bodies can solve this difficulty. We first construct a hierarchy which is rather complete in its concepts, but whose content remains mostly empty. We fill in the knowledge of director's planning step by step, starting from the root of the hierarchy. Then, once SWAN feels short of methods to implement an abstract ingredient, it can goes back along the path of the hierarchy toward its root, and take the nearest father node as a rough solution for the current problem.

8 Camera Planning

8.1 The Camera Planning Language Morning Glow

While making a movie, the work of a director of photograph is very important. S/he must cooperate well with the movie director to accomplish a masterpiece of film art.

In SWAN, this task is also done by the computer. We call it as camera planning. This function is realized by a separate module of SWAN, of which the way of planning is a hierarchical one. It works in a top down fashion. Given that the story is already analyzed, the main roles with their properties and characters determined, the monolithic story divided in a series of acts, the important events in detailed plots developed, then the camera planning of SWAN is produced in the following steps.

1. Generate a set of director's planning requirement specification (DPRS) for each act. Note that DPRS is also used for other planning tasks, e.g. director planning (chapter seven), light and color planning (chapter nine), etc.
2. Use the set of DPRS to produce a set of routine camera statements (RCS).
3. Translate each RCS into high level camera primitives (HLCP).
4. Translate the high level camera primitives into basic camera primitives of the Rainbow Language (BCP).
5. Compile the BCP of the Rainbow language into quantitative camera statements in Evergreen form (QCS).

The set of DPRS, RCS, HLCP, BCP, and QCS elements form a hierarchy of camera planning representation. This set {RCS, HLCP, BCP} can be considered as an independent language for camera planning. We give it the name: Morning Glow. We have introduced DPRS in chapter seven in details. In this chapter, we will describe Morning Glow in detail.

The reader may wonder why we need so many steps to produce a camera plan. Our answer is that the camera planning is a very complicated task. Let us compare the camera planning with software engineering.

DPRS planning ←→ Software Requirement Specification
RCS Planning ←→ Software Architecture Design
HLCP Planning ←→ Function and Module Design
BCP Planning ←→ Higher Level Language Programming
QCP Planning ←→ Compiling and Implementation

R. Lu and S. Zhang: Automatic Generation of Computer Animation, LNAI 2160, pp. 255-285, 2002.

From another point of view, we can make the following interpretation:

1. DPRS specifies the director's understanding and intention about the situation of the story. It does not involve the audience's point of view.
2. RCS specifies the audience's point of view. It does not involve any camera technique.
3. HLCP specifies the camera technique which should be used to implement the RCS. It does not involve the concrete use of cameras.
4. BCP specifies the qualitative use of cameras. It does not involve the quantitative aspects of camera position and camera movement.
5. QCP specifies everything quantitatively.

8.2 The Work of Edit

After the set of DPRS is given, the next step is to transform these DPRS into RCS representation which is the first member of our language family Morning Glow. Before explaining what RCS is, we would like to introduce a technique of film production which has been adopted by SWAN: the technique of edit. Editing is a very important part of film production. As said by Roy Thompson: "this is the name given to the complete process of putting an entire film together. The operations are carried out with different machines" [Thompson, 1993]. He explained further: "The edit is a transition between two shots" In SWAN, edit is used to restructure the DPRS before they are transformed into RCS, in order to reach the goal which is followed by the script adapter and movie director when they are cutting the film they have made. Traditionally, it takes one of the three forms: the cut, the mix and the fade. In this section we only describe the part of SWAN which implements the cut function.

According to [Thompson, 1993], there are six elements of the edit, which must be kept in mind by any cameraman. They are: the motivation (there must be a reason to make a cut), the information (a cut must bring in new information), the composition (relation between two shots following each other), sound (a problem of synchronization), the camera angle (the camera should be on a different angle from the previous shot), and the continuity(jumps undesirable). In SWAN, we can not include all forms of cut. But we have found out conditions which can be judged by a computer as to where and how to make an appropriate cut.

There is a big difference between the way of realizing a cut in movie studios and in our SWAN system. In the movie studios, cut will be made after all the camera work has been done. The traditional way of making cut is to take the produced film in the hand, and to use scissors and clues to put the shots together. Nowadays, people have got rid of scissors and clues and have used computer to make the so-called non-linear cut. They can put any sets of shots together at their will. But the fact that the procedure of cut is done after the movie has been filmed remains unchanged.

In SWAN, the work of cut is done before the movie frames are produced in later steps. It belongs to the module of camera planning, as we will see below.

Definition 8.2.1

Two ingredients are said to have a relation with each other, when at least one of the following conditions is fulfilled.

1. They belong to the same class of ingredients (e.g. sentiment), but with different values (e.g. happy and angry) and with respect to different persons (e.g. John is happy and Mary is angry).
2. Another example: the director's attitude is appreciative towards John, but depreciative towards Mary.
3. One of the two is the cause or result of the another, for example, one performs a key action to change the sentiment of the another (e.g. John beats Mary in a chess match).

Definition 8.2.2

An ingredient is said to be co-relative, if one of the following conditions is fulfilled.

1. It indicates a bad relation between two principal roles, for example hate each other, or struggle against each other.
2. It indicates a good relation between two principal roles to a high degree, for example love each other very much.

In this case, the both sides related by the co-relative ingredient are called the related partners.

Definition 8.2.3

An ingredient is said to be focus making, if one the following conditions is fulfilled.

1. It mentions some important thing, for example a key props, a key body part or a key environment.
2. It mentions some characteristic of a principal role (e.g. sentiment), which the other principal roles do not have, for example, his sentiment = good.

In this case, this important thing or this principal role is called the implied focus.

Algorithm 8.2.1 (Cut Making)

1. Assume a DPRS is given, with a basic scenario bs and a sequence of additional ingredients sai = { ings[i] | i=1,2,...,n }, where each ings[i] is the set of ingredients in the time interval $[s_i, s_{i+1}]$. The time interval of each ingredient is the same as that of bs is $[S_1, S_{n+1}]$.
2. If there are two or more centers of focus (COF) in any time interval $[S_i, S_{i+1}]$, then split this interval into a sequence of subintervals such that:

   2.1. for each COF, there is at least one subinterval containing only this COF,
   2.2. except in the case of 2.3 below, no two neighboring subintervals contain the same COF, we use again the notation $[s_i, s_{i+1}]$ to denote the new sequence of time intervals, i = 1,..., k.
   2.3. there is at least one subinterval which contains all COF of the original interval.
3. If there is a set of two or more ingredients in the same ings [i], which have a relation to each other (definition 8.2.1), then let the set of these ingredients be i, and split the time interval $[s_i, s_{i+1}]$ into some subintervals such that:
   3.1. for each ingredient of I, there is at least one subinterval which contains only this ingredient.
   3.2. with exception of 3.3, no two neighboring subintervals contain the same ingredient from I.
   3.3. there is at least one subinterval which contains all ingredients. (We use again the notation $[s_i, s_{i+1}]$ to denote the new sequence of time intervals, i = 1,…,j)
4. If there is a ingredient ing in ings [i], which is co-relative, then split the time interval $[s_i, s_{i+1}]$ into some subintervals such that:
   4.1. for each partner of the co-relation, there is at least one subinterval which contains this partner as the only principal role,
   4.2. with exception of 4.3, no two neighboring subintervals contain the same principal role,
   4.3. there is at least one subinterval which contains all partners. (We use again the notation $[s_i, s_{i+1}]$ to denote the new sequence of time intervals, i = 1,…,h)
5. If there is a ingredient ing in ings [i], which is difference making, then split the time interval $[s_i, s_{i+1}]$ into some subintervals such that:
   5.1. there is at least one subinterval which contains the difference maker as the only principal role.
   5.2. with exception of 5.3, no two neighboring subintervals contain the same difference maker.
   5.3. there is at least one subinterval which contains all principal roles.
6. Repeat step 3, 4, 5 until there is no more such ingredients.
7. The result is a sequence of DPRS after cut.

End of Algorithm

Example 8.2.1

Consider example 7.4.1.once again. There we have generated a series of five time intervals

People dance [t1, t2]
People dance, Tom and Mary dance [t2, t3]
People dance, Tom and Mary dance, John watches [t3, t5]
People dance, Tom and Mary dance [t5, t6]
People dance [t6, t8]

With the sentiments: Tom and Marry are happy. John is jealous.

With definition 8.2.1, John's sentiment of being jealous is a result of Tom and Mary's sentiment of being happy. So jealous and happy have a relation to each other. On the other hand, with definition 8.2.3, John's sentiment of being jealous is also focus making, because no other main roles (Tom and Mary) have this sentiment. Besides that, John and the pair (Tom, Mary) form two separate focuses of center. All these provide reasons for cut making. The result is:

People dance [t1, t2]
  People dance, Tom and Mary dance [t2, t3]
  People dance, John watches [t3, t4]
  People dance, Tom and Mary dance [t4, t5]
  People dance, Tom and Mary dance, John watches [t5, t6]
  People dance, Tom and Mary dance [t6, t7]
  People dance, John watches [t7, t8]
  People dance, Tom and Mary dance [t8, t9]
  People dance [t9, t10]

Now we have nine time intervals after cut. Each time interval may be a scene or a shot, according to its degree of complexity. The first two and last two new intervals are the same as the old ones. The old middle time interval (third one) is developed into five small new ones by algorithm 8.2.1.

Example 8.2.2

According to an ancient legend of China, once upon a time there were ten suns in the sky. They produced a terrible heat such that everything was made scorched. A great hero called Hou Yi shot down nine of the ten suns and thus rescued the earth.

SWAN has produced an animation of this legend, of which one scene shows the procedure of a sun being shot down. The sun first laughed at Hou Yi and then got scared and began to enter a panic. This scene was cut into small pieces by the algorithm 8.2.1. The result is given in form of frame pictures from picture 1 to picture 11 in the appendix of this book.

8.3 The Routine Camera Statements

The routine camera statements form an intermediate level between camera planning requirement specification and high level camera statements.

We differentiate between DPRS and RCS. The DPRS is camera independent and does not involve camera technical primitives. Each DPRS includes just a list of characteristics of the plot description, which may play a role while deciding about which camera design techniques can be used. For example, "a small group of people is having a meeting" may be one of such DPRS. In this specification, we have information about the number of the roles (a small group), though somewhat in a fuzzy way. We have also information about the position of people with respect to each other (a meeting). Apart from that, we also have information about the possible attitudes of the roles (having a meeting). Therefore a DPRS usually has parameters, for example, the exact number of participants, the chair person, the meeting place, etc. are all useful parameters for generating appropriate RCS from the current DPRS "meeting".

The roles of RCS can be explained by a metaphor. They are just like the basic function modules in a software program. The translation process from DPRS into RCS is the most important step in our camera planning. We will introduce the library of RCS in section 8.3.1, and explain the translation process from DPRS into RCS in section 8.3.2.

8.3.1 Classification of Routine Camera Statements

The language of motion picture is a language of art. It expresses the intention of directors in an abstract way, or in a way of symbolic meaning. We can illustrate this idea with the example of using colors in our daily life. The colors are usually divided in two classes: the warm colors and the cold ones. Further, red means often "revolution", "danger", "hot", "halt!", etc. Yellow means often "rich", "royal", etc. Green means often "life", "young", "spring", "the way is free of obstacle", etc. White means often "peace", "clean", "pure", and "winter". Black means often "terror", "death", "serious", "noble", etc. The language of motion picture also uses the technique of symbolic meaning to express what the director wants to show to the audience. In SWAN, the routine camera statements are classified according to the principle of abstract symbolic meaning of director's intention. Following is an incomplete list of RCS statements, where we omit the parameters to improve the simplicity. The semantics of most of them can be understood by their names. We have added a few notes to help the reader's understanding.

1. Introducing a single person
   1.1. step_in_approach (target1)
        # Introduction with stepwise refinement. That means: the position of the observer approaches the target closer and closer #
   1.2. step_out_approach (target1)
        # Introducting a person in a reverse way than 1.1. The position of the observer leaves the target more and more #
   1.3. top_down_scan (target1)
        # Introduction with part for part scanning. The observer observes the target in a top down way. #
   1.4. bottom_up_scan (target1)
   1.5. part_to_whole_scan (target1)
        # Introduction in a part-to-whole way. Starting from a key body part or from some key props connected to the target's body. #
   1.6. whole_to_part_scan (target1)
        # Introduction in a whole-to-part way. Starting from the target body and towards some key body part or some key props connected to the target's body. #

1.7. partial_round_observe (target1, target2)
  # Observe target1 from different sides. The view includes target2 #
  # Both targets may be a group #
1.8. one_round_observe (target)
  # Observe the target(s) from all sides #

2. Introducing two persons
   2.1. With equal weights:
      2.1.1. side_by_side (target1, target2) # in parallel direction #
      2.1.2. face_to_face (target1, target2)
      2.1.2. one_after_another (target1, target2)
   2.2. With unequal weights
      2.2.1. side_by_side_with_contrast (target1, target2)
      2.2.2. face_to_face_with_contrast (target1, target2)
      2.2.3. one_after_another_with_contrast (target1, target2) # target1 is important #

3. Introducing more than two persons
   3.1. Introduction with equal weight.
      3.1.1. normal_group_shot (group1) # all targets on the screen #
      3.1.2. respectively_group_shot (group1) # all targets shown one after another #
      3.1.3. triangle_three_shot (group1) # targets form a triangle #
   3.2. Introduction with unequal weights
      3.2.1. three_one_shot (group1, group2, group3) # group1 is important #
      3.2.2. three_two_shot (group1, group2, group3)
      # group1 and group2 are important #
      3.2.3. three_two_one_shot (group1, group2, group3)
      # combination of the above two #
      3.2.4. three_exchanging_two (group1, group2, group3)
      # group1 fixed, two other groups appear alternatively #

4. Introducing many persons
   4.1. fixed_observe_many (group1) # observer fixed #
   4.2. moving_observe_many (group1) # observer moving #

5. Presenting the sentiment
   5.1. facial expression
      5.1.1. one_expression (target1)
      # demonstrate the facial expression of a single person #
      5.1.2. sorrow_or_lonely (target1) # demonstrate sorrow or loneliness #
      5.1.3. anogant_shot (target1)
      5.1.4. madness_shot (target1)
   5.2. key props
      5.2.1. static_focus_of_attention (target1) # target fixed #
      5.2.2. dynamic_focus_of_attention (target1) # target moving #

6. Observing the movement
   6.1. move_and_back (target1, dir1)
   6.2. right_angle_turn_around (target1, dir1, dir2)
   6.3. move_and_stop (target1)
   6.4. to_and_from (target1)

7. Observing two persons' movement
   7.1. one_move_to_one (target1, target2) # target1 approaches target2 #
   7.2. one_follow_another (target1, target2)
   7.3. one_near_another (target1, target2)
   7.4. one_seeing_another_off (target1, target2)
   7.5. walking_in_opposite_direction (target1, target2)
   7.6. coming_together (target1, target2)

8. Observing two persons' action
   8.1. fighting (target1, target2)
   8.2. object_passing (target1, target2, object)
   8.3. one_touch_another (target1, target2)
   8.4. cross_attention (target1, target2) # alternating focus of attention #

9. Introducing a group
   9.1. around_a_meeting (group1)
   9.2. around_a_table (group1)
   9.3. diagonal_table_shot (group1)
   9.4. middle_line_table_shot (group1)
   9.5. conspiracy_shot (group1)
   # despise a group of bastards who are getting together to make some conspiracy #

10. Pushing persons forward from many others
    10.1. pushing one person forward
       10.1.1. one_face_many (target1, group1) # target1 faces group1 #
       10.1.2. principal_role_pushed_forward # focusing on the principal role #
       10.1.3. principal_role_surrounded # principal role observed from all sides #
       10.1.4. one_stands_out_gradually # principal role becomes more and more clear #
    10.2. pushing two persons forward
       10.2.1. two_persons_outstanding (target1, target2)
       10.2.2. two_persons_surrounded (target1, target2)
       10.2.3. two_persons_from_a_table (target1, target2)
       10.2.4. two_fight_shot (target1, target2)
       # two targets fighting against each other #

11. Many persons in the middle of focus
    11.1. many persons only

11.1.1. scan_and_return (group1) # scan a group from left to right and return #
11.1.2. many_focuses (group1)
11.1.3. many_changing_focuses (group1)
11.1.4. circling_around_many_persons (group1)
11.2. many persons with someone else
11.2.1. one_circles_many (target1, group1)
principal role circles around many people
11.2.2. one_meets_many (target1, group1)
11.2.3. half_circle (target1, group1) # compare it with 12.2.1 #

12. Many persons in action
12.1. three_persons_moving_in_line (target1, target2, target3)
12.2. many_persons_moving_in_line (group1)
12.3. parallel_go_through_the_frame (group1)
13. More than one group
13.1. two_equal_groups (group1, group2)
13.2. many_triangles (group1)
14. Observe the environment
14.1. bird's_view
14.2. look_around

From the classification above, it is easy to notice that this is only a very small subset of all possible routine camera statements it should include. For example, the RCS listed above are mainly people-centered. They do not care the huge variability of different actions a man or several people may perform. There should be different routine camera techniques for representing different kinds of actions. Those given above only serve as some examples to illustrate the content of the knowledge base. In fact, the total amount of possible RCS may be infinite. At the first stage of building the knowledge base, our task is only to establish the basic framework of this knowledge base and to collect the most important RCS for testing the usefulness and appropriateness of this kind of knowledge. Then, the user can add more and more RCS to the knowledge base when there is a need to do so.

Here is the simple syntax of RCS:

<RCS> := <Name of RCS> [(<Sequence of RCS Parameters >)]
<RCS Parameter> := <Group Role> | <Single Role>
<Group Role> ::= group [<Digit>]
<single Role> ::= target [<Digit>]

We see that a RCS has no parameters other than those describing (group or single) roles. The semantics of a RCS can be seen by its name. The name of each RCS specifies a particular camera technique which is further realized by the corresponding HLCP plan which consists of a finite sequence of high level camera primitives (HLCP). The number and types of these HLCP components are quite different for different RCS. In the following, we will list some RCS with their HLCP components.

8.3.2 From DPRS to RCS (1): A Rough Generator of RCS

Now it is time to attack the problem about how to translate the DPRS into a real camera plan. That is, how to make a camera plan consisting of a series of RCS. The main difficulty of transforming a DPRS into a RCS plan is the irregular correspondence between DPRS and RCS plans. The mapping, if we could talk about a mapping at all, between DPRS elements (i.e. ingredients) and RCS is not one to one, but usually many to many. To solve the problem of generating routing camera statements, we use mainly knowledge about technique of film photography, but also some commonsense knowledge.

Algorithm 8.3.1 (Rough RCS planner)

1. Assume a DPRS is given, with a basic scenario bs and a sequence of additional ingredients sai.
2. Perform algorithm 8.3.2 to order the ingredients according to their time intervals and to produce a sequence of DPRS based on the inputted one. (Note that part of this work has been done in algorithm 8.2.1)
3. For each DPRS which is a member of the DPRS sequence produced in step 2, perform algorithm 8.2.1 to edit them, and thus to get a refined series of DPRS.
4. For each refined DPRS, use algorithm 8.3.3 to produce a series of RCS plans if possible. If algorithm 8.3.3 fails, use the case_based planning of algorithms 8.3.4 and 8.3.5 to get an approximate solution. If this solution is still not satisfying, try to use the modification approach of algorithm 8.3.6 to refine the solution.

End of Algorithm

Algorithm 8.3.2 (Order the Ingredients)

1. Assume a DPRS is given, with a basic scenario bs and a sequence of additional ingredients sai.
2. Assume the time interval of bs is $[t_0, t_0']$, assume further sai consists of a finite number of ingredients ing [i], each attached with a time interval $[t_i, t_i']$, i = 1, ..., n.
3. Arrange all t_i and t_I' (i = 0, 1, ..., n) in a total order according to the natural order of integers. We get a sequence of m increasing time points $s_1, s_2, \ldots, s_m$, where $s_1 = t_0$, $s_m = t_0'$.
4. For each interval $[s_i, s_{i+1}]$, consider all intervals $[t_j, t_j']$ which have a nonempty intersection with $[s_i, s_{i+1}]$, build a union of all ingredients of these intervals and define it as the ingredients ings [i] of the interval $[s_i, s_{i+1}]$. In this way we get a sequence cp[i] of DPRS, i = 1, 2, ..., m-1. Each cp[i] inherits the basic scenario bs from the inputted DPRS and has ings[i] as its set of ingredients.

5. If there is a contradiction within any of the ings [i] (for example, some role is happy and angry at the same time), issue an error message and stop the algorithm.
6. Otherwise is the algorithm finished.

End of Algorithm

Now we will sketch an algorithm for establishing a RCS plan only based on a DPRS, without making use of any existing RCS plan. This algorithm is an additive one. It examines the individual ingredients separately, considers the contribution of each ingredient to the generation of RCS, and then integrates the partial results to a whole solution. There are six elements which we should consider in this generation process. They are:

1. Introduce the whole environment,
2. Introduce the group roles,
3. Introduce the individual roles (main minor roles),
4. Introduce the main roles,
5. Introduce the relations between main roles and the main minor roles,
6. Introduce the relations between individual roles and group roles.

It is just for this purpose that we have made the classification of RCS in section 8.3.1. Now we list the rough principles of an algorithm transforming DPRS into RCS:

Algorithm 8.3.3 (Sketch)

Solo without moving → RCS group1,
Solo with moving → RCS group 2, 6,
Double without moving → RCS group 8,
Double with moving → RCS group 7, 8,
Few without action → RCS group 3, 9,
Few with action → RCS group 6,
Few times Few → RCS group 3,
Many without moving → RCS group 4, 11.1,
Many with moving → RCS group 12,
Few plus Many → RCS group 10, 11.2,
Few Times Many → RCS group 13,
Many times Few → RCS group 14.

End of Algorithm

One will find from the discussion above that there are yet many details to be determined, for example,

1. Which RCS group should be selected if there are more than one choices for a basic scenario?
2. Which RCS should be taken from the RCS group selected for a basic scenario?
3. How about the roles of the ingredients in the selection of RCS?

These problems will be solved partly in the algorithm itself, whose details are omitted here. We will only mention that the ingredients are used to help the selection of RCS plans, which is in principle not unique when only based on the basic scenario.

8.3.3 From DPRS to RCS (2): Ingredient Forest

We have introduced the concept of ingredients in chapter seven, where all ingredients have only simple values. In this chapter, however, we will extend this concept a little bit and let each ingredient have a tree of subclasses of ingredients as its value. That means, each ingredient class stands for a whole tree of ingredients classes and values.

Definition 8.3.1 (Ingredient Forest)

1. A node of a tree is called a total node, if all its direct subnodes (i.e. son nodes) are arranged in a total order. Note that a leaf node is always a total node.
2. A tree consists of total nodes only is called an ordered tree. Otherwise it is called a partially ordered tree.
3. An ingredient tree is an ordered or partially ordered tree where the root is an ingredient class (together with its basic scenario), and where a non leaf node is a subclass of its father node, and where each non root node is a value of its father node.
4. An ingredient forest is a set of ingredient trees.
5. An ingredient vector is a n-tuple of values, where each its value corresponds to a non root node of a ingredient tree, and none two of them coexist in the same ordered tree or have an ancestor_son relation in an ingredient tree.

In our notation, members of a total order are marked with pure numerical indices. Other members are marked with alphabetical indices.

Example 8.3.1

The values of the ingredient class "weather" form an ordered tree:

Weather → (1) Good Weather → (1.1) Sunny
→ (1.2) slightly cloudy
→ (1.3) cloudy
→ (2) Bad Weather → (2.1) Overcast
(2.2) Foggy
(2.3) Rainy
(2.4) snowy
→ (3) Very Bad Weather → (3.1) Rain Storm
→ (3.2) Thunder Storm
→ (3.3) Snow Strom

In this example, good weather, bad weather and very bad weather are values of the root node "weather". Sunny, slightly cloudy and cloudy are values of their father node "good weather", etc. If the knowledge base were so that it contains only this ingredient tree "weather", then all ingredient vectors have the lengths 1, and the number of all possible ingredient vectors in 13.

Example 8.3.2

The values of the ingredient class "character" form a partially ordered tree:

Character → (1) Good Character → ($1.x_1$) Diligent
→ ($1.x_2$) Honest
→ ($1.x_3$) Kind → ($1.x_3.1$) warm-hearted
→ ($1.x_3.2$) helpful
→ ($1.x_3.3$) sympathizing
→ (2) Bad Character → ($2.x_1$) Lazy
→ ($2.x_2$) Sly
→ ($2.x_3$) Not helpful → ($2.x_3.1$) Indifferent
→ ($2.x_3.2$) Selfish

We see that diligent, honest and kind are not comparable. But warm-hearted is more than helpful which is again more than just sympathising. The reader may find that the organization of the tree in example 8.3.2 is not very reasonable for our purpose. In our real life, a diligent person must not be lazy at the same time. A honest person must not be sly at the same time. But an ingredient vector may contain "diligent" and "lazy" at the same time, or "honest" and "sly" at the same time, which is a contradiction. Therefore, a better organization of the same tree may be:

Character → (x_1) Attitude towards work → ($x_1.1$) Diligent
→ ($x_1.2$) Lazy
→ (x_2) Attitude of Honestness → ($x_2.1$) Honest
→ ($x_2.2$) Sly
→ (x_3) Attitude of Kindness → ($x_3.1$) warm-hearted
→ ($x_3.2$) helpful
→ ($x_3.3$) sympathizing
→ ($x_3.4$) Indifferent
→ ($x_3.5$) Selfish

This way of tree organization raises a new problem because "attitude towards work (of honest ness, of kindness)" can not be a value for the ingredient class "character". In the following we call such nodes idle nodes which are not allowed to appear in any ingredient vector.

It follows that the organization of the ingredient knowledge base needs to be very careful in order to obtain an ideal result. It has had also an influence on the design of our DPRS language. In fact, whether an ingredient tree should be total or partial, depends often on the flavor of the knowledge base designer. In the process of knowledge refinement, more and more total order trees will become partial.

Definition 8.3.2 (Sort of an Ordered Tree or Partially Ordered Tree)

If a subtree T' of a tree T is a partially ordered tree, then all leaf nodes of T' may be arranged in a total order according to the principle:

1. Node a is smaller than node b ($a < b$), if a and b have the same father node which is a total node and a is marked with an index smaller than that of b.
2. Node a is smaller than node b if the father of a is smaller than (the father of) b.
3. Two nodes a and b are called comparable, if either $a < b$ or $b < a$ is valid.

Definition 8.3.3 (Maximal Ordered Tree)

If nodes a and b of a tree T are comparable, then the maximal ordered tree determined by a and b, denoted with MOT (a, b), is that ordered subtree T' of T, which contains a and b, and there is no other subtree T'' of T with the same property, such that T'' contains T'. The ordered list of leaf nodes of MOT (a, b) is denoted as OLL (a, b).

Proposition 8.3.1

For any pair of comparable nodes a and b, there exists one and only one MOT (a,b).

Definition 8.3.4 (Similarity of Brother Nodes)

The function length (le) denotes the length of an ordered list le. It is equal to the number of items of this list minus 1. The function dis (a, b) denotes the distance between two items a and b in an ordered list. It is equal to $n + 1$, where n is the number of items between a and b.

Two nodes a and b of an ingredient tree T have no similarity, denoted as simh (a, b) = 0, if they are not comparable.

Two leaf nodes a and b of an ordered have the horizontal similarity:

simh (a, b) = (length (OLL (a, b)) - dis (a, b)) / length (OLL (a, b))

Definition 8.3.5 (Similarity of Family Nodes)

If nodes a and b belong to the same ingredient tree, $a \neq b$, then,

1. If a is a node of the sub-tree with b as the root node, then the vertical similarity of a and b is
   simv (a, b) = (length (OLP (a, b)) - dis (a, b)) / length (OLP (a, b))
   where OLP (a, b) is the path from the root to a leaf node containing a and b, and is considered as an ordered list.
2. If there is no path connecting a with b, but a and b are comparable, then the horizontal similarity of a and b is:
   simh (a, b) = (length (OLL (a, b)) - tdis (a, b)) / length (OLL (a, b))
   where
   tdis = length (dis (a, b)), if a and b belong to OLL (a, b),
   tdis = length (OLL (a, c)) + 1/2 length (dev (B)), if a is a leaf node, B is the sub-tree with b as root, dev (B) is the ordered list of all leaf nodes of B, c is that leaf node in dev (B), which is most close to a ,
   tids = 1/2 length (dev (A)) + 1/2 length (dev (B)) + dis(c,d), if neither a nor b is a leaf node, where A is the sub-tree with a as root, c is

the leaf node in dev (A) most close to dev (B), b is the leaf node in dev (B) most close to dev (A).

Example 8.3.3

In Example 8.3.2, length (OLL (cloudy, rainstorm)) = 5, the maximal ordered tree containing cloudy and rain storm is the whole "weather" tree, length (dev ("weather") = 9, simh (cloudy, rainstorm) = 4/9, simv (good weather, cloudy) = 1/2, simh (bad weather, snow storm) = 1/2, simh (bad weather, good weather) = 11/18.

8.3.4 From DPRS to RCS (3): The Case Based RCS Planner

People often make complaints that using knowledge based method to produce a master piece of art such as movie or animation by computer will have the disadvantage of "always producing the similar" result under similar situation, thus ignoring the creative vigor of human artists, for example the creative vigor of movie directors. While we admit that the computer will never become a movie director as great as the best human director, we still think that efforts towards making computer behave more and more similar to the human movie directors will not be wasted in vain. In this section, we will introduce an intelligent method which will make the computer more "artistic" and avoid, to some extent, the problem of "always producing similar results". Our method is based on fuzzy inference and case based planning. We combine these two techniques and propose a new technique, called case based fuzzy planning.

The basic components of case based fuzzy planning includes: a fuzzy dictionary for camera planning use, a fuzzy case base for RCS planning, a case based RCS planner and a normal RCS planner (already presented in the last section 8.3.3). We need a normal RCS planner because of two reasons. First, sometimes we do not want to take benefit of the flexibility of case based planning. We just want to get the same results for the same input parameters. Second, we need an initial set of cases in our case library. The normal RCS planner spreads seeds in the empty case library.

Among the components mentioned above, the most important part of the knowledge base is the DPRS forest. This forest consists of a tree of basic scenarios and a forest of ingredient trees. The tree of basic scenarios has only two levels: the quantity scenario level and the quality scenario level. The former consists of eight branches (Solo, Double, Few, etc.). Each of these branches has some sub-branches, of which the types and values depend on the types of quantity scenarios (e.g. the three sub-branches of Solo are no action, body action and moving, see chapter seven).

At each leaf node of the basic scenario tree is attached a forest of ingredients. The composition and content of the latter depends on the type of the former. For example, at the leaf node Solo.No_Action is attached the following ingredient forest:

Solo.No_Action→ Tree of social position,
Tree of role's character,
Tree of role's sentiment,
Tree of role's age,
Tree of spatial position,
Tree of role's figure,
Tree of figure change,
Other relevant ingredient trees……

As we said before, the combined tree is called a DPRS tree.

The case library is organized in form of a DPRS transducer. A DPRS transducer is a set of translation pairs ((basic scenario, ingredient vector), RCS plan), where the basic scenario is a leaf node of the basic scenario tree, and the ingredient vector is constructed using values of the ingredient forest attached to this leaf node.

The initial state of the case library is a DPRS transducer, where the RCS plans of some translation pairs may be empty, but for each basic scenario, there is at least one ingredient vector containing this basic scenario, whose corresponding RCS plan is not empty.

Now we present the main algorithms of our case based planning. This algorithm has the following assumptions:

The DPRS produced by the director planning module always:

1. Carries a basic scenario which equals to one of the leaf nodes of the basic scenario tree in the knowledge base,
2. Carries a non empty set of ingredients,
3. The values of its ingredients form an ingredient vector of the ingredient forest, which is attached to the leaf node mentioned in 1.

Algorithm 8.3.4 (Case based RCS Planning)

1. Given a DPRS tree in the knowledge base with rt as its root, a new DPRS pdp produced by the director planning module which contains a basic scenario bs and a non empty set of ingredients sin.
2. Find that translation pair ele in the case library, where the first item of ele equals to pdp. (such a translation pair must exist)
3. If the second item of ele is not empty, then go to 10.
4. For each i and the value of the i-th ingredient sin [i] of sin, find all nodes nd [i,j] of the corresponding i-th ingredient tree, which have a similarity value
   match (nd [i,j], sin [i]) $\leq$ thr1,
   where thr1 is a threshold value > 0, the value of match is calculated by algorithm 8.3.5.
5. Calculate the total similarity:
   Similarity (nd, sin) = $\sum$ (match (nd[i], sin[i]))/n
   Where nd = {nd[1], nd[2], …, nd[n]} is an ingredient vector, for which
   5.1. Each nd[i] satisfies the condition in 4.
   5.2. There is a translation pair ele = ((bs, nd), rp), where rp is a nonempty RCS plan.

5.3. Similarity (nd, sin) ≤ thrz, where thrz > 0 and sin = {sin[1], sin[2], ..., sin[n]}.

6. If there is no nd which satisfies the conditions 5.1, 5.2 and 5.3, then go to 8.
7. Select that nd which satisfies 5.1, 5.2 and 5.3, and whose similarity value takes the maximum. Go to 9.
8. Ask the human expert to provide an appropriate RCS plan for pdp, and ask the system manager to maintain the knowledge base by filling the second slot of the corresponding ingredient pair with this new RCS plan. This plan is at the same time the wanted result. Algorithm finished.
9. Take the second term of ele, which is a RCS plan. Modify this plan according to algorithm 8.3.6 based on the difference between the original DPRS and the first term of ele. .
10. If the system SWAN works in the "automatic" mode, then this is the wanted result. Algorithm finished.
11. Otherwise, ask the human expert to check this RCS plan.
12. If the human expert agrees with it, then this plan is the wanted result. Algorithm finished, otherwise go to 8.

End of Algorithm

Algorithm 8.3.5 (Calculate Similarity)

For a node nd [i] in an ingredient tree, a given ingredient sin [i] in this tree, examine all paths starting from root, going through sin [i] and until some leaf node.

If the node nd [i] is on such a path, then calculate and return the vertical similarity simv (nd [i], sin [i]).

Otherwise, if the node nd [i] is not on such a path, then calculate and return the horizontal similarity simh (nd [i], sin [i]).

End of Algorithm

The idea is as follows: first try to have an exact match (of an existing case with the new case). If successful, then we get the wanted RCS plan. But this is not enough, we still have to ask an expert for comments and suggestions if the system does not work in "automatic" mode, since there may very well be details in the plot which have not been considered before. If not successful, try to find a similar case in the knowledge base and to infer a plan for the current DPRS based on the old one. This plan has also to be checked by the expert. Only if no similar case can be found, then ask the expert to provide an appropriate RCS plan for the current case. In each of these situations, there is a chance to let the user examine the plan generated and revise the plan according to his aesthetic point of view. Of course the user's modification will be used to improve the knowledge base if the user is an expert.

Details have to be added to this algorithm, which will be provided by the following definitions and algorithm.

8.3.5 The Virtual Ingredient Forest

The number of possibilities of using Chinese Natural Language to describe a role, an object, a background, a sentiment, a relation, a natural phenomenon, etc., is immense. It is not wise to try to construct a DPRS transducer to include all these possibilities. A way to enlarge the functionality of the DPRS transducer is to make benefit of our commonsense knowledge base Pangu.

Definition 8.3.6

A node nd of the ingredient tree is said to have a rough match with an ingredient ing, if nd does not match ing, but it does match an ancestor of ing in the terminology hierarchy of the commonsense knowledge base. We say that a path of the ingredient tree has as many rough matches with a set of ingredients as the nodes on it have.

Example 8.3.4

If the DPRS ts produced by the director planning module contains an ingredient "sentiment = rage". But the concept "rage" is not an ingredient class (or value) of our DPRS knowledge base. Nevertheless, we have in our case library a translation pair tp = ((bs, sin), RCS plan), where sin contains the ingredient "sentiment = angry". The second term of this translation pair contains a RCS plan. Obviously rage is not equal to angry. But after examining the commonsense knowledge base, SWAN discovers that angry is a father concept of rage. Thus sentiment = angry has a rough match with sentiment = rage. That means, if there is no other difference, the RCS plan stored in tp can be used for ts "roughly".

Definition 8.3.7 (Virtual Ingredient Tree)

Let ing be an ingredient class. Consider the ingredient tree itr with ing as its root. For any non root node nrd of itr we consider its corresponding agent in Pangu kanwledge base. In order to enhance the clarity, we call the nrd in itr as itr(nrd), and that nrd in Pangu as Pangu(nrd). If:

1. In Pangu there is a son agent Pangu(sa) of Pangu(nrd),
2. Pangu(sa) does not appear in itr,

Then we can extend itr by adding a branch to itr(nrd). This branch consists of Pangu(nrd) and all its son agents in Pangu. The extended tree is called a virtual ingredient tree.

Do this for all ingredient classes defined in DPRS knowledge base and all nodes in their ingredient trees, we obtain a virtual ingredient forest, extended by Pangu.

We call the extended trees and forest virtual. That means we do not construct them really. We only make use of this concept if there is a need for searching a rough match for some ingredient. We can calculate the vertical similarity function simv (Pangu(nrd), Pangu(sa)) to make it useful in algorithm 8.3.4.

Algorithm 8.3.6 (Infer a RCS Plan from an Old One)

1. Given an old DPRS nd, a new DPRS ts and an old RCS plan ndp, which corresponds to nd.
2. Establish four lists:
   List 1. those ingredient classes which appear in ts but not in nd.
   List 2. those ingredients classes which appear in nd but not in ts.
   List 3. those ingredients which appear in ts and also in nd, but with different values.
   List 4. those ingredients which appear in ts and also in nd, and with the same values.
3. Establish three lists:
   List 5. those RCS groups in ndp, which are produced by ingredients in list 2 only.
   List 6. those RCS groups in ndp, which are produced by ingredients in list 3 only.
   List 7. those RCS groups in ndp, which are contributed by ingredients in list 4.
4. Give up the algorthm, if at least one of the following conditions is true.
   4.1. length (list 1) > c1
   4.2. length (list 2) > c2
   4.3. length (list 3) > c3
   where c1, c2, c3 are constants.
5. Delete from ndp all RCS groups of list 5.
6. For each group g of list 6, use case_based reasoning mentioned above to get the corresponding RCS groups with new values of ingredients.
7. Use case_based reasoning to get RCS groups for List 1.
8. Add the results of 5, 6, 7 and list 7 together to get a new RCS plan.

End of Algorithm

Example 8.3.5

We reconsider a small piece of example 7.3.2:

Double.Talking (Tom, Mary) [t2, t3]
Relative position = equal,
Attitude to each other = harmonic,
Sentiment (Tom, Mary) = happy ,
Background people = many ,

The RCS plan produced from this DPRS is the following:
look_around,

two_persons_outstanding (Tom, Mary)
face_to_face (Tom, Mary)
one_expression (Tom)
one_expression (Mary)

Now we have a new RCPS which is "similar" to the old one:

Double.Talking (Tom, Mary) [t2, t3]
Relative position = master-slave,
Director's attitude = sympathizing (Mary),
Sentiment (Tom) = angry,
Sentiment (Mary) = sorrow,

Use algorithm 8.3.6, we calculate:

List 1: director's attitude
List 2: attitude to each other, background people
List 3: relative position, sentiment
List 4: empty
List 5: two_persons_outstanding, look_around, (contributed by "background")
face_to_face, one_after_another, (contributed by "attitude to each other")
List 6: face_to_face, one_after_another,(contributed by "sentiment" and "relative position")
List 7: empty

The final result of case based planning is:

RCS (sin) – list 5 – list 6 + changed (list 6) + RCS (list 1) =
{ face_to_face_with_contrast (Tom, Mary)
one_after_another_with_contrast (Tom, Mary)
one_expression (Tom),
one_expression (Mary)
sorrow_or_lonely (Mary),
step_in_approach (Mary) }

8.4 High Level Camera Primitives

8.4.1 Overview

Just as its name "High Level Camera Primitive" reminds, a HLCP is a basic unit of camera technique, which can be used to film some state or some action of a person, or a group of persons, or the environment. As we said before, the HLCP differ from the RCS in that they are represented in jargon of camera directors, while the RCS (and DPRS) are represented in camera independent terminology. In other words, RCS describe the effects of camera one wishes to achieve, while HLCP describe the camera techniques used to achieve these effects. On the other hand, HLCP differ also from their next level representation: BCP. Each BCP describes a simple or complex shot, while each HLCP describes a combination of several simple or complex shots. The HLCP are summarized based on the practice and experience of directors and cameramen. Each of them has its own pragmatics. For example, the HLCP in_contra and out_contra (see below) can be used to film a face-to-face conversation between two partners; right_angle can be used to film two conversation partners who are standing in right angle to each other; n_parallel can be used to introduce more than one focus of attention; n_coaxiale can be used to stress some special effect, etc. The HLCP level of representation is necessary in Morning Glow, because both DPRS and RCS are rather abstract such that their direct translation into BCP (ADL camera statements) would be too difficult. We will first give a simple syntax of HLCP and then illustrate this by some typical examples.

<HLCP> ::= <Name of HLCP> (<Sequence of HLCP Parameters>)
<HLCP Parameter> ::= <Target> | <Shot> | <Direction> | <Position>
| <Angle> | <Speed> | <Time>
<Target> ::= <Target Name> | {<Sequence of Target Names>}
<Shot> ::= BCU | CU | MCU | MS | MLS | LS | VLS | ELS
<Direction> ::= left | right | front | back | beneath | above | <Direction>
<Direction>
<Position> ::= left | right | middle
<Angle> ::= up | down | a little <Angle> | moderate <Angle> | largely <Angle>
<Speed> ::= quickly | slowly | a little <Speed> | quite <Speed> | very <Speed>
<Time> ::= long | short | a little <Time> | quite <Time> | very <Time>

In the following examples we have simplified their syntactical representation whenever there is no ambiguity.

Example 8.4.1

right_angle (<Target>, <Target>, <Shot>, <Shot>, <Direction>, <Time>)

It means: use camera 1 to film the first <Target> from the <Direction> and with the first shot type <Shot>. At the same time use camera 2 to film the second <Target> with the second shot type <Shot>. The direction of camera 2 does not need to be specified because it should form a right angle with <Direction>.

For example: right_angle (king, minister, LS, CU, front, medium long)

Example 8.4.2

3_parallel (<Target>, <Target>, <Target>, <Shot>, <Shot>, <Shot>,
<Direction>, <Time>)

This primitive makes use of three parallel cameras to film three targets at the same time. Since the directions of three cameras are the same (parallel), there is no need to specify the directions of other two cameras.

For example: 3_parallel (girl1, girl2, girl3, CU, CU, CU, front, short)

Example 8.4.3

4_coaxile (<Target>, <Shot>, <Shot>, <Shot>, <Shot>, <Direction>, <Time>)

This primitive makes use of four cameras one after another on the same axis towards the same target. By editing pieces of films (shot by these four cameras) together one can produce a view effect of stepwise approaching the target.

For example: 4_coaxile (princess, LS, MLS, MS, MCU, front, slowly)

8.4.2 Syntax of HLCP

An incomplete list of HLCP is as follows:

1. out_contra (<Target>, <Target>, <Shot>, <Time>)
   Two cameras. Each behind one of two conversation partners. See figure 8.4.1.
2. in_contra (<Target>, <Target>, <Shot>, <Time>)
   Two cameras. Each before one of two conversation partners and towards another one. See figure 8.4.2
3. rightangle (<Target>, <Target>, <Shot>, <Shot>, <Direction>, <Time>)
4. 2_parallel (<Target>, <Target>, <Shot>, <Shot>, <Direction>, <Time>)
5. 3_parallel (<Target>, <Target>, <Target>, <Shot>, <Shot>, <Shot>, <Direction>, <Time>)
   See figure 8.4.3.
6. 4_parallel (<Target>, <Target>, <Target>, <Target>, <Shot>, <Shot>, <Shot>, <Shot>, <Direction>, <Time>)
7. multi_parallel (<Sequence of Targets>, <Sequence of Shots>, <Direction>, <Time>)
8. 2_coaxile (<Target>, <Shot>, <Shot>, <Direction>, <Time>)
9. 3_coaxile (<Target>, <Shot>, <Shot>, <Shot>, <Direction>, <Time>)
   See figure 8.4.4.
10. 4_coaxile (<Target>, <Shot>, <Shot>, <Shot>, <Shot>, <Direction>, <Time>)
11. multi_coaxile (<Target>, <Sequence of Shots>, <Direction>, <Time>)
12. reverse_shot (<Target>, <Target>, <Shot>, <Shot>, <Direction>, <Time>)
    Two (back to back) cameras looking at two opposite targets.
13. up_shot (<Target>, <Shot>, <Direction>, <Time>)
    The camera points to <Target> in <Direction> upwards.
14. down_shot (<Target>, <Shot>, <Direction>, <Time>)
    The camera points to <Target> in <Direction> downwards.
15. contrast_shot (<Target>, <Shot>, <Shot>, <Direction>, <Time>)
    Towards the same <Target,> contrast one shot with another one.
16. front_shot (<Target>, <Shot>, <Direction>, <Time>)
    See figure 8.4.5.
17. back_shot (<Target>, <Shot>, <Direction>, <Time>)
    See figure 8.4.6.
18. introduce_shot (<Sequence of Targets>, <Shot> , <Direction>)
    Introduce the targets one after another.
19. vertex_shot (<Target>, <Target>, <Shot>, <Direction>);
    Camera towards the middle of two targets. See figure 8.4.7.

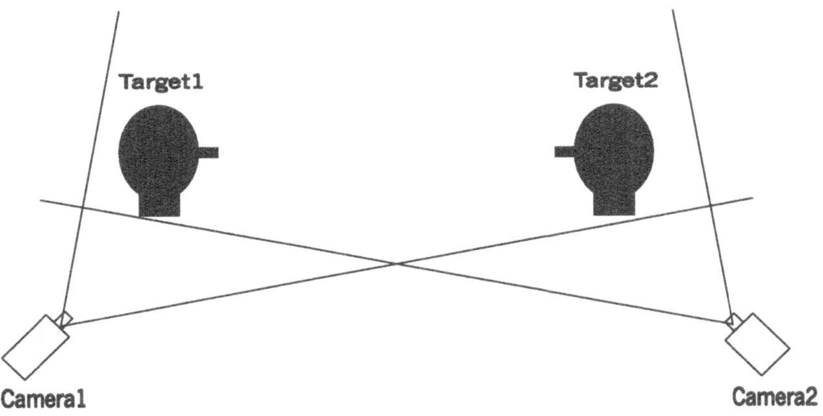

Figure 8.4.1 Out-contra

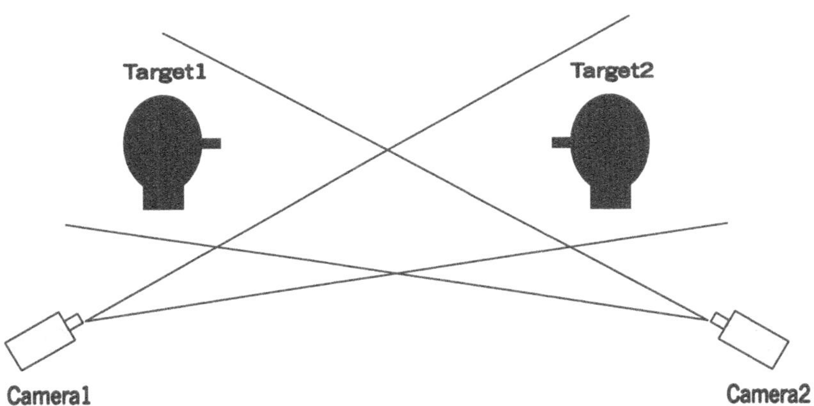

Figure 8.4.2 In-contra

20. own_fix (<Target>, <Target>)
    Subjective view of the first <Target> about the second <Target>. Camera moves with the first <Target>. See figure 8.4.8.
21. return_move (<Target>, <Target>, <Shot>, <Shot>, <Direction>, <Direction>, <Time>)
    Repeat moves towards the first <Target> and the second <Target> in an alter nating way.

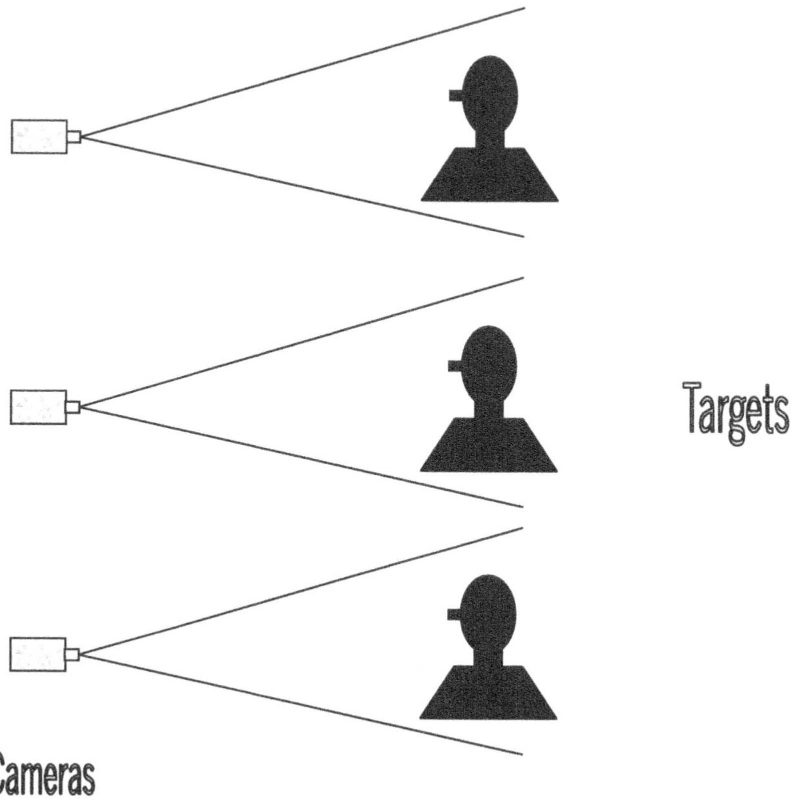

Figure 8.4.3 Three-parallel

22. return_pan (<Target>, <Target>, <Shot>, <Direction>, <Time>)
    Repeat pans between the first <Target> and the second <Target> in an alter nating way.
23. return_track (<Target>, <Shot>, <Shot>, <Direction>, <Time>)
    Repeat tracks between the first <Shot> and the second <Shot> in an alternating way
24. down_normal (<Target>, <Shot>, <Direction>, <Time>)
    Camera looks forwards and slightly down.
25. pan_fixed (<Target>, <Target>, <Shot>, <Direction>, <Speed>, <Time>)
    First pan and then fixed. The following five HLCP are similar

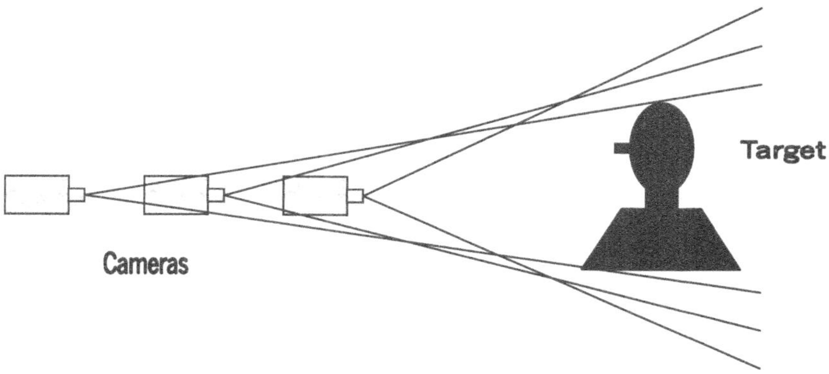

Figure 8.4.4 Three-coaxile

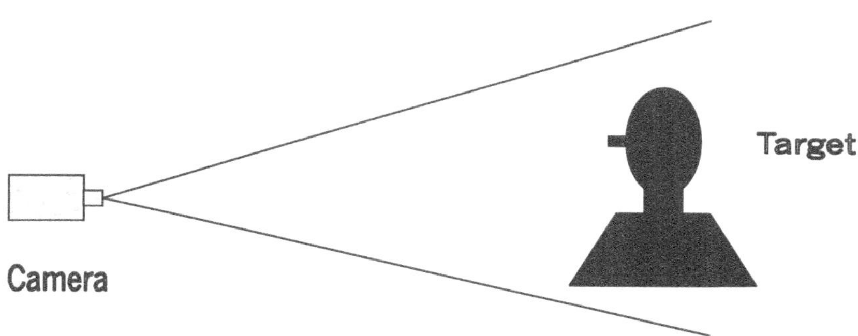

Figure 8.4.5 Front-shot

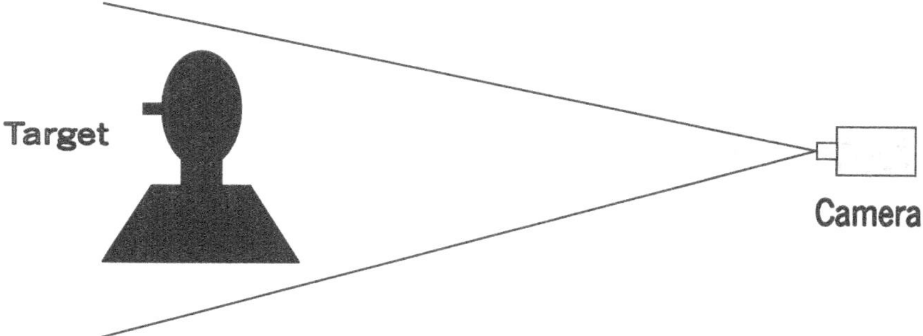

Figure 8.4.6 Back-shot

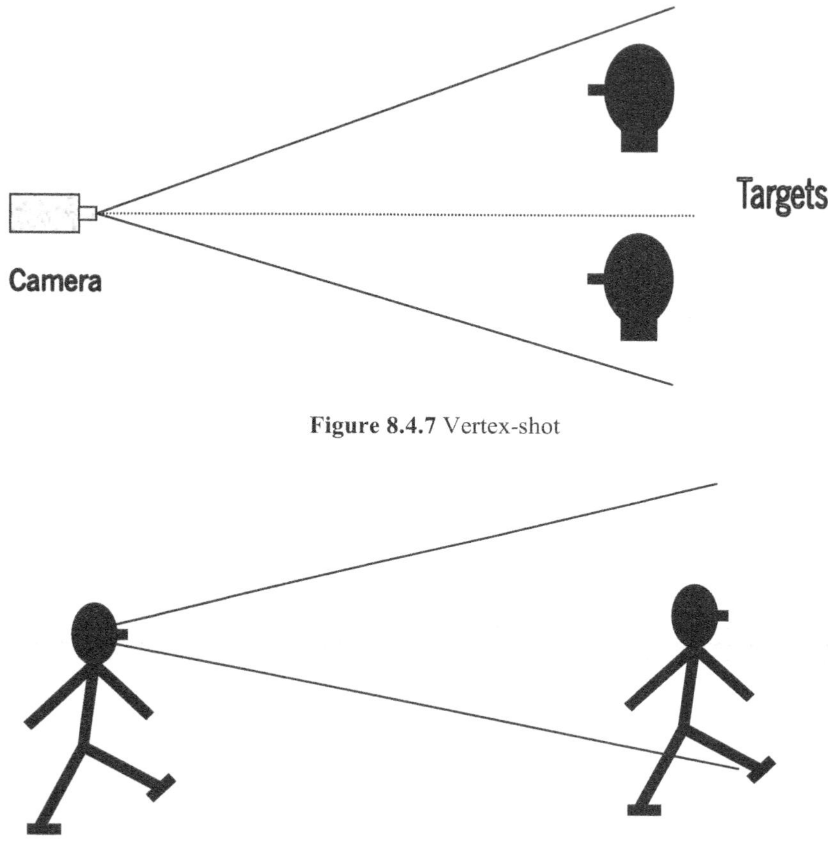

Figure 8.4.7 Vertex-shot

Figure 8.4.8 Own-fix

26. move_fixed (<Target>, <Target>, <Shot>, <Shot>, <Direction>, <Direction>, <Speed>, <Time>)
27. fixed_pan (<Target>, <Target>, <Shot>, <Direction>, <Speed>, <Time>)
28. fixed_move (<Target>, <Target>, <Shot>, <Shot>, <Direction>, <Direction>, <Speed>, <Time>)
29. track_fixed (<Target>, <Shot>, <Shot>, <Direction>, <Speed>, <Time>)
30. fixed_track (<Target>, <Shot>, <Shot>, <Direction>, <Speed>, <Time>)
31. over_shoulder_shot (<Target>, <Target>, <Shot>, <Speed>, <Time>)
    See figure 8.4.9.

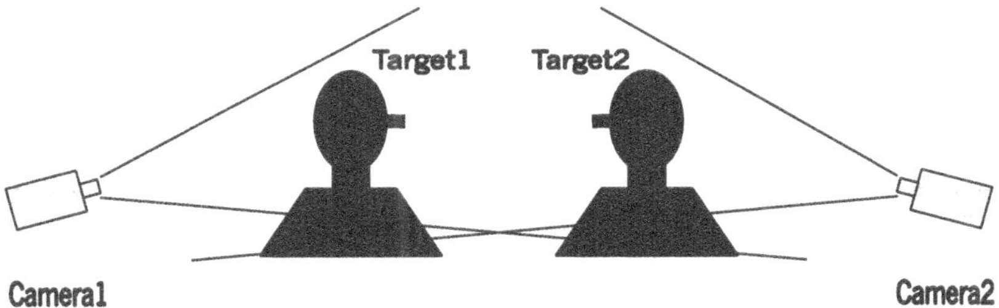

Figure 8.4.9 Over-shoulder-shot

8.4.3 From RCS to HLCP

In order to show how the HLCP work, we will list a few examples of translating RCS into HLCP, where all time parameters are omitted. The translation is in principle based on pattern matching.

1. Introducing a person
   RCS: one_round_observe (target)
   # Observe the target from all sides #
   HLCP: front_shot (target, MS) ;
   back_shot (target, MCU) ;
   front_shot (target, MCU).

2. Introducing two persons
   2.1 Two persons side by side with equal weights
   RCS: side_by_side (target1, target2);
   # Two targets stand or sit side by side #
   HLCP: out_contra (target1, target2, MCU) .
   2.2. Two persons face to face with equal weights
   RCS: face_to_face (target1, target2)
   HLCP: over_shoulder_shot (target1, target2, MCU).
   Picture 16 of appendix is an over shoulder shot of the king and the new queen.
   2.3. Two persons with unequal weights
   RCS: face_to_face_with_contrast (target1, target2);
   # Emphasize target 1 #
   HLCP: front_shot (target1, MCU, right);
   back_shot (target2, MCU, right);

3. Introducing more than two persons
   3.1. With equal weights
   RCS: respectively_group_shot (group1);
   # Several persons introduced one after another #

HLCP: introduce_shot (group1, LS, front);
first an overview
front_shot (target1.face, BCU, front);
then one after another
....
front_shot (target n.face, BCU, front).

3.2. With unequal weights
RCS: three_one_shot (group1, group2, group3);
HLCP: intruduce_shot (group1, group2, group3, LS, front);
first an overview
vertex_shot (group2, group3, MCU, front);
then show the two less important groups
front_shot (group1, CU, front).
then show the most important one

4. Facial expression
RCS: one_expression (target1);
demonstrate the facial expression of a single person
HLCP: push (target1, LS, MCU, front).
push is also a BCP

5. Focus of attention
RCS: static_focus_of_attention (target1)
HLCP: fix_shot (target1, CU, front).

6. Director's sympathy
RCS: step_in_approach (target1)
show the director's sympathy
HLCP: track_fixed (target1, MCU, CU, front, slowly).

7. Relative move
RCS: one_move_to_one (target1, target2);
target1 approaches target2
HLCP: pan_fixed (target1, target2, MS, front, fast);
2_coaxile (target2□LS□MCU, target2.left);
out_contra (target1, target2, MCU).

8. Fight against each other:
RCS: fighting (target1, target2)
HLCP: vertex_shot (target1, target2, LS, target1.left);
an overview from target1's left side
own_fix (target1, target2);
own_fix (target2, target1).

9. One to many:
RCS: one_face_many (target1, group1)
target1 faces group1

HLCP: back_shot (target1, right, MCU);
front_shot (target1, left, MCU);
introduce_shot (group1, MCU, front).

8.5 The Basic Camera Primitives

First we will introduce some useful definitions, most of which have been cited from the book of Roy Thomson [Thompson, 1993], but with some modifications according to the reality of SWAN.

Definition 8.5.1 (Shot)

A shot is a series of pictures of a basic activity or happening or action in the story. A shot may be either minutes in length or only seconds in length. Each shot is subject to four basic elements: the lens, the camera, the mounting and the target. Either of them may be fixed or moving. (compare it with the definition in section 6.1)

In SWAN, the factor of lens is not considered since it would involve a lot of complicated geometrical and optical calculations if we were to simulate the effects of lens by using a computer. Further we combine the effect of camera and its mounting to an integrated one, because a difference between these two is only meaningful when we talk about mechanical devices. For the computer, it is easy to simulate both of them in a combined way. So, in the rest of this book, if we are talking about the camera, we mean practically the combination of camera and its mounting.

Definition 8.5.2 (Simple Shot)

A simple shot has no lens movement, no camera movement, no mounting movement and possibly only a simple target movement. In SWAN, the simple shots are only classified according to the distance between the camera and the target(s).

1. BCU (Big Close Up): The face (or some body part) of the target occupies the whole screen.
2. CU (Close Up): The face (or some body part) of the target occupies almost the whole screen. For example, with the target's whole face one can see also the target's shoulder. Picture 2 of appendix is a CU picture of a sun.
3. MCU (Medium Close Up): About one third of the target's body, including the chest, appears on the screen.
4. MS (Medium Shot): About two fifths of the target's body, including the waist, appear on the screen.
5. MLS (Medium Long Shot): About three quarters of the target's body, sometimes including the knees, appear on the screen. Picture 12 of appendix is a MLS picture of Hou Yi who is just getting angry.
6. LS (Long Shot): The target occupies almost the whole screen. There is little space above the head and beneath the feet of the target.

7. VLS (Very Long Shot): The targets appear only as small objects on the screen. The height of a target is only about half of the height of the screen. Picture 13 of appendix is VLS of the frog prince who is jumping out from a well.
8. ELS (Extremely Long Shot): The targets are so small on the screen that they are hard to be seen

Definition 8.5.3 (Complex Shot)

A simple shot plus one or several following additional factors is called a complex shot:

1. Posture of camera: Up (pointing upwards) and Down
2. Vertical move of camera: Move Up and Move Down.
3. Horizontal peripheral move of camera: Move Left and Move Right.
4. Horizontal radial move of camera: Track In and Track Out.
5. Vertical rotation of camera: Tilt Up and Tilt Down.
6. Horizontal rotation of camera: Pan Left and Pan Right.

In the design of BCP, we have combined the factors 2 and 3 in definition 8.5.3 and give it a unified name: move. Similarly, we have combined the factors 5 and 6 to one and call it simply pan. Thus the syntax of BCP is as follows.

```
<BCP> ::= <Type of BCP> (<Parameter Sequence>)
<Parameter Sequence> ::= <First Parameter of Target> , [<Second Parameter of
        Target>,] [<Sequence of Fuzzy Parameters>,] <Time Interval>
<First Parameter of Target> ::= <Shot Parameter>
  (<Direction Parameter>(<Sequence of Target Parameters>)) | <Sequence of
        Target Parameters>
<Second Parameter of Target> ::=<Shot Parameter>(<Direction Parameter>
        (<Target Parameter>)) | <Target Parameter> | <Shot Parameter> (<Target
        Parameter>)
<Fuzzy Parameter> ::= <Angle Parameter> | <Speed Parameter>
        |<Time Parameter> | <Position Parameter>
<Type of BCP> ::= fixed | middle | part_2 | part_3 | pan | tilt | track | move
        | ownfix | ownpan | introduction | follow
```

The number and types of parameters are different for different BCP. In order to explain the BCP in more details, we list a more concrete syntax of a few of BCP in the following.

```
<BCP1> ::= fixed (<Shot Parameter>(<Direction Parameter>(<Sequence of
           Target Parameters>)), {<Angle Parameter>,} <Time Parameter>,
           <Time Interval> )
<BCP2> ::= middle (<Shot Parameter> (<Direction Parameter>(<Target Pa-
           rameter>, <Target Parameter>)), {<Angle Parameter>,} <Time Pa-
           rameter>, <Time Interval> )
<BCP3> ::= part_2 (<Shot Parameter> (<Direction Parameter>(<Sequence of
           Target Parameters>)), <Position Parameter>, {<Angle Parame-
           ter>,} <Time Parameter>, <Time Interval> )
```

<BCP4> ::= pan (<Shot Parameter > (<Direction Parameter>(<Sequence of Target Parameters>)), <Target Parameter>, {<Angle Parameter>,} <Time Parameter>,<Time Interval>)
<BCP5> ::= tilt (<Shot Parameter > (<Direction Parameter>(<Target Part>)), <Target Part>, {<Angle Parameter>,} <Time Parameter>,<Time Interval>)
<BCP6> ::= track (<Shot Parameter > (<Direction> Parameter (<Sequence of Target Parameters>)), <Shot Parameters> (<Sequence of Target Parameters>),{<Angle Parameter>,} <Time Parameter>, <Time Interval>)
<BCP7> ::= move (<Shot Parameter > (<Direction Parameter>(<Sequence of Target Parameters>)), {<Angle Parameter>,} <Shot Parameter> (<Direction Parameter> (<Sequence of Target Parameters>)), {<Angle Parameter>,} <Time Parameter>, <Time Interval>)
<BCP8> ::= ownfix (<Observer>, <Time Parameter>, <Time Interval>)
<Time Interval> ::= <Time Mark>, <Time Mark>
<Time Mark> ::= t <Sequence of Digits>
<Observer> ::= <Role Name>
<Target Part> ::= <Part Name>

In the appendix of this book, we attach two pictures to show the effect of the direction parameter in the BCP statements, where picture 14 shows a top-down shooting and picture 15 a bottom-up shooting.

Definition 8.5.4 (Semantics of BCP)

1. Fixed means a simple shot.
2. Middle means a virtual target between two physical targets.
3. Part_2 means the screen is divided into two halves. The targets are in the left (right) half of the screen.
4. Pan means the camera pans from pointing to the first group of targets to pointing to the second one.
5. Tilt means the camera tilts from pointing to the first part of the target to pointing to the second one.
6. Track means the camera tracks (in or out) from the shot type of the first group of targets to the shot type of the second group of targets. Note that either the first group of targets is a subset of the second one (in case of track out) or the second group of targets is a subset of the first one (in case of track in).
7. Move means the camera moves from pointing to the first group of targets to pointing to the second one. Note that here the directions of the two target groups may be different. So a pure parallel move may be not enough. Apart from that, there may be obstacles between the two groups of targets. In this case, a path planning for camera moving like that for target moving is required. If the path planning fails, then this BCP implies a run time error of SWAN.
8. Follow means the camera always follows the targets while they are moving.
9. Ownfix means the camera's position coincides with the observer's eyes. This observer is also a role in the script.

9 Light, Color, and Role Planning

9.1 Light Planning

9.1.1 Glorious: A Language for Light Planning

The light planning in SWAN is accomplished in four procedures.

The first procedure is to determine the environmental conditions of light planning for each script. In daily life, different environments determine different view effects of light. If the environment (background) has been determined in the specification of the script, then the use of light has to follow this specification in order to reproduce the wanted effect. The environmental factors which have an influence on the view effect of light include different seasons (spring, summer, autumn, winter), different weathers (sunny, rainy, cloudy, etc.), different daytimes (dawn, morning, noon, afternoon, evening, etc.), different locations (indoor, outdoor, open field, valley, etc.)

The second procedure is to determine the director's intention on the design of the view effect of light. By using different layouts of light, the director may want to create some atmosphere in the scene (happy, sorrow, terrifying, shocking, mysterious, etc.) or to mould some appearance of a role (old, young, kind, cruel, fierce, happy, sorrow, etc.) It is a special technique of camera directors to make the same actor have different appearances by using different light combinations. For example, using a sided front light makes someone look normal, while using a top light may make the same person look fierce.

The third procedure is to determine the final effect of light use. That is what we want to see after the light planning has been implemented. This effect involves the global layout of illumination (balanced, unbalanced, etc.), light style (hard, soft, etc.), light form (light field, light beam, light fleck, light shadow, etc.).

The fourth procedure is to determine the technique of light use in order to implement the final light effect determined in the third procedure.

Note that the first two procedures have been completed in chapter seven, the director planning phase. Therefore the job of this chapter is only to complete the last two procedures. Just as we have done in chapter eight for camera planning, we have also designed a special language for light planning, called Glorious. It consists of three sub-languages: the general light effect specification language Dragon, the particular light effect specification language Poplar and the light source description language BLP. Glorious is the global name of all these three. Each time when a specification in form of DPRS and the corresponding camera plan are produced, a front end compiler of Glorious analyses the DPRS and the

R. Lu and S. Zhang: Automatic Generation of Computer Animation, LNAI 2160, pp. 287-313, 2002.

camera plan and produces a Dragon program. Then the DPRS, the camera plan and the thus produced Dragon program together produce a Poplar program. Then the Dragon and the Poplar program together produce a BLP specification which is a part of the qualitative planning program coded in Rainbow.

9.1.2 Sublanguage Dragon: General Light Effect Specification

The first step of implementing the director planning requirement specification with technique of light planning is to specify the effect of light in an animation. In another word, we first specify the point of view of the audience. By general effects of light we mean the way of illumination of all the objects, roles and environments in an animated film. These effects are in essential objective effects. That means they are produced by (explicitly or implicitly specified) objective light sources, such as the sun, the moon, the lamps, etc. It is expressed in a language called Dragon. We first summarize its syntax as follows.

<Dragon Program> ::= Dragon (<Program Name>)
<Series of Light Effects>
End of Dragon
<Light Effect> ::= Light Style : <Light Style> | Light Form : <Light Form>
| Light Layout : <Light Layout>

9.1.2.1 Light Style

<Light Style> ::= soft | hard | high | low | little <Light Style> | very <Light Style> | moderately <Light Style>

Hard light is also called straight illuminating light. It projects directly on targets and produces clear shadows. Soft light is also called scattering light. It does not produce clear shadows and the light is diffused in the whole space homogeneously. High light produces relatively bright scenes in general. Low light produces relatively dark scenes in general.

9.1.2.2 Light Form: Field Light

<Light Form> ::= < Field Light > | < Fleck Light > | < Beam Light >
| <Light Shadow> | <Light Source>
< Field Light > ::= daylight (<Daytime>,<Weather>,<Place>)|
moonlight(<Moon>, <Cloud>, <Place>) |
room-light(<Light Distribution>)
<Daytime> ::= dawn | morning | noon | afternoon | evening | night
<Weather> ::= sunny | rainy | <Cloud> | foggy
<Cloud> ::= slightly-cloudy | cloudy | overcast
<Place> ::= indoor | outdoor
<Moon> ::= full-moon | first-quarter-moon | last-quarter-moon

<Light Distribution> ::= [Group-of-] <Lamp Light> (<Light Color>,
<Intensity>) | <Lamp Light> and <Light Distribution>
<Lamp Light> ::= top-lamp | wall-lamp | desk-lamp

Light form is the spatial distribution of light in a scene. Field Light is a homogenous light distribution in the whole space. In most cases, the source of a field light is a natural one, for example the sun or the moon. But there is another kind of light sources other than the natural light sources. These are the sources of room light which is also homogeneous in the intern of the room. Note that a field light does not imply the appearance of a visible light source. Whether the light source is visible or not depends on the context of the story and the director's design.

In the appendix of this book, we collect pictures with light effect produced by SWAN. Picture 17 shows a normal day light (it is sunny), while picture 19 shows a typical moon light (quarter moon). All of them are outdoor light.

Note that in a Dragon program, there may be several light effect specifications, several light form specifications, etc. These specifications may contradict each other, because they are not all independent. For example, the light source specification may be not consistent with the light shadow specification. It is difficult for the programmers to check all these consistency conditions efficiently. Therefore, the Dragon compiler would do the following:

1. Check the consistency of each current specification item with all previous specification items in the same program. If inconsistency is detected, then remove the current specification item.
2. The Dragon compiler presents the thus modified Dragon program to the programmer, who then could compare this program with the end result of light programming.
3. If the result is not satisfactory, the programmer can revise the Dragon program to achieve the wanted result.

In this way, programming in Dragon has a flavor of fault tolerance. Any mistake of the programmer made with respect to inconsistency will be removed.

9.1.2.3 Light Form: Fleck Light

<Fleck Light> ::= Light-fleck: <Fleck Sort> (<Fleck Description>)
| <Fleck Light>; <Fleck Sort> (<Fleck Description>)
<Fleck Sort> ::= sun-fleck | moon-fleck | lamp-fleck
<Fleck Description> ::= number: <Fleck Number> | form: <Fleck Form>|
motion: <Fleck Motion> | size: <Fleck Size> |
color: <Light Color> | intensity: <Intensity> |
<Fleck Description>, <Fleck Description>
<Fleck Number> ::= single | few | many
<Fleck Form> ::= piece | string | stripe | parallels | matrix
<Fleck Motion> ::= <Fleck Position> | moving: <Fleck Trace>
<Fleck Position> ::= fixed: <Object Name> | cover: <Object Name>
<Fleck Trace> ::= from <Fleck Position> to <Fleck Position> |

drift-around <Object Name>
<Fleck Size> ::= very-large | large | small

A fleck light is an isolate piece of illumination on a target lighted by some light source. We often see such scenes: on the day, the sun light pierces through the window and produces yellow sun light flecks on the desk and bed. In the night, the moon light penetrates the same window and produces white moon light flecks.

A fixed fleck occupies only a part of the target object. A cover fleck illuminates the whole object.

For the definition of <Light Color> and <Intensity>, see section 9.1.2.6.

9.1.2.4 Light Form: Beam Light

< Beam Light > ::= Light-beam :<Beam> | <Beam Light>; <Beam>
<Beam> ::= <Sun Beam> | <Moon Beam> | <Flashlight> | <Other Beam>
<Sun Beam> ::= Sun_beam: <SB Description>
<Moon Beam> ::= Moon_beam: <MB Description>
<Flashlight> ::= Flashlight: <FB Description>
<Other Beam> ::= Other_beam: <OB Description>
<SB Description> ::= Time (<SB time>), Place (<SB Place>), Direction
(<SB Direction>)
<SB Time> ::= morning | noon | afternoon
<SB Place> ::= forest | indoor
<SB Direction> ::= left | right | front | back
<MB Description> ::= Time (<MB time>), Place (<MB Place>), Direction
(<MB Direction>)
<MB Time> ::= midnight | early night | late night
<MB Place> ::= outdoor | indoor
<MB Direction> ::= left | right | front | back
<FB Descriptor> ::= Source:<Object Name>, Angle: <Rate>, Intensity
(<Intensity >), Direction: <Beam Direction>
<Rate> ::= very large | large | middle small | no
<Beam Direction> ::= Fixed: <Target Direction> |
Changing: around <Target Direction> with <Rate> deviation
<Target Direction> ::= <Sequence of Object Names>| <SB Direction>
<OB Description> ::= Source:<Object Name>, Angle: <Rate>, Intensity
(<Intensity >),
Color (<Light Color>), Direction: <Beam Direction>,
Number (<Beam Number>), Period (<Beam Period>)
<Beam Number> :: = single | <Number> | few | many
<Beam Period> ::= <Working Length> working | <Working Length> pause
| stochastic | <Number> / minite | <Beam Period> and <Beam Period>
<Working Length> ::= long | short

If you are walking in a forest in the morning, you will observe the sun light beams penetrating the forest from the sky. If you are walking in a dark night with a flesh light, the light beam produced by this flesh light will help you to find the rood. We have also seen search light beams which helped us to detect airplanes in the dark sky. All of them are examples of light beams. In computer animation, the existence of a light source does not guarantee to produce a beam light. Each time when we need a beam light, we construct a lighting object to simulate its effect.

9.1.2.5 Light Shadow

<Light Shadow> ::= light-shadow :<Shadow Sort> (<Shadow Description>) |
<Light Shadow>; <Shadow Sort> (<Shadow Description>)
<Shadow Sort> ::= sun | moon | lamp
<Shadow Description> ::= producer: <Shadow Producer> | form: <Shadow Form>|
position: <Shadow Position> | Size: <Shadow Size> |
<Shadow Description>, <Shadow Description>
<Shadow Producer> ::= [<Numeral>] <Object or Role Name> | unknown
| <Shadow Producer> and <Shadow Producer>
<Numeral> ::= <Number> | few | many
<Shadow Form> ::= piece | [Slanting-]Stripe | [Slanting-]Parallels
<Shadow Position> ::= cover: <Object Name> | inside: <Object Name> |
cross: <Object Name> | lying: from <Position> to <Position>
<Shadow Size> ::= very large | large | small

Both picture 17 and 20 in the appendix show scenes with light shadow.

9.1.2.6 Light Sources

<Light Source> ::= light-source (<Source Position> [, <Light Direction>]
[, <Source Intensity>] [, <Light Color>])
<Source Position> ::= fixed : <Object Name> | moving : <Trace>
<Light Direction> ::= fixed : <Direction> | changing : <Scan>
<Scan> ::= horizontal | vertical | big round | small round |
from <Direction> to <Direction> | <Scan> and <Scan>
<Source Intensity> ::= Constant : <Intensity>| Variable : <I-change>
<Intensity> ::= very bright | bright | normal | weak | dark
<I-change> ::= increasing | decreasing | slowly-changing | rapidly-changing |
glimmer-light
<Light Color> ::= Constant : <Color> | Variable : <C-change>
<C-change> ::= from <Color> to <Color> | <C-change> and <C-change>
<Trace> ::= <Moving Object Name>
<Color> ::= <Color Name> | <RGB Representation>

Light sources are either specified in the original script description, or produced by the Dragon compiler in a default way according to the otherwise specified light effects. The former are called explicit light sources, while the latter are called implicit ones. The syntax <Light Source> describes only explicit light sources.

9.1.2.7 Light Layout

```
<Light Layout> ::= <Balanced Illumination>|<Unbalanced Illumination>
<Balanced Illumination> ::= Balanced(<Intensity>)
<Unbalanced Illumination> ::= Unbalanced (<Series of Unbalanced Cases>)
<Unbalanced Case> ::= <Unbalanced Environment> (<Environment Partition>)|
        <Unbalanced Roles>
<Unbalanced Environment> ::= top-bright-bottom-dark |
        top-dark-bottom-bright | left-bright-right-dark |
        side-dark-middle-bright
<Environment Partition> ::= <Number>, <Number>
<Unbalanced Roles> ::= Illumination (<Series of Illumination Cases>)
<Illumination Case> ::= <Intensity> : <Illuminated Part>
<Illuminated Part>::= <Part Denotation> | (<Series of Part Denotations>)
<Part Denotation> ::= <Role Name> | <Role Part> of <Role Name> |
        <Part Position> of <Role Part> of <Role Name>
<Role Part> ::= face | head | left_arm | right_arm | left_hand |
        right_hand | left_leg | right_leg | left_foot |
        right_foot | body | chest | belly | back | neck |
        arms | legs | hands | feet
<Part Position> ::= upper_part | lower_part | left_part | right_part
```

Almost all pictures in appendix are balanced illuminations. Only in picture 21 we can see an unbalanced role: the new queen. Her front side is illuminated while the back side not.

Light layout specification realizes the director's intention. It is produced, like the other parts of the Dragon language, by a Glorious front end compiler. For more details see below, section 9.1.3.2 and section 9.1.5.

9.1.3 Sublanguage Poplar: Particular Light Effect Specification

The next step is to "program" the light plan in some language which consists of the terminology of a professional cameraman (i.e. not a computer scientist). This language is called Poplar. A specification in Poplar is an artist level program of light planning. The difference between a specification in Dragon and one in Poplar is that the light effects specified in Poplar are more artificial. They reflect the intention of the movie directors, especially their intention about how to portray the roles in a movie.

In the following, we list the main statements of Poplar in programming light planning.

9.1.3.1 Light Combination

```
<Light Combination> ::= <Series of Functional Lights>
<Functional Light> ::= <Key Light> | <Second Key Light> | <Full Light>
      | <Environmental Light> | <Modification Light>
```

<Key Light> ::= key (<Lighting Procedure>)
<Second Key Light> ::= second key (<Lighting Procedure>)
<Full Light> ::= full (<Series of Lighting Procedures>)
<Environmental Light> ::= environment (<Series of Lighting Procedures>)
<Modification Light> ::= modification (<Sequence of Typed Modifications>)
<Typed Modification> ::= <Background Modification> | <Outline Modifica tion> | <Eye Expression Modification> | <Special Effect Modification>
<Background Modification> ::= props (<Lighting Procedure>)
| background [<Key Point Name>] (<Lighting Procedure1>)
<Outline Modification> ::= outline (<Lighting Procedure2>)
<Eye Expression Modification> ::= eye (<Lighting Procedure1>)
<Special Effect Modification> ::= effect (<Lighting Procedure>)
<Lighting Procedure> ::= (<Light Description>, <Time Interval>)
<Lighting Procedure1> ::= (<Light Description1>, <Time Interval>)
<Lighting Procedure2> ::= (<Light Description2>, <Time Interval>)
<Light Description> ::= <Light Position> ,
<Light Description1> ::= <Light Position1> ,
<Light Description2> ::= <Light Position2> ,

For the definitions of <Light Position>, <Light Position1> and <Light Position2>, see section 9.1.3.2.

Semantics:

1. Key light
   This is the light which plays a very important role in the illumination. Under the word "important role" we mean its importance when portraying (molding) the principal roles. Therefore it is also called "the portraying light". Besides that, the key light plays also a major role in determining the effect of view of the environment. For example, the weather, the daytime, outdoor or indoor, etc. all these factors have an influence on the selection of key light.

2. Second key light
   There is no essential difference between key light and second key light. While the key light illuminates the place where the principal roles stay most of the time in the current scene, the second key light illuminates those places where the principal roles otherwise appear. Therefore, we can consider the second key light just as a translated key light. Therefore, the compiler will check the time interval of key light and that of the second key light, in order to assure they have no common subinterval.

3. Full light
   This is that light which plays a complementary role besides the key light. If there were only the key light, the illumination would be too monotone and less colorful. Some part of the screen picture would be over bright. Other parts would be covered by shadow. In total, the contrast between different parts of the picture would be too striking. The full light is used to fill in the remaining place not illuminated by the key light. Its introduction can weaken the contrast

and produce a more mild and more harmonic image. It is used to strengthen the intensity of the shadowed parts, to enhance the depth of field and to make the overall picture style more mild. Therefore we give the name full light. The intensity of the full light should not surpass that of the key light. The Dragon compiler will check it to make sure that the latter will never be weaker than the former. Light sources can be classified according to their functions in a scene. There are light sources used to mould roles, actions, relations between roles, to show the backgrounds and to push some parts of roles or objects forward to attract the audience's attention.

4. Environmental light
   It is used to let the audience have a feeling about the environment, mainly in three aspects: the weather (sunny, rainy, etc.), the time (season and day time) and the background (indoor, outdoor, etc.). Environmental light is mostly used as full light.
5. Modification light
   It is used to illuminate some parts of the roles, objects or the environment to reach special effects wanted by the director. The parts illuminated by this kind of light include parts of human body (head, hands, feet, face, eye expression, etc.), whole or parts of objects, parts of the environment, etc. It is according to this principle that the modification light is classified in background light, outline light, eye expression light and special effect light. While the portrait light is often used as key light, the modification light is also used as full light.
6. Background light
   In fact, this is another kind of environmental light. While the environmental light often has a function of full light, the background light is implemented as modification light. It illuminates only part of the background or some props or part of some props.
7. Outline light
   In fact, this is another kind of portrait light. If one does not want to show the whole portrait in detail, but only its outline (contour), then this kind of light can be used. It is implemented by an adverse light or a combination of adverse light and side light. When we take a picture, we can reach this effect by holding the camera towards the sun.
8. Eye expression light
   This is yet another kind of portrait light. It portraits a main role by stressing his/her special eye expression. One can use key light or full light to display and to strengthen roles' eye expression. One can also use special eye expression light (usually with small light sources) to do that. A typical example was the processing of the eye expression of Othello by the director of the soviet film "Othello". It has really a shocking effect to see his eye expression when Othello decided to kill his wife.

In picture 22 of appendix, the mian role princess Snow White get the key light, while other roles get the full light. Picture 18, 19 and 21 show examples of environmental light, where the palace is lightened by an environmental light represented by the moon light. In picture 18, a modification is used to illuminate the chest of the hunter, otherwise his chest would be dark since the key light source is behind him.

9.1.3.2 Light Position

Given a target, how do we arrange the light sources so that the light effect will meet the requirement of the director (cameraman)? This does not meant the direction of light sources. Obviously the light source should face its target. Thus the global direction of the light source is already determined. The factors which have not been determined are the place and posture of the light source.

<Light Position> ::= [horizontal : <Horizontal Light Position>]
[vertical : <Vertical Light Position>]
<Light Position1> ::= [horizontal : <Horizontal Light Position1>]
[vertical : <Vertical Light Position1>]
<Light Position2> ::= [horizontal : <Horizontal Light Position2>]
[vertical : <Vertical Light Position2>]
<Horizontal Light Position> ::= front | front and <Side> | <Side> | adverse
| adverse and <Side>
<Vertical Light Position> ::= front and top | top | adverse and top | <Bottom>
<Horizontal Light Position1> ::= front | front and <Side> | <Side>
<Vertical Light Position1> ::= front and top | top | front and bottom
<Horizontal Light Position2> ::= adverse | adverse and <Side>
<Vertical Light Position2> ::= adverse and top | adverse and bottom
<Side> ::= left | right
<Bottom> ::= front and bottom | adverse and bottom

Semantics:

Since sometimes the terminology used in the community of cameramen is rather ambiguous and confusing from the point of view of a computer implementation, we have to determine its meaning in a more rigorous way. In the language Poplar, the light direction does not specify the relative positions of the light sources with respect to the roles in the film, but specifies their relative positions with respect to the camera. Thus, for horizontal light positions, the term "front light" means that the light and the camera have the same direction, no matter whether the cameraman sees the front side or the back side of the target person. Similarly, the term "adverse light" means that the light and the camera have opposite directions.

Note that the camera direction is always pointing to the screen, because the direction of the camera is the same as that of the point of view of the audience. In most of the cases, our definition of light direction corresponds to the convention of movie directors. But in some cases, they are different. For example, if somebody is lying on the ground. Both the camera and the light source are above this person. We still consider the light as a front light, while the movie director may call it a top light. For the sake of implementation and programming, we need a rather strict definition of light directions.

1. Front light
   The light source and the camera are in the same direction with respect to the roles or objects being photographed. This direction is horizontal with respect to the screen.

Example 9.1.1

In figure 9.1.1, the role is standing on the ground. Both the camera and the light source are in front of him. In figure 9.1.2, the role is lying on the ground, both the camera and the light source are above him. We call all these two cases as front light, no matter whether the light source is in front of or above the role.

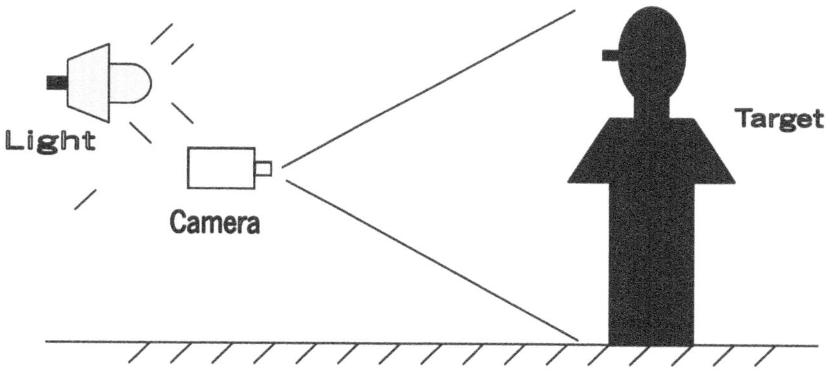

Figure 9.1.1 One Front Light

2. Adverse light
   The light source and the camera are in opposite directions with respect to the roles or objects being photographed. Adverse lights are often used to produce outline lights and silhouettes of roles.

3. Side light
   The light source and the camera are in orthogonal directions with respect to the roles or objects being photographed. Both directions are horizontal.

4. Top light
   The light source and the camera are in orthogonal directions with respect to the roles or objects being photographed. The light direction is top down from the point of view of the camera.

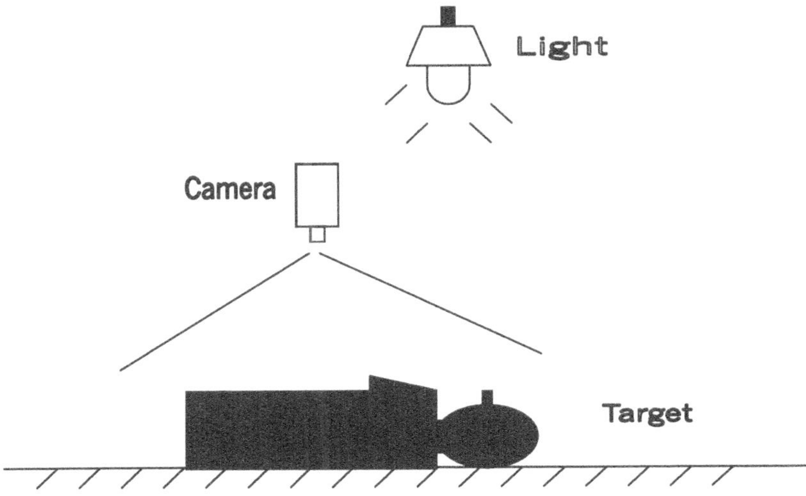

Figure 9.1.2 Another Front Light

5. Bottom light
   The light source and the camera are in orthogonal directions with respect to the roles or objects being photographed. The light direction is bottom up from the point of view of the camera.

6. Combination of different directions
   A combination of more than one light direction described above is possible, provided that no two of the light sources are directly opposite. For example: (front, right) light or (front, left) light is typical for making harmonic human portraits. Two remarks. The first remark: If we write down a "front and right" light specification, then that means there is only one single light source, which is in the same direction with the camera, but on its right side. If the specification is "front" light and "right" light, then there are two separate light sources, one for front and one for right. Second remark: the exact angle scope for a light position is 90 degree. For example, the angle for a front light is from –45 to +45 degree, given that the camera position is 0 degree. Under the same condition, the angle for a right light is from +45 degree to + 135 degree.

In appendix, almost all pictures take the front light, with exception of picture 14, 17, 18, 19, 20 and 21, where picture 14, 18 and 21 take the bottom-and-side light, which makes the new queen look viperous. On the other hand, picture 19 presents a scene of top-side light because of the existence of the moon. Picture 20 is a typical adverse light which shows an outline of the hero Hou Yi.

9.1.4 Generation of Dragon and Poplar Specifications

Based on summarizing the professional experiences of movie directors, we have established a rule base for generating Dragon and Poplar statements from the DPRS produced in chapter seven and the camera plan produced in chapter eight. The inference engine running on this rule base is called the front end compiler of Glorious. The current version of this rule base is quite simple and by no means complete. We just list some of them in the following.

9.1.4.1 Generation of Dragon Statements from DPRS

Some of the rules are:

1. On the light form
   Outdoor, street, open field (sunny and daytime)→ white field light
   Outdoor, street, open field (overcast and daytime)→ gray field light
   Outdoor, street, open field (nighttime)→ dark blue field light
   Indoor (nighttime) → yellow field light,
   Search light, flesh light → white beam light,
   Lamp, candle → yellow light source,
   Projection, flesh light → light fleck,
2. On the light style
   Sunny, slightly cloud → high light,
   Happy, lively, bustling atmosphere → high light,
   Overcast, foggy → low light,
   Sorrow, lonely atmosphere → low light,
   Mysterious, terrifying → hard light,
   Old men and women, people doing labor work → (possible) hard light
   Children, baby, young lady→ soft light,
   Harmonic, friendly → soft light,
3. On shadow and silhouette
   Morning or evening sun light → long stripe shadow
   Conspiracy making persons → (possibly) long stripe shadow
   Very powerful or terrifying things → (possibly) long stripe or immense shadow
   Loving pair behind a curtain → normal shadow
   Display some event indirectly → shadows on the wall or on the ground
   Soft representation of complicated sentiments → semi silhouette,
   Hard representation of complicated sentiments → silhouette,
4. On light layout
   Paradigm is realistic or romantic → balanced illumination,
   Attitude is extolling or appreciating → balanced illumination
   Paradigm is heavy or terrifying → unbalanced illumination,
   Attitude is stressing or contrasting → unbalanced illumination,
   Attitude is critiquing → unbalanced illumination

In the appendix, almost all pictures take a soft light, only some of them take a hard light. For example, the pictures showing the mysterious meeting of the new queen with the hunter are presented with hard light. There is a clear contrast between the illumination of the roles and the environment.

The shadows in picture 17 and 20 are different. The former is normal and the latter tends to be long and immense, reflecting the fact that trees are normal plants but Hou Yi is a very powerful hero.

In the current version of SWAN, we have not yet integrated presentations of dynamic natural phenomena in our background or light planning, though the integration would help SWAN to produce very lively scenes. For example, in the traditional movie director's routine, a sharp conflict between two persons, during which at least one of the two partners of the conflict feels very sorrow, usually takes place under a whether of thunder and lightning. Such functions do not exist in our current library. We expect to integrate packages of dynamic natural phenomena presentations in the next version of SWAN.

9.1.4.2 Generation of Poplar Statements from DPRS

Some of the rules are:

1. default light → front and <Side> light.
   It is said that the first artist using this light was the Netherlands's famous painter Rembrandt. This light can be used whenever no further specification is given
2. For displaying roles' characteristics:
   2.1. cruel, sinister, ruthless persons→ top light or bottom light,
   2.2. very old, old → hard light,
3. For displaying roles' sentiments:
   very angry or very sorrow sentiment → eye expression light,
4. For displaying roles' portray
   To produce a perfect portray of a role→ <Side> light,
   To produce a semi silhouette → adverse and <Side> light,
   To show the contour (silhouette) of the role → adverse light,
5. For producing deep impression about the environment
   To separate the roles from the background → adverse and <Side> light,
   To emphasize the depth of field → adverse and <Side> light,
   To produce a strong contrast of lighting → adverse and <Side> light,
6. For implementing light style:
   6.1. hard light → adverse and/or <Side> light
   6.2. soft light → front and <Side> light

9.1.5 Sublanguage BLP: Light Source Specification

In the last two sections 9.1.3 and 9.1.4, we have presented the languages Dragon and Poplar which are designed to do light planning for general and particular light effects. In this section, we will go a step further and present another language which is designed to program light sources on the level of a computer scientist. This is the language BLP (Basic Light Primitive). Note that the Dragon statements and Poplar statements are independent. A synthesis of these two groups of statements produces a program of BLP. During this process, a consistency check of Dragon and Poplar statements is made to ensure the correctness of resulted BLP statements. Remember we have introduced a camera planning language BCP in chapter eight. BLP is about at the same level of programming like BCP.

1. Homogeneous light source

This kind of light is distributed homogeneously in the whole environment and in the whole room. Its intensity is always the same, independent of time and space, no matter whether the space is separated by walls or something else. For example, when it is overcast, the light outdoor is homogeneous. There are no shadows. Or, in the evening, the illumination in a small room is also homogeneous. The corresponding BLP is:

Homo_light (<Intensity>, <Color>, <Time Interval>);

Note that a homogeneous light may undergo an intensity change. For example, the changing intensity of a room light, or that of the sky light due to the change of day time.

2. Infinite Light Source

The infinite light source is also homogeneous, with the exception that the obstacles play a role. The light has a fixed direction, determined by an infinite line in the three dimensional space. Any obstacle will produce a shadow in the target direction. Its BLP has the following form:

Infi_light (<Source Direction>, <Intensity>, <Color>, <Time Interval>);

where

<Source Direction> ::= <Relative Direction> (<Target>)

<Relative Direction> ::= above | left | right | back | front | [<Direction Modification>] <Relative Direction> and [<Direction Modification>] <Relative Direction>

<Direction Modification> ::= little | more

For example, left and front and above (house) is a legal source direction. Little left and more front (house) is also a valid source direction. In fact, the source light comes from an infinitely far place. For example, the sun light is an infinite light source.

3. Diffusing light source

This is a finite light source which is a finite three dimensional object sending light to all directions. The illumination is distributed in the whole space. But its intensity is diminishing gradually towards all directions, with exception of those directions where there are obstacles. In the latter case, the obstacles will produce shadows. For example, a lampe in an open field is a diffusing light source. A BLP displaying diffusing light source is as follows:

Diff_light (<Light Source>, <Radius>, <Intensity Change>,
<Intensity Attenuation>, <Color>, <Time Interval>);

where

<Intensity Change> ::= <Intensity>
<Intensity Attenuation> ::= <Positive Number ≤ 1>
<Light Source> ::= <Object Name>
<Radius> ::= <Positive Number> | <Quantity Concept>
<Quantity Concept> ::= large | small | middle | quite <Quantity Concept>

The intensity of each diffusing light source attenuates from the light source to the surface of a ball with the light source as center and <Radius> as radius. The term "intensity attenuation" denotes the rate of the intensity at the surface of the light ball to the initial intensity of the light source. For example, if the initial intensity of the light source is 100, the intensity attenuation is 0.7, then the intensity at the surface of the light ball is 70.

On the other hand, we do not have to specify the position of the light source extra, because the light source has already been specified as an object sending light, which is assigned a position. Note that there should be an "appear" statement of this object in the plot part of the scene. Otherwise there will be no light at all. For example,

```
# Light
 Diff_light (candle.flame, large, bright, 0.01, yellow, t1, t2 );
# End of Light
# Plot
 standing (candle, middle (room), t1, t2 );
# End of Plot
```

which means that a candle flame is quite bright in its neighborhood, but the illumination diminishes very rapidly towards outside.

4. Projecting light source

This is a special kind of diffusing light source. The source is a finite three dimensional object. The light is distributed only in a spatial angle. Examples are flesh light and search light beams.

Proj_light (<Light Object>, <Light Angle>, <Time Interval>);

where

<Light Object> ::= <Object Name> | {<Sequence of Object Names>}
<Light Angle>::=<Rate>

5. Moving light source

All light sources mentioned above are fixed light sources, if nothing else is specified. These sources always remain at the same place and are mostly used sources in animation. The only factor which may change is their intensity. Another kind of light sources is the moving and rotating sources, for example, the front light of a car or the flash light brought by a human being. In order to specify a moving light source, we use a macro statement of object moving in the plot part. For example,

```
# Light
  Proj_light (lfront_light, middle, t1, t2 );
  Proj_light (rfront_light, middle, t1, t2 );
  ...........................
# End of Light
# Plot
  Drive (car, foot (hill), in_front_of (house), t1, t2 );
  ............................
# End of Plot
```

describes a car driving with two head lights lfront_light and rfront_light

6. Group Light Source

We have already seen an example of group light sources. It was a pair of car head lights. Besides that, we can make use of another syntactic possibility of grouping several light sources in the same light specification statement:

```
Proj_light ({lfront_light, rfront_light}, middle, t1, t2 );
```

Yet another possibility is to write a group source definition:

```
Define_light ((lfront_light, rfront_light), front_light);
```

With this definition one may write:

```
Proj_light (front_light, middle, t1, t2 );
```

9.1.6 A Wide Spectrum Language

Glorious is a wide spectrum language. That means it contains three different languages with statements at different levels. Those at higher levels will be compiled and produce corresponding statements at lower levels. In this section, it is necessary to explain the relations among the three languages.

9.1.6.1 From Dragon to Dragon

The source of the Dragon statements is the plot plan produced by the plot planning module, the DPRS produced by the director planning module and the camera plan produced by the camera planning module. But the information which Dragon can use is a wide spectrum one. For example, it may require that the light style should be hard (abstract information), that there is a shadow in the middle of the room (concrete information without giving light source), and that there is a lamp on the desk (concrete information with light source). Dragon accepts all of them. That means, Dragon itself is a wide spectrum language. Therefore, we must first transform the abstract part of information of Dragon in its concrete form.

We list some default principles of the Dragon compiler.

1. If only light effects, but no corresponding light sources are specified, then additional light sources corresponding to the specified light effects will be added by the compiler and light planner.
2. Projecting lights are produced by point like light sources.
3. Light flecks are produced by point like light sources and/or light grids which are not light sources but light obstacles in form of a plane board with single or several holes on it. This board will be added by the compiler to the Dragon program automatically as an additional (not necessary visible) object.
4. Light beams will be implemented as lighting objects with transparent material characteristics. These objects will be also automatically produced and added to the Dragon program by the compiler.
5. In most of the cases, light shadows are produced by light sources and light obstacles cooperatively. If at least one of the both is missing in the script specification, then it should be added by the Dragon compiler automatically to the program (not necessary visible, either).
6. Hard lights are implemented by diminishing the scattering coefficients of targets' material, while soft lights are implemented by enhancing these coefficients.
7. High lights are implemented by enhancing the intensity of light sources, while low lights are implemented by diminishing the light intensity of the sources.
8. In many cases, the unbalanced illumination specification may be partly redundant to that of light flecks. It is the job of the compiler to synthesize these two specifications to produce a combined light effect.

9.1.6.2 From Dragon to Poplar

Basically, Poplar gets information directly from the DPRS. The relation between Dragon and Poplar is in its essence not a source-target relation. Both of them are targets of DPRS. But on the other hand, there is really information in Dragon which is useful for generating Poplar statements. The function of such information is twofold. The first function is to produce new Poplar statements. The second one is to check the consistency of DPRS requirements by checking the consistency between Dragon and Poplar statements. Here we list some examples.

If the light style in Dragon is hard, then the key light in Poplar must be a <Side> and/or adverse light.

If the light style in Dragon is soft, then the key light in Poplar must be a front [and <Side>] light.

The direction of shadows (specified in Dragon) must be consistent with the direction of key light (specified in Poplar).

In case of unbalanced illumination (Dragon), the illuminated part must be in the scope of key light (Poplar).

In case of balanced illumination (Dragon), there must be a full light (Poplar).

9.1.6.3 From Dragon and Poplar to BLP

The BLP generator combines the information provided by Dragon and Poplar statements and produces a BLP program. The information contained in Dragon and that contained in Poplar are essentially complementary. Some of the principles on generating BLP statements have been mentioned above. Here we list some further ones which are important for the BLP generator.

If neither light effect, nor light source is specified in Dragon and Poplar, then produce a BLP statement of homogeneous light. The default is daylight.

All fixed lights are implemented as BLP diffusing lights or project lights, except the sun and moon light which are implemented as infinite lights.

If a full light is specified, then generate a BLP homogeneous light with low intensity.

If there are special modification lights (e.g. eye expression light), then generate appropriate BLP light source statements (e.g. small light sources with low intensity close to the eyes of the main role).

While producing BLP statements based on light source specification of Dragon, use Poplar statements to determine the position of light sources and their illumination direction (e.g. a front light specification determines that the light source with highest intensity must be in front of the main role)

9.2 Color Planning

9.2.1 The Importance of Color Use

The use of color constitutes a very important technique of movie shooting. In the earlier stage of development of movie technique, people knew only black white films. Even at that time, the film directors tried a lot to use different degrees of grayness (intermediate colors between black and white) to express his/her attitude towards the events and roles in the movie. Since the birth of color films, movie directors have developed a great lot of techniques to use colors in film making. It is just these theories and experiences of movie directors in color use which constitute a basis for our color planning in SWAN. Thanks to a systematic analysis of movie color technique in the book "The Technique and Theory of Cinematography" [Ge and ShenS, 1988], we have summarized the principal content of these techniques and transformed them in computer realizable color planning rules and schemas in SWAN.

In the history, many famous movie directors have expressed their point of view towards color use with excellent words. The soviet movie director Dovrenko said: "People tend to compare color films with oil paintings. In fact, this comparison is incorrect and superficial. The color in a film is always rich of layers and impulse. It is dynamic and is always in motion. Therefore, if compared with oil paintings, the color in a film is more similar to music". He said furthermore: the color in movie is a music of vision! Eisenstein, another famous director, said "There is no difference between color processing and music processing. If you understand how to process music, then you also understand how to process colors".

These points of view constitute the principal guideline of color planning in SWAN.

9.2.2 Jade: A Language for Color Requirement Planning

Just as we have done in camera planning and light planning, the planning of color use should also go through a process of requirement specification and implementation. Our language for color planning requirement statement is called Jade whose simplified syntax is as follows.

9.2.2.1 Global Color Planning

<Jade Program> ::= Jade (<Program Name>)
<Color Signature>
End of Jade
<Color Signature> ::= signature : (<Global Schema> <Detail Schema>)
<Global Schema> ::= global : [<Keynote Color>;] [<Color Layout>;] [<Color Contrast>;]
<Keynote Color> ::= keynote : (<Color Declaration>)
<Color Declaration> ::= <Sequence of Color Specifications>
<Color Specification> ::= <Color Type> | <Color Palette>
<Color Type> ::= tone : (<Sequence of Color Tones>)
<Color Tone> ::= optical = <Optical Tone> | thermal = <Thermal Tone> | tint = <Colorful Tone>
<Optical Tone> ::= hard | soft | a little <Optical Tone> | very <Optical-Tone>
<Thermal Tone> ::= cold | warm | a little <Thermal Tone> | very <Thermal Tone>
<Colorful Tone> ::= gaudy | simple | black_white | red | green | blue
<Color Palette> ::= <Color Name> | <RGB Representation> | <Heuristic Color> | <Color Palette> and <Color Palette>
<Color Layout> ::= <Sequence of Global Colors>

<Global Color> ::= <Global Role Color> | <Global Thread Color>
<Global Role Color> ::= global_role : <Sequence of Role Names> (<Color Specification>)
<Global Thread Color> ::= global_thread : <Sequence of Scene Numbers> (<Color Specification>)
<Color Contrast> ::= contrast : <Sequence of Color Contrast Items>
<Color Contrast Item> ::= <Role Contrast> | <Thread Contrast> | <Role Fate Contrast> | <Thread Phase Contrast>
<Role Contrast> ::= role : (<Sequence of Role Contrast Pairs>)
<Role Contrast Pair> ::= (<Sequence of Role Names> : <Sequence of Color Tones>, <Sequence of Role Names> : <Sequence of Color Tones>)
<Thread Contrast> ::= thread : (<Sequence of Thread Contrast Pairs>)
<Thread Contrast Pair>::=(<Sequence of Scene Numbers >: <Sequence of Color Tones>, <Sequence of Scene Numbers > : <Sequence of Color Tones>)
<Role Fate Contrast> ::= fate : <Sequence of Role Names> (<Series of Role Fates>)
<Role Fate> ::= <Key Event> : <Sequence of Color Tones>
<Key Event> ::= <Abstract Action Name>
<Thread Phase Contrast> ::= phase : <Sequence of Scene Numbers > (<Series of Thread Phases>)
<Thread Phase> ::= <Key Event> : <Sequence of Color Tones>

9.2.2.2 Semantics of Global Color Planning

1. Global Color Planning

   Global color planning is a set of guidelines which have different scopes. Guidelines of each scope should be valid for the whole process of animation with respect to this scope. In the <Global Schema>, the <Keynote Color> and <Color Type> specification determine the basic color paradigms for the whole animation. Their scopes are the whole movie. The scope of <Color Layout> is either the characteristic of colors of a role in the whole animation (in case of a <Role Color> specification), or the characteristic of colors of a development thread (see chapter five for its definition). The scope of <Color Contrast> is the characteristic of the colors of the contrasted roles, role fates, threads or thread phases.

2. Priority Principles

   In case that two scopes with different color characteristics intersect, we have contradictions. Note that it is impossible to avoid such contradictions completely, because the colors of the real life are not monotone. The information provided by a story may also be inherently inconsistent. For example, it is a routine to take the green color as the basic color for a scene describing the spring season. But it is possible to have two ladies in black suits appearing in this scene. To solve these (seemingly) contradictions, we use priority principles:

If any color specification x violates the keynote color, then keep x unchanged.
If role x appears in a role contrast specification y, and color (x) violates the color of x in y, then change color (x) to conform to the latter.
If thread phase x appears in a thread contrast specification y, and color (x) violates the color of x in y, then change color (x) to conform to the latter.
If role x appears in thread y, but color (x) violates color (y), then keep color (x) unchanged.
If x is a fate of the role y in a role fate contrast specification, and color (x) violates the color (y), then keep color (x) unchanged.
If x is a phase of the thread y in a thread phase contrast specification, and color (x) violates the color (y), then keep color (x) unchanged.

3. Keynote Color

   This is the realization of the key note of the whole film with respect to color use. The key note color may be one single color, or a combination of several neighboring colors. The symbolic meaning of the keynote color of a movie reflects the intention of the director. Usually, the keynote color of an animation is sanguine, lucid and lively, because its main audience are the children. Exceptions are "little girl selling matches" and "daughter of the see" of Anderson and "happy prince" of Walder.

4. Color Schema

   A summary of color use in the whole movie which determines the guidelines of characteristic colors of all roles, all backgrounds and all scenes, and their changes in the movie.

5. Global Role Color

   Refers to the characteristic color for a role, which does not change in the whole movie. For example, the little girl in the children story "little red hat" is always happy and does not know any danger. Her characteristic color is red. On the other hand, the big gray wolf has gray as its characteristic color which portraits a cruel figure of the wolf.

6. Global Thread Color

   Refers to the contrast between different threads. In the fifth chapter we have discussed techniques of dividing a story in a bunch of plot development threads. Usually a movie director will use different colors for different plot development threads. Consider the two plot threads in the animation "lion king". The life and struggle of the old lion king and its son, the future new lion king, constitute a positive thread whose characteristic color is warm (the color of the screen is warm whenever their activity dominates the screen). On the other hand, the conspiracy of the old lion king's brother forms another plot thread, the negative thread, whose characteristic color is cold.

7. Role Fate Contrast

   Refers to the change of a role's fate during the progress of a movie and its reflection in the change of colors. Above we have seen that it is possible to specify a characteristic color for some role in the whole movie. But this is not always true. Usually the fate or sentiment of a role changes from time to time in a movie. In this situation, different colors are needed in different scenes for the same role. In the film "Jane Eyre", Jane, the leading role, wore a dark dress at the beginning. Later, as she knew that her master fell in love with her, she put on a dress with sanguine color. But when she heard that her master would marry another woman, she changed on her dark dress again. These three states of her wearing reflect three different sentiments of her. We call it "three fates" of Jean according to our syntax.

   We did not define the syntax of <Role Fate> with "key scenes" but with "key events" because the fates of a role depend on events which are in general abstract ones in the terminology of chapter six and need to be developed in several scenes.

8. Thread Phase Contrast

   Refers to the change of colors reflecting the progressing of plot in a movie. While the role fate contrast refers to the change of a role's color in the whole movie, the thread phase contrast refers to the change of scenes' colors in this thread. In the example of lion king, the thread "old_new_lion_king" has experienced a happy phase (birth of the lion prince, congratulations from many animals), a sorrow phase (death of the old lion king) and a new happy phase (coronation of the new lion king). These three phases are certainly worth three different colors.

9.2.2.3 Detailed Color Planning

<Detail Schema> ::= detail : <Sequence of Scene Colors>
<Scene Color> ::= scene : <Sequence of Scene Numbers>
    (<Series of Scene Color Specifications>)
<Scene Color Specification> ::= <Color Specification>
    | (<Sequence of Local Colors>; <Space Color Layout>)
<Local Color> ::= <Role Color> | <Background Color> | <Props Color>
<Role Color> ::= role : <Sequence of Role Names> (<Color Specification>)
<Background Color> ::= background : [<Sequence of Key Point Names>]
    (<Color Specification>)
<Props Color> ::= props : <Sequence of Props Names> (<Color Specification>)
<Space Color Layout> ::= <Part to Whole> | <Double Parties>
    | <Triple Combination> | <Sequence of Color Tones>
<Part to Whole> ::= focus : <Focus Part> , from : <Other Part>
<Focus Part> ::= <Object Name> | <Role Name>

<Part> ::= background | <Sequence of Objects> | <Sequence of Role Names>
<Other Part> ::= other | <Part>
<Double Parties> ::= contrast : <Part>, with : <Other Part>
<Triple Combination> ::= differentiate : <Part>, with : <Part>, and : <Other Part>
<Heuristic Color> ::= <Active Color> | <Passive Color> | <Poor Color>
| <Tragic Color> | <Happy Color> | <Striking Color>
| <Simple Color> | <Noble Color> | <Vulgar Color>
| <Adequate Color> | <Sanguine Color> | <Mysterious Color> | ......
<Active Color> ::= red | green | yellow | purple | ......
<Passive Color> ::= white | black | gray |......
<Poor Color> ::= black | gray
... ...
<Noble Color> ::= <Oriental Noble Color> | <Western Noble Color>
<Oriental Noble Color> ::= gold | yellow
<Western Noble Color> ::= white | black | gold | silver
... ...

In the appendix, we have some pictures showing heuristic colors. Among them, picture 23 has a happy color, picture 22 has a tragic color and picture 14 has a mysterious color and a striking color as well.

9.2.2.4 Semantics of Detailed Color Planning

1. General Semantics

   The detailed color planning is used for specifying the color use in individual scenes.

2. Further Priority Principles

   If a detail color specification x violates a global color specification y, then keep x unchanged.

   If x is a key point name of the background y, and color (x) violates color (y), then keep x unchanged. Note that the same background may have different characteristic colors at different key points.

   Let color (x, y) denote the color specification of x in y, where x is a role or object in the scene y. If color (x, y) violates the space color layout of y, then change color (x, y) to conform to the latter.

3. Similarity and Difference of colors

   If we take that segment of the optical spectrum, which starts from purple (shortest wave length) to red (longest wave length), and connect the two ends purple and red with an intermediate color in the middle, e.g. pinkish red, then we get a ring of colors, in which the neighboring colors are similar (for example red and orange), and colors on the two ends of a diameter are opposite (for example orange and blue).

4. Cold and warm colors

   Take the segment of the optical spectrum again. This time not to produce a ring, but to consider it as a strip. There are two classes of colors in this color strip : the cold colors and the warm colors. Those colors with shorter wave length (green, blue, dark blue, purple) are called cold colors. Those with longer wave length (red, orange, yellow) are called warms colors. Each class has its own symbolic meaning.

5. Scene Color

   The meaning of a scene color is twofold. On the one hand, a scene color means the dominating color in the whole scene. On the other hand, a scene color is a group concept. It specifies the local characteristic colors of roles, of the background and of the props in this scene. These two meanings are useful under different situations. The former is often used in a scene with a unified atmosphere. For example, the red color may dominate a scene “wedding”. The latter is used when the scene’s color design needs to be refined. For example, it is difficult to give a unified color to the scene where the lovely girl “little red hat” is facing the big gray wolf.

6. Heuristic Color

   Heuristic colors are introduced for easing the programming. There should be no fixed and rigorous definitions for heuristic colors, such as what is an “active color” or “passive color”. They are parts of our animation knowledge base. It is depending on the knowledge base designer’s taste and director(user)’s taste that a definition is given. One can modify it and add new definitions to the knowledge base at any time.

   In picture 19 of the appendix, the scene color specification can be as follows:

```
detail: scene: queen’s conspiracy
 (tone: (optical = hard,
      thermal = cold,
      tint = blue );
     (role : new queen
        (tone: (optical = hard,
              thermal = warm,
              tint = red ));
      role: hunter
        (tone: (optical = soft,
              thermal = warm,
              tint = purple ))
```

The picture 18 is almost equal to picture 19, except that the moon in picture 19 disappears in picture 18. As a trade off, in picture 18, the lamp light passes through the window and adds some warm light flavor to the whole cold light picture.

9.2.3 Generation of Jade Statements

9.2.3.1 Generating Standard Jade Statements

These colors, e.g. cold color, warm color, etc. are built-in knowledge of SWAN. We list only a few examples.

Night, overcast, foggy → cold color,
Funeral, sorrow atmosphere → cold color,
Hospital, class room, laboratory → cold color,
Spring → green color,
Sunny → warm color,
Celebration, pub, ball → warm color,
Chinese wedding → red color,
Western wedding → white color,
Poor family → simple color,

9.2.3.2 Generating Heuristic Jade Statements

Heuristic knowledge is inputted by the user. The definitions of the various kinds of colors, e.g. active color, passive color, etc., depend on the taste of the user.

1. Keynote Color → (x_1) Comedy → Happy Color
→ …………
→ (x_2) Tragedy → Sorrow Color
→ ……..
→ (x_3) Educational → Active Color
→ (x_4) Terrifying → Striking Color

2. Role → (x_1) Little Girl → (x_1. y_1) Character → (x_1. y_1.1) Lively → Active Color
→ (x_1. y_1.2) Normal → Adequate Color
→ (x_1. y_2) Fate → (x_1.y_2.1) Very Well → Active Color
→ (x_1.y_2.2) Normal → Adequate Color
→ (x_1. y_2.3) Bad → Passive Color
→ (x_1. y_2.4) Very Bad → Poor Color
→ (x_2) Woman → (x_2. y_1) Character →(x_2. y_1.z_1) Hot → Active Color
→ (x_2. y_1.z_2) Cruel → Striking Color
→ (x_2. y_1.z_3) Kind → Simple Color
→ (x_2. y_2) Social Position → (x_2. y_2. z_1) Noble → Noble Color
→ (x_2. y_2. z_2) Rich → Vulgar Color

3. Thread → (x_1. 1) Chain of Positive Role Actions → Active Color
→ ……..

→ (x_1. 2) Chain of Negative Role Actions → Passive Color
→ ……

4. (An Event in) Role Fate Contrast → (1) Always Success→ Happy Color
→ (2) Good Fate → Active Color
→ (3) Fight and Struggle → Striking Color
→ (4) Bad Fate → Passive Color

5. (An Event in) Thread Phase Contrast → (1) Good Fate for Positive Roles → Active Color
→ (2) Bad Fate for Positive Roles → Passive Color
→ (3) Negative Roles' conspiracy → Mystery Color
→……………..

Finally note the difference between color planning and the other two: camera planning and light planning. While the latter two produce extra camera statements (BCP) and light statements (BLP), the former does not produce any "color statements". The result of color planning is contained in that of light planning (remember that the light sources may have colors), that of background and props selection (from the background and object library) and that of figure and props planning (by coloring and clothing, see next chapter).

9.3 Role Portraying

In certain sense, the task of portraying roles is the most important one in the mind of a director. We could have developed a great package in SWAN for portraying roles and written a big chapter for it in this book. But due to the time limit of developing SWAN we have only implemented part of our idea. In SWAN, the task of portraying roles includes behavior planning, outlook planning and facial expression planning. Many of these procedures have been already discussed and are scattered in past chapters. In this section, we just summarize the main ideas and techniques used in the current version of SWAN for portraying a person.

9.3.1 Behavior Planning

A very important part of roles' behavior planning has already been discussed in the camera planning part (chapter eight) and in the light planning part (section 9.1). For example, to portray a cruel person we used top light. To portray an arrogant and wildly conceited person we used tilt up camera positions etc.

Another way of displaying the particular behavior of a person is to assign a special set of characteristic actions to him/her. There are two possibilities. The first one is to detect the characteristic behavior of a person during the story analysis phase. (For example, a sly person always rolls his/her eyeballs.) We can then use this behavior set to design characteristic actions of this person. The second technique is simpler. We just determine the characteristic actions of a person according to his age, carrier and social positions. (For example, an old man always walks slowly) It is not an ideal technique, but is a useful one. SWAN took the second approach.

9.3.2 Outlook Planning

There is another dimension of techniques used for portraying the outlook of roles. It includes mainly the figure, the color and the clothing.

The figure planning is mainly done in the phase of character construction (section 10.5). There, we have designed a special parameter for modifying the figure of a person: the scaling. It can be used to make some articulates of a person long or short, fat or thin. The guideline of determining the scaling factor is the same as it was said in the last section 9.3.1. For example, the figure of a princess is always thin, except if we define a particular "fat princess".

The color planning for a person's outlook is a part of clothing planning. It is determined by the cloth image selected for this purpose. Since the cloth image sub-library is organized in a classification hierarchy (see section 10.5.4), a relatively appropriate image will be selected each time.

10 Knowledge Base and Libraries

The work of SWAN is supported by a group of knowledge bases and Libraries.

10.1 The Pangu Commonsense Knowledge Base

10.1.1 Commonsense Knowledge and Commonsense Knowledge Bases

It is a common point of view of many AI experts that the processing of commonsense knowledge is a core and the most difficult problem of AI. The level of achievements of AI depends to a great extent on the progress of research in the field of commonsense knowledge. The study on commonsense knowledge is not only theoretically significant. It has also a great practical meaning in many fields of software and computer science. In our SWAN system, the application of commonsense knowledge also plays an important role. It is to this end that we have designed and implemented a large-scale commonsense knowledge base called Pangu.

Commonsense knowledge is a counterpart of expert knowledge. Many people are well informed about the importance of expert knowledge. But only few people outside the circle of computer scientists are aware of this importance. For example, McCarthy has pointed out many years ago, that the lack of commonsense knowledge has made most of the expert systems fragile. For example, a medical expert system does not understand the concept of life and death [McCarthy, 1968].

A very important direction of research on commonsense knowledge is its representation, its mathematical and logical models. It involves the various kinds of representations (first order logic, production systems, semantic networks, neural networks, etc.) and mechanisms of commonsense reasoning (deduction, induction, qualitative reasoning, fuzzy reasoning, non-monotonic reasoning, para-consistent reasoning, etc.). Research on commonsense knowledge and commonsense reasoning has made great progress. But there is still a very long way to go until many interesting problems can be solved. In fact, our understanding on the essence of commonsense knowledge is still very poor.

Feigenbaum stressed the importance of knowledge from another point of view [Lenat and Guha, 1990]. He has proposed a so-called knowledge principle according to which the great goal of AI can be reached in a three-step program. In the first step, one will construct a massive knowledge base, such that a huge set of

R. Lu and S. Zhang: Automatic Generation of Computer Animation, LNAI 2160, pp. 315-349, 2002.

problems can be solved with this knowledge base. In the second step, much more knowledge will be added to this knowledge base so that it can answer questions whose solutions do not exist in the knowledge base. The mechanism of answering such questions is based on an analogical reasoning. In the third step, even more knowledge will be added to the knowledge base so that it can start to invent new knowledge.

The CYC program proposed by Lenat is often considered as a serious effort aiming at realizing the dream of Feigenbaum [Lenat and Guha, 1990]. This is a very ambitious program. There has been a live discussion about CYC [McDermott, 1993].

In the framework of a key project supported by NSFC (Natural Science Foundation of China), we have been attacking the problem of studying commonsense knowledge for three years. We have started to build up a large-scale commonsense knowledge base called Pangu. Our goal is not only to study the theoretical issues of commonsense knowledge, but also its application in some practical fields, like natural language understanding, automatic generation of computer animation, etc.

A key issue of establishing such a knowledge base is its architecture. Roughly, it consists of three layers. The basic level is the commonsense knowledge itself, organized in agents and ontology bodies. The top one is the level of application. There will be a lot of application programs built on this level. Between these two is the level of mediators. It accepts the requests sent by the application programs, analyzes them and tries to solve the problems relying upon the basic level.

Below is a list of applications:

Commonsense Query: "Why we shouldn't stay under sunlight too long?"
Commonsense Check: Is the statement "We swim in a desk" reasonable?
Plot Development: Please give details of "Prince and princess get married"
Situation Analysis: "John is all over wet". What happened?
Forecast: "There are dark clouds in the sky". What will happen?
Associative Thinking: "The bikes are on sell". What should we do?
Disambiguation: "John hit Jack. He is angry". Who is angry?

These functions are useful for many fields, including natural language understanding, machine translation, pattern recognition, adaptive man machine interface, automatic generation of computer animation, etc. In order to implement them, we have investigated various known representation forms of knowledge. Usually the expert systems take rules, production systems and frames to represent knowledge. Note that to represent expert knowledge is easier than to represent commonsense knowledge, because the former is much easy to formalize. But it is totally different with respect to commonsense knowledge. People call it "knowledge soup", "knowledge cloud" due to its fuzzy and non deterministic scope, structure and content. The CYC system of Lenat takes first order logic plus frame architecture as its basic representation. The frame architecture is used to represent basic facts (a classification hierarchy of mental and physical objects). The first order logic is used to program inference procedures. For each problem domain, they constructed a micro theory (an axiomatic system). After more than 10 years effort, a knowledge base with more than one million assertions has been built up.

10.1.2 Characteristic Features of Pangu

For our purpose of representing and applying commonsense knowledge, we have taken another approach. The principles for establishing the Pangu knowledge base are:

1. The commonsense knowledge should be modularized. Each knowledge unit represents a human expert in the relevant domain. This expert is assumed to be capable to answer any question in the relevant domain. We call it an agent.
2. The agents form a hierarchy of inheritance. For example, the agent "pine" inherits all properties from its father agent "tree".
3. Agents belonging to the same discourse form an ontology. We have defined seven types of ontology. Their ontology bodies are all different. The ontologies organize the agents in an associative way.
4. The agents cooperate to solve the problems in a distributed way.
5. There is fuzzy inference, inexact reasoning and nonmonotonic reasoning.
6. The knowledge base is evolutionary. It may improve its knowledge during the procedure of service.
7. The communication among the agents is based on an extension of KQML, called XQML.

10.1.3 The Agent Architectures and Their Function Layers

In order to establish an agent oriented commonsense knowledge base, we have to determine two architectures: one about the architecture of a single agent, another one about that of the whole knowledge base. We first consider the former one.

Based on the research reported in literature, we can divide the various kinds of agents in six global classes: the passive agents, the reactive agents, the BDI agents, the social agents, the evolutionary agents and the personalized agents. The main characteristics of these agents are:

1. Passive agents. They are very similar to the objects in conventional object oriented languages and possess similar functions, e.g. data encapsulation, attribute inheritance, message passing etc. They are the least intelligent class of agents. They will be activated only when receiving message from other agents.
2. The reactive agents. A reactive agent can monitor the environment according to a predefined pattern. Whenever the state of the environment is changed, this change will be detected by reactive agents. The latter will take necessary measure to react to this change. The most typical application of reactive agents is robotics. Remember the robot insects of Brookes.
3. The BDI agents. This is the most typical intelligent agent (or autonomous agent) in the current research. A BDI agent has its own belief, desire and inten-

tion. A typical kind of BDI agents is a software agent, an agent which collects information and knowledge from the internet for its master. A high level robot is also a BDI agent.

4. The social agents. A social agent lives in a society of agents which is also called a multi agent society. The social agents may have common interest (they cooperate to perform a job) or contradicting interest (they compete for a job or a resource). Therefore, these agents have both functions of cooperation and competition.
5. The evolutionary agents. An evolutionary agent can learn from the environment and from its own experience. A single agent can learn from its interaction with the environment. But in most cases the agents learn from events in a multi agent society. These agents can be used to mimic a biological society, such as the society of ants and bees.
6. The personalized agents. These agents can not only think, but can also have sentiment. There is relatively few study on personalized agents in the literature. But they may have important application, for example in story understanding, where each character of the story can be represented as a personalized agent.

After a thorough analysis, we came to the conclusion that non of these agent classes may serve as a unique representation to fulfil our task satisfactorily. Our commonsense agent is an autonomous unit for solving a class of problems. The function of a passive agent is too weak to complete this task. A reactive agent is also not powerful enough because it still lacks the ability of sound thinking and inference. A BDI agent has powerful mental functions. But it is not appropriate to integrate these functions into every commonsense agent. It is better to have simpler commonsense agents (they are the main content of the knowledge base) and to organize some mental functions as separate functional agents other than the commonsense knowledge agents. Similarly, the cooperation and competition functions of social agents are all needed when doing inference on our knowledge base. It is better to have independent functional agents for organizing cooperation and competition among the commonsense knowledge agents.

Therefore, we have designed a special architecture of agents, called CBS agent, as a representation of commonsense knowledge units, which is different from all the agent architectures mentioned above. Before introducing the details of CBS agents, we notice that all the agent forms mentioned above are needed in our knowledge base Pangu. Their functions except those of passive agents are illustrated in table 10.1.1.

10.1.3.1 CBS Agent

In this section, we will discuss the architecture and functions of CBS agents which are the basic knowledge representation units in Pangu. In principle, the CBS agents must possess the ability of representing and processing any kind of human commonsense knowledge. CBS means capability, belief and strategy. Each CBS agent has two kinds of knowledge: the static knowledge (Belief) and the dynamic knowledge (Strategy). Generally speaking, the belief part of a CBS agent mimics

Table 10.1.1 Use of Different Agents in Pangu

	Knowledge representation	Knowledge management, user interface	Knowledge based reasoning	Learning, evolution	Application
CBS Agent	Yes	no	yes	No	yes
Reactive agent	no	yes	no	yes	yes
BDI agent	No	no	yes	yes	yes
Evolutionary agent	No	no	no	yes	yes
Social agent	No	no	no	yes	yes
Personalized agent	No	no	no	no	yes

the memory of a human agent. Its strategy part mimics the ability of a human expert of using his/her static knowledge to solve complex problems. Therefore we call the CBS agent's dynamic knowledge also its meta-knowledge. In order to improve the efficiency of problem solving, each CBS agent has a Capability part as an abstract of its knowledge. If a CBS agent is requested to solve a problem, it first matches this problem against its Capability part and starts the solution process only if the Capability part says yes.

Each CBS agent is divided into two parts: the implicit part and the explicit part, where the explicit part is programmed by the user and the implicit part is established by the system. Their syntax is roughly the following:

<CBS Agent> ::= <Implicit Part> <Explicit Part>
<Implicit Part> ::= Input : <Input Mail Box>
Output : <Output Mail Box>
History : <Session Protocol>
Buffer : <Working Buffer>
<Explicit Part> ::= Name : <Agent Name>
Father : <Sequence of Father Class Names>
Capability : <Sequence of Capability Items>
Belief : <Sequence of Belief Items>
Strategy : <Inference Engine>
<Capability Item> ::= <Knowledge Triple>
<Belief Item> ::= <CS-net Semantic Network> | <Rule Base>
| <Data Dictionary> | <Relational Data Base> | <Ontology Pointer>
| <Fuzzy Dictionary> | <HTML Text>
<Inference Engine> ::= <CS-Prolog Program>

Now let us explain the five components of the explicit part of a CBS agent.

The Father Component. It specifies all father nodes of this agent. In Pangu, a CBS agent may have more than one father agent. The multi inheritance mechanism is different from those reported in the literature. It is not based on a fixed order of father nodes, for example a depth first order, but based on a dynamic selection principle. Each time when the inheritance is needed, the father node will be selected by the CS-prolog program of the Strategy part. Furthermore, this CS-prolog program may call more than one father node within the same inference procedure. In this way, the flexibility of inference is enhanced.

The Belief Component. Many problems of commonsense knowledge are posed in form of natural language. The semantic network is a suitable tool for representing natural language statements. Therefore, even though there are different knowledge representations used in the Belief component, the most important representation is the CS-net. CS-net is a special form of semantic network proposed by the authors to represent commonsense knowledge. For example, the question: "can a human being eat everything which an ox eats?" can be represented with CS-net in the following form:

```
? ( human    can (eat )    all (food : L) )
L: (food     can(be(eat))      ox    )
```

Where the keyword "all" is a universal quantifier, the second triple headed by the label L is a modification to the concept "food" followed by the same label L. The modal verb "can" is a modification to the verb "eat". One of the possible answers to this question could be:

```
( truth(L)   is   false )
L: ( human   can(eat)   all(food: M) )
M: ( food   can(be(eat)   ox )
```

They represent that the proposition labeled by L is false. Please note that the label is only unique inside the same semantic net.

Here is the appropriate place to define the concept of a semantic network. We consider each triple as a node. If there is a label which appears in two triples, then we say that there is an arc connecting these two triples. In this way, a semantic network can be defined as a connected graph with triples as nodes and labels as arcs.

The Capability Component. Being an outline of Belief and Strategy, Capability represents what the agent can process and solve. The tasks of Capability involve:

1. matching the query from outside, and roughly deciding if it can be solved;
2. if yes, starting the corresponding inference engine in Strategy part;
3. entering a bid when competing for an application task.

If every agent did not know whether it could solve some problem until it searched all of its knowledge and inference functions, the efficiency of searching the problem solving space would be very low. Due to this reason, Capability is established to list the outline of the problem solving abilities of an agent. For each item of Capability, the main (first) triple of some CS-net semantic network (describing the problem solving ability in details), represents one problem solving ability. The other part of the CS-net semantic network involves the modification and additional conditions to the main (first) triple. If a query from another agent can not match any item of Capability of agent x, nor match Capability of any father of x, then agent x does not have the ability to answer this query. On the other hand, if a query can match Capability of x or some father of x, it is quite possible that x can process this query (certainly it is also possible that x can not after reasoning). Therefore, the use of Capability could reduce the searching space, and no solutions would be missing.

The Strategy Component. It executes Belief interpretatively and provides answers to questions. As we said before, Belief is the core resource of agent knowledge, and it is static. It is uncertain that Belief can solve problems directly, and static knowledge could be ambiguous or vague. We need some dynamic knowledge to control the use of Belief knowledge. This type of meta-knowledge is what the inference engine needs in Strategy part. The inference engines of Knowledge are responsible for solving complicated problems with supplement or modification to the knowledge in Belief part. This meta-knowledge is represented by the extended Prolog. The tasks of the inference engines involve:

1. Use the items of Capability to match the query statements (of XQML, an improved version of KQML). If the matching fails, generate a refusing letter.
2. If the match works, try to use Belief to answer the query, and send the result out.
3. If it is necessary to ask for knowledge from other agents during the processing, generate and send the XQML query statements to the relevant agents.
4. Synthesize the knowledge collected, generate the XQML solution statements and send them out.

Apparently Prolog is the appropriate language for coding such inference engines. But the general Prolog program can only reason on its own database (Prolog clauses). What we need is to reason on the semantic network in Strategy part. Therefore the extension to Prolog becomes necessary, including the extension of Prolog's procedure predicates and functions. We will introduce CS-net semantic network and CS-Prolog in the next two sections, they are the static and dynamic knowledge representation of CBS Agent, respectively.

10.1.3.2 CS-net: Commonsense Knowledge Oriented Semantic Network Description Language

CS-net was designed based on Snetl [Lu, 1994b] according to commonsense knowledge reasoning. A CS-net program is a sequence of triples, where before each triple there could be a label, called the definition label. The first and third item of the triple are concept nodes, and the second item semantic relation. A label inside the triple is called decoration label. A decoration label :L appearing after some concept represents that the concept is decorated by the triple defined by L. Labels are begun with English capital letters, input variables in lower-case letters, and output variables in lower-case letters with "!" before them. A triple with output variables is a query sentence. A triple without output variables nor definition label is a proposition. A proposition with "?" is also a query sentence. A triple with definition label functions as the decorative phrase in natural language. Input variables exist in Capability and Belief part, as the formal parameters of the procedures.

In order to enhance the descriptive and reasoning ability of commonsense knowledge, we introduce a group of special language components to CS-net, including:

1. semantic case descriptors describe the various aspects of a concept or a proposition, such as: cause, reason, result, place, time, size, time length, way, state, procedure, tool, truth.
2. relation descriptors describe the relations among concepts, such as: the relation between a and b: relation(a,b), a's influence on b: influence(a,b).
3. verbal decorative words, including modal verbs, adverbs, negation, etc., such as: may, must, should, will, hope, possibly, very, not.
4. adjective decorative words, such as: very, a bit, quite, not, completely.

10.1.3.3 CS-prolog: Commonsense Knowledge Oriented Extended Prolog

The extension mainly includes adding new built-in predicates and some functions. Here we only list 8 predicates and 2 functions.

1. Inherit(x): inherit all the knowledge from father node x (not necessarily a direct father).
2. Getbel(x): take the next untested belief x.
3. Getinfo(x,y,z): obtain information (value) x from agent y and assign x to z. (All the values processed by Pangu are represented in the form of triple [u,v,w] where u stands for the value itself, v the certainty, and w the additional conditions to u.)
4. Fzgr(x,y,z): compare x with y, and assign the result (a triple) to z.
5. Numcompa(x,y): compare directly the numerical belief x (e.g., "there are 1.2 billion people in China")with the current query (e.g., "are there more than 1 billion people in China?"), and assign the result to y.
6. Bqmatch(x,y): match belief x to the current query directly, and assign the result to y.
7. Answer(x,y,z): construct a return letter y for solution x, indicating that y is for answering letter z.
8. Reply(x,y,z,t): call procedure "reply" of agent x with belief t, get return letter y (which answers the query letter z) by calling "answer", and send return letter y to the post agent.
9. Val(i): get the i-th item of the query triple.
10. Core(x): delete all the parentheses of x and take its most inner part.

In order to illustrate the extension in Prolog of Pangu, we give a small reasoning example in the following. Suppose the query is "ox is bigger than sheep?", by

CS-net it is "?(ox more(big) sheep)", the agents involved in solving the problem are (agent sheep omitted since it is similar to agent ox):

```
Agent ( size-comparison )
  Father: comparison
  Capability: ( all(size-comparison)  is  !x  )
  Belief: … …(Omitted)
  Strategy:  reply (size-comparison, t, s, x) :-
    getinfo (volume (val(1)), core(val(1)), [q, r, h]),
    getinfo (volume (val(2)), core(val(2)), [u, v, w]),
    fzgr ([q, r, h], [u, v, w], [m, n, k]),  answer ([m, n, k], t, s);

Agent ( physical-object )
  Father: no
  Capability: … …
  Belief: … …
  Knowledge:  reply(physical-object, t, s, x) :-
           numcompa(x, [u, v, w]), answer([u, v, w], t, s);
          reply(physical-object, t, s, x) :-
           bqmatch(x, [u, v, w]), answer([u, v, w], t, s);

Agent ( animal )
  Father: living-things
  Capability: ( all(animal)  is   !x  )
  Belief:  1. ( number(leg(animal))   is    4  )
       2. ( number(head(animal))   is    1  )
       3. ( number(tail(animal))   is    1  )
  Strategy:  reply(animal, t, s, x) :-
        getbel(x), inherit(physical-object), reply(physical-object, t, s, x);

Agent ( large-domestic-animal )
  Father: animal
  Capability: (all(large-domestic-animal)  is   !x  )
  Belief:  1. ( volume(large-domestic-animal )  average(is)   3:L    )
         L: ( unit   is    meter  )
       2 …….
  Strategy:  reply(large-domestic-animal,t,s,x) :-
        getbel(x),inherit(physical-object),  reply(physical-object, t, s, x);
       reply(large-domestic-animal, t, s, x) :-
        inherit(animal), reply(animal, t, s, x);

Agent ( ox )
  Father: large-domestic-animal
  Capability: (all(ox)   is   !x   )
  Belief:  (usage(ox)  is  cultivation  )
  Strategy:   reply(ox, t, s, x) :-
         getbel(x), inherit(physical-object), reply(physical-object, t, s, x);
        reply(ox, t, s, x) :-
         inherit(large-domestic-animal), reply(large-domestic-animal, t, s, x);
```

The problem solving process is as follows. Firstly the query is sent to agent "size-comparison". In Capability part of this agent there is information about "all" representing that the agent involves all the knowledge about size comparison (thus not necessary to check other agents anymore). The capability matching succeeds, so the solving process starts. It sends letters to agent ox and agent sheep asking for their body volumes. Agent ox tries to use its own Belief by only inheriting the reasoning rules from agent physical-object to solve the problem, but fails. Then it turns to agent large-domestic-animal for help by inheriting also its Belief information. Agent large-domestic-animal tells that its average body volume is 3 meters. If the average volume of sheep is 2 meters, the answer is [true, average,], meaning ox is bigger than sheep by average. This is a half-certain comparison, so the result is also a half-certain information. Agent ox can also answer questions such as "how many legs does ox have?", "what is the usage of ox?", etc.

10.1.4 The Ontology Structure of Pangu

As we said before, another important feature of Pangu is that it organizes knowledge in horizontal mechanism (ontology association) as well as vertical (generic inheritance).

Recently international research on ontology is getting hotter and hotter. Originally being a philosophical concept for describing the essence of things [XiaoK and LiD, 1987], ontology was used by knowledge engineers for the purpose of domain knowledge acquisition while developing knowledge-based systems [Lu, 1994c]. Nowadays information system researchers began to use ontology concept to simulate enterprise structure, techniques such as virtual enterprise [Stader, 1996] are being developed. Like agent, ontology can also be used to describe domain knowledge, with different aspect and granularity. Agent emphasizes encapsulation and inheritance, concentrating on the vertical connection among things; while ontology emphasizes the knowledge structure, concentrating on the horizontal connection. Usually agent has small granularity, and ontology large. As a matter of fact, ontology method is a very good complement to agent method.

A concept or a thing could be studied from various aspects. Correspondingly, their ontology descriptions could be in variety, too. Among them the most important ones are the static ontology and dynamic ontology. Static ontology describes the components of a thing or concept and the static connections among these components, while dynamic ontology describes the movement and change of thing or concept. For example, ER graph is a static ontology, whereas data flow chart dynamic. The reason for Pangu to introduce ontology is that it needs to do commonsense reasoning on the connections among things and concepts, such as, what can we infer if we read "Zhang-San saw a bloody knife", or "Li-Si put fish on the board"? According to generic relations, "blood" and "knife", "fish" and "board" differ a lot. But if we know that "blood" and "knife" all belong to the ontology of "murder-case", and "fish" and "board" to "cooking", it would not be too difficult to do corresponding reasoning or mental association.

In Pangu, an ontology description is divided into three parts: set of static extensions, set of dynamic extensions and Ontonet, where Ontonet is a semantic network as well, constructed by all the agents belonging to the ontology. Every ontology description belongs to Belief part of some agent, while this agent is called the topic of the ontology. All of the Ontonets form the ontology structure of Pangu. One agent can belong to many ontologies. One can see the complexity of the knowledge base structure from a crisscross network of the Ontonet.

Let us see a simplified example of ontology description.

Ontology murder-case
Static Extension murderer, lethal-weapon, killing, victim, scene-of-crime, time-of-crime, motive-of-crime, consequence-of-crime, detective, judge, judgement
Dynamic Extension procedure-of-crime, detection-procedure, trial
Ontonet (m is murder-case: H : S: W)
H: (procedure-of-crime(murder-case) is K)
K: (murderer[x] kill: L: M: N: Q: R victim[y])
L: (tool(kill) is lethal-weapon[z])
M: (location(kill) is scene-of-crime[p])
N: (time(kill) is time-of-crime[t])
Q: (motive (kill) is motive-of-crime[g])
R: (consequence(kill) is consequence-of-crime[t])
S: (detection-procedure(murder-case) is P)
P: (detective[u], investigate: T m)
T: (procedure(investigate) is w)
W: (trial(murder-case) is U then V)
U: (judge[v] try x)
V: (judge[v] pronounce judgement[r])

Following comes a commonsense conversation example based on the above ontology.

User: "Our neighbor Lao-Wang was murdered by a knife"
Computer: "Who is the murderer?"
User: "A tramp"
Computer: "Was it for robbing money?"
User: "Yes. It is said that several 10 thousands of money was robbed"
Computer: "what was the judgement?"
User: "Not yet declared"
Computer: "Please let me know as soon as it is declared"

In order to generate such a "simple" conversation, complicated reasoning has to be done by Pangu roughly as follows. Agent "knife" has a father agent "lethal weapon" which belongs to the same ontology "murder-case" with agent "kill". Therefore Pangu decides to take murder-case as the conversation topic. From ontology "murder-case", "murderer" is selected and a question is generated accordingly. Afterwards, "motive-of-crime" is selected, one of its son agents is agent "money-robbery", so another question is generated accordingly. And so on and so on, where a lot of technical details are omitted here. Actually during the period of early AI research, people already attempted to generate intelligent conversation programs. ELIZA [Barr and Feigenbaum, 1981] was one of them, but it only adopted pattern matching, and no systematic technology was developed. We use ontology method to construct the mental relations between two "speakers" based on commonsense knowledge so as to make their conversation natural.

10.1.5 The Working Mechanism of Pangu

Commonsense reasoning and problem solving tasks are raised by application programs or through user interface, in the form of XQML.A memory-resident interface program of Pangu recognizes the orders and calls a group of system built-in agents including task distribution agent, post agent, log agent, etc. Pangu adopts a heuristic hierarchical control mechanism for task distribution and task acceptance. Task distribution agent recognizes the current task, devises strategies, calls a series of relevant agents from knowledge the base, sends the XQML letter through post agent to one or several most competitive agents, now the problem solving program starts. Every agent which accepts the task is responsible for solving the problems within its own knowledge field. Whenever necessary every one of such agents can function as task distribution agent by calling other agents for help. The interface program returns the solution to the application or user. Roughly speaking, Pangu consists of several components shown in Fig 10.1, where the related ones are connected by lines, and every one is connected with the knowledge base.

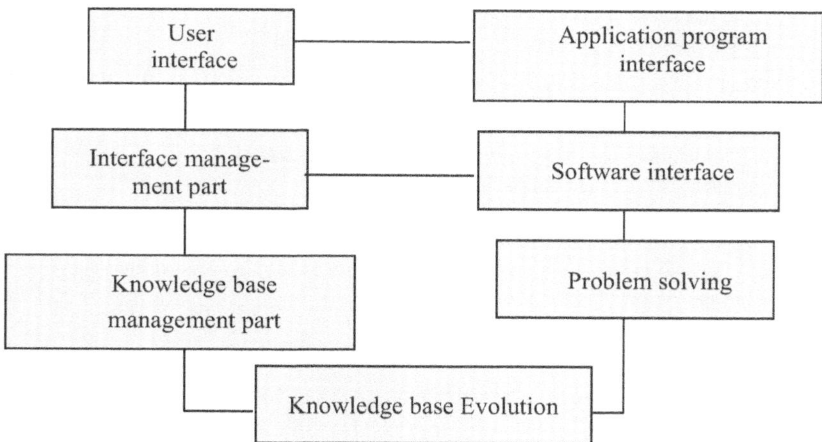

Figure 10.1.1 The Components of Pangu

The left column of the above figure can be organized into 8 levels as follows.

Table 10.1.2 Multi-Level Organization of Pangu

Function	Level	Main Functions	Function Examples
1	Application level	Interaction with applications	Transformation between external and internal representation
2	Problem level	Problem division into tasks	Problem decomposition, solution synthesis
3	Task level	Concrete task processing	Task distribution, sub-solution synthesis
4	Cooperation level	Multi-agent cooperating	Inviting bidding and bidding
5	Communication level	Communication between agents	Communication management, deadlock detection
6	Searching level	Knowledge searching	Searching according to generic knowledge hierarchy and ontology
7	Reasoning level	Using the knowledge of the agent to do reasoning	Heuristic reasoning
8	Representation level	Basic knowledge representation	Knowledge management

We would like to mention the difference between a problem and a task. Problems differ along with the applications. They are very domain-dependent. Let us list a few problems relating to the commonsense knowledge application: disambiguation of natural language understanding, translation of natural language sentences, commonsense consistency checking in natural language story understanding, plot planning in automatic animation generation, word usage design in composition, etc. All these problems are related to application domains with large granularity. A task is a basic subprogram in commonsense knowledge processing, domain-independent with small granularity, and shared by many problem solvers. Here are some of such tasks: search for concept definition, for procedure development, for reason, for result, for regularity, for example, for counterexample, for equivalence, for conflict, etc. Chandrasekaren did the related research with respect to expert systems [Lu, 1994c]. There are thousands of expert system application domains, he analyzed and synthesized to get less than 20 typical tasks.

10.2 The Swanlake Knowledge Base

In last section we have introduced the Pangu commonsense knowledge base. As we said there, the Pangu base contains only commonsense knowledge and is designed for public use in many application fields. Apart from the commonsense knowledge, we also need professional knowledge of animation producer and director, and we need it as much as possible. All professional knowledge of SWAN is collected in an expert knowledge base called Swan Lake. We have mentioned the different components of this knowledge base already in the relevant chapters. Here we just mention the names of these knowledge bases as a summary:

Knowledge Base of Chinese Language
Knowledge Base of Chinese Parser
Knowledge Base of Story Parsing Rules
Knowledge Base of Plot Planning
Knowledge Base of Director Planning
Knowledge Base of Camera Planning
Knowledge Base of Color and light Planning.

Apart from these knowledge bases, there is still a set of knowledge bases with representations at "lower" levels which serve as basis for animation generation and are introduced in the following section.

10.3 The Element Library

An element is a basic component for building up characters (roles) and objects. The element library is established by interactive graphics work through a man-machine interface. It consists of two parts: the element archive and the element index.

10.3.1 The Element Archive

Following is a short syntax of the element archive:

```
<Element Archive> ::= <Sequence of Elements>
<Element> ::=
    $
    element name <Element File Name>
    type <Element File Type>
    project movie
    articulate <Sequence of Articulate Names>
    male_female_other  <Sex Indication>
    size <Length Width Height>
    center <Original Point of Coordinates>
    $
```

<Element File Type> ::= <Face File> | <Patch File>
<Face File> ::= f
<Patch File> ::= p
<Sex Indication> ::= m | f | n
< Length Width Height > ::= <Length> <Width> <Height>
<Length> ::= <Positive Number>
<Width> ::= <Positive Number>
<Height> ::= <Positive Number>
< Original Point of Coordinates > ::=
  <Value at X Coordinate> <Value at Y Coordinate> <Value at Z Coordinate>
<Value at X Coordinate> ::= <Real Number>
<Value at Y Coordinate> ::= <Real Number>
<Value at Z Coordinate> ::= <Real Number>

where

<Element File Name> : corresponds to a Face graphics file while Face is a polygonal object modeler. Another type of graphics file is Patch file while Patch is a curved surface object modeler.
<Articulate Name> : specifies those articulates to which this element can be attached.

The center of an object locates at the origin when the object is put at a coordinate system.

Example 10.3.1 (Specification of an Element)

To be specified is a left upper arm for a male character. This arm can be attached to the articulate called uparm_lhbmr_y. The three real numbers of the term "size" denote the minimal three dimensional cuboid which just contains this element. The three real numbers of the term "center" denote the relative coordinates of this element when it is attached to the articulate, assumed that the coordinates of the articulate are (0, 0, 0).

```
<Element> ::=
$
element name  arm_l_upper_m_y
type  f
project  movie
articulate  uparm_lhbmr_y
male_female_other  m
size  1.799166 3.799516  0.799531
center  0.283519 -1.448721 0.000000
$
```

10.3.2 The Element Index

The element index locates the address of the element in the library. Its syntax is:

<Element Index> ::= <Sequence of Element Index Items>
<Element Index Item> ::= <Element Name> <Address of Element Name>
<Address of Element Name> ::= <Integer>

Example 10.3.2

7 arm_l_upper_m_y 785

10.4 The Structure Library

A structure library consists of a structure archive (structure_lib.str) and a structure index (structure_lib.ndx).

10.4.1 Definition of a Structure

In order to integrate a set of elements to assemble a character, we have to first define a structure which consists of an architecture of articulates. There are two kinds of articulates: the virtual ones and the real ones. If we consider a structure as a function definition, then the virtual articulates are the name of the function together with the parentheses and separators. They are only used to connect the real articulates. The real articulates are the formal parameters whose values are yet to be filled by real parameters. As we will see in the next section, the real parameters used to replace the formal parameters (real articulates) are just the elements.

Now the syntax of a structure:

<Structure Archive> ::= <Sequence of Structures>
<Structure> ::= #
structure <Structure Name>
class <Structure Type Name>
sex <Sex Indication>
$
<Structure Tree>
<String of Montage Articulates>
#
<Structure Tree> ::= <Mixed Branch> <Block of Virtual Branches>

<Montage Articulate> ::= <Montage Virtual Articulate>
| <Montage Real Articulate> | <Montage Mixed Articulate>
<Montage Virtual Articulate> ::= articulate <Articulate Name>

```
            type  <Virtual Type>
            t <Translation>
<Montage Real Articulate> ::= articulate  <Articulate Name>
            type  <Real Type>
            size  <Length Width Hight>
            center <Original Point of Coordinates>
<Montage Mixed Articulate> ::= articulate  <Articulate Name>
            type  <Virtual Type>
            size  <Length Width High>
            center <Original Point of Coordinates>
            t  <Translation>
<Mixed Branch> ::= <Mixed Articulate>  [<Flow of Virtual Articulates>]
<Virtual Branch> ::= <Virtual Articulate> <Real Articulate>
                [<Flow of Virtual Articulates>]
<Mixed Articulate> ::= <Articulate Name>
<Virtual Articulate> ::= <Articulate Name>
<Real Articulate> ::= <Articulate Name>
    <Translation> ::= <X Translation> <Y Translation> <Z Translation>
    <X Translation> ::= <Real Number>
    <Y Translation> ::= <Real Number>
    <Z Translation> ::= <Real Number>
<Articulate Type> ::= <Virtual Type> | <Real Type>
<Virtual Type> ::= v
<Real Type> ::= r
```

Note that the two terms "size" and "center" exist only in the syntax of real articulates, not in that of virtual articulates.

Example 10.4.1

We reproduce here a simplified structure of a male human being which has only a head, a neck, a trunk, a waist, two arms, two legs, two hands and two feet.

```
442 #
443 structure  boy
444 class   human
445 sex  m
446 $
447 body  waist_dhbmv_y                          # body #
448 waist_dhbmv_y  waist_dhbmr_y  trunk_dhbmv_y
    upleg_lhbmv_y  upleg_rhbmv_y                 # waist #
449 trunk_dhbmv_y  trunk_dhbmr_y  uparm_lhbmv_y
    uparm_rhbmv_y  neck_dhbmv_y                  # trunk #
450 upleg_lhbmv_y  upleg_lhbmr_y  lwleg_lhbmv_y     # left thigh #
450 upleg_rhbmv_y  upleg_rhbmr_y  lwleg_rhbmv_y     # right thigh #
451 uparm_lhbmv_y  uparm_lhbmr_y  lwarm_lhbmv_y  #left upper arm #
452 uparm_rhbmv_y  uparm_rhbmr_y  lwarm_rhbmv_y #right upper arm #
453 neck_dhbmv_y  neck_dhbmr_y  head_dhbmv_y  # neck #
```

```
454 lwleg_lhbmv_y lwleg_lhbmr_y boot_lhbmv_y # left shank #
455 lwleg_rhbmv_y lwleg_rhbmr_y boot_rhbmv_y # right shank #
456 lwarm_lhbmv_y lwarm_lhbmr_y hand_lhbmv_y #left lower arm #
457 lwarm_rhbmv_y lwarm_rhbmr_y hand_rhbmv_y #right lower arm #
458 head_dhbmv_y head_dhbmr_y    # head #
459 boot_lhbmv_y boot_lhbmr_y    # left foot #
460 boot_rhbmv_y boot_rhbmr_y    # right foot #
461 hand_lhbmv_y hand_lhbmr_y    # left hand #
462 hand_rhbmv_y hand_rhbmr_y    # right hand #
463 $
464 articulate body
465 type v
466 size 7.362255 20.591351 2.901772
467 center 0.000000 -1.668089 0.052424
468 t 0.000000 0.000000 0.000000
469 $
470 articulate waist_dhbmv_y
471 type v
472 t 0.000000 0.000000 0.000000
473 $
474 articulate waist_dhbmr_y
475 type r
476 size 5.696099 2.443497 2.617380
477 center 0.000000 -1.070603 -0.024235
478 $
479 articulate trunk_dhbmv_y
480 type v
481 t 0.000000 0.000000 0.000000
482 $
483 articulate upleg_lhbmv_y
484 type v
485 t 1.050000 -1.150000 0.000000
486 $
487 articulate upleg_rhbmv_y
488 type v
489 t -1.050000 -1.150000 0.000000
490 $
491 articulate trunk_dhbmr_y
492 type r
493 size 5.246451 5.195490 2.186598
494 center -0.000001 2.026593 0.141987
................................
```

From label 447 to 462, we have written 46 articulates. Among them there are 15 repetitions. In the remaining 31 articulates, there are 15 virtual articulates and the corresponding 15 real articulates. The first articulate, body, is a mixed one.

This structure includes a specification for each articulate. We have only written seven of them to save the space.

10.4.2 The Structure Index

Syntax:

<Structure Index> ::= <Sequence of Structure Index Items>
<Structure Index Item> ::= <Structure Name> <Structure Address>
<Structure Address> ::= <Integer>

Example 10.4.2

7 boy 8423

10.4.3 The Structure Forest

This section is talking about the relation between characters and actions. At an early stage of SWAN implementation, we have attached the actions to roles. Each character had its own set of actions. Soon, we detected the irrationality of this arrangement. Many characters have the same structure. But we had nevertheless to construct the same actions for these characters separately. For example, the king, the prince and the big frog of the "frog prince" script have the same structure "man". Once during a demon, the visitor asked us to turn the statement " the prince jumped into the well" into an animation. But we could not find the action "jump into" for prince in our library, though we did have this same action for other two characters: the king and the big frog. So we had to enrich our action library on the spot.

From that time on, we have improved the architecture of our structure library in the way that we have defined a new organization of structures called structure forest which is essentially a hierarchy of structures from simple ones to complex ones. The actions are attached to the different nodes of this hierarchy. The complex ones can inherit all actions which are enabled by simple ones.

Note that the possibility of performing a predefined action by a character depends on the organization of articulates of this character. Generally speaking, if some action AC involves a set SA of articulates, then each character CH which has a set SC of articulates, which is a superset of SA, can perform the action AC. In this case we say that the action AC is enabled by the character CH. From this analysis it is easy to see that the organization of the structure hierarchy is designed based on the stepwise addition of new articulates.

Now we give the syntax of the structure forest in the following:

<Structure Forest> ::= structure forest <Structure Forest Name>
<Structure Forest Content>
<Structure Forest Content> ::= <Root Node> <Block of Structure Nodes>
| <Root Node>

<Root Node> ::= <Structure Name> [(<Sequence of Action Names>)]
<Structure Node> ::= <New Structure Name> : <Old Structure Name> :
<Virtual Articulate> [(<Sequence of Action Names>)]

Each structure node introduces a new sub-forest of the structure forest, which is itself a structure forest. If x and y are the new structure and old structure names in the same structure node, then x inherits all actions of y. If x inherits all actions of y and y inherits all actions of z, then x inherits all actions of y and z.

Example 10.4.3

The figure of a boy in a movie may not be always complete. He may lack a leg, a foot, an arm, a hand, or something else. But the structure "boy" given in last section is not decomposable. In order to show a boy with one leg only, it would be necessary to construct another boy, and another action set. Using the concept of a structure forest, we can now construct the boy structure in a step by step way, starting from his body, until everything is okay.

Structure forest (boy structure)
1446 boy (move)
1447 boy1 : boy : waist_dhbmv_y
1448 boy2 : boy1 : trunk_dhbmv_y (wrench)
1449 boy3 : boy2 : upleg_lhbmv_y
1450 boy4 : boy3 : lwleg_lhbmv_y
1451 boy5 : boy4 : boot_lhbmv_y (jump_with_left_leg)
1452 boy6 : boy2 : upleg_rhbmv_y
1453 boy7 : boy6 : lwleg_rhbmv_y
1454 boy8 : boy7 : boot_rhbmv_y (jump_with_right_leg)
1455 boy9 : boy8 : upleg_lhbmv_y
1456 boy10 : boy9 : lwleg_lhbmv_y
1457 boy11 : boy10 : boot_lhbmv_y (jump, walk, run, ...)
1458 boy12 : boy2 : uparm_lhbmv_y
1459 boy13 : boy12 : lwarm_lhbmv_y
1460 boy14 : boy13 : hand_lhbmv_y (shake_with_left_hand)
1461 boy15 : boy2 : uparm_rhbmv_y
1462 boy16 : boy15 : lwarm_rhbmv_y
1463 boy17 : boy16 : hand_rhbmv_y (shake_with_right_hand)
1464 boy18 : boy17 : uparm_lhbmv_y
1465 boy19 : boy18 : lwarm_lhbmv_y
1466 boy20 : boy19 : hand_lhbmv_y (shake_hand, applaud, ...)
1467 boy21 : boy20 : upleg_lhbmv_y
1468 boy22 : boy21 : lwleg_lhbmv_y
1469 boy23 : boy22 : boot_lhbmv_y
1470 boy24 : boy20 : upleg_rhbmv_y
1471 boy25 : boy24 : lwleg_rhbmv_y
1472 boy26 : boy25 : boot_rhbmv_y
1473 boy27 : boy26 : upleg_lhbmv_y

1474 boy28 : boy27 : lwleg_lhbmv_y
1475 boy29 : boy28 : boot_lhbmv_y (dance, play_basketball, ...)

Here, actions are attached to the sub-structures: trunk without legs and arms, trunk with right hand, trunk with left hand, trunk with right and left hands, trunk with right foot, trunk with left foot, trunk with right and left feet, trunk with all hands and all feet. It is easy to see that there are still many nodes in this structure forest where one can insert a set of actions.

10.5 The Character Library

The character library consists of four parts: a character archive (character_lib.ch), a character index (character_lib.ndx), an element index (character_lib.ele_ndx) and a structure index (character_lib.str_ndx).

10.5.1 Character Archive

A character is different from a structure in three sense. First, the real articulates of a structure are replaced by elements in a character. Note that a character is not necessary a person. It may denote any object with articulates. Second, the elements used to fill in the framework of a structure may change its position and posture by a translation and rotation. It may also be modified by a scaling. For example the elements may be made thinner or fatter before being attached to the articulates. Even the structure itself (as an integrated whole of the set of elements) may be deformed. Third, some real articulates of the structure may be replaced by exotic elements which otherwise do not appear at these places. For example, the real articulate “body” in example 10.4.1 may be replaced by a football, “upbody” replaced by a cucumber and “skirt” replaced by a glass bottle.

In the character library, the characters are either organized as independent structures, or in tree forms where the different characters are attached at the nodes of the trees. In this section, we first introduce characters represented as independent structures.

<Character Archive> ::= <Sequence of Characters>
<Character> ::=
#
<Character Name> (<Sex Indication> <Structure Name>) : <Root Link>
<Structure Tree>
$
<Articulate Name>
type <Type Indication>
[element name <Element Name>]
[size <Length Width High>]
[center <Original Point of Coordinates>]
[r <Rotation>]

```
    [t <Translation>]
    [h <Scaling> ]
<Root Link> ::= <Articulate Name>
<Type Indication> ::= <Virtual Articulate> | <Element File Type>
<Rotation> ::= <x Axis Rotation> <y Axis Rotation> <z Axis Rotation>
<Scaling> ::= <x Axis Scaling> <y Axis Scaling> <z Axis Scaling>
<Any Rotation> ::= <Real Number>
<Any Scaling> ::= <Positive Number>
```

where Any means x, y or z Axis, and the "size" and "center" items in square brackets exist only for real articulates.

Example 10.5.1

This time we will consider the construction of a bird in our character library. For saving space, we take a part of it.

```
bird1(neutral,bird):body          # Begin of the Structure Tree #
body neck_add chest_add leg_l_add leg_r_add wing_l_add wing_r_add ;
neck_add head_add neck_art ;       # neck #
chest_add chest_art tail_add ;     # chest #
leg_l_add leg_l_1_add ;            # left leg #
leg_r_add leg_r_1_add ;            # right leg #
wing_l_add wing_l_1_add ;          # left wing #
wing_r_add wing_r_1_add ;          # right wing #
head_add head_art ;                # head #
tail_add tail_art ;                # tail #
leg_l_1_add leg_l_art foot_l_add ;   # left foot #
leg_r_1_add leg_r_art foot_r_add ;   # right foot #
wing_l_1_add wing_l_1_art wing_l_2_add ;
wing_r_1_add wing_r_1_art wing_r_2_add ;
foot_l_add foot_l_art ;
foot_r_add foot_r_art ;
wing_l_2_add wing_l_2_art ;
wing_r_2_add wing_r_2_art ;        # End of the Structure Tree #
$
body                        # First Virtual Articulate #
type v
size 8.644571 1.468310 3.725065
center 4.163981 -0.001185 0.015078
$
neck_add                    # Second Virtual Articulate #
type v
t 0.000000 0.000000 0.000000
r 0.000000 0.000000 0.000000
h 1.000000 1.000000 1.000000
..............................
```

```
neck_art                 # First Real Articulate #
type p
elementname zyneck
size 0.541664 0.605282 0.779616
center 0.209953 0.000000 -0.009607
t 0.000000 0.000000 0.000000
r 0.000000 0.000000 0.000000
h 1.000000 1.000000 1.000000
$
chest_art                # Second Real Articulate #
type p
elementname zybody
size 4.301876 1.468310 1.853049
center 1.992634 -0.001185 -0.005298
t 0.000000 0.000000 0.000000
r 0.000000 0.000000 0.000000
h 1.000000 1.000000 1.000000
......................................
```

10.5.2 The Indices

The Syntax of character index is:

<Character Index> ::= <Sequence of Character Index Items>
<Character Index Item> ::= <Character Name> <Character Address>
<Character Address> ::= <Integer>

Example 10.5.2

2 Apple 145

The syntax of element index (in the character library) is:

<Element Index in Character Library> ::= <Sequence of EICL Items>
<EICL Item> ::= <Element Name> <Master Character Name>

where master character refers to character which takes this element as one of its articulates.

The syntax of structure index (in the character library) is:

<Structure Index in Character Library> ::= <Sequence of SICL Items>
<SICL Item> ::= <Structure Name> <Master Character Name>

where master character refers to character which takes this structure as its basic architecture.

10.5.3 The Cloth Library

The cloth library consists of three sub-libraries: the cloth material library (fur, silk, cotton, etc.), the cloth image library (those images printed on the cloth) and the suit product library (sweater. skirt, coat, etc.). In fact, it is organized as a forest of structures. Each structure represents a special form of suit. The syntax and semantics of a suit product structure is very similar to that of a character structure (explained in section 10.4) and thus is omitted here.

The cloth material sub-library partly makes use of a package provided by the TDI™. The cloth image sub-library has been established by ourselves. It is organized in a classification hierarchy based on the principles of role qualities. These principles are very similar to those explained in section 9.2 about color planning and thus are omitted here.

10. 6 The Action Library

10.6.1 Context Sensitivity of Verb Meanings

To transform the abstract events into concrete ones is not the only job we have while planning a script. We notice that there is no one-to-one correspondence between events (or actions) and verbs.

Example 10.6.1

"Eat apple", "eat orange", "eat noodle", "eat rice", and "eat ice-cream" are five different events (actions). Their presentations are quite different:

Eat apple: hold the apple in the hand,
  [pare the apple with a knife,]
  eat the apple bite by bite,
  throw away the skin and the pit.
Eat orange: hold the orange in the hand,
  Shell the orange with hand,
  Take the orange capsule one by one and eat it,
  Throw away the skin.
Eat noodle: Use a pair of chopsticks to pick up some strips of noodle,
  Put into the mouth.
Eat rice: hold a spoon in the hand,
  Take a spoonful rice from a bowl,
  Put the rice into the mouth.
Eat ice cream: hold the ice cream in the hand,
  Lick the ice cream for several times.

But they use the same verb: eat! In Chinese, even the action "take medicine" will be spoken as "eat medicine". On the other hand, "people eat apples" and "birds eat apples" are completely different. "People eat rice" and "chicken eat rice" are also completely different. Another example: let us consider the verb "give". To present the event "The new queen gave an apple to Snow White", it is enough to design the following micro-action chain: "The new queen is holding an apple in the right hand. The new queen stretches the right hand toward Snow White. The new queen opens the right hand. Snow White grapes the apple and takes it". But what would happen if the story were "The king gave a house to Snow White"? It is impossible for a human-being to hold a (real) house in the hand. So it is better to illustrate it as follows: "The king and Snow White are standing by a house. The king points to the house with his right hand and says to Snow White that he would like to give this house to her".

We call this phenomenon the context sensitivity of verbs. That means, the meaning of a verb is sensible to its context in the sentence, not only sensible to its object, but also to its subject. Taking this "one-to-many" correspondence of verb-event relations into account, it is easy to conclude that one can not determine the presentation of an event only on the basis of the abstract, context free meaning of the verb whose action represents this event. On the other hand, It is also not practical to build our knowledge base with all the concrete actions. Such a plot knowledge base would contain "eat apple" and "eat pear" as different knowledge items. It would also contain "give a watch" and "give a chocolate" as two different knowledge items. Our plot knowledge base (a part of the commonsense knowledge base) consists of a hierarchy of verbs together with their plot specifications.

10.6.2 Consistency of Concurrent Actions

The context sensitivity exists also in the relationship between different concurrent actions. In a script we may specify concurrent actions. The following three concurrent actions are possible:

> Walking (John, in_front_of (window), near_to (door), t_1, t_2);
> holding (John, right (hand), book, t_1, t_2);
> whistling (John, t_1, t_2);

They happen even in the same time interval $[t_1, t_2]$. But this consistency does not exist among all concurrent actions. In fact, one action may have an influence on another one. For example, everybody has only one mouth. Therefore any two actions involving the use of the mouth are inconsistent. Our parents told us always: "Do not try to eat and speak at the same time". Thus:

Example 10.6.2

> Eat (John, apple, t_1, t_2);
> Speak (John, Mary, "delicious!", t_1, t_2);

are inconsistent.

We will give two other examples which are of different types than the above one.

Example 10.6.3

Sleep (John, t_1, t_3);
Open-eye (John, both, t_2, t_4);

are inconsistent, because the time intervals [t_1, t_3] and [t_2, t_4] have a non empty intersection (it is always assumed $t_n < t_{n+1}$), and one does not open his/her eye while sleeping.

Example 10.6.4

Sleep (John, t_1, t_2);
Roll-eye (John, t_2, t_3);

are inconsistent because the time intervals [t_1, t_2] and [t_2, t_3] are successive, and it is impossible for a person to roll his/her eyes immediately following a sleep.

It is important to check such inconsistency when compiling a Rainbow or Evergreen program. But it is not enough to only check the inconsistency and then simply reject it, because the script may be rational in its whole and a small modification of the script may be enough to make it consistent again. There are different types of modification according to semantics of the two contradicting actions.

Definition 10.6.1

Given two actions act1 [t_1, t_2] and act2 [t_3, t_4] which are inconsistent.

1. Modification of interruption type: The consistency will be recovered if we can reduce the time interval of the first or second action to let them do not intersect.
2. Modification of insertion type: The consistency will be recovered if we can insert an appropriate new action between the two given ones.
3. Modification of interleaving type: The consistency will be recovered if we can cut the intervals of both given actions in several pieces and let them interleave.

Example 10.6.5

It is easy to see that the examples 10.6.3, 10.6.4 and 10.6.2 can be made consistent with modification of interruption, insertion and interleaving types, respectively, namely:

1. Sleep (John, t_1, t_2);
   Open-eye (John, both, t_2, t_4);
2. Sleep (John, t_1, t_2);
   Open-eye (John, both, t_2, t_3);
   Roll-eye (John, t_3, t_4);
3. Eat (John, apple, t_1, t_2);
   Speak (John, Mary, "delicious!", t_2, t_3);
   Eat (John, apple, t_3, t_4);
   Speak (John, Mary, "delicious!", t_4, t_5);

In order to do that, we have analyzed the semantics and relative relations of the actions and constructed a table of consistency check and modification which is done automatically by the corresponding SWAN module. This table is, of course, not complete. Much more time and space are needed for a trial to construct a complete table. A small piece of this table is shown in the following, where the action x in the first column never follows any y in the sixth column immediately. There must always be an action z from the seventh column inserted between y and x.

Table 10.6.1 Consistency of Actions

Action Name	Implies or canses	Interrupts	Interrupted by	Interleaving with	Never Follows	Must insert
Eye_ closed			open_eye		Twinkle, roll_eye, cry, smile, see	close_eye
close_eye	eye_closed	Twinkle, roll_eye, cry, smile, see, eye_opened			eye_ closed	open_eye
eye_ opened			close_eye	twinkle	sleep, eye_ closed	open_eye
open_eye	eye_opened	Eye_closed, sleep			eye_ opened	close_eye
speak	eye_opened			eat, drink, read	1.eye_ closed, 2. holding in mouth	1.open_ eye, 2. spit or swallow
watch	eye_opened				eye_ closed, sleep,	open_eye
eat	eye_opened, holding_in _mouth			speak, drink,	1.eye_ closed, 2. holding in mouth	1.open_ eye, 2. spit or swallow
walk	eye_opened	Standing	Standing	jump, run	sitting, lying	stand_up
stand_up	Standing	Sitting			lying	sit_up

10.6.3 The Action Archive

The action library consists of an action archive (action_lib.act), an action index (action_lib.ndx) and an action list (action_lib.tab).

Syntax of the action archive:

<Action Archive> ::= <String of Action Definitions>
<Action Definition> ::=
#
<Action Name> <Action Type>
{ <State Denotation> <State Denotation> <Time> } $_{1-n}$
{ $
<State Denotation>
{ <Articulate Name> [r <Rotation>] [t <Translation>] [h <Scaling>]
} $_{1-n}$ }
<Action Type> ::= <Single Action> | <Repeating Action>
<Single Action> ::= single
<Repeating Action> ::= loop
<State Denotation> ::= <Integer Number>
<Time> ::= <Positive Integer>

where "single" means that the action will be performed only once. "Loop" means that the action will be performed repeatedly. "State denotation" means a particular state of the articulate. The unit of time is frame. In a word, this specification says that the first state is transformed into the second state during <Time> frames.

Example 10.6.6

The action man1_y_walkto consists of eight states. These states are described below in text form and also in sketched image form.

```
$
man1_y_walkto loop
1 2 2
2 3 2
3 4 2
4 5 2
5 6 2
6 7 2
7 8 2
8 1 2

$
1
waist_dhbmv_y (r 0.000000 0.000000 0.000000)
trunk_dhbmv_y (r 0.000000 0.000000 0.000000)
upleg_lhbmv_y (r 0.000000 0.000000 0.000000)
upleg_rhbmv_y (r 0.000000 0.000000 0.000000)
```

```
uparm_lhbmv_y (r  0.000000  0.000000  0.000000)
uparm_rhbmv_y (r  0.000000  0.000000  0.000000)
lwleg_lhbmv_y (r  30.000000  0.000000  0.000000)
lwleg_rhbmv_y (r  0.000000  0.000000  0.000000)
lwarm_lhbmv_y (r  0.000000  0.000000  0.000000)
lwarm_rhbmv_y (r  0.000000  0.000000  0.000000)
$
2
waist_dhbmv_y (r  0.000000  0.000000  0.000000)
trunk_dhbmv_y (r  0.000000  0.000000  0.000000)
upleg_lhbmv_y (r  -10.000000  0.000000  0.000000)
upleg_rhbmv_y (r  10.000000  0.000000  0.000000)
uparm_lhbmv_y (r  7.500000  0.000000  0.000000)
uparm_rhbmv_y (r  -5.000000  0.000000  0.000000)
lwleg_lhbmv_y (r  30.000000  0.000000  0.000000)
lwleg_rhbmv_y (r  0.000000  0.000000  0.000000)
lwarm_lhbmv_y (r  0.000000  0.000000  0.000000)
lwarm_rhbmv_y (r  0.000000  0.000000  0.000000)
$
3
waist_dhbmv_y (r  0.000000  0.000000  0.000000)
trunk_dhbmv_y (r  0.000000  0.000000  0.000000)
upleg_lhbmv_y (r  -20.000000  0.000000  0.000000)
upleg_rhbmv_y (r  20.000000  0.000000  0.000000)
uparm_lhbmv_y (r  15.000000  0.000000  0.000000)
uparm_rhbmv_y (r  -15.000000  0.000000  0.000000)
lwleg_lhbmv_y (r  0.000000  0.000000  0.000000)
lwleg_rhbmv_y (r  0.000000  0.000000  0.000000)
lwarm_lhbmv_y (r  0.000000  0.000000  0.000000)
lwarm_rhbmv_y (r  -10.000000  0.000000  0.000000)
$
4
waist_dhbmv_y (r  0.000000  0.000000  0.000000)
trunk_dhbmv_y (r  0.000000  0.000000  0.000000)
upleg_lhbmv_y (r  -10.000000  0.000000  0.000000)
upleg_rhbmv_y (r  10.000000  0.000000  0.000000)
uparm_lhbmv_y (r  7.500000  0.000000  0.000000)
uparm_rhbmv_y (r  -7.500000  0.000000  0.000000)
lwleg_lhbmv_y (r  0.000000  0.000000  0.000000)
lwleg_rhbmv_y (r  30.000000  0.000000  0.000000)
lwarm_lhbmv_y (r  0.000000  0.000000  0.000000)
lwarm_rhbmv_y (r  -5.000000  0.000000  0.000000)
$
5
```

```
waist_dhbmv_y (r 0.000000 0.000000 0.000000)
trunk_dhbmv_y (r 0.000000 0.000000 0.000000)
upleg_lhbmv_y (r 0.000000 0.000000 0.000000)
upleg_rhbmv_y (r 0.000000 0.000000 0.000000)
uparm_lhbmv_y (r 0.000000 0.000000 0.000000)
uparm_rhbmv_y (r 0.000000 0.000000 0.000000)
lwleg_lhbmv_y (r 0.000000 0.000000 0.000000)
lwleg_rhbmv_y (r 30.000000 0.000000 0.000000)
lwarm_lhbmv_y (r 0.000000 0.000000 0.000000)
lwarm_rhbmv_y (r 0.000000 0.000000 0.000000)
$
6
waist_dhbmv_y (r 0.000000 0.000000 0.000000)
trunk_dhbmv_y (r 0.000000 0.000000 0.000000)
upleg_lhbmv_y (r 10.000000 0.000000 0.000000)
upleg_rhbmv_y (r -10.000000 0.000000 0.000000)
uparm_lhbmv_y (r -7.500000 0.000000 0.000000)
uparm_rhbmv_y (r 7.500000 0.000000 0.000000)
lwleg_lhbmv_y (r 0.000000 0.000000 0.000000)
lwleg_rhbmv_y (r 30.000000 0.000000 0.000000)
lwarm_lhbmv_y (r 0.000000 0.000000 0.000000)
lwarm_rhbmv_y (r 0.000000 0.000000 0.000000)
$
7
waist_dhbmv_y (r 0.000000 0.000000 0.000000)
trunk_dhbmv_y (r 0.000000 0.000000 0.000000)
upleg_lhbmv_y (r 20.000000 0.000000 0.000000)
upleg_rhbmv_y (r -20.000000 0.000000 0.000000)
uparm_lhbmv_y (r -15.000000 0.000000 0.000000)
uparm_rhbmv_y (r 15.000000 0.000000 0.000000)
lwleg_lhbmv_y (r 20.000000 0.000000 0.000000)
lwleg_rhbmv_y (r 0.000000 0.000000 0.000000)
lwarm_lhbmv_y (r -10.000000 0.000000 0.000000)
lwarm_rhbmv_y (r 0.000000 0.000000 0.000000)
$
8
waist_dhbmv_y (r 0.000000 0.000000 0.000000)
trunk_dhbmv_y (r 0.000000 0.000000 0.000000)
upleg_lhbmv_y (r 10.000000 0.000000 0.000000)
upleg_rhbmv_y (r -10.000000 0.000000 0.000000)
uparm_lhbmv_y (r -7.500000 0.000000 0.000000)
uparm_rhbmv_y (r 7.500000 0.000000 0.000000)
lwleg_lhbmv_y (r 30.000000 0.000000 0.000000)
lwleg_rhbmv_y (r 0.000000 0.000000 0.000000)
```

```
lwarm_lhbmv_y (r -5.000000 0.000000 0.000000)
lwarm_rhbmv_y (r 0.000000 0.000000 0.000000)
#
```

10.7 Bit Image Libraries

10.7.1 The Gold Fish Content Based Background Library

In the current version of SWAN, a background is always a two dimensional bit image whose content can not be changed. The two dimensions are x and z axes. Using background has a disadvantage that it can not display dynamic scenes, such as a raining weather. But the backgrounds are very useful if we want to create some environment or atmosphere without wasting lots of time to design objects and to do complicated calculations to simulate physical or natural phenomena. The key of making good use of backgrounds is to maintain a content based background index and an intention based rule base containing rules for selecting backgrounds from the index. These are the two main parts of our background library. Note that after director planning it is almost everything determined qualitatively in the DPRS. It is the job of the Rainbow compiler to pick the best suitable background from the background base by using this index.

Now we give its syntax which specifies a forest of backgrounds:

<Background Archive> ::= <Series of Background Archive Items>
< Background Archive Item> ::= <Background Item Name> :
<Background Item Content>
<Background Item Content> ::= <Sequence of Background Packages>
<Background Package> ::= <Background Name> (<Background Description>)
[: (<Block of Background Branches>)]
<Background Branch> ::= <Sequence of Background Ingredients>
: <Background Name>
<Background Ingredient> ::= <Background Ingredient Class> =
<Background Ingredient Value>
<Background Ingredient Class> ::= place | environment | weather | light | season
| daytime | atmosphere | ......
<Background Ingredient Value> ::= indoor | outdoor | mountain | city | street
| office | sunny | foggy | cloudy | delighted | dark | spring | summer
| autumn | winter | morning | afternoon | evening | night
| happy | sorrow | desolation | ......

Example 10.7.1

The background package "outdoor".

Outdoor : mountain (<Background Description>) :
(season = spring, ort = southern : bt_mountain),
(season = winter, ort = northeast : sf_mountain);

```
country_side (<Background Description>) :
  (season = spring, ort = European : ws_village),
  (season = spring, ort = China_southern : rp_village);
.........................

bt_mountain (<Background Description>) :
  (weather = sunny, daytime = morning : sm_mountain),
  (weather = rainy, daytime = night : rn_mountain);
........................
rp_village (<Background Description>) :
  (weather = rainy, work = rice_planting : rr_village),
.........................
```

There are two kinds of backgrounds: the normal backgrounds and the extended ones. A normal background's size is equal to the screen's size roughly. It will not change during the whole scene. But an extended background's size is larger than that of a screen. It is used to enable a long shot which shows the roles' movement along a moving trace. For example, to show a policeman chasing a thief along a street, the camera moves together with the two roles along the same street. In such situations, extended backgrounds are necessary.

Often, a background is used in a scene together with some additional props. Sometimes it is important to determine the relative positions of these props with respect to the background. For a hill background, where should we pose a pavilion, on top of the hill or at the foot of the hill? Generally, it is better to pose it on the top of the hill. But how can we specify a position in a two dimensional image? This is the reason why we define the so-called key points for a background. These points are given in absolute coordinates. Now we can give the rest of the syntax.

```
<Background Description> ::= <Background Type> , <Background Image> ,
        <Sequence of Background Key Points>
<Background Type> ::= <Normal Type> | <Extended Type>
<Normal Type> ::= normal
<Extended Type> ::= extended (<Horizontal Extension>, <Vertical Extension>)
<Horizontal Extension> ::= <Positive Number > 1> | <empty>
<Vertical Extension> ::= <Positive Number > 1> | <empty>
<Background Image> ::= <Background Number> [<Background Center>]
<Background Number> ::= <Positive Integer>
<Background Center> ::= (<Real Number>, <Real Number>)
<Background Key Point> ::= (<Key Point Name> : <Point Coordinates>)
<Point Coordinates> ::= (<Real Number>, <Real Number>)
```

where the horizontal and vertical extension means the horizontal and vertical extension rate of the background's size with respect to the screen's size. The coordinates of the key points are their geometric centers and are given with respect to the coordinates of the background center which is in the middle of symmetry of the background by default. But an otherwise specification is also possible.

Example 10.7.2

Background Description of a street:

extended (5,), 681120 (0, 0), bank_building : (0, 9.8), post_office : (8.4, 6.7), school : (-7.34, 2.33), tree1 : (4, 5.44), tree2 : (-4, 5.44), tree3 : (8, 5.44), tree4 : (-8, 5.44), tree5 : (12, 5.44), tree6 : (-12, 5.44)

10.7.2 The Duckweed Facial Expression Library

In the first stage of SWAN implementation, the faces of our characters did not have articulates. No part of a face can do any action. Thus, all characters are quite dull-looking. This situation was not changed until we installed a library of facial expressions. This section explains the design and implementation of facial expressions in SWAN.

10.7.2.1 Design of Facial Expressions

We divide the construction process of an facial expression into three stages: the basic expression, the intermediate expression and the macro expression. A basic expression consists essentially of a micro action, i.e. a simple movement of an articulate. An intermediate expression is a group of a few basic actions which do not yet have an independent meaning. A macro expression is a macro action involving only facial outlooks.

Example 10.7.3

Basic Expressions: open_mouth, close_mouth, open_eye, close_eye,
Intermediate Expression bascule_mouth = loop : (open_mouth; close_mouth)
Intermediate Expression twinkle = loop : (open_eye; close_eye)
Macro Expression speak = parallel : (bascule_mouth, twinkle)

From the example above we can see that we need a small language to describe how the intermediate expressions are composed from basic expressions, and how the macro expressions are composed from intermediate ones. Here we only use four basic operations. They are:

A semicolon ":" means a sequential chain of basic or intermediate expressions.
A colon "," means a concurrent set of basic or intermediate expressions.
Key word "loop" means repeated execution.
Key word "parallel" means parallel execution.

This tiny language can be used by the user to add new facial expressions to the duckweed library. Note that macro expressions constitute an additional ingredient to the Rainbow language. They appear there as macro actions. The intermediate and basic expressions form components of the Evergreen language.

10.7.2.2 Implementation of Facial Expressions

The basic technique for implementing the facial expressions is interpolation. We divide the facial structure in several parts, e.g. the eyebrows, the eyes, the nose, etc. First we consider the file temp.data which collects the macro expressions used in Rainbow program. This file is produced by the compiler from Rainbow to Evergreen. We pick a Rainbow statement from the story about Houyi. If the Rainbow statement is:

Laugh (sun, once, t1, t2);

Search the duckweed library, we get the decomposition of laugh:

```
$ laugh_open_mouth    0      (open mouth)
$ lbrow_laugh         0      (left eyebrow)
$ rbrow_laugh         0      (right eyebrow)
$ laugh_con_open      1      (keep laughing)
$ laugh_close_mouth   1      (close mouth)
```

where the number 0 means concurrent actions, and 1 means sequential actions. Then the format of a temp.data file is about the following:

```
# sun head_being c1,
$ open_mouth          1   10   1
$ laugh_open_mouth    11  13   1
$ lbrow_laugh         11  13   1
$ rbrow_laugh         11  13   1
$ laugh_con_open      14  20   1
$ laugh_close_mouth   21  23   1
```

where the data are initial frame numbers, terminal frame numbers and loop numbers, respectively.

We still have to build up a library inter.exp for articulate interpolation whose format is as follows.

Table 10.7.1 Interpolation for Laugh Expression

Expression to be interpolated	Structure involved	Articulate involved	First real articulate	Second Real articulate
Opcl_mouth	Head_being	Head	Head1	Head2
Laugh_open_ mouth	Head_being	Head	Head1	Head2
Laugh_con_ Open	Head_being	Head	Head1	Head2
Laugh_close_ mouth	Head_being	Head	Head1	Head2
Lbrow_laugh	Head_being	Lbrow	Lbrow1	Lbrow2
Rbrow_laugh	Head_being	Rbrow	Rbrow1	Rbrow2

The Rainbow compiler reads data from the temp.data file, searches interpolation library for real articulates to be interpolated, and writes down them in the Script program. The resulted program piece looks like:

Interp : facet interpolation (head1 → head2 → head1 → head1 → head1 → head2 → head2 → head2 → head1, interp0. Trj, 1 → 22),
C1. Head _dsndr : Interp0 color movie / head1;
Interp1 : facet interpolation (lbrow1 → lbrow2 → lbrow1, Interp1. Trj, 11 → 13),
C1 : eybr → lsndl : Interp1 color movie / lbrow1;
Interp2 : facet interpolation (rbrow1 → rbrow2 → rbrow1, Interp2. Trj, 11-13),
C1 : eybl → rsndr : Interp2 color movie / rbrow1

The corresponding trace file looks like follows:

key point	frame number	from-state	to-state
0	1	0	0
1	5	1	0
2	10	2	0
3	11	3	0
4	13	4	0
5	14	5	0
6	20	6	0
7	21	7	0
8	23	8	0

The result of this interpolation is given in the appendix as an image picture taken from the animation.

Appendix

Pic. 1

R. Lu and S. Zhang: Automatic Generation of Computer Animation, LNAI 2160, pp. 351-362, 2002.

Pic. 2

Pic. 3

Pic. 4

Pic. 5

Pic. 6

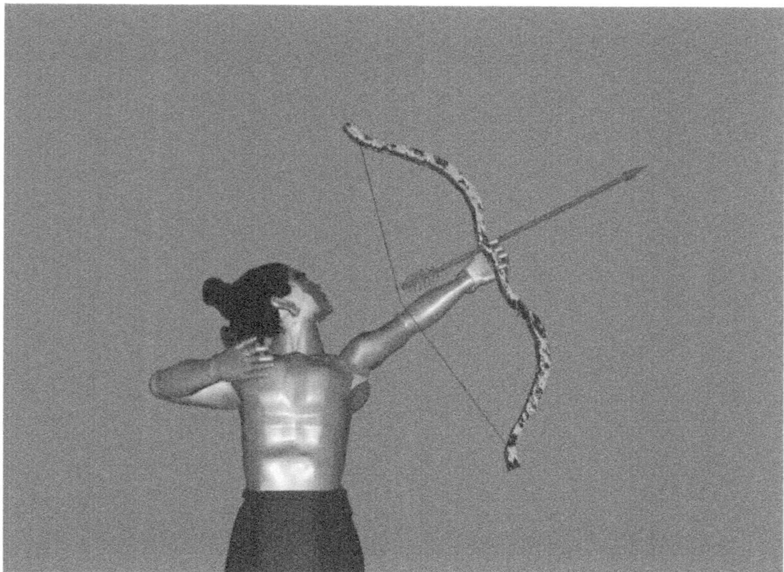

Pic. 7

Pic. 8

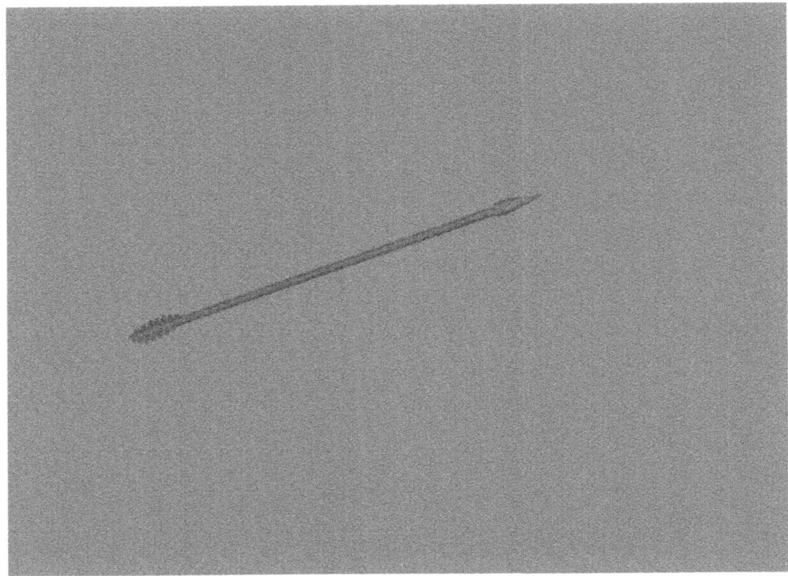

Pic. 9

Pic. 10

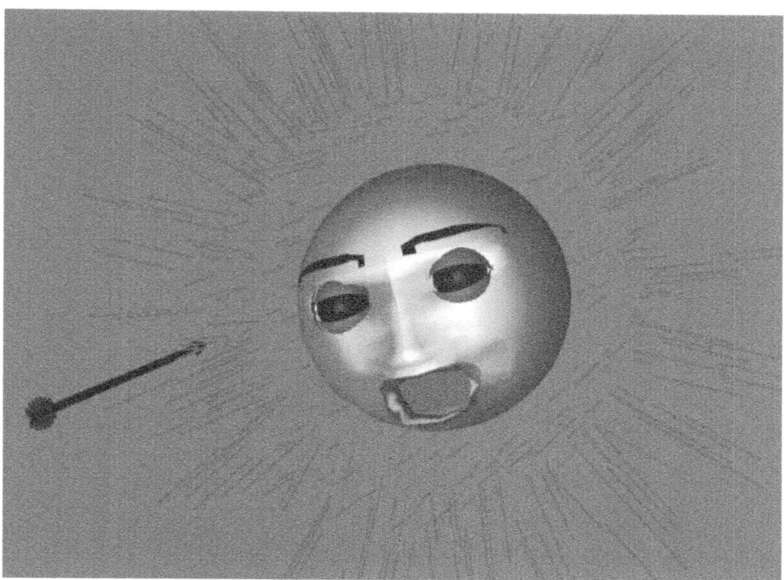

Pic. 11

Pic. 12

Pic. 13

Pic. 14

Pic. 15

Pic. 16

Pic. 17

Pic. 18

Pic. 19

Pic. 20

Pic. 21

Pic. 22

Pic. 23

References

Part One

[Aho and Ullmann, 1972] A.V.Aho and J.D.Ullmann, *The Theory of Parsing, Translation and Compiling, Vol.1: Parsing*, Prentics-Hall, Inc., 1972

[Alterman, Zito-Wlf and Carpenter, 1998] R.Alterman, R.Zito-Wlf and T.Carpenter, Pragmatic Action, *Cognitive Science*, Vol.22, No.1, 1998, pp53-105

[Arnold, 1989] V.I.Arnold, *Mathematical Methods in Classical Mechanics*, New York: Springer Verlag, 1989

[Arijon, 1976] D.Arijon, *Grammar of the Film Language*, Communication Arts Books, New York: Hastings House, Publishers, 1976

[Badler, 1991] N.I.Badler, et al., Animation from Instructions, Chapter three, in N.I.Badler et al. (Eds.), *Making them Move: Mechanics, Control, and Animation of Articulated Figures*, Morgan Kaufmann, 1991, pp51-93

[Badler, 1993] N.I.Badler, et al., *Simulating Humans: computer graphics, animation and control*, Oxford University Press, 1993

[Badler, O'Rourke and Kaufman, 1980] N.I.Badler, J.O'Rourke and B.Kaufman, Special Problems in Human Movement Simulation, *Computer Graphics*, Vol.14, No.3, 1980, pp189-197

[Badler, O'Rourke, Smoliar and Weber, 1978] N.I.Badler, J.O'Rourke, S.Smoliar and L.Weber, The Simulation of Human Movement by Computer, Technical Report, University of Pennsylvania, 1978

[Baltsan and Sharir, 1988] A.Baltsan and M.Sharir, On the Shortest Paths between Two Convex Polyhedral, *Journal of ACM*, Vol.35, No.2, 1988, pp267-287

[Barr, 1992] A.H.Barr, et al., Smooth Interpolation of Orientations with Angular Velocity Constraints using Quaternions, *Computer Graphics*, Vol.26, No.2, 1992, pp313-320

[Barr and Feigenbaum, 1981] A.H.Barr and E.A.Feigenbaum (Eds.), *The Handbook of Artificial Intelligence, Volume 1*, Los Altos, CA: Williamm Kaufmann, 1981

[Bechmann and Dubreuil, 1995] D.Bechmann and N.Dubreuil, Order-Controlled Free-Form Animation, *The Journal of Visualization and Computer Animation*, Vol.6, 1995, pp11-32

[Black and Wilensky, 1979] J.B.Black and R.Wilensky, An Evaluation of Story Grammars, *Cognitive Science* 3, 1979, pp213-230

[Brotman, 1988] L.S.Brotman, et al, Motion Interpolation by Optimal Control, *Computer Graphics*, Vol.22, No.4, 1988, pp179-188

[Bruderlin and Calvert, 1989] A.Bruderlin and T.W.Calvert, Goal-Directed Dynamic Animation of Human Walking, *Computer Graphics*, Vol.23, No.3, 1989, pp233-242

R. Lu and S. Zhang: Automatic Generation of Computer Animation, LNAI 2160, pp. 363-374, 2002.

[Buck and Schoemer, 1998] M.Buck and E.Schoemer, Interactive Rigid Body Manipulation with Obstacle Contacts, *The Journal of Visualization and Computer Animation*, Vol.9, No.4, 1998, pp243-257

[Calvert, Bruderlin, Dill, Schiphorst and Welman, 1993] T.Calvert, A.Bruderlin, J.Dill, T.Schiphorst and C.Welman, Desktop Animation of Multiple Human Figures, *IEEE Computer Graphics and Applications*, May 1993, pp18-26

[Canny and Reif, 1987] J.Canny and J.Reif, New Lower Bound Techniques for Robot Motion Planning Problems, *Proc. of the 28th Annual IEEE Symposium on Foundations of Computer Science*, New York, 1987, pp49-60

[Charniak, 1977] E.Charniak, Ms.Malaprop: A Language Comprehension Program, *Proc. of IJCAI'77*, 1977

[Charniak, 1978] E.Charniak, On the Use of Framed Knowledge in Language Comprehension, *Artificial Intelligence*, Vol.11, No.3, 1978

[Chen, Qian and Sun, 1980] H.Chen, J.Qian and Y.Sun, *Compiling Theory of Programming Languages*, Beijing: Defense Industry Press, 1980

[Chiba, Muraoka, Takahashi and Miura, 1994] N.Chiba, K.Muraoka, H.Takahashi and M.Miura, Two-dimensional Visual Simulation of Flames, Smoke and the Spread of Fire, *The Journal of Visualization and Computer Animation*, Vol.5, 1994, pp37-53

[Chiba, Ohkawa, Muraoka and Miura, 1994] N.Chiba, S.Ohkawa, K.Muraoka and M.Miura, Visual Simulation of Botanical Trees based on Virtual Heliotropism and Dormancy Break, *The Journal of Visualization and Computer Animation*, Vol.5, 1994, pp3-15

[Clay and Wilhelms, 1996] S.R.Clay and J.Wilhelms, Put: Language-based Interactive Manipulation of Objects, *IEEE Computer Graphics and Applications*, March 1996, pp31-39

[Cohen and Perrault, 1979] P.R.Cohen and C.R.Perrault, Elements of a Plan-based Theory of Speech Acts, *Cognitive Science*, Vol.3, 1979

[Courcelle and Engelfriet, 1995] B.Courcelle and J.Engelfriet, A Logical Characterization of the Sets of Hypergraphs Defined by Hyperedge Replacement Grammars, *Mathematical Systems Theory*, Vol.28, 1995, pp515-552

[Cullingford, 1978] R.E.Cullingford, *Script Application: Computer Understanding of Newspaper Stories*, PhD Thesis, Yale University, New Haven, CT. Res. Rep.116, 1978

[De Jong, 1979] G.F.De Jong, Skimming Stories in Real Time: An Experiment in Integrated Understanding, Research Report 158, Yale University, 1979

[Denavit and Hartenberg, 1955] J.Denavit and R.Hartenberg, A Kinematic Notation for Lower-Pair Mechanism based on Matrices, *Journal of Applied Mechanics*, Vol.77, 1955, pp215-221

[Deransart and Jourdan, 1990] P.Deransart and M.Jourdan (Eds.), Attribute Grammars and their Applications, *LNCS* 461, Berlin: Springer-Verlag, 1990

[Dyer, 1983a] M.G.Dyer, Understanding Stories through Morals and Remindings, *Proc. of IJCAI'83*, 1983

[Dyer, 1983b] M.G.Dyer, The Role of Affect in Parsing, *Artificial Intelligence*, Vol.7, 1983

[Ehrenfeucht, Pas and Rozenberg, 1994] A.Ehrenfeucht, P.Pas and G.Rozenberg, Context-free Text Grammars, *Acta Informatica*, Vol.31, 1994, pp161-206

[Ehrenfeucht and Rozenberg, 1993] A.Ehrenfeucht and G.Rozenberg, *T*-structures, *T*-functions, and Texts, *Theorectical Computer Science*, Vol.116, 1993, pp227-290

[Elvins, 1997] T.T.Elvins, VisFiles: Presentation Technologies for Time-Series Data, *Computer Graphics*, Vol.31, No.4, 1997, pp14-16

[Erkan and Ozguc, 1995] B.Erkan and B.Ozguc, Object-Oriented Motion Abstraction, *The Journal of Visualization and Computer Animation*, Vol.6, 1995, pp49-65

[Esakov and Badler, 1989] J.Esakov and N.I.Badler, An Architecture for Human Task Animation Control, P.A.Fishwick and R.S.Modjeski (Eds.), *Knowledge-based Simulation: Methodology and Applications*, New York: Springer Verlag, 1989

[Fillmore, 1968] Ch.J.Fillmore, The Case for Case, E.Bach and R.T.Harms(Eds.), *Universal in Linguistic Theory,* London: Holt, Rinehart and Winston, 1968, pp1-90

[Frisch and Perlis, 1981] A.Frisch and D.Perlis, A Re-Evaluation of Story Grammars, *Cognitive Science*, Vol.5, 1981, pp79-86

[Fu, 1977] K.S.Fu, *Syntactic Pattern Recognition Applications*, Berlin: Springer-Verlag, 1977

[Fu, 1982] K.S.Fu (Eds.), *Application of Pattern Recognition*, Florida: CRC Press, Inc., 1982

[Ge and ShenS, 1988] D.Ge and S.Shen, *The Technique and Theory of Cinematography* (in Chinese), Beijing: China Film Press, 1988

[Gerevini and Schubert, 1995] A.Gerevini and L.Schubert, Efficient Algorithms for Qualitative Reasoning about Time, *Artificial Intelligence*, Vol.74, 1995, pp207-248

[Giertsen, 1994] C.Giertsen, Direct Volume Rendering and Multiple Scalar Fields, *The Journal of Visualization and Computer Animation*, Vol.5, 1994, pp69-84

[Girard, 1987] M.Girard, Interactive Design of 3-D Computer Animated Legged Animal Motion, *IEEE Computer Graphics and Applications*, Vol.7, No.6, 1987, pp39-51

[Girard and Maciejewski, 1985] M.Girard and A.A.Maciejewski, Computational Modeling for the Computer Animation of Legged Figures, *Computer Graphics*, Vol.19, No.3, 1985, pp263-270

[Gleicher and Litwinowicz, 1998] M.Gleicher and P.Litwinowicz, Constraint-based Motion Adaptation, *The Journal of Visualization and Computer Animation*, Vol.9, No.2, 1998, pp65-94

[Gonzalez and Thomason, 1977] R.C.Gonzalez and M.G.Thomason, *Syntactic Pattern Recognition*, 1977

[Gordon and Hendrick, 1998] P.C.Gordon and R.Hendrick, The Representation and Processing of Coreference in Discourse, *Cognitive Science*, Vol.22, No.4, 1998, pp389-424

[Gries, 1971] D.Gries, *Compiler Construction for Digital Computer*, New York: John Wiley & Sons, Inc., 1971

[Grosz, 1985] B.Grosz, *The Structure of Discourse Analysis*, New York: Garland Publishing, 1985

[Guenter, 1990] B.Guenter, et al., Computing the Arc Length of Parametric Curves, *IEEE Computer Graphics and Applications*, Vol.10, No.3, 1990, pp72-78

[He, Cohen and Salesin, 1996] L.He, M.Cohen and D.Salesin, *The Virtual Cinematographer: A Paradigm for Automatic Real-Time Camera Control and Directing*, Technical Report, August 1996

[Hearst, 1997] M.A.Hearst, TextTiling: Segmenting Text into Multi-Paragraph Subtopic Passages, *Computational Linguistics*, Vol.23, No.1, 1997, pp33-64

[Hiller and Isaacson, 1959] L.Hiller and L.Isaacson, *Experimental Music*, New York: McGraw-Hill, 1959

[Huang, 1992] G.Huang, *Essentials of Text Analysis* (in Chinese), Changsha: Human Education Press, 1992

[HuangT and Tang, 1996] T.S.Huang and L.Tang, 3D Face Modeling and its Applications, *International Journal of Pattern Recognition and Artificial Intelligence*, Vol.10, No.5, 1996, pp491-520

[HuangYK and Ahuja, 1992] Y.K.Huang and N.Ahuja, Gross Motion Planning – A Survey, *ACM Computing Survey*, Vol.24, No.3, 1992, pp218-291

[Huls and Bos, 1998] C.Huls and E.Bos, Studies into Full Integration of Language and Action, *LNCS 1374*, Berlin: Springer-Verlag, 1998, pp313-325

[IKAN, 2000] Inverse Kinematics using ANalytical methods, software package, *http://hms.upenn.edu/software/ik/contact.html*, 2000

[Jin, Bao and Peng, 1997] X.Jin, H.Bao and Q.Peng, A Survey of Computer Animation (in Chinese), *Software Journal*, Vol.8, No.4, 1997, pp241-251

[John and James, 1994] H.R.John and A.S.James, A Single-Exponential Bound for Finding Shortest Paths in Three Dimensions, Journal of ACM, Vol.41, No.5, 1994, pp1013-1019

[Joseph, 1987] S.B.M.Joseph et al., The Discrete Geodesic Problem, *SIAM Journal of Computing*, Vol.16, No.4, 1987, pp647-667

[Jung, Badler and Toma, 1994] M.Jung, N.Badler and T.Toma, Animated Human Agents with Motion Planning Capability for 3D-Space Postural Goals, *The Journal of Visualization and Computer Animation*, Vol.5, 1994, pp225-246

[Kastens and Waite, 1994] U.Kastens and W.M.Waite, Modularity and Reusability in Attribute Grammars, *Acta Informatica*, Vol.31, 1994, pp601-627

[Kehler, 1997] A.Kehler, Current Theories of Centering for Pronoun Interpretation: A Critical Evaluation, *Computational Linguistics*, Vol.23, No.3, 1997, pp467-475

[Kehler and Shieber, 1997] A.Kehler and S.Shieber, Squibs and Discussions: Anaphoric Dependencies in Ellipsis, Computational Linguistics, Vol.23, No.3, 1997, pp457-466

[Kim, Park and Lee, 1994] M.Kim, E.Park and H.Lee, Modelling and Animation of Generalized Cylinders with Variable Radius Offset Space Curves, *The Journal of Visualization and Computer Animation*, Vol.5, 1994, pp189-207

[Knuth, 1968] D.E.Knuth, Semantics of Context-Free Languages, *Mathematical System Theory*, Vol.2, No.2, 1968, pp127-145

[Koenig, 1970a] G.M.Koenig, Project 1: A Programme for Musical Composition, *Electric Music Reports* 2, 1970, pp32-44

[Koenig, 1970b] G.M.Koenig, Project 2: A Programme for Musical Composition, *Electric Music Reports* 3, 1970, pp1-16

[Komura, Shinagawa and Kunii, 1998] T.Komura, Y.Shinagawa and T.L.Kunii, Calculation and Visualization of the Dynamic Ability of the Human Body, *The Journal of Visualization and Computer Animation*, Vol.10, No.2, 1998, pp57-78

[Kuhn and DeMori, 1995] R.Kuhn and R.DeMori, The Application of Semantic Classification Trees to Natural Language Understanding, *IEEE Transactions on Pattern Analysis and Machine Intelligence*, Vol.17, No.5, 1995, pp449-460

[Lebowitz, 1983] M.Lebowitz, Memory-based Parsing, *Artificial Intelligence*, Vol.21, 1983, pp363-404

[Lee and Preparata, 1984] D.T.Lee and F.P.Preparata, Euclidean Shortest Paths in the Presence of Rectilinear Barriers, *Networks*, Vol.14, 1984

[Lee and Stenning, 1998] J.Lee and K.Stenning, Anaphora in Multimodal Discourse, *LNCS 1374*, Berlin: Springer-Verlag, 1998, pp251-263

[Lehnert, 1981] W.G.Lehnert, Plot Units and Narrative Summarization, *Cognitive Science*, Vol.4, 1981, pp293-331

[Lehnert, 1983] W.G.Lehnert, et al., Boris - An Experiment in In-depth Understanding of Narratives, Artificial Intelligence, Vol.20, No.1, 1983

[Lenat and Guha, 1990] D.B.Lenat and P.V.Guha, Building Large Knowledge Based Systems: Representation and Inference in the CYC Project, Reading, MA: Addison Wesley, 1990

[Lester and Porter, 1997] J.C.Lester and B.W.Porter, Developing and Empirically Evaluating Robust Explanation Generators: The KNIGHT Experiments, Computational Linguistics, Vol.23, No.1, 1997

[Leven and Sharir, 1987] D.Leven and M.Sharir, An Efficient and Simple Motion Planning Algorithm for a Ladder Moving in Two-dimensional Space Amidst Polygonal Barriers, Journal of Algorithms, Vol.8, 1987, pp192-215

[LiuY, Pan and Gu, 1983] Y.Liu, W.Pan and H.Gu, Chinese Grammar (in Chinese), Xian: Foreign Language Tutoring and Research Press, 1983

[Lozano-Perez and Wesley, 1979] T.Lozano-Perez and M.A.Wesley, An Algorithm for Planning Collision-Free Paths among Polyhedral Obstacles, Communications of ACM, Vol.22, 1979, pp560-570

[MacIntyre and Feiner, 1998] B.MacIntyre and S.Feiner, A Distributed 3D Graphics Library, Proc. of ACM SIGGRAPH'98, 1998, pp361-370

[Maiocchi, 1990] R. Maiocchi, et al., Directing an Animation Scene with Autonomous Actors, The Visual Computer, Vol.6, No.6, 1990, pp351-371

[Mallinder, 1995] H.Mallinder, The Modeling of Large Waterfalls using String Texture, The Journal of Visualization and Computer Animation, Vol.6, 1995, pp3-10

[Mandler and Johnson, 1977] J.M.Mandler and N.S.Johnson, Remembrance of Things Parsed: Story Structure and Recall, Cognitive Psychology, Vol.7, 1977, pp111-151

[Mandler and Johnson, 1980] J.M.Mandler and N.S.Johnson, On Throwing out the Baby with the Bath Water: A Reply to Black and Wilensky's Evaluation of Story Grammars, Cognitive Science, Vol.4, 1980, pp305-312

[Marcus, 1997] S.Marcus, Contextual Grammars and Natural Languages, in G.Rozenberg and A.Salomaa (Eds.), *Handbook of Formal Languages, Volume 2*, 1997, pp215-235

[Marcus, Martin-Vide and Paun, 1998] S.Marcus, C.Martin-Vide and G.Paun, Contextual Grammars as Generative Models of Natural Languages, *Computational Linguistics*, Vol.24, No.2, 1998, pp245-274

[Mathews and Pierce, 1991] M.V.Mathews and J.R.Pierce, *Current Directions in Computer Music Research (System Development Foundation Benchmark Series, 2)*, 1991

[McCarthy, 1968] J.McCarthy, Programs with Common Sense, *Proc. of Symposium on Mechanism of Thought*, M.L.Minsky (Eds.), *Semantic Information Processing*, Cambridge□MA: MIT Press, 1968, pp403-418

[McDermott, 1993] D.McDermott, (Book Review) D.B.Lenat and R.V.Guha, Building Large Knowledge-Based Systems: Representation and Inference in the Cyc Project, *Artificial Intelligence*, Vol.61, No.1, 1993, pp53-63

[McRoy, Ali, Restificar and Channarukul, 1999] S.W.McRoy, S.S.Ali, A.Restificar and S. Channarukul, Building Intelligent Dialog Systems, *Intelligence*, Vol.10, No.1, 1999, pp14-23

[McRoy and Hirst, 1995] S.W.McRoy and G.Hirst, The Repair of Speech Act Misunderstandings by Abductive Inference, *Computational Linguistics*, Vol.21, No.4, 1995, pp435-478

[Meduna, 1995] A.Meduna, Syntactic Complexity of Scattered Context Grammars, *Acta Informatica*, Vol.32, 1995, pp285-298

[Meehan, 1981] J.Meehan, TALE-SPIN, R.C.Schank and C.K.Riesbeck (Eds.), *Inside Computer Understanding*, Hillsdale, NJ: Lawrence Erlbaum Associates, 1981

[Milne, 1997] M.Milne, Entertaining the Future: the Virtual Question, *Computer Graphics*, Vol.31, No.4, 1997, pp7-8

[Multon, France, Cani-Gascuel and Debunne, 1999] F.Multon, L.France, M.Cani-Gascuel and G.Debunne, Computer Animation of Human Walking: a Survey, *The Journal of Visualization and Computer Animation*, Vol.10, 1999, pp39-54

[Nakamura, Kaku, Hyun, Noma and Yoshida, 1994] J.Nakamura, T..Kaku, K.Hyun, T.Noma and S.Yoshida, Automatic Background Music Generation based on Actor's Mood and Motions, *The Journal of Visualization and Computer Animation*, Vol.5, 1994, pp247-264

[Noma, 1987] T.Noma, Story Driven Animation, *Proc. CHI + GI'87*, 1987, pp149-153

[Noma, Kai, Nakamura and Okada, 1992] T.Noma, K.Kai, J.Nakamura and N.Okada, Translating from Natural Language Story to Computer Animation, *SPICIS'92*, pp475-480

[O'Rorke and Ortony, 1994] P.O'Rorke and A.Ortony, Explaining Emotions, *Cognitive Science*, Vol.18, 1994, pp283-323

[Overveld, 1994] C.W.A.M.van Overveld, A Simple Approximation to Rigid Body Dynamics for Computer Animation, *The Journal of Visualization and Computer Animation*, Vol.5, 1994, pp17-36

[Overveld and Ko, 1994] C.W.A.M.van Overveld and H.Ko, Small Steps for Mankind: Towards a Kinematically Driven Dynamic Simulation of Curved Path Walking, *The Journal of Visualization and Computer Animation*, Vol.5, 1994, pp143-165

[Paakki, 1995] J.Paakki, Attribute Grammar Paradigms—A High-Level Methodology in Language Implementation, *ACM Computing Survey*, Vol.27, No.2, 1995, pp196-255

[Paun and Rozenberg, 1994] G.Paun and G.Rozenberg, Prescribed Teams of Grammars, *Acta Informatica*, Vol.31, 1994, pp525-537

[Phillips and Badler, 1988] C.Phillips and N.I.Badler, Jack: A Toolkit for Manipulating Articulated Figures, *ACM/SIGGRAPH Symposium on User Interface Software*, Banff, Canada, 1988, pp221-229

[Platt and Barr, 1988] J.C.Platt and A.H.Barr, Constraint Method for Flexible Models, *Computer Graphics*, Vol.22, No.4, 1988, pp279-288

[Polack, 1990] M.Polack, *Plans as Complex Mental Attitudes, Intentions in Communication*, in J.M.P. Cohen and M.Polack (Eds.), Cambridge: MIT Press, MA, 1990

[Radev and Mckeown, 1998] D.R.Radev and K.R.Mckeown, Generating Natural Language Summaries from Multiple On-Line Sources, *Computational Linguistics*, Vol.24, No.3, 1998, pp469-500

[Raibert, 1991] M.H.Raibert, et al., Animation of Dynamic Legged Locomotion, *Computer Graphics*, Vol.25, No.4, 1991, pp349-358

[Rumelhart, 1975] D.E.Rumelhart, Notes in a Schema for Stories, D.G.Bobrow and A.Collins (Eds.), *Representation and Understanding: Studies in Cognitive Science*, New York: Academic Press, 1975

[Rumelhart, 1977a] D.E.Rumelhart, Understanding and Summarizing Brief Stories, D.LaBerge and S.J.Samuels (Eds.), *Basic Processes in Reading: Perception and Comprehension*, Hillsdale, NJ: Lawrence Erlbaum Associates, 1977

[Rumelhart, 1977b] D.E.Rumelhart, Toward an Interactive Model of Reading, S.Dornic (Eds.), *Attention and Performance VI*, Hillsdale, NJ: Lawrence Erlbaum Associates, 1977

[Rumelhart, 1980] D.E.Rumelhart, On Evaluation Story Grammars, *Cognitive Science*, Vol.4, 1980, pp313-316

[Ruprecht and Mueller, 1994] D.Ruprecht and H.Mueller, Deformed Cross-Dissolves for Image Interpolation in Scientific Visualization, *The Journal of Visualization and Computer Animation*, Vol.5, 1994, pp167-181

[Schabes and Waters, 1995] Y.Schabes and R.C.Waters, Tree Insertion Grammar: A Cubic-Time, Parsable Formalism that Lexicalizes Context-Free Grammar without Changing the Trees Produced, *Computational Linguistics*, Vol.21, No.4, 1995, pp479-513

[Schank, 1977] R.C.Schank, et al., *Scripts, Plans, Goals, and Understanding*, 1977

[Schank, 1980] R.C.Schank, Language and Memory, *Cognitive Science*, Vol.4, 1980

[Schank, 1982] R.C.Schank, Reminding and Memory Organization: An Introduction to MOPs, *Strategies for Natural Language Processing*, 1982

[Schwartz and Sharir, 1983] J.T.Schwartz and M.Sharir, On the "Piano Moves" Problem I. The Case of a Two-dimensional Rigid Polygonal Body Moving Amidst Polygonal Barriers, *Communications on Pure and Applied Mathematics*, Vol.36, 1983, pp345-398

[Sgouros, 1997] N.M.Sgouros, Dynamic, User-Center Resolution for Interactive Stories, *Proc. of 15th International Joint Conference on Artificial Intelligence (IJCAI-97)*, Nagoya, Japan, 1997

[Sgouros, 1999] N.M.Sgouros, Dynamic Generation, Management and Resolution of Interactive Plots, *Artificial Intelligence*, Vol.107, No.1, 1999, pp29-62

[Sharir, 1985] M.Sharir, Intersection and Closest-Pair Problems for a Set of Planar Discs, *SIAM Journal of Computing*, Vol.14, 1985, pp448-468

[Sharir, 1987] M.Sharir, On Shortest Paths Amidst Convex Polyhedral, *SIAM Journal of Computing*, Vol.16, No.3, 1987

[Sharir and Baltsan, 1986] M.Sharir and A.Baltsan, On Shortest Paths Amidst Convex Polyhedral, *Proc. of the 2nd Annual ACM Symposium on Computational Geometry*, 1986

[Sharir and Schorr, 1986] M.Sharir and A.Schorr, On Shortest Paths in Polyhedral Spaces, *SIAM Journal of Computing*, Vol.15, 1986, pp193-215

[Shoemake, 1985] K.Shoemake, Animating Rotation with Quaternion Curves, *Computer Graphics*, Vol.19, No.3, 1985, pp245-254

[Shinya, Mori and Osumi, 1998] M.Shinya, T.Mori and N.Osumi, Periodic Motion Synthesis and Fourier Compression, *The Journal of Visualization and Computer Animation*, Vol.9, No.2, 1998, pp95-107

[Sifrony and Sharir, 1987] S.Sifrony and M.Sharir, An Efficient Motion Planning Algorithm for a Rod Moving in Two-dimensional Polygonal Space, *Algorithmica*, Vol.2, 1987, pp367-402

[Simmons and Bennett-Novak, 1975] R.F.Simmons and G.Bennett-Novak, Semantically Analyzing and English Subset for the Clowns Microworld, *American Journal of Computational Linguistics*, Microfiche 18, 1975

[Stader, 1996] J.Stader, *Results of the Enterprise Project*, Technical Report AIAI-TR-209, University of Edinburg, 1996

[Steketee and Badler, 1985] S.N.Steketee and N.I.Badler, Parametric keyframe interpolation incorporating kinetic adjustment and phrasing control, *Computer Graphics*, Vol.19, No.3, 1985, pp255-262

[Strurmann, 1986] D.Strurmann, Interactive Keyframe Animation of 3-D Articulated Models, *Graphics Interface '86*, 1986

[Taboada, Marin, Mira and Macias, 1996] M.Taboada, R.Marin, J.Mira and M.Macias, Representation of Human-Computer Interaction by Means of Behavior Rules, *Applied Artificial Intelligence*, Vol.10, 1996, pp163-185

[TangX, TangZ, MaH and ZhaoC, 1998] X.Tang, Z.Tang, H.Ma and C.Zhao, The Application of XYZ System in the Animation Field (in Chinese), *Software Journal*, Vol.9, No.1, 1998

[Terasawa and Kimura, 1994] M.Terasawa and F.Kimura, Collision Response for Deformable Models based on Hertz's Contact Theory, *The Journal of Visualization and Computer Animation*, Vol.5, 1994, pp209-224

[Thompson, 1993] R.Thompson, *Grammar of the Edit*, Oxford: Focal Press, 1993

[Thorndyke, 1977] P.W.Thorndyke, Cognitive Structures in Comprehension and Memory of Narrative Discourse, *Cognitive Psychology*, Vol.7, 1977, pp77-110

[Thorup, 1996] M.Thorup, Disambiguating Grammars by Exclusion of Sub-Parse Trees, *Acta Informatica*, Vol.33, 1996, pp511-522

[Vanecek, 1994] G.Vanecek Jr., Back-face Culling Applied to Collision Detection of Polyhedra, *The Journal of Visualization and Computer Animation*, Vol.5, 1994, pp55-63

[Vilaplana and Pueyo, 1994] J.Vilaplana and X.Pueyo, Multilevel Use of Coherence for Complex Radiosity Environments, *The Journal of Visualization and Computer Animation*, Vol.5, 1994, pp129-141

[Wang and Verriest, 1998] X.Wang and J.P.Verriest, A Geometric Algorithm to Predict the Arm Reach Posture for Computer-aided Ergonomic Evaluation, *The Journal of Visualization and Computer Animation*, Vol.9, 1998, pp33-47

[WangB and WuB, 1988] B.Wang and B.Wu, *Formal Language*, Beijing: Press of National University of Defense Technology, 1988

[Waters, 1995] R.C.Waters, The 1995 AAAI Spring Symposia Report; Interactive Story Systems: Plot and Character, *AI Magazine*, Vol.16, No.3, 1995

[Webber, 1998] B.Webber, Instructing Animated Agents: Viewing Language in Behavioral Terms, *LNCS 1374*, Berlin: Springer-Verlag, 1998, pp89-99

[Wells, 1998] A.J.Wells, Turing's Analysis of Computation and Theories of Cognitive Architecture, *Cognitive Science*, Vol.22, No.3, 1998, pp269-294

[Wiebe, 1994] J.M.Wiebe, Tracking Point of View in Narrative, *Computational Linguistics*, Vol.20, No.1, 1994, pp232-287

[Wilensky, 1978] R.Wilensky, Why John Married Mary: Understanding Stories Involving Recurring Goals, *Cognitive Science*, Vol.2, 1978

[Winograd, 1983] T.Winograd, *Language as a Cognitive Process*, Addison-Wesley Publishing Company, Inc., 1983

[Wu and Hou, 1988] J.Wu and X.Hou, Modern Chinese Language Sentence Parsing (in Chinese), Beijing: Press of Peking University, 1988

[XiaoK and LiD, 1987] K.Xiao and D.Li, Ontology, *China Encyclopedia, Philosophy Volume I* (in Chinese), Beijing: Encyclopedia Press, 1987, 35

[XuN, 1986] N.Xu et al., Dictionary of Film Art (in Chinese), Beijing: Chinese Film Press, 1986

[Zeltzer, 1982] D.Zeltzer, Motor Control Techniques for Figure Animation, *IEEE Computer Graphics and Applications*, Vol.2, No.9, 1982, pp53-59

[Zeltzer, 1983] D.Zeltzer, Knowledge-based Animation, *ACM SIGGRAPH/SIGART, Workshop on Motion*, 1983, pp187-192

[Zeltzer, Pieper and Sturman, 1989] D.Zeltzer, A.Pieper and D.Sturman, An Integrated Graphical Simulation Platform, *Proc. of Graphics Interface 89*, London, Ontario, 1989, pp266-274

[Zimmermann, 1995] D.Zimmermann, Exploiting Models of Musical Structure for Automatic Intention-based Composition of Background Music, G.Widmer (Eds.), *Proc. of the IJCAI'95 Workshop on Artificial Intelligence and Music*, Menlo Park, CA: AAAI Press, 1995

[ZhuW, 1992] W.Zhu, *Social Linguistics: An Introduction* (in Chinese), Changsha: Human Education Press, 1992

Part Two

[Lu, 1985] Ruqian Lu, *Expert Union - United Service of Expert Systems*, Technical Report 85-6, University of Minnesota, Duluth, 1985

[Lu, 1988] Ruqian Lu, *Artificial Intelligence (I)* (in Chinese), Beijing: Science Press, 1988

[Lu, 1992] Ruqian Lu, *Formal Semantics of Computer Languages* (in Chinese), Beijing: Science Press, 1992

[Lu, 1993] Ruqian Lu, A true concurrency model of CCS semantics, *Theoretical Computer Science,* Vol.113, 1993, pp231-258

[Lu, 1994a] Ruqian Lu, Automatic Knowledge Acquisition by Understanding Pseudo-Natural Languages, *Theory and Pracxis of Machine Learning*, Dagstuhl Seminar Report 91 (9426), 1994, pp11-12

[Lu, 1994b] Ruqian Lu et al., *Expert System Development Environment* (in Chinese), Beijing: Science Press, 1994

[Lu, 1994c] Ruqian Lu, *New Approaches to Knowledge Acquisition*, Singapore: World Scientific, 1994

[Lu, 1996] Ruqian Lu, *Artificial Intelligence (II)* (in Chinese), Beijing: Science Press, 1996

[Lu, 2000] Ruqian Lu, Knowledge Science and its Research Frontiers, *Invited Talk of the 5th International Symposium on Future Software Technology*, China, August, 2000

[Lu, Cao, 1990] Ruqian Lu, Cungen Cao, Towards Knowledge Acquisition from Domain Books, *Current Trends in Knowledge Acquisition*, IOC, Amsterdam, 1990, pp289-301

[Lu, Han, Ma, ZhangW, WangW, 1997] Ruqian Lu, Ke Han, Yinghao Ma, Wenyan Zhang, Wenbiao Wang, Intelligent VR Training, *Proc. of EPIA'97, LNAI 1323*, 1997, pp111-118

[Lu, Ji, 2000] Ruqian Lu, Guangfeng Ji, Research on Common Sense (in Chinese), *Knowledge Engineering and Knowledge Science*, Beijing: Tsinghua University Press, 2000

[Lu and Li, 1992] Ruqian Lu, Xiaobin Li, Progress in Study of Story Understanding (in Chinese), *Pattern Recognition and Artificial Intelligence*, Vol.5, No.3, 1992, pp196-206

[Lu, LiuH, Li, 1989] Ruqian Lu, Yinghui Liu, Xiaobin Li, Computer-aided Grammar Acquisition in the Chinese Understanding System CUSAGA, *Proc. of 11th IJCAI*, Detroit, 1989, pp1550-1555

[Lu, ShiC, Zhang, Mao, Xu, Yang and Fan, 2000] Ruqian Lu, Chunyi Shi, Songmao Zhang, Xiping Mao, Jinhui Xu, Ping Yang and Lu Fan, Agent-Oriented Commonsense Knowledge Base, *Scientia Sinica*, Series E, 2000 (to appear)

[Lu, Zhang, 2000] Ruqian Lu, Songmao Zhang, Pangu – An Agent-Oriented Knowledge Base, *Proc. of Intelligent Information Processing*, 16th World Computer Congress, China, August, 2000, pp486-493

[Lu, Zhang, JinZ, Liu, Ji, Yang and Fan, 1999] Ruqian Lu, Songmao Zhang, Zhi Jin, Lengning Liu, Guangfeng Ji, Ping Yang, Lu Fan, Talk to Computers in Natural Way, *Proc. of the 4th International Symposium on Future Software Technology*, China, October, 1999, pp343-345

[Lu, Zhang, Shi and Yu, 1995] Ruqian Lu, Songmao Zhang, Haihu Shi, Lixin Yu, The Quantification Problem in Animation Generation, *Proc. of ANZIIS'95* (The 3rd Australian and New Zealand Conference on Intelligent Information Systems), 1995

[Lu, Zhang, Shi and Yu, 1995] Ruqian Lu, Songmao Zhang, Haihu Shi, Lixin Yu, Solving the Quantification Problem in Animation Generation, *Australian Journal of Intelligent Information Processing Systems*, Vol.2, No.4, 1995, pp35-45

[Lu, Zhang and Wei, 1999] Ruqian Lu, Songmao Zhang, Zichu Wei, Generate Computer Animation from Natural Language Stories, *Proc. of Pacific Asian Conference on Expert Systems*, Los Angeles, USA, 1999

[Lu, Ying, 1998] Ruqian Lu, Mingsheng Ying, A Model of Knowledge Reasoning, *Scientia Sinica*, Series E, Vol.41, No.5, 1998, pp527-534

[Zhang, 1992a] Songmao Zhang, *Research on Story Parsing* (in Chinese), PhD Thesis, Institute of Mathematics, Academia Sinica, 1992

[Zhang, 1992b] Songmao Zhang, Story Representation and High-dimensional Grammars (in Chinese), *Artificial Intelligence in China 1992*, 1992, pp139-146

[Zhang, 1993] Songmao Zhang, SPARS - A Story Parsing System (in Chinese), *Proc. of Conference on China Artificial Intelligence*, 1993, pp254-259

[Zhang, 1994a] Songmao Zhang, Forest Grammar (I), *Scientia Sinica*, Series A, Vol.37, No.6, 1994, pp761-768

[Zhang, 1994b] Songmao Zhang, Forest Grammar (II), *Scientia Sinica*, Series A, Vol.37, No.8, 1994, pp998-1008

[Zhang, 1994c] Songmao Zhang, Story Parsing Grammar, *Journal of Computer Science and Technology*, Vol.9, No.3, 1994, pp215-228

[Zhang, 1994d] Songmao Zhang, Story Grammar-a failed approach or a promising technique? *Proc. 14th Int'l Conference on AI, KBS, Expert Systems and Natural Language*, Paris, France, June, 1994

[Zhang, 1994e] Songmao Zhang, Research on Correlated Weak Precedence Story Parsing Grammar (in Chinese), *Chinese Journal of Computer*, Vol.17, No.6, 1994, pp477-480

[Zhang, 1994f] Songmao Zhang, Story Parsing Grammar with Unordered Productions (in Chinese), *Journal of Software*, Vol.5, No.1, 1994, pp11-18

[Zhang, 1995a] Songmao Zhang, Weak Precedence Story Parsing Grammar, *Journal of Compute Science and Technology*, Vol.10, No.1, 1995, pp53-64

[Zhang, 1995b] Songmao Zhang, A Heuristic Approach for Acquiring the Sketch of Story, *Proc. of Pacific-Asian Conference on Expert Systems*, China, May, 1995

[Zhang, 1997] Songmao Zhang, Story Parsing Grammar with Attributes, *Proc. 10th International Conference of FLAIRS*, Florida, USA, March, 1997

[Zhang, 1999] Songmao Zhang, After-Development Collaboration between Academia and Industry: Success and Failure, *Proc. of PAIRS'99*, Japan, December, 1999

[Zhang, 2000] Songmao Zhang, Formal Grammars and Story Understanding (in Chinese), *Knowledge Engineering and Knowledge Science*, Beijing: Tsinghua University Press, 2000

Part Three

[Geng, 1991] Qing Geng, *Design and Implementation of CAL-A Language for Computer Automation of 3D Animation* (in Chinese), Master's Thesis, Institute of Mathematics, Academia Sinica, 1991

[Zhu, 1992] Wenhong Zhu, *Design and Implementation of ADL-An Animation Description Language* (in Chinese), Master's Thesis, Institute of Mathematics, Academia Sinica, 1992

[JinZH, 1992] Zhenghao Jin, *Design and Implementation of the Management System of Animation Libraries* (in Chinese), Bachelor's Thesis, Institute of Mathematics, Academia Sinica, 1992

[YangD, 1992] Dejie Yang, *Design and Implementation of the Management System of Story Parsing Rulebase* (in Chinese), Bachelor's Thesis, Institute of Mathematics, Academia Sinica, 1992

[Li, 1993] Xiaobin Li, *Research on Story Pragmatics* (in Chinese), PhD Thesis, Institute of Mathematics, Academia Sinica, 1993

[ChenZ, 1993] Zhaobing Chen, *3D Reconstruction of Simple Geometrical Objects* (in Chinese), Master's Thesis, Institute of Mathematics, Academia Sinica, 1993

[Zhao, 1993] Ying Zhao, *Constructing Process of Animation Figures and Analysis of Some Examples* (in Chinese), Bachelor's Thesis, Institute of Mathematics, Academia Sinica, 1993

[Luo, 1993] Yi Luo, *Implementation of a Story Parsing System* (in Chinese), Bachelor's Thesis, Institute of Mathematics, Academia Sinica, 1993

[GaoB, 1993] Bo Gao, *CATN - An Improved Chinese ATN* (in Chinese), Bachelor's Thesis, Institute of Mathematics, Academia Sinica, 1993

[LiY, 1994] Yizhen Li, *Design and Implementation of Adding Quantitative Description to ADL* (in Chinese), Bachelor's Thesis, Institute of Mathematics, Academia Sinica, 1994

[WangY, 1994] Yujie Wang, *The Augmented Management System of Animation Libraries* (in Chinese), Bachelor's Thesis, Institute of Mathematics, Academia Sinica, 1994

[Zhou, 1994] Yuejiao Zhou, *The Improved CATN* (in Chinese), Bachelor's Thesis, Institute of Mathematics, Academia Sinica, 1994

[LiL, 1995] Lu Li, *Several Issues in the Action Planning in 3D Animation* (in Chinese), Bachelor's Thesis, Institute of Mathematics, Academia Sinica, 1995

[Du, 1995] Haixia Du, *Static Scene Planning in Animation* (in Chinese), Bachelor's Thesis, Institute of Mathematics, Academia Sinica, 1995

[Shi, 1996] Haihu Shi, *Research on Motion Planning* (in Chinese), PhD Thesis, Institute of Mathematics, Academia Sinica, 1996

[Yang, 1996] Ping Yang, *Transplantation and Improvement of ADL* (in Chinese), Bachelor's Thesis, Institute of Mathematics, Academia Sinica, 1996

[Fan, 1996] Lu Fan, *Design and Implementation of the Special-Effect Action Library* (in Chinese), Bachelor's Thesis, Institute of Mathematics, Academia Sinica, 1996

[ChenH, 1996] Hongjie Chen, *Compiling Techniques of Animation Software* (in Chinese), Technical Report, Institute of Mathematics, Academia Sinica, 1996

[Zhou, 1997] Yuejiao Zhou, *Commonsense Knowledge based Natural Language Disambiguation* (in Chinese), Technical Report, Institute of Mathematics, Academia Sinica, 1997

[Liu, 1997] Lengning Liu, *Prolog based Chinese Natural Language Understanding System* (in Chinese), Bachelor's Thesis, Institute of Mathematics, Academia Sinica, 1997

[Ji, 1997] Guangfeng Ji, *Design and Implementation of Transplantation of "Full Life Cycle Automation of Computer Animation" System from WAVEFRONT to 3D STUDIO Platform* (in Chinese), Bachelor's Thesis, Institute of Mathematics, Academia Sinica, 1997

[ZhangX, 1997] Xuesheng Zhang, *Computer Simulation and Implementation of Facial Expressions* (in Chinese), Bachelor's Thesis, Institute of Mathematics, Academia Sinica, 1997

[Du, 1998] Haixia Du, *Camera Planning in Animation Automation* (in Chinese), Master's Thesis, Institute of Mathematics, Academia Sinica, 1998

[YangF, 1998] Fan Yang, *Emotional Commonsense Knowledge based Pronoun Anaphora Decision* (in Chinese), Bachelor's Thesis, Institute of Mathematics, Academia Sinica, 1998

[JinX, 1998] Xiaolong Jin, *Knowledge Base based Plot Planning and Scene Planning* (in Chinese), Bachelor's Thesis, Institute of Mathematics, Academia Sinica, 1998

[SunC, 1998] Chengmin Sun, *ADL File Generation and the Construction of Knowledge Base of Camera Requirement Primitives* (in Chinese), Bachelor's Thesis, Institute of Mathematics, Academia Sinica, 1998

[Meng, 1998] Xiangliang Meng, *The Most Reliable 2D Path Planning* (in Chinese), Bachelor's Thesis, Institute of Mathematics, Academia Sinica, 1998

[JinZH, 2000] Zhenghao Jin, *Research on the Director Planning System in Animation Automation*, Institute of Mathematics, Master's Thesis, Academia Sinica, 2000

Index

Lecture Notes in Artificial Intelligence (LNAI)

Vol. 2005: W. Ziarko, Y. Yao (Eds.), Rough Sets and Current Trends in Computing. Proceedings, 2000. XV, 670 pages. 2001.

Vol. 2086: M. Luck, V. Mařík, O. Stěpánková, R. Trappl (Eds.), Multi-Agent Systems and Applications. Proceedings, 2001. X, 437 pages. 2001.

Vol. 2100: R. Küsters, Non-Standard Inferences in Description Logics. X, 250 pages. 2001.

Vol. 2101: S. Quaglini, P. Barahona, S. Andreassen (Eds.), Artificial Intelligence in Medicine. Proceedings, 2001. XIV, 469 pages. 2001.

Vol. 2103: M. Hannebauer, J. Wendler, E. Pagello (Eds.), Balancing Reactivity and Social Deliberation in Multi-Agent Systems. VIII, 237 pages. 2001.

Vol. 2109: M. Bauer, P.J. Gmytrasiewicz, J. Vassileva (Eds.), User Modeling 2001. Proceedings, 2001. XIII, 318 pages. 2001.

Vol. 2111: D. Helmbold, B. Williamson (Eds.), Computational Learning Theory. Proceedings, 2001. IX, 631 pages. 2001.

Vol. 2112: R. Kowalczyk, S.W. Loke, N.E. Reed, G. Williams (Eds.), Advances in Artificial Intelligence. Proceedings, 2000. IX, 363 pages. 2001.

Vol. 2116: V. Akman, P. Bouquet, R. Thomason, R.A. Young (Eds.), Modeling and Using Context. Proceedings, 2001. XII, 472 pages. 2001.

Vol. 2117: M. Beynon, C.L. Nehaniv, K. Dautenhahn (Eds.), Cognitive Technology: Instruments of Mind. Proceedings, 2001. XV, 522 pages. 2001.

Vol. 2120: H.S. Delugach, G. Stumme (Eds.), Conceptual Structures: Broadening the Base. Proceedings, 2001. X, 377 pages. 2001.

Vol. 2123: P. Perner (Ed.), Machine Learning and Data Mining in Pattern Recognition. Proceedings, 2001. XI, 363 pages. 2001.

Vol. 2132: S.-T. Yuan, M. Yokoo (Eds.), Intelligent Agents: Specification, Modeling, and Application. Proceedings, 2001. X, 237 pages. 2001.

Vol. 2143: S. Benferhat, P. Besnard (Eds.), Symbolic and Quantitative Approaches to Reasoning with Uncertainty. Proceedings, 2001. XIV, 818 pages. 2001.

Vol. 2148: A. Nareyek (Ed.), Local Search for Planning and Scheduling. Proceedings, 2000. IX, 171 pages. 2001.

Vol. 2155: H. Bunt, R.-J. Beun (Eds.), Cooperative Multimodal Communication. Proceedings, 1998. VIII, 251 pages. 2001.

Vol. 2157: C. Rouveirol, M. Sebag (Eds.), Inductive Logic Programming. Proceedings, 2001. X, 261 pages. 2001.

Vol. 2159: J. Kelemen, P. Sosík (Eds.), Advances in Artificial Life. Proceedings, 2001. XIX, 724 pages. 2001.

Vol. 2160: R. Lu, S. Zhang, Automatic Generation of Computer Animation. XI, 380 pages. 2002.

Vol. 2166: V. Matoušek, P. Mautner, R. Mouček, K. Taušer (Eds.), Text, Speech and Dialogue. Proceedings, 2001. XIII, 542 pages. 2001.

Vol. 2167: L. De Raedt, P. Flach (Eds.), Machine Learning: ECML 2001. Proceedings, 2001. XVII, 618 pages. 2001.

Vol. 2168: L. De Raedt, A. Siebes (Eds.), Principles of Data Mining and Knowledge Discovery. Proceedings, 2001. XVII, 510 pages. 2001.

Vol. 2173: T. Eiter, W. Faber, M. Truszczynski (Eds.), Logic Programming and Nonmonotonic Reasoning. Proceedings, 2001. XI, 444 pages. 2001.

Vol. 2174: F. Baader, G. Brewka, T. Eiter (Eds.), KI 2001: Advances in Artificial Intelligence. Proceedings, 2001. XIII, 471 pages. 2001.

Vol. 2175: F. Esposito (Ed.), AI*IA 2001: Advances in Artificial Intelligence. Proceedings, 2001. XII, 396 pages. 2001.

Vol. 2182: M. Klusch, F. Zambonelli (Eds.), Cooperative Information Agents V. Proceedings, 2001. XII, 288 pages. 2001.

Vol. 2190: A. de Antonio, R. Aylett, D. Ballin (Eds.), Intelligent Virtual Agents. Proceedings, 2001. VIII, 245 pages. 2001.

Vol. 2198: N. Zhong, Y. Yao, J. Liu, S. Ohsuga (Eds.), Web Intelligence: Research and Development. Proceedings, 2001. XVI, 615 pages. 2001.

Vol. 2203: A. Omicini, P. Petta, R. Tolksdorf (Eds.), Engineering Societies in the Agents World II. Proceedings, 2001. XI, 195 pages. 2001.

Vol. 2225: N. Abe, R. Khardon, T. Zeugmann (Eds.), Algorithmic Learning Theory. Proceedings, 2001. XI, 379 pages. 2001.

Vol. 2226: K.P. Jantke, A. Shinohara (Eds.), Discovery Science. Proceedings, 2001. XII, 494 pages. 2001.

Vol. 2246: R. Falcone, M. Singh, Y.-H. Tan (Eds.), Trust in Cyber-societies. VIII, 195 pages. 2001.

Vol. 2250: R. Nieuwenhuis, A. Voronkov (Eds.), Logic for Programming, Artificial Intelligence, and Reasoning. Proceedings, 2001. XV, 738 pages. 2001.

Vol. 2253: T. Terano, T. Nishida, A. Namatame, S. Tsumoto, Y. Ohsawa, T. Washio (Eds.), New Frontiers in Artificial Intelligence. Proceedings, 2001. XXVII, 553 pages. 2001.

Vol. 2256: M. Stumptner, D. Corbett, M. Brooks (Eds.), AI 2001: Advances in Artificial Intelligence. Proceedings, 2001. XII, 666 pages. 2001.

Vol. 2258: P. Brazdil, A. Jorge (Eds.), Progress in Artificial Intelligence. Proceedings, 2001. XII, 418 pages. 2001.

Lecture Notes in Computer Science

Vol. 2226: K.P. Jantke, A. Shinohara (Eds.), Discovery Science. Proceedings, 2001. XII, 494 pages. 2001. (Subseries LNAI).

Vol. 2227: S. Boztaş, I.E. Shparlinski (Eds.), Applied Algebra, Algebraic Algorithms and Error-Correcting Codes. Proceedings, 2001. XII, 398 pages. 2001.

Vol. 2228: B. Monien, V.K. Prasanna, S. Vajapeyam (Eds.), High Performance Computing – HiPC 2001. Proceedings, 2001. XVIII, 438 pages. 2001.

Vol. 2229: S. Qing, T. Okamoto, J. Zhou (Eds.), Information and Communications Security. Proceedings, 2001. XIV, 504 pages. 2001.

Vol. 2230: T. Katila, I.E. Magnin, P. Clarysse, J. Montagnat, J. Nenonen (Eds.), Functional Imaging and Modeling of the Heart. Proceedings, 2001. XI, 158 pages. 2001.

Vol. 2232: L. Fiege, G. Mühl, U. Wilhelm (Eds.), Electronic Commerce. Proceedings, 2001. X, 233 pages. 2001.

Vol. 2233: J. Crowcroft, M. Hofmann (Eds.), Networked Group Communication. Proceedings, 2001. X, 205 pages. 2001.

Vol. 2234: L. Pacholski, P. Ružička (Eds.), SOFSEM 2001: Theory and Practice of Informatics. Proceedings, 2001. XI, 347 pages. 2001.

Vol. 2235: C.S. Calude, G. Păun, G. Rozenberg, A. Salomaa (Eds.), Multiset Processing. VIII, 359 pages. 2001.

Vol. 2236: K. Drira, A. Martelli, T. Villemur (Eds.), Cooperative Environments for Distributed Systems Engineering. IX, 281 pages. 2001.

Vol. 2237: P. Codognet (Ed.), Logic Programming. Proceedings, 2001. XI, 365 pages. 2001.

Vol. 2239: T. Walsh (Ed.), Principles and Practice of Constraint Programming – CP 2001. Proceedings, 2001. XIV, 788 pages. 2001.

Vol. 2240: G.P. Picco (Ed.), Mobile Agents. Proceedings, 2001. XIII, 277 pages. 2001.

Vol. 2241: M. Jünger, D. Naddef (Eds.), Computational Combinatorial Optimization. IX, 305 pages. 2001.

Vol. 2242: C.A. Lee (Ed.), Grid Computing – GRID 2001. Proceedings, 2001. XII, 185 pages. 2001.

Vol. 2243: G. Bertrand, A. Imiya, R. Klette (Eds.), Digital and Image Geometry. VII, 455 pages. 2001.

Vol. 2244: D. Bjørner, M. Broy, A.V. Zamulin (Eds.), Perspectives of System Informatics. Proceedings, 2001. XIII, 548 pages. 2001.

Vol. 2245: R. Hariharan, M. Mukund, V. Vinay (Eds.), FST TCS 2001: Foundations of Software Technology and Theoretical Computer Science. Proceedings, 2001. XI, 347 pages. 2001.

Vol. 2246: R. Falcone, M. Singh, Y.-H. Tan (Eds.), Trust in Cyber-societies. VIII, 195 pages. 2001. (Subseries LNAI).

Vol. 2247: C. P. Rangan, C. Ding (Eds.), Progress in Cryptology – INDOCRYPT 2001. Proceedings, 2001. XIII, 351 pages. 2001.

Vol. 2248: C. Boyd (Ed.), Advances in Cryptology – ASIACRYPT 2001. Proceedings, 2001. XI, 603 pages. 2001.

Vol. 2249: K. Nagi, Transactional Agents. XVI, 205 pages. 2001.

Vol. 2250: R. Nieuwenhuis, A. Voronkov (Eds.), Logic for Programming, Artificial Intelligence, and Reasoning. Proceedings, 2001. XV, 738 pages. 2001. (Subseries LNAI).

Vol. 2251: Y.Y. Tang, V. Wickerhauser, P.C. Yuen, C.Li (Eds.), Wavelet Analysis and Its Applications. Proceedings, 2001. XIII, 450 pages. 2001.

Vol. 2252: J. Liu, P.C. Yuen, C. Li, J. Ng, T. Ishida (Eds.), Active Media Technology. Proceedings, 2001. XII, 402 pages. 2001.

Vol. 2253: T. Terano, T. Nishida, A. Namatame, S. Tsumoto, Y. Ohsawa, T. Washio (Eds.), New Frontiers in Artificial Intelligence. Proceedings, 2001. XXVII, 553 pages. 2001. (Subseries LNAI).

Vol. 2254: M.R. Little, L. Nigay (Eds.), Engineering for Human-Computer Interaction. Proceedings, 2001. XI, 359 pages. 2001.

Vol. 2255: J. Dean, A. Gravel (Eds.), COTS-Based Software Systems. Proceedings, 2002. XIV, 257 pages. 2002.

Vol. 2256: M. Stumptner, D. Corbett, M. Brooks (Eds.), AI 2001: Advances in Artificial Intelligence. Proceedings, 2001. XII, 666 pages. 2001. (Subseries LNAI).

Vol. 2257: S. Krishnamurthi, C.R. Ramakrishnan (Eds.), Practical Aspects of Declarative Languages. Proceedings, 2002. VIII, 351 pages. 2002.

Vol. 2258: P. Brazdil, A. Jorge (Eds.), Progress in Artificial Intelligence. Proceedings, 2001. XII, 418 pages. 2001. (Subseries LNAI).

Vol. 2259: S. Vaudenay, A.M. Youssef (Eds.), Selected Areas in Cryptography. Proceedings, 2001. XI, 359 pages. 2001.

Vol. 2260: B. Honary (Ed.), Cryptography and Coding. Proceedings, 2001. IX, 416 pages. 2001.

Vol. 2264: K. Steinhöfel (Ed.), Stochastic Algorithms: Foundations and Applications. Proceedings, 2001. VIII, 203 pages. 2001.

Vol. 2273: A.R. Coden, E.W. Brown, S. Srinivasan (Eds.), Information Retrieval Techniques for Speech Applications. XI, 109 pages. 2002.

GPSR Compliance

The European Union's (EU) General Product Safety Regulation (GPSR) is a set of rules that requires consumer products to be safe and our obligations to ensure this.

If you have any concerns about our products, you can contact us on ProductSafety@springernature.com

In case Publisher is established outside the EU, the EU authorized representative is:

Springer Nature Customer Service Center GmbH
Europaplatz 3
69115 Heidelberg, Germany

Batch number: 09625304

Printed by Printforce, the Netherlands